The

Bessie Parmet Kannerstein '32

Memorial Fund

Established by

MR. JOSEPH PARMET

for the purchase of

REFERENCE BOOKS

for the

CEDAR CREST COLLEGE

LIBRARY

Twentieth-Century Short Story Explication

Supplement IV to Third Edition

With Checklists of Books and Journals Used

WARREN S. WALKER
Horn Professor Emeritus of English
Texas Tech University

THE SHOE STRING PRESS, INC.
1989

Third Edition, Supplement IV
© 1989 The Shoe String Press, Inc.
Hamden, Connecticut 06514

Printed in the United States of America

First edition published 1961
Supplement I to first edition published 1963
Supplement II to first edition published 1965
Second edition published 1967
Supplement I to second edition published 1970
Supplement II to second edition published 1973
Third edition published 1977
Supplement I to third edition published 1980
Supplement II to third edition published 1984
Supplement III to third edition published 1987

The paper in this book meets the minimum requirements
of American National Standard for Information Sciences—Permanence
of Paper for Printed Library Materials, ANSI Z39.48–1984. ∞

Library of Congress Cataloging-in-Publication Data
(Revised for volume 4)

Walker, Warren S.
Twentieth-century short story explication.
Includes indexes.
1. Short stories—Indexes. 2. Short story—
Bibliography. I. Title.
Z5917.S5W33 1977, Suppl. 016.8093'1 80–16175
[PN3373]
ISBN 0–208–02188–4 (3rd Ed. S. IV)
ISBN 0–208–01813–1 (v. 1)

For
Laurence Perrine,
from whose work many of us have learned
much about the short story.

CONTENTS

PREFACE

This eleventh volume of *Twentieth-Century Short Story Explication* includes more than 4,500 entries. Of the 660 short story writers represented, 249 appear for the first time in this volume, increasing to 2,016 the total number of authors covered in the Third Edition and its four Supplements. The newcomers are mainly women writers, Third World authors, and the creators of fantasy and science fiction.

Whatever the original language of the stories themselves, the explications are here limited to those published in the major languages of Western Europe. Although these parameters may seem unduly restrictive, the fact of the matter is that they encompass the vast majority of critical studies on the genre. The growing numbers of competent Indian writers, for example, are far more frequently discussed in English than they are in Hindi or Bengali or Tamil. Similarly, despite the emphasis on indigenous languages among African states that were once colonies, their literary journals are usually printed in French or English.

Twentieth-Century Short Story Explication is a bibliography of interpretations that have appeared since 1900 of short stories published since 1800. The term *short story* here has the same meaning it carries in the Wilson Company's *Short Story Index:* "A brief narrative of not more than 150 average-sized pages." By *explication* I suggest simply interpretation or explanation of the meaning of a story, including observations on theme, symbol, and sometimes structure. This excludes from the bibliography what are essentially studies of sources, biographical data, and background materials. Occasionally there are explicatory passages cited in works otherwise devoted to these external considerations. All page numbers refer strictly to interpretive passages, not to the longer works in which they occur.

The profusion of interpretations generated in the "knowledge explosion" of recent decades required that, beginning with the Third Edition (1977), we adopt a system of coding and consequently a format different from that used in the first two editions and their Supplements. Each book is cited by author or editor and a short title; the full title and publication data are provided in "A Checklist of Books Used." For an article in a journal or an essay in a critical collection, the full publication information is provided in the text the first time the study is cited. In subsequent entries, only the critic's or scholar's name and a short title are used as long as these entries appear under the name of the same short story author; if an article or essay explicates stories by two or more authors, a complete initial entry is made for each author. As in Supplements I, II, and III, we have again included "A Checklist of Journals Used." This should be especially helpful to students who may not be familiar with titles of professional journals, much less the abbreviations for such titles.

Supplement III to the Third Edition carried forward the coverage of short story interpretations through 31 December 1984. Supplement IV extends this coverage through 31 December 1986. Although most of the entries in Supplement IV were published during 1985 and 1986, there are also included (1) earlier interpretations that had been overlooked previously, and (2) new reprintings of earlier studies. An asterisk preceding an entry indicates that the item is a reprinting of an explication listed in the Third Edition.

In the preparation of this book I have been indebted to the editors of such journals as *PMLA, Modern Fiction Studies, Studies in Short Fiction,* and *Journal of Modern Literature.* I wish to extend thanks to the Interlibrary Loan Department of Texas Tech University Library, especially to its chairperson, Amy Chang, and her industrious assistant, Carol Roberts. As usual, I am most grateful to my wife, Barbara K. Walker, for her continuous encouragement and assistance.

Warren S. Walker
Texas Tech University

KHWAJA AHMAD ABBAS

"Seven Hindustani"
Kalinnikova, Elena J. *Indian-English Literature* . . . , 120–121.

"The Umbrella"
Kalinnikova, Elena J. *Indian-English Literature* . . . , 112–113.

WALTER ABISH

"Crossing the Great Void"
Jardine, Alice A. *Gynesis* . . . , 50–52.

ALICE ADAMS

"Roses, Rhododendron"
Bohner, Charles H. *Instructor's Manual* . . . , 1–2.

"To See You Again"
Bohner, Charles H. *Instructor's Manual* . . . , 2–3.

FRANCIS ADAMS

"The Hut by the Tanks"
Hadgraft, Cecil, Ed. *The Australian Short Story* . . . , 31.

SHMUEL [SHAY] YOSEF AGNON [SHMUEL YOSEF CZACZKES]

"Agunot"
Aberbach, David. *At the Handles* . . . , 19–20.
Shaked, Gershon. "Midrash and Narrative: Agnon's 'Agunot,'" in Hartman, Geoffrey H., and Sanford Budick, Eds. *Midrash and Literature*, 285–303.

"Another Face"
Aberbach, David. *At the Handles* . . . , 29–30, 95–96.

"Another Talit"
Aberbach, David. *At the Handles* . . . , 104–105.

"The Black Canopy"
Aberbach, David. *At the Handles* . . . , 155–156.

"The Doctor's Divorce"
Aberbach, David. *At the Handles* . . . , 78–79, 128–130.

"Edo and Enam"
Aberbach, David. *At the Handles* . . . , 98, 153–154.

1

"The Face and the Image"
Aberbach, David. *At the Handles* . . . , 102–104.

"The First Kiss"
Aberbach, David. *At the Handles* . . . , 71–72.

"Forevermore"
Fuchs, Esther. "Wherefrom Did Gediton Enter Gumlidata? Realism and Comic
    Subversiveness in 'Forevermore,'" *Mod Lang Stud*, 15, iv (1985), 64–79.

"Friendship"
Aberbach, David. *At the Handles* . . . , 123–124.

"The Hill of Sand"
Aberbach, David. *At the Handles* . . . , 154–155.

"In the Prime of Her Days"
Aberbach, David. *At the Handles* . . . , 20–21.

"The Kerchief"
Aberbach, David. *At the Handles* . . . , 143–144.

"The Lady and the Pedlar"
Aberbach, David. *At the Handles* . . . , 45–46.

"The Last Bus"
Aberbach, David. *At the Handles* . . . , 73–74.

"The Legend of the Scribe"
Aberbach, David. *At the Handles* . . . , 66–67.

"The Letter"
Aberbach, David. *At the Handles* . . . , 111–114.

"The Orchestra"
Aberbach, David. *At the Handles* . . . , 149–150.

"Ovadiah the Lame"
Aberbach, David. *At the Handles* . . . , 48–49.

"The Song Which Is Sung"
Aberbach, David. *At the Handles* . . . , 135–136.

"To the Doctor"
Aberbach, David. *At the Handles* . . . , 42–43.

"The Well of Miriam"
Aberbach, David. *At the Handles* . . . , 164–165.

"A Whole Loaf"
Aberbach, David. *At the Handles* . . . , 57–58, 77–78.

IQBAR AHMAD

"The Kumbh Fair"
Suganasiri, Suwanda. "Reality and Symbolism in the South Asian Canadian Short Story," *World Lit Written Engl*, 26 (1986), 98–99.

KASSIM AHMAD

"A Common Story"
Gooneratne, Yasmine. "Lloyd Fernando's *Twenty-Two Malaysian Stories*," in Goodwin, K. L., Ed. *Commonwealth Literature . . .*, 122.

AI WU

"In the Mountain Gorge"
Anderson, Marston. "The Morality of Form: Lu Xun and the Modern Chinese Short Story," in Lee, Leo Ou-fan, Ed. *Lu Xun . . .*, 51.

"A Lesson in Life"
Anderson, Marston. "The Morality of Form . . . ," 50.

ROBERT AICKMAN

"Compulsory Games"
Clute, John. "Robert Aickman," in Bleiler, E. F., Ed. *Supernatural Fiction Writers . . .*, II, 962–963.

"The Fetch"
Clute, John. "Robert Aickman," 959.

"The Stain"
Clute, John. "Robert Aickman," 963.

VASILIY PAVLOVICH AKSENOV

"Colleagues"
Busch, R. L. "The Exotic in the Early Novellas of Aksenov," in Mozejko, Edward, Boris Briker, and Per Dalgard, Eds. *Vasiliy Pavlovich Aksenov . . .*, 54–57.

"Halfway to the Moon"
Meyer, Priscilla. "Basketball, God, and the Ringo Kid: Philistinism and the Ideal in Aksenov's Short Stories," in Mozejko, Edward, Boris Briker, and Per Dalgard, Eds. *Vasiliy Pavlovich Aksenov . . .*, 123–124.

"It's Time, My Friend, It's Time"
Busch, R. L. "The Exotic . . . ," 63–66.

"The Local Hooligan Abramashvili"
Meyer, Priscilla. "Basketball . . . ," 124–126.

"Oranges from Morocco"
Busch, R. L. "The Exotic . . . ," 60–63.

"Papa, What Does It Spell?"
Meyer, Priscilla. "Basketball . . . ," 126–127.

"Parachuting"
Meyer, Priscilla. "Basketball . . . ," 126.

"A Ticket to the Stars"
Busch, R. L. "The Exotic . . . ," 57–60.

"Victory"
Meyer, Priscilla. "Basketball . . . ," 127–128.
Zholkovsky, Alexander. "Aksenov's 'Victory': A Post-Analysis," in Mozejko, Edward, Boris Briker, and Per Dalgard, Eds. *Vasiliy Pavlovich Aksenov . . . ,* 224–240.

"The Village of Sviyazhsk"
Meyer, Priscilla. "Basketball . . . ," 128–130.

AKUTAGAWA RYŪNOSUKE

"The Horrors of Hell"
Morrison, John W. *Modern Japanese Fiction,* 91–93.

"The Nose"
Morrison, John W. *Modern Japanese Fiction,* 91.

"Rashōmon"
Morrison, John W. *Modern Japanese Fiction,* 90–91.

LEOPOLDO ALAS

"El dúo de la tos"
Romera Castillo, José. "Espacio y tiempo, elementos connotadores, en 'El dúo de la tos' de Clarín," *Letras de Deusto,* 15 (1985), 199–206.

"Pipá"
Landeiro, Ricardo. "'Pipá': Maníqueismo, ironía y tragedia en un relato de Leopoldo Alas," in Boudreau, H. L., and Luis T. González-del-Valle, Eds. *Studies in Honor . . . ,* 129–144.

SALIM AL-BUSTANI

"A Shot from No Shooter" [same as "A Bolt from the Blue"]
Haywood, John A. *Modern Arabic Literature . . . ,* 126–127.

LOUISA MAY ALCOTT

"Behind a Mask"
Strickland, Charles. *Victorian Domesticity . . .* , 93–96.

"Cupid and Chow-Chow"
Keyser, Elizabeth. "'Playing Puckerage': Alcott's Plot in 'Cupid and Chow-Chow,'" *Children's Lit,* 14 (1986), 105–122.

"Love and Self Love"
Strickland, Charles. *Victorian Domesticity . . .* , 58–59.

"Pauline's Passion and Punishment"
Strickland, Charles. *Victorian Domesticity . . .* , 65–67.

SHOLOM ALEICHEM

"Another Page from the Song of Songs"
Gittleman, Sol. *Sholom Aleichem . . .* , 162.

"An Aytzeh"
Roback, A. A. "The Humor of Sholom Aleichem," in Grafstein, M. W., Ed. *Sholom Aleichem Panorama,* 21.

"Bandits"
Aarons, Victoria. *Author as Character . . .* , 90–94.

"Boaz the Teacher"
Gittleman, Sol. *Sholom Aleichem . . .* , 155.

"The Bubble Burst"
Gittleman, Sol. *Sholom Aleichem . . .* , 109–112.

"Chava"
Gittleman, Sol. *Sholom Aleichem . . .* , 118–122.

"Cnards"
Gittleman, Sol. *Sholom Aleichem . . .* , 93–95.

"Competitions"
Gittleman, Sol. *Sholom Aleichem . . .* , 169–170.

"The Dreydl"
Gittleman, Sol. *Sholom Aleichem . . .* , 147–148.

"An Easy Fast"
Grafstein, M. W. "Sholom Aleichem's Tiny People," in Grafstein, M. W., Ed. *Sholom Aleichem Panorama,* 43.

"Final Pages from the Song of Songs"
Gittleman, Sol. *Sholom Aleichem . . .* , 164–165.

"The Purim Feast"
Gittleman, Sol. *Sholom Aleichem* . . . , 145–146.

"Shprintze"
Gittleman, Sol. *Sholom Aleichem* . . . , 122–124.

"Station Baranovich"
Aarons, Victoria. *Author as Character* . . . , 101–109.

"Summer Romances"
Gittleman, Sol. *Sholom Aleichem* . . . , 99.

"The Tenth Man"
Gittleman, Sol. *Sholom Aleichem* . . . , 168–170.

"Tevye Goes to Palestine"
Gittleman, Sol. *Sholom Aleichem* . . . , 124–127.

"Tevye Reads the Psalms"
Gittleman, Sol. *Sholom Aleichem* . . . , 129–130.

"Tevye Wins a Fortune"
Gittleman, Sol. *Sholom Aleichem* . . . , 106–109.

"Three Little Heads"
Gittleman, Sol. *Sholom Aleichem* . . . , 170–171.

"Two Shalachmones"
Gittleman, Sol. *Sholom Aleichem* . . . , 62–63.

"Visiting with King Ahasuerus"
Gittleman, Sol. *Sholom Aleichem* . . . , 156.

WILLIAM ALEXANDER

"The Authentic History of Peter Grundie"
Donaldson, William. *Popular Literature* . . . , 108–115.

PETER ALTENBERG

"A Letter from Africa"
Gilman, Sander L. "Black Sexuality and Modern Consciousness," in Grimm, Reinhold, and Jost Hermand, Eds. *Blacks and German Culture*, 40–45.

JORGE AMADO

"A Carnaval Story"
Vieira, Nelson H. "Myth and Identity in Short Stories by Jorge Amado," *Stud Short Fiction*, 23 (1986), 28–30.

"The Deaths and the Victory of Rosalinda"
Vieira, Nelson H. "Myth and Identity . . . ," 33–34.

"How the Mulatto Porciuncula Got the Corpse Off His Back"
Vieira, Nelson H. "Myth and Identity . . . ," 30–32.

KINGSLEY AMIS

"I Spy Strangers"
Pickering, Jean. "The English Short Story in the Sixties," in Vannatta, Dennis,
    Ed. *The English Short Story, 1945–1980,* 107–108.

MULK ANAND

"Birth"
Naik, M. K. "Infinite Variety: A Study of the Short Stories of Mulk Raj Anand,"
    in Sharma, K. K., Ed. *Perspectives . . . ,* 42–43.

"A Kashmir Idyll"
Naik, M. K. "Infinite Variety . . . ," 46.

"Lullaby"
Naik, M. K. "Infinite Variety . . . ," 42.

"The Silver Bangles"
Naik, M. K. "Infinite Variety . . . ," 47–48.

"The Thief"
Naik, M. K. "Infinite Variety . . . ," 48.

"The Tractor and the Corn Goddess"
Naik, M. K. "Infinite Variety . . . ," 45–46.

"A Village Idyll"
Naik, M. K. "Infinite Variety . . . ," 43.

TRYGGVE ANDERSEN

"Anne Catherine Bühring"
Schiff, Timothy. *Scenarios . . . ,* 41–42.

"Captain Tebetmann's Daughter"
Schiff, Timothy. *Scenarios . . . ,* 36–37.

"The Dead Man"
Schiff, Timothy. *Scenarios . . . ,* 95–96.

"East Among the Skerries"
Schiff, Timothy. *Scenarios . . . ,* 102–106.

"The Golden Revenge"
Schiff, Timothy. *Scenarios* . . . , 87.

"The Great Success"
Schiff, Timothy. *Scenarios* . . . , 85, 106–107.

"Gullik Hauksveen"
Schiff, Timothy. *Scenarios* . . . , 94–96.

"In Difficult Waters"
Schiff, Timothy. *Scenarios* . . . , 85–86.

"The Journey Home"
Schiff, Timothy. *Scenarios* . . . , 87–88.

"The Last Nights"
Schiff, Timothy. *Scenarios* . . . , 91–94.

"The Night Watch"
Schiff, Timothy. *Scenarios* . . . , 86–87.

"Old People"
Schiff, Timothy. *Scenarios* . . . , 89–90.

"The Story About the Major"
Schiff, Timothy. *Scenarios* . . . , 97–98.

POUL ANDERSON

"The Queen of Air and Darkness"
Tweet, Roald. "Poul Anderson," in Bleiler, E. F., Ed. *Supernatural Fiction Writers* . . . , II, 976–977.

"Sam Hall"
Bergen, Albert I. "*Analog Science Fiction/Science Fact*," in Tymn, Marshall B., and Mike Ashley, Eds. *Science Fiction . . . Magazines*, 83.

SHERWOOD ANDERSON

"An Awakening"
Bredahl, A. Carl. "'The Young Thing Within': Divided Narrative and Sherwood Anderson's *Winesburg, Ohio*," *Midwest Q*, 27 (1986), 434–436.
Bruyère, Claire. *Sherwood Anderson* . . . , 322–324.
Ward, J. A. *American Silences* . . . , 43–44.

"A Chicago Hamlet"
Bruyère, Claire. *Sherwood Anderson* . . . , 84–85.

"Daughters"
Bruyère, Claire. *Sherwood Anderson* . . . , 157–158.

"Death in the Woods"
Bruyère, Claire. *Sherwood Anderson . . .* , 332–339.
Colquitt, Clare. "The Reader as Voyeur: Complicitous Transformations in 'Death in the Woods,'" *Mod Fiction Stud*, 32 (1986), 175–190.
Sheidley, William E., and Ann Charters. *Instructor's Manual . . .* , 65–66; rpt. Charters, Ann, William E. Sheidley, and Martha Ramsey. *Instructor's Manual . . .* , 2nd ed., 67–68.

"The Egg"
Bohner, Charles H. *Instructor's Manual . . .* , 3–4.
Bruyère, Claire. *Sherwood Anderson . . .* , 232–240.

"The Flood"
Bruyère, Claire. *Sherwood Anderson . . .* , 91–92.

"Hands"
Bredahl, A. Carl. "'The Young Thing Within' . . . ," 427–428.
Bruyère, Claire. *Sherwood Anderson . . .* , 41–42.
Gerlach, John. *Toward the End . . .* , 95–100.
Sheidley, William E., and Ann Charters. *Instructor's Manual . . .* , 63; rpt. Charters, Ann, William E. Sheidley, and Martha Ramsey. *Instructor's Manual . . .* , 2nd ed., 65.

"I Want to Know Why"
Bohner, Charles H. *Instructor's Manual . . .* , 5–6.
Bruyère, Claire. *Sherwood Anderson . . .* , 153–155.

"I'm a Fool"
Bruyère, Claire. *Sherwood Anderson . . .* , 146–147.

"Loneliness"
Bredahl, A. Carl. "'The Young Thing Within' . . . ," 433–434.
Bruyère, Claire. *Sherwood Anderson . . .* , 194–196.

"The Man Who Became a Woman"
Bruyère, Claire. *Sherwood Anderson . . .* , 168–174.

"Mother"
Bredahl, A. Carl. "'The Young Thing Within' . . . ," 428–429.

"Paper Pills"
Bredahl, A. Carl. "'The Young Thing Within' . . . ," 425.

"The Philosopher"
Bruyère, Claire. *Sherwood Anderson . . .* , 124–125.

"Queer"
Ward, J. A. *American Silences . . .* , 45–46.

"Respectability"
Bredahl, A. Carl. "'The Young Thing Within' . . . ," 426–427.

"The Sad Horn Blowers"
Bruyère, Claire. *Sherwood Anderson* . . . , 174–175.

"Seeds"
Bruyère, Claire. *Sherwood Anderson* . . . , 185–189.

"Sophistication"
Ward, J. A. *American Silences* . . . , 47–50.

"The Strength of God"
Bredahl, A. Carl. " 'The Young Thing Within' . . . ," 429–432.

"The Teacher"
Bredahl, A. Carl. " 'The Young Thing Within' . . . ," 432–433.

"The Thinker"
Ward, J. A. *American Silences* . . . , 40–41.

IVO ANDRIĆ

"Ex Ponto"
Juricić, Zelimir. "All of Alija's Women: Andrić's Realization of 'Ex Ponto' Visions," in Bristol, Evelyn, Ed. *East European Literature,* 23–32.

ANONYMOUS

"Azakia: A Canadian Story"
Current-García, Eugene. *The American Short Story before 1850* . . . , 14–15.

"The Counterfeiters"
Current-García, Eugene. *The American Short Story before 1850* . . . , 22–23.

"Ellen Linn, the Needlewoman"
Kestner, Joseph. *Protest and Reform* . . . , 149–150.

"Narrative of the Unpardonable Sin"
Current-García, Eugene. *The American Short Story before 1850* . . . , 15–16.

"The Story of Constantius and Pulchera"
Current-García, Eugene. *The American Short Story before 1850* . . . , 16.

"The Three Homes: A Tale of the Cotton Spinners"
Gallagher, Catherine. *The Industrial Reformation* . . . , 142–146.

S. ANSKY [S. Z. RAPPAPORT]

"The Tower of Rome"
Knapp, Bettina L. *Archetype, Architecture* . . . , 45–66.

JOSÉ MARÍA ARGUEDAS

"La agonía de Rasu-Ñiti"
Shaw, Bradley A. "Narrative Distance in Arguedas' 'La agonía de Rasu-Ñiti,'"
in González-de Valle, Luis T., and Catherine Nickel, Eds. *Selected Proceedings* . . . , 159–165.

"Los escoleros"
Crovetto, Pier L. " 'Los escoleros' di José María Arguedas: Dalla nostalgia arcadica all'antagonismo sociale," in Cattaneo, Mariateresa, and Silvana Serafin, Eds. *Studi di letteratura* . . . , 279–289.

RONALD FRANCIS ARIAS

"The Castle"
Gingerich, Willard. "Ronald Francis Arias," in Martínez, Julio A., and Francisco A. Lomelí, Eds. *Chicano Literature* . . . , 55.

"Chinches"
Gingerich, Willard. "Ronald Francis Arias," 55–56.

"A House on the Island"
Gingerich, Willard. "Ronald Francis Arias," 54–55.

"The Interview"
Gingerich, Willard. "Ronald Francis Arias," 54.

"The Mago"
Gingerich, Willard. "Ronald Francis Arias," 53–54.

"A Story Machine"
Gingerich, Willard. "Ronald Francis Arias," 55.

"The Wetback"
Gingerich, Willard. "Ronald Francis Arias," 54.

AYI KWEI ARMAH

"An African Fable"
Wright, Derek. "The Early Writings of Ayi Kwei Armah," *Research African Lit*, 16 (1985), 507–511.

"Asemka"
Wright, Derek. "The Early Writings . . . ," 489–491.

"Contact"
Wright, Derek. "The Early Writings . . . ," 499–506.

"The Offal Kind"
Wright, Derek. "The Early Writings . . . ," 495–499.

"Yaw Manu's Charm"
Wright, Derek. "The Early Writings . . . ," 491–493.

DAVID ARNASON

"Sylvie"
Hughes, Kenneth J. *Signs of Literature* . . . , 198–221.

ISAAC ASIMOV

"The Bicentennial Man"
Charters, Lawrence I. "Binary First Contact," in Hassler, Donald A., Ed. *Patterns*
    . . . *II,* 52–53.

"Breeds There a Man . . . ?"
Berger, Harold L. *Science Fiction* . . . , 114–115.

"The Evitable Conflict"
Berger, Harold L. *Science Fiction* . . . , 36–37.

GERTRUDE ATHERTON

"The Bell in the Fog"
Holt, Marilyn J. "Gertrude Atherton," in Bleiler, E. F., Ed. *Supernatural Fiction*
    Writers . . . , II, 778.

"The Dead and the Countess"
Holt, Marilyn J. "Gertrude Atherton," 779.

"Death and the Woman"
Holt, Marilyn J. "Gertrude Atherton," 779–780.

"The Eternal Now"
Holt, Marilyn J. "Gertrude Atherton," 780.

"The Striding Place"
Holt, Marilyn J. "Gertrude Atherton," 779.

MARGARET ATWOOD

"The Man from Mars"
Bohner, Charles H. *Instructor's Manual* . . . , 6–7.

"Rape Fantasies"
Bohner, Charles H. *Instructor's Manual* . . . , 8–9.

"The Resplendent Quetzal"
Davey, Frank. "Alternate Stories: The Short Fiction of Audrey Thomas and
    Margaret Atwood," *Canadian Lit,* 109 (1986), 11.

WILLIAM AUSTIN

"The Man with the Clocks"
Fisher, Benjamin F. "William Austin," in Bleiler, E. F., Ed. *Supernatural Fiction
    Writers . . . ,* II, 694–695.

"Peter Rugg, the Missing Man"
Current-García, Eugene. *The American Short Story before 1850 . . . ,* 23.
Fisher, Benjamin F. "William Austin," 695.

MARTIN AVERY

"Santa's Village"
Vauthier, Simone. "Fantaisie sur Saint Nicolas et la 45° parallele," *Recherches
    Anglaises et Américaines,* 18 (1985), 197–212.

FRANCISCO AYALA

"Un *quid pro quo, o Who Is Who*"
Altisent, Marta E. "Periodismo y Ficcion en un cuento de Francisco Ayala,"
    Hispanic J, 7, ii (1986), 57–64.

ISAAC BABEL

"After the Battle"
Ehre, Milton. *Isaac Babel,* 82–83.

"Argamak"
Ehre, Milton. *Isaac Babel,* 83–85.

"Awakening"
Ehre, Milton. *Isaac Babel,* 98–102.

"Berestechko"
Ehre, Milton. *Isaac Babel,* 73–75.

"Childhood at Grandmother's"
Ehre, Milton. *Isaac Babel,* 39–40.

"The Church at Novograd"
Ehre, Milton. *Isaac Babel,* 72–73.

"Crossing into Poland"
Ehre, Milton. *Isaac Babel,* 71–72.

Ehre, Milton. *Isaac Babel,* 83–86.

"The Road"
Ehre, Milton. *Isaac Babel,* 137–139.

"Sashka the Christ"
Ehre, Milton. *Isaac Babel,* 79–81.

"The Sin of Jesus"
Ehre, Milton. *Isaac Babel,* 55–56.

"Squadron Commander Trunov" [originally titled "There Were Ten"]
Ehre, Milton. *Isaac Babel,* 58–59.
Sicher, Efraim. *Style and Structure* . . . , 82–83.

"The Story of My Dovecote"
Bar-Yosef, Hamutal. "On Isaac Babel's 'The Story of My Dovecote,'" *Prooftexts,*
    6 (1986), 264–271.
Bohner, Charles H. *Instructor's Manual* . . . , 9–10.
Ehre, Milton. *Isaac Babel,* 87–91.

"There Were Nine"
Ehre, Milton. *Isaac Babel,* 58–59.

"Through the Fanlight"
Ehre, Milton. *Isaac Babel,* 61–62.

"Treason"
Ehre, Milton. *Isaac Babel,* 65–66.

"The Trial"
Ehre, Milton. *Isaac Babel,* 140–142.

"With Old Man Makhno"
Ehre, Milton. *Isaac Babel,* 57–58.

"You Were Too Trusting, Captain"
Ehre, Milton. *Isaac Babel,* 59–61.

"Zamoste"
Ehre, Milton. *Isaac Babel,* 75–76.

INGEBORG BACHMANN

"Ein Schritt nach Gomorrha"
Namowicz, Tadeusz. "Begreifen und Benennen: Zur sprachlichen Struktur der
    Erzählung 'Ein Schritt nach Gomorrha' von Ingeborg Bachmann," in
    Klein, Michael, and Sigurd P. Scheichl, Eds. *Thematisierung* . . . , 93–101.

VLADLEN BAKHNOV

"How the Sun Went Out"
McGuire, Patrick L. *Red Star...*, 75–76.

ANDREI BALABUKHA

"Appendix"
McGuire, Patrick L. *Red Star...*, 56.

JAMES BALDWIN

"Sonny's Blues"
Bohner, Charles H. *Instructor's Manual...*, 10–11.
Clark, Michael. "James Baldwin's 'Sonny's Blues': Childhood Light and Art,"
    Coll Lang Assoc J, 29 (1985), 197–205.

JURGI LABRAIL BALIT

"A Man with Two Wives"
Haywood, John A. *Modern Arabic Literature...*, 128.

J. G. BALLARD

"The Ultimate City"
Firsching, Lorenz J. "J. G. Ballard's Ambiguous Apocalypse," *Sci-Fiction Stud*,
    12 (1985), 299–301.

HONORÉ BALZAC

"An Episode Under the Terror"
Schuerewegen, Franc. "'Un épisode sous la Terreur': une lecture expiatoire,"
    L'Année Balzacienne, N.S. 6 (1985), 247–263.

"Louis Lambert"
Young, Michael. "Beginnings, Endings and Textual Identities in Balzac's 'Louis
    Lambert,'" *Romanic R*, 77 (1986), 343–358.

"The Message"
Kelly, Dorothy J. "What *Is* the Message in Balzac's 'Le Message'?" *Nineteenth-
    Century French Stud*, 13, ii–iii (1986), 45–58.

"The Succubus"
Nesci, Catherine. "'Le Succube' ou l'itinéraire de Tours en Orient: Essai sur
    les lieux du poétique balzacien," *L'Année Balzacienne*, N.S. 5 (1984), 263–
    265.

"Venial Sin"
Nesci, Catherine. "Étude drolatique de femmes: Figures et fonctions de la fém-
    inité dans les *Contes drolatique*," *L'Année Balzacienne*, N.S. 6 (1985), 247–
    263.

TONI CADE BAMBARA

"A Girl's Story"
Byerman, Keith E. *Fingering the Jagged Grain* . . . , 115–117.

"Gorilla, My Love"
Hargrove, Nancy D. "Youth in Toni Cade Bambara's *Gorilla, My Love*," *Southern
    Q*, 22, i (1983), 85–87; rpt. Prenshaw, Peggy W., Ed. *Women Writers* . . . ,
    218–220.

"The Hammer Man"
Hargrove, Nancy D. "Youth . . . ," 92–94; rpt. Prenshaw, Peggy W., Ed. *Women
    Writers* . . . , 225–227.

"Happy Birthday"
Hargrove, Nancy D. "Youth . . . ," 83–85; rpt. Prenshaw, Peggy W., Ed. *Women
    Writers* . . . , 216–218.

"The Johnson Girls"
Byerman, Keith E. *Fingering the Jagged Grain* . . . , 111–114.

"The Lesson"
Bohner, Charles H. *Instructor's Manual* . . . , 11–12.
Hargrove, Nancy D. "Youth . . . ," 87–90; rpt. Prenshaw, Peggy W., Ed. *Women
    Writers* . . . , 220–223.

"Maggie of the Green Bottles"
Hargrove, Nancy D. "Youth . . . ," 95–97; rpt. Prenshaw, Peggy W., Ed. *Women
    Writers* . . . , 228–230.

"Mississippi Ham Rider"
Byerman, Keith E. *Fingering the Jagged Grain* . . . , 108–111.

"My Man Bovanne"
Byerman, Keith E. *Fingering the Jagged Grain* . . . , 105–108.

"The Organizer's Wife"
Byerman, Keith E. *Fingering the Jagged Grain* . . . , 117–119.

"Raymond's Run"
Hargrove, Nancy D. "Youth . . . ," 97–98; rpt. Prenshaw, Peggy W., Ed. *Women
    Writers* . . . , 230–232.

"Sweet Town"
Hargrove, Nancy D. "Youth . . . ," 90–92; rpt. Prenshaw, Peggy W., Ed. *Women
    Writers* . . . , 223–225.

"Witchbird"
Byerman, Keith E. *Fingering the Jagged Grain* . . . , 119–123.

A[UDREY] L[ILIAN] BARKER

"Domini"
Baldwin, Dean. "The English Short Story in the Fifties," in Vannatta, Dennis, Ed. *The English Short Story, 1945–1980,* 39–40.

"Here Comes a Candle"
Baldwin, Dean. "The English Short Story . . . ," 70.

"The Iconoclasts"
Baldwin, Dean. "The English Short Story . . . ," 26.

DJUNA BARNES

"Aller et Retour"
Plumb, Cheryl. *Fancy's Craft* . . . , 62–65.

"The Beauty"
Plumb, Cheryl. *Fancy's Craft* . . . , 27–28.

"Cassation" [originally titled "A Little Girl Tells a Story to a Lady"]
Plumb, Cheryl. *Fancy's Craft* . . . , 67–69.

"The Coward"
Plumb, Cheryl. *Fancy's Craft* . . . , 52–54.

"The Grande Malade"
Plumb, Cheryl. *Fancy's Craft* . . . , 69–72.

"The Jest of Jests"
Plumb, Cheryl. *Fancy's Craft* . . . , 51–52.

"A Night Among the Horses"
Plumb, Cheryl. *Fancy's Craft* . . . , 56–57.

"The Passion"
Plumb, Cheryl. *Fancy's Craft* . . . , 72–74.

"The Rabbit"
Plumb, Cheryl. *Fancy's Craft* . . . , 57–59.

"Spillway"
Plumb, Cheryl. *Fancy's Craft* . . . , 65–67.

"The Valet"
Plumb, Cheryl. *Fancy's Craft* . . . , 59–61.

JOHN BARTH

"Ambrose His Mark"
Kim, Seong-Kon. *Journey into the Past . . .* , 68–69.
Walkiewicz, Edward P. *John Barth*, 91–94.

"Anonymiad"
Walkiewicz, Edward P. *John Barth*, 107–109.

"Bellerophoniad"
Walkiewicz, Edward P. *John Barth*, 117–119.

"Dunyazadiad"
Walkiewicz, Edward P. *John Barth*, 112–114.
Ziegler, Heide. "A Room of One's Own: The Author and the Reader in the
    Text," in Chénetier, Marc, Ed. *Critical Angles . . .* , 54–56.

"Life-Story"
Lemon, Lee T. *Portraits . . .* , 196–198.
Walkiewicz, Edward P. *John Barth*, 103–105.

"Lost in the Funhouse"
Bohner, Charles H. *Instructor's Manual . . .* , 12–13.
Robinson, Douglas. *American Apocalypse . . .* , 211–213.
Sheidley, William E., and Ann Charters. *Instructor's Manual . . .* , 170–172; rpt.
    Charters, Ann, William E. Sheidley, and Martha Ramsey. *Instructor's Man-
    ual . . .* , 2nd ed., 185–187.
Walkiewicz, Edward P. *John Barth*, 94–98.

"Menelaiad"
Lemon, Lee T. *Portraits . . .* , 167–169.
Verschueren, Walter. "'Voice, Tape, Writing': Original Repetition in *Lost in the
    Funhouse* (Beyond Phenomenology: Barth's 'Menelaiad')," *Delta*, 21 (Octo-
    ber, 1985), 79–93.
Walkiewicz, Edward P. *John Barth*, 105–107.

"Night-Sea Journey"
Kim, Seong-Kon. *Journey into the Past . . .* , 67–68.
Walkiewicz, Edward P. *John Barth*, 89–91.

"Perseid"
Kim, Seong-Kon. *Journey into the Past . . .* , 74–75.
Walkiewicz, Edward P. *John Barth*, 114–116.
Weixlemann, Joe and Sher. "Barth and Barthelme Recycle the Perseus Myth:
    A Study of Literary Ecology," *Mod Fiction Stud*, 25 (1979), 191–207.

"Water-Message"
Lemon, Lee T. *Portraits . . .* , 152–153.

DONALD BARTHELME

"The Abduction from the Seraglio"
Upton, Lee. "Failed Artists in Donald Barthelme's *Sixty Stories*," *Critique*, 26, i
    (1984), 12–13.

"The Balloon"
Couturier, Maurice, and Regis Durand. *Donald Barthelme*, 62–63, 69–70.
Gerlach, John. *Toward the End* . . . , 148–150.

"A City of Churches"
Bohner, Charles H. *Instructor's Manual* . . . , 14–15.

"The Death of Edward Lear"
Upton, Lee. "Failed Artists . . . ," 16.

"The Dolt"
Upton, Lee. "Failed Artists . . . ," 14–15.

"The Falling Dog"
Upton, Lee. "Failed Artists . . . ," 13–14.

"How I Write My Songs"
Upton, Lee. "Failed Artists . . . ," 13.

"The Indian Uprising"
Evans, Walter. "Comanches and Civilization in Donald Barthelme's 'The Indian
    Uprising,'" *Arizona Q*, 42 (1986), 45–52.

"Kierkegaard Unfair to Schlegel"
Couturier, Maurice, and Regis Durand. *Donald Barthelme*, 30–32.
Wilde, Alan. "Barthelme Unfair to Kierkegaard: Some Thoughts on Modern
    and Postmodern Irony," *Boundary*, 2, v (1976), 45–70.

"The Phantom of the Opera's Friend"
Upton, Lee. "Failed Artists . . . ," 16–17.

"Robert Kennedy Saved from Drowning"
Couturier, Maurice, and Regis Durand. *Donald Barthelme*, 36–38.

"The Sandman"
Couturier, Maurice, and Regis Durand. *Donald Barthelme*, 42–43.

"A Shower of Gold"
Upton, Lee. "Failed Artists . . . ," 15–16.
Weixlemann, Joe and Sher. "Barth and Barthelme Recycle the Perseus Myth:
    A Study of Literary Ecology," *Mod Fiction Stud*, 25 (1979), 191–207.

"Views of My Father Weeping"
Couturier, Maurice, and Regis Durand. *Donald Barthelme*, 38–41.
Durand, Regis. "On the Pertinaciousness of the Father, the Son, and the Sub-

ject: The Case of Donald Barthelme," in Chénetier, Marc, Ed. *Critical Angles* . . . , 159–161.

GIORGIO BASSANI

"Ai tempi della Resistenza"
Schneider, Marilyn. *Vengeance* . . . , 189–192.

"Apologo (No. 1)"
Schneider, Marilyn. *Vengeance* . . . , 204–206.

"Una corsa ad Abbazia"
Schneider, Marilyn. *Vengeance* . . . , 182–186.

"Cuoio grasso"
Schneider, Marilyn. *Vengeance* . . . , 196–200.

"Una Lapide in via Mazzini"
Schneider, Marilyn. *Vengeance* . . . , 77–81.

"Lida Mantovani"
Schneider, Marilyn. *Vengeance* . . . , 154–158.

"La necessità è il velo di Dio"
Schneider, Marilyn. *Vengeance* . . . , 186–188.

"Una notte del '43"
Schneider, Marilyn. *Vengeance* . . . , 66–74; 115–118.

"L'odore del fieno" [originally titled "Il muro di cinta"]
Schneider, Marilyn. *Vengeance* . . . , 173–175.

"La paseggiata prima di cena"
Schneider, Marilyn. *Vengeance* . . . , 43–50, 158–161.

"Pelandra"
Schneider, Marilyn. *Vengeance* . . . , 200–203.

"La ragazza dei fucili"
Schneider, Marilyn. *Vengeance* . . . , 164–166, 180–182.

"Ravenna"
Schneider, Marilyn. *Vengeance* . . . , 193–196.

"Le scarpe da tennis"
Schneider, Marilyn. *Vengeance* . . . , 207–209.

"Un topo nel formaggio"
Schneider, Marilyn. *Vengeance* . . . , 206–207.

"Gli ultimi anni di Clelia Trotti"
Schneider, Marilyn. *Vengeance* . . . , 139–151.

H. E. BATES

"The Bride Comes to Evenford"
Flora, Joseph M. *The English Short Story* . . . , 134–135.

"The Cruise of the *Breadwinner*"
Stinson, John J. "The English Short Story, 1945–1950," in Vannatta, Dennis,
Ed. *The English Short Story, 1945–1980*, 3.

"The Flag"
Flora, Joseph M. *The English Short Story* . . . , 119–120.

"The Major of Hussars"
Flora, Joseph M. *The English Short Story* . . . , 118–119.

"The Place Where Shady Lay"
Pickering, Jean. "The English Short Story in the Sixties," in Vannatta, Dennis,
Ed. *The English Short Story, 1945–1980*, 101–102.

"The Waterfall"
Flora, Joseph M. *The English Short Story* . . . , 131–132.

CHARLES BAUDELAIRE

"La Fanfarlo"
Chambers, Ross. "Le fade et le pimenté: Modes de séduction dans 'La Fanfarlo'
de Baudelaire," in Tobin, Ronald W., Ed. *Littérature* . . . , 175–201.

ANN BEATTIE

"The Burning House"
Murphy, Christina. *Ann Beattie*, 84–88.

"The Cinderella Waltz"
Hill, Jane B. "Ann Beattie's Children as Redeemers," *Critique*, 27 (1986), 205.
Murphy, Christina. *Ann Beattie*, 93–98.

"A Clever-Kid Story"
Hill, Jane B. "Ann Beattie's Children . . . ," 202.

"Colorado"
Murphy, Christina. *Ann Beattie*, 63–64.

"Desire"
Murphy, Christina. *Ann Beattie*, 98–102.

"Dwarf House"
Hill, Jane B. "Ann Beattie's Children . . . ," 199–200.
Murphy, Christina. *Ann Beattie*, 20–23.

"Fancy Flight"
Murphy, Christina. *Ann Beattie*, 34–40.

"Friends"
Murphy, Christina. *Ann Beattie*, 52–55.

"Imagined Scenes"
Murphy, Christina. *Ann Beattie*, 29–34.

"It's Just Another Day in Big Bear City, California"
Hill, Jane B. "Ann Beattie's Children . . . ," 201.
Porter, Carolyn. "Ann Beattie: The Art of the Missing," in Rainwater, Catherine, and William J. Scheick, Eds. . . . *Narrative Strategies*, 12–13.

"Jacklightning"
Murphy, Christina. *Ann Beattie*, 91–93.

"The Lawn Party"
Murphy, Christina. *Ann Beattie*, 65–66.

"Learning to Fall"
Murphy, Christina. *Ann Beattie*, 88–91.
Porter, Carolyn. "Ann Beattie . . . ," 20–21.

"The Lifeguard"
Hill, Jane B. "Ann Beattie's Children . . . ," 203.

"Marshall's Dog"
Porter, Carolyn. "Ann Beattie . . . ," 14–16.

"Octascope"
Hill, Jane B. "Ann Beattie's Children . . . ," 204.
Murphy, Christina. *Ann Beattie*, 55–58.

"The Parking Lot"
Murphy, Christina. *Ann Beattie*, 26–29.

"Playback"
Hill, Jane B. "Ann Beattie's Children . . . ," 202–203.

"Running Dreams"
Porter, Carolyn. "Ann Beattie . . . ," 21.

"Snakes' Shoes"
Murphy, Christina. *Ann Beattie*, 23–26.

"Vermont"
Hill, Jane B. "Ann Beattie's Children . . . ," 203–204.

"A Vintage Thunderbird"
Murphy, Christina. *Ann Beattie,* 58–63.

"Waiting"
Sheidley, William E., and Ann Charters. *Instructor's Manual* . . . , 191; rpt. Char-
    ters, Ann, William E. Sheidley, and Martha Ramsey. *Instructor's Man-
    ual* . . . , 2nd ed., 226–227.

"Winter: 1978"
Hill, Jane B. "Ann Beattie's Children . . . ," 205–206.
Porter, Carolyn. "Ann Beattie . . . ," 22–24.

"Wolf Dreams"
Porter, Carolyn. "Ann Beattie . . . ," 13–14.

SAMUEL BECKETT

"Assumption"
Ben-Zvi, Linda. *Samuel Beckett,* 34–36.

"The Calmative"
Ben-Zvi, Linda. *Samuel Beckett,* 77–78.

"A Case in a Thousand"
Ben-Zvi, Linda. *Samuel Beckett,* 43–44.

"Dante and the Lobster"
Hanson, Clare. *Short Stories* . . . , 143–145.
Stevenson, Kay G. "Belacqua in the Moon: Beckett's Revision of 'Dante and the
    Lobster,'" in McCarthy, Patrick A., Ed. *Critical Essays on Samuel Beckett,* 36–
    46.

"The End"
Ben-Zvi, Linda. *Samuel Beckett,* 78–79.

"Enough"
Brienza, Susan. "Beckett's 'Enough': The Style of Delusion and Revision," *Style,*
    9, i (1985), 50–65.

"First Love"
Ben-Zvi, Linda. *Samuel Beckett,* 76–77.

"Imagination Dead Imagine"
Ben-Zvi, Linda. *Samuel Beckett,* 115–116.
Hanson, Clare. *Short Stories* . . . , 149–150.

"Old Earth"
Hanson, Clare. *Short Stories* . . . , 152–153.

"Ping"
Hanson, Clare. *Short Stories* . . . , 150–151.

"Still"
Hanson, Clare. *Short Stories . . .* , 151–152.

SAUL BELLOW

"Cousins"
Fuchs, Daniel. "On *Him with His Foot in His Mouth and Other Stories*," *Saul Bellow J*, 5, i (1986), 7–11.
Knight, Karl F. "Bellow's 'Cousins': The Suspense of Playing It to the End," *Saul Bellow J*, 5, ii (1986), 32–35.

"Him with His Foot in His Mouth"
Fuchs, Daniel. "On *Him with His Foot . . .* ," 13–15.
Roudane, Matthew C. "Discordant Timbre: Saul Bellow's 'Him with His Foot in His Mouth,'" *Saul Bellow J*, 4, i (1985), 52–61.

"Looking for Mr. Green"
Abbott, H. Porter. *Diary Fiction . . .* , 172–174.

"Mosby's Memoirs"
Abbott, H. Porter. *Diary Fiction . . .* , 175–178.

"Seize the Day"
Ancona, Francesco A. *Writing the Absence . . .* , 35–48.
Bouson, J. Brooks. "The Narcissistic Self-Drama of Wilhelm Adler: A Kohutian Reading of Bellow's 'Seize the Day,'" *Saul Bellow J*, 5, ii (1986), 3–14.
Clayton, John J. "Saul Bellow's 'Seize the Day': A Study in Mid-Life Transition," *Saul Bellow J*, 5, i (1986), 34–47.
Goldman, Leila H. *Saul Bellow's Moral Vision . . .* , 61–84.
Marotti, Maria O. "Concealment and Revelation: The Binary Structure of 'Seize the Day,'" *Saul Bellow J*, 5, ii (1986), 46–51.
Weiss, Daniel. *The Critical Agonistes . . .* , 185–213.
Wilson, Jonathan. *On Bellow's Planet . . .* , 96–111.

"A Silver Dish"
Fuchs, Daniel. "On *Him with His Foot . . .* ," 11–13.

"What Kind of Day Did You Have?"
Fuchs, Daniel. "On *Him with His Foot . . .* ," 3–7.

JUAN BENET

"Por los suelos"
Perrin Bussiere, Annie. "Identification de un homme: 'Por los suelos' de Juan Benet," *Les Langues Néo-Latines*, 80, iii–iv (1986), 37–51.

STEPHEN VINCENT BENÉT

"The Angel Was a Yankee"
Bromley, Robin. "Stephen Vincent Benét," in Bleiler, E. F., Ed. *Supernatural Fiction Writers . . .* , II, 801.

"The Devil and Daniel Webster"
Bromley, Robin. "Stephen Vincent Benét," 798–799.

"Doc Mellhorn and the Pearly Gates"
Bromley, Robin. "Stephen Vincent Benét," 800.

"The Gold Dress"
Bromley, Robin. "Stephen Vincent Benét," 802.

"Johnny Pye and the Fool-Killer"
Bromley, Robin. "Stephen Vincent Benét," 800.

"The King of the Cats"
Bromley, Robin. "Stephen Vincent Benét," 799–800.

"The Land Where There Is No Death"
Bromley, Robin. "Stephen Vincent Benét," 802.

"The Minister's Books"
Bromley, Robin. "Stephen Vincent Benét," 801–802.

"O'Halloran's Luck"
Bromley, Robin. "Stephen Vincent Benét," 800.

"Sea Serpent"
Bromley, Robin. "Stephen Vincent Benét," 799.

"A Tooth for Paul Revere"
Bromley, Robin. "Stephen Vincent Benét," 800–801.

"William Riley and the Fates"
Bromley, Robin. "Stephen Vincent Benét," 802.

GREGORY BENFORD

"And the Sea Like a Mirror"
Samuelson, David N. "From Aliens to Alienation: Gregory Benford's Variations
  on a Theme," *Foundation*, 14 (1978), 6.

"Deeper Than the Darkness"
Samuelson, David N. "From Aliens to Alienation . . . ," 7.

EDWARD FREDERIC BENSON

"Naboth's Vineyard"
Morgan, Chris. "E. F. Benson," in Bleiler, E. F., Ed. *Supernatural Fiction Writers* . . . , I, 494–495.

"Pirates"
Morgan, Chris. "E. F. Benson," 495.

ALEXANDER A. BESTUZHEV-MARLINSKY
[ALEXANDER BESTUZHEV]

"Ammalat-Bek"
Moser, Charles A. *The Russian Short Story* . . . , 12–13.

"Eisen Castle"
Landsman, Neil B. "Decembrist Romanticism: A. A. Bestuzhev-Marlinsky," in
   Reid, Robert, Ed. *Problems* . . . , 82–83.

"An Evening at a Bivouac"
Simpson, Mark S. *The Officer* . . . , 54–57.

"Neuhausen Castle"
Landsman, Neil B. "Decembrist Romanticism . . . ," 81–82.

"The Reval Tournament"
Landsman, Neil B. "Decembrist Romanticism . . . ," 82.

"The Test"
Moser, Charles A. *The Russian Short Story* . . . , 10–11.

"Wenden Castle"
Landsman, Neil B. "Decembrist Romanticism . . . ," 81.

GEOFFREY BEWLEY

"Passage from India"
Bennett, Bruce. "Asian Encounters in the Contemporary Australian Short
   Story," *World Lit Written Engl*, 26 (1986), 59–60.

AMBROSE BIERCE

"The Damned Thing"
Wymer, Thomas L. "Ambrose Bierce," in Bleiler, E. F., Ed. *Supernatural Fiction
   Writers* . . . , II, 735.

"The Death of Halpin Frayser"
Butterfield, Herbie. "'Our Bedfellow Death': The Short Stories of Ambrose
   Bierce," in Lee, A. Robert, Ed. . . . *American Short Story*, 141–142.
Wymer, Thomas L. "Ambrose Bierce," 736–737.

"The Famous Gilson Bequest"
Wymer, Thomas L. "Ambrose Bierce," 735–736.

"Moxon's Master"
Bleiler, E. F. "Who Was Moxon's Master?" *Extrapolation*, 26 (1985), 181–189.

"An Occurrence at Owl Creek Bridge"
Bohner, Charles H. *Instructor's Manual* . . . , 15–16.

Cheatham, George. "Point of View in Bierce's 'Owl Creek Bridge,'" *Am Lit Realism*, 18 (1985), 219–225.
Sheidley, William E., and Ann Charters. *Instructor's Manual...*, 20–21; rpt. Charters, Ann, William E. Sheidley, and Martha Ramsey. *Instructor's Manual...*, 2nd ed., 23–24.

ADOLFO BIOY CASARES

"Cómo perdí la vista"
Meehan, Thomas C. "The Motifs of the Homunculus and the Shrinking Man in Two Versions of a Short Story by Adolfo Bioy Casares," *Hispano*, 28, ii (1985), 79–87.

ANDREI GEORGIEVICH BITOV

"The Departing Monakhov"
Moser, Charles A. *The Russian Short Story...*, 176–177.

ALGERNON BLACKWOOD

"The Damned"
Punter, David. "Algernon Blackwood," in Bleiler, E. F., Ed. *Supernatural Fiction Writers...*, I, 465–466.

"The Man Whom the Trees Loved"
Punter, David. "Algernon Blackwood," 464–465.

"The Pikestaffe Case"
Punter, David. "Algernon Blackwood," 467.

CLARK BLAISE

"A North American Education"
Lecker, Robert. "Frankie's 'Demimonde': Notes on Clark Blaise's 'A North American Education,'" *Lit R*, 28 (1985), 351–360.

"Notes Beyond a History"
Lecker, Robert. "'The Other Side of Things': Notes on Clark Blaise's 'Notes Beyond a History,'" *Canadian Lit*, 111 (1986), 117–127.

"The Salesman's Son Grows Older"
Darling, Michael. "The Psychology of Alienation: Clark Blaise's 'The Salesman's Son Grows Up,'" in Struthers, J. R., Ed. *The Montreal Story Tellers...*, 140–147.

ROBERT BLOCH

"The Cloak"
Daniels, Les. "Robert Bloch," in Bleiler, E. F., Ed. *Supernatural Fiction Writers* . . . , II, 902.

"The Dark Isle"
Larson, Randall D. *Robert Bloch,* 15–16.

"The Feast in the Abbey"
Larson, Randall D. *Robert Bloch,* 11–12.

"Iron Mask"
Larson, Randall D. *Robert Bloch,* 47–48.

"The Shadow from the Steeple"
Larson, Randall D. *Robert Bloch,* 22–23.

"The Shambler from the Stars"
Larson, Randall D. *Robert Bloch,* 19–20.

"Slave of the Flames"
Larson, Randall D. *Robert Bloch,* 13–14.

"Terror in Cut-Throat Cove"
Larson, Randall D. *Robert Bloch,* 23–24.

"That Hell-Bound Train"
Daniels, Les. "Robert Bloch," 904.
Larson, Randall D. *Robert Bloch,* 48–49.

"Yours Truly, Jack the Ripper"
Larson, Randall D. *Robert Bloch,* 54–55.

LOUISE BOGAN

"Dove and Serpent"
Frank, Elizabeth. *Louise Bogan* . . . , 217–219.

"Journey Around My Room"
Frank, Elizabeth. *Louise Bogan* . . . , 215–217.

"Keramik"
Frank, Elizabeth. *Louise Bogan* . . . , 207–209.

"The Short Life of Emily"
Frank, Elizabeth. *Louise Bogan* . . . , 212–213.

HEINRICH BÖLL

"Like a Bad Dream"
Bohner, Charles H. *Instructor's Manual . . . ,* 16–17.

JORGE LUIS BORGES

"Abenjacán the Bojarí, Dead in His Labyrinth" [same as "Ibn Hakkam al-
Bokhari, Dead in His Labyrinth"]
Agheana, Ion T. *The Prose . . . ,* 237–240.
Gai, Adam. "Abenjacán el Borges: Conjetura e 'hipalage,'" *Explicación de Textos
Literarios,* 14, i (1986), 91–97.
Reisz de Rivarola, Susana. "Borges: Teoría y Praxis de la ficción fantastica: A
propósito de 'Abenjacán el Bojarí, muerto en su laberinto,'" *Lexis,* 6 (1982),
161–202.

"The Aleph"
Agheana, Ion T. *The Prose . . . ,* 136–141.
Pavel, Thomas G. *Fictional Worlds,* 96–97.

"The Babylonian Lottery"
Agheana, Ion T. *The Prose . . . ,* 173–179.

"Borges and I"
Miller, Karl. *Doubles . . . ,* 32–36.

"The Congress"
Continez, Carlos. "Hacia el extasis: 'El congresso' de Borges," *Hispanic R,* 54
(1986), 313–322.

"Death and the Compass"
Agheana, Ion T. *The Prose . . . ,* 234–237.
Bedell, Jeanne F. "Borges' Study in Scarlet: 'Death and the Compass' as Detec-
tive Fiction and Literary Criticism," *Clues,* 6, ii (1985), 109–122.
Boruchoff, David A. "In Pursuit of the Detective Genre: 'La muerte y la brújula'
of J. L. Borges," *Inti,* 21, i (1985), 13–26.
Dyson, John P. "On Naming in Borges's 'La muerte y la brújula,'" *Comp Lit,* 37
(1985), 140–168.
Franco, Jean. "Plotting Women: Popular Narratives for Women in the United
States and Latin America," in Chevigny, Bell G., and Gari Laguardia, Eds.
Reinventing the Americas . . . , 254–255.
Hanson, Clare. *Short Stories . . . ,* 154–155.
Irwin, John T. "Mysteries We Reread, Mysteries of Rereading: Poe, Borges,
and the Analytic Detective Story; Also Lacan, Derrida, and Johnson," *Mod
Lang Notes,* 101 (1986), 1188–1211.
McGurk, B. J. "Seminar on Jorge Luis Borges' 'Death and the Compass,'"
Renaissance & Mod Stud, 27 (1983), 47–60.
Solotorevsky, Myrna. "'La Muerte y la brújula,' parodia irónica de una conver-
ción genetica," *Neophilologus,* 70 (1986), 547–554.
Sussman, Henry. "Kafka in the Heart of the Twentieth Century: An Approach
to Borges," in Udoff, Alan, Ed. *Kafka's Contextuality,* 218–221.

"Deutsches Requiem"
Agheana, Ion T. *The Prose . . .* , 121–124.

"Emma Zunz"
Agheana, Ion T. *The Prose . . .* , 285–287.
Brodzki, Bella. "'She was unable not to think': Borges' 'Emma Zunz' and the Female Subject," *Mod Lang Notes*, 100 (1985), 330–347.
Stavans, Ilan. "Emma Zunz: The Jewish Theodicy of Jorge Luis Borges," *Mod Fiction Stud*, 32 (1986), 469–475.

"The Encounter"
Wheelock, Carter. "Borges and the 'Death' of the Text," *Hispanic R*, 53 (1985), 160.

"The End of the Duel"
Bohner, Charles H. *Instructor's Manual . . .* , 17–18.
Sheidley, William E., and Ann Charters. *Instructor's Manual . . .* , 115–116; rpt. Charters, Ann, William E. Sheidley, and Martha Ramsey. *Instructor's Manual . . .* , 2nd ed., 114–115.

"Everything and Nothing"
Stephens, Michael. *The Dramaturgy of Style . . .* , 22–23.

"Funes the Memorious"
Agheana, Ion T. *The Prose . . .* , 135–136.
Hanson, Clare. *Short Stories . . .* , 157–158.
Nuño, Juan. "El montón de espejos rotos: 'Funes el memorioso,'" *Escritura*, 8 (January–June, 1983), 105–109.
Shapiro, Henry L. "Memory and Meaning: Borges and 'Funes el memorioso,'" *Revista Canadiense de Estudios Hispánicos*, 9 (1985), 257–265.

"The Garden of Forking Paths"
Agheana, Ion T. *The Prose . . .* , 124–126.
Hanson, Clare. *Short Stories . . .* , 155–156.
Sussman, Henry. "Kafka in the Heart . . . ," 216–217.

"The God's Script" [same as "The Writing of the Lord"]
Agheana, Ion T. *The Prose . . .* , 187–188.

"The House of Asterion"
Anderson-Imbert, Enrique. "Un cuento de Borges: 'La casa de Asterión,'" *Revista Iberoamericana*, 25 (January–June, 1960), 33–43.
Harrison, Regina. "Mythopoesis: The Monster in the Labyrinth According to Supervielle, Gide, Borges, and Cortázar," *Kentucky Romance Q*, 32, ii (1985), 127–137.
McGrady, Donald. "El redentor del Asterión de Borges," *Revista Iberoamericana*, 52 (1986), 531–535.
Thirouin, Laurent. "Astérion, ou l'impatience de lire," *Poétique*, 14 (1983), 282–292.

"Juan Murana"
Wheelock, Carter. "Borges and the 'Death' . . . ," 159–160.

"The Library of Babel"
Agheana, Ion T. *The Prose* . . . , 181–187.
Knapp, Bettina L. *Archetype, Architecture* . . . , 100–124.
Pavel, Thomas G. *Fictional Worlds*, 58–59.
Thiher, Allen. *Words in Reflection* . . . , 163–164.

"The Life of Isidoro Cruz (1829–1874)"
Kadir, Djelal. *Questing Fictions* . . . , 16–21.

"The Man on the Threshold"
Gutiérrez Mouat, Ricardo. "De Te Fabula Narratur: 'El hombre en el umbral'
de Borges," *Romance Notes*, 26, ii (1985), 90–94.

"Pierre Menard, Author of *Quixote*"
Hume, Kathryn. *Fantasy and Mimesis* . . . , 95–96.
Thiher, Allen. *Words in Reflection* . . . , 160–161.

"The Secret Miracle"
Agheana, Ion T. *The Prose* . . . , 108–113.
Zlotchew, Clark M. "La experencia directa de la obsesiva fantasía en Borges y
en Robbe-Grillet," *Káñina*, 4, i (1980), 61–67.

"The Theme of the Traitor and the Hero"
Agheana, Ion T. *The Prose* . . . , 127–131.

"Tlön, Uqbar, Orbis Tertius"
Sussman, Henry. "Kafka in the Heart . . . ," 191–213.
Thiher, Allen. *Words in Reflection* . . . , 161–162.

"The Zahir"
Agheana, Ion T. *The Prose* . . . , 141.
Feenberg, Andrew. "Le Désordre économique et erotique," in Dumouchel,
Paul, Ed. *Violence et vérité* . . . , 201–210.

JUAN BOSCH

"Luis Pie"
Fernández Olmos, Margarita. "El haitiano en la literatura dominicana: Un análisis de 'Luis Pie,'" *Stud Afro-Hispanic Lit*, 2–3 (1978–79), 231–243.

"The Woman"
Olmos, Margarita de. "'La mujer': Un análisis estetico-cultural," *Ciencia & So-
ciedad* (Santo Domingo), 5, i (1980), 149–162.

ELIZABETH BOWEN

"Ann Lee's"
Hanson, Clare. *Short Stories* . . . , 117–118.

"The Cat Jumps"
Partridge, A. C. "Language and Identity in the Shorter Fiction of Elizabeth
    Bowen," in Sekine, Masaru, Ed. *Irish Writers . . .* , 174–175.

"The Cheery Soul"
Sanders, Joe. "Elizabeth Bowen," in Bleiler, E. F., Ed. *Supernatural Fiction Writ-
    ers . . .* , II, 570–571.

"The Demon Lover"
Sanders, Joe. "Elizabeth Bowen," 571–572.

"The Disinherited"
Haule, James M. "*She* and the Moral Dilemma of Elizabeth Bowen," *Colby Lib
    Q,* 22 (1986), 208–211.

"Green Holly"
Sanders, Joe. "Elizabeth Bowen," 573–574.

"The Happy Autumn Fields"
Sanders, Joe. "Elizabeth Bowen," 572.

"Her Table Spread"
Touhy, Frank. "Five Fierce Ladies," in Sekine, Masaru, Ed. *Irish Writers . . .* ,
    204.

"The Inherited Clock"
Sanders, Joe. "Elizabeth Bowen," 571.

"Ivy Gripped the Steps"
Partridge, A. C. "Language and Identity . . . ," 179–180.
Sanders, Joe. "Elizabeth Bowen," 573.

"Joining Charles"
Partridge, A. C. "Language and Identity . . . ," 173–174.

"The Little Girl's Room"
Hanson, Clare. *Short Stories . . .* , 118–121.

"Maria"
Partridge, A. C. "Language and Identity . . . ," 175–177.

"Mysterious Kôr"
Hanson, Clare. *Short Stories . . .* , 123–124.
Haule, James M. "*She* and the Moral Dilemma . . . ," 211–213.
Sanders, Joe. "Elizabeth Bowen," 574.

"Pink May"
Sanders, Joe. "Elizabeth Bowen," 573.

"Songs My Father Sang Me"
Sanders, Joe. "Elizabeth Bowen," 571.

"Summer Night"
Hanson, Clare. *Short Stories* . . . , 121–123.
Partridge, A. C. "Language and Identity . . . ," 178–179.

PAUL BOWLES

"Allal"
Pounds, Wayne. *Paul Bowles* . . . , 120–126.

"The Circular Valley"
Pounds, Wayne. *Paul Bowles* . . . , 68–71.
Wagner, Linda W. "Paul Bowles and the Characterization of Women," *Critique*,
    27, i (1985), 19.

"The Dismissal"
Pounds, Wayne. *Paul Bowles* . . . , 132.

"Doña Faustina"
Ditsky, John. *"The Time of Friendship:* The Short Stories of Paul Bowles," *San
    José Stud*, 12, ii (1986), 70–71.

"The Eye"
Pounds, Wayne. *Paul Bowles* . . . , 134–137.

"Fqih"
Pounds, Wayne. *Paul Bowles* . . . , 126–127.

"A Friend of the World"
Ditsky, John. *"The Time* . . . ," 67–68.

"The Frozen Field"
Ditsky, John. *"The Time* . . . ," 73–74.
Wagner, Linda W. "Paul Bowles . . . ," 19–20.

"The Garden"
Ditsky, John. *"The Time* . . . ," 70.

"Here to Learn"
Pounds, Wayne. *Paul Bowles* . . . , 131–132.

"The Hours After Noon"
Ditsky, John. *"The Time* . . . ," 65–67.

"The Hyena"
Ditsky, John. *"The Time* . . . ," 69–70.

"I Should Open My Mouth"
Ditsky, John. *"The Time* . . . ," 72–73.

"Istikhar, Anaya, Medagan and the Medaganat"
Pounds, Wayne. *Paul Bowles* . . . , 127–128.

"Kitty"
Pounds, Wayne. *Paul Bowles* . . . , 129–130.

"The Little House"
Pounds, Wayne. *Paul Bowles* . . . , 132–134.

"Reminders of Bouselham"
Pounds, Wayne. *Paul Bowles* . . . , 128–129.

"The Scorpion"
Pounds, Wayne. *Paul Bowles* . . . , 65–68.

"The Story of Lahcen and Idir"
Ditsky, John. "*The Time* . . . ," 68.

"The Successor"
Ditsky, John. "*The Time* . . . ," 65.

"Tapiama"
Ditsky, John. "*The Time* . . . ," 71–72.

"Things Gone and Things Still Here"
Pounds, Wayne. *Paul Bowles* . . . , 111–120.

"The Time of Friendship"
Ditsky, John. "*The Time* . . . ," 62–65.
Pounds, Wayne. *Paul Bowles* . . . , 97–100.

"The Wind at Beni Midar"
Ditsky, John. "*The Time* . . . ," 68–69.

HJALMAR HJORTH BOYESEN

"A Good-for-Nothing"
Sollors, Werner. *Beyond Ethnicity* . . . , 155–156.

KAY BOYLE

"Begin Again"
Spanier, Sandra W. *Kay Boyle* . . . , 187.

"Big Fiddle"
Spanier, Sandra W. *Kay Boyle* . . . , 136–138.

"Black Boy"
Spanier, Sandra W. *Kay Boyle* . . . , 108–109.

"The Bridegroom's Body"
Spanier, Sandra W. *Kay Boyle* . . . , 133–136.

"The Canals of Mars"
Spanier, Sandra W. *Kay Boyle* . . . , 157.

"The Crazy Hunter"
Spanier, Sandra W. *Kay Boyle* . . . , 138–142.

"Decision" [originally titled "Passport to Doom"]
Spanier, Sandra W. *Kay Boyle* . . . , 181–182.

"Defeat"
Spanier, Sandra W. *Kay Boyle* . . . , 154–155.

"Episode in the Life of an Ancestor"
Spanier, Sandra W. *Kay Boyle* . . . , 50–52.

"The First Lover"
Spanier, Sandra W. *Kay Boyle* . . . , 106.

"Frankfurt in Our Blood"
Spanier, Sandra W. *Kay Boyle* . . . , 188–189.

"French Harvest"
Spanier, Sandra W. *Kay Boyle* . . . , 182.

"I Can't Get Drunk"
Spanier, Sandra W. *Kay Boyle* . . . , 104–105.

"Madame Tout Petit"
Spanier, Sandra W. *Kay Boyle* . . . , 47–48.

"Maiden, Maiden"
Spanier, Sandra W. *Kay Boyle* . . . , 110–111.

"Major Alshuster"
Spanier, Sandra W. *Kay Boyle* . . . , 109–110.

"Major Engagement in Paris"
Spanier, Sandra W. *Kay Boyle* . . . , 155–156.

"Men"
Spanier, Sandra W. *Kay Boyle* . . . , 153.

"On the Run"
Spanier, Sandra W. *Kay Boyle* . . . , 37–38.

"Polar Bears and Others"
Spanier, Sandra W. *Kay Boyle* . . . , 52–53.

"Portrait"
Spanier, Sandra W. *Kay Boyle* . . . , 38–39.

"Rest Cure"
Spanier, Sandra W. *Kay Boyle* . . . , 105–106.

"Seeing the Sights of San Francisco"
Spanier, Sandra W. *Kay Boyle* . . . , 202–203.

"Spring Morning"
Spanier, Sandra W. *Kay Boyle* . . . , 41–42.

"Summer"
Spanier, Sandra W. *Kay Boyle* . . . , 48–50.

"They Weren't Going to Die"
Spanier, Sandra W. *Kay Boyle* . . . , 153–154.

"This They Took with Them"
Spanier, Sandra W. *Kay Boyle* . . . , 156–157.

"Three Little Men"
Spanier, Sandra W. *Kay Boyle* . . . , 107–108.

"Vacation-Time"
Spanier, Sandra W. *Kay Boyle* . . . , 39–41.

"Wedding Day"
Spanier, Sandra W. *Kay Boyle* . . . , 42–45.

"The White Horses of Vienna"
Spanier, Sandra W. *Kay Boyle* . . . , 113–116.

"Winter Night"
Spanier, Sandra W. *Kay Boyle* . . . , 157–158.

T. CORAGHESSAN BOYLE

"A Women's Restaurant"
Gerlach, John. *Toward the End* . . . , 13–15.

LEIGH BRACKETT

"The Beast-Jewel of Mars"
Carr, John L. "Leigh Brackett," in Bleiler, E. F., Ed. *Supernatural Fiction Writers* . . . , II, 911.

"Mars Minus Bisha"
Carr, John L. "Leigh Brackett," 911–912.

"Purple Priestess of the Mad Moon"
Carr, John L. "Leigh Brackett," 912.

"The Road to Sinharat"
Carr, John L. "Leigh Brackett," 912.

LEIGH BRACKETT and RAY BRADBURY

"Lorelei of the Red Mist"
Clareson, Thomas D. *"Planet Stories,"* in Tymn, Marshall B., and Mike Ashley,
    Eds. *Science Fiction . . . Magazines,* 478.

MALCOLM BRADBURY

"A Goodbye for Evadne Winterbottom"
Evans, Walter. "The English Short Story in the Seventies," in Vannatta, Dennis,
    Ed. *The English Short Story, 1945–1980,* 144–145.

RAY BRADBURY

"August 2002: Night Meeting"
Bohner, Charles H. *Instructor's Manual . . . ,* 18–19.

"Cistern"
Touponce, William F. *Ray Bradbury . . . ,* 43–54.

"The Golden Apples of the Sun"
Touponce, William F. *Ray Bradbury . . . ,* 59–77.

"The Sea Shell"
Touponce, William F. *Ray Bradbury . . . ,* 21–41.

ERNEST BRAMAH

"The Eastern Mystery"
Routley, Erik. *The Puritan Pleasures . . . ,* 79–80.

"The Strange Case of Cyril Bycourt"
Routley, Erik. *The Puritan Pleasures . . . ,* 77–78.

RICHARD BRAUTIGAN

"The Post Office of Eastern Oregon"
Klinkowitz, Jerome. *The American 1960s . . . ,* 41–43.

"Winter Rug"
Horvath, Brooke K. "Wrapped in a Winter Rug: Richard Brautigan Looks at
    Common Responses to Death," *Notes Mod Am Lit,* 8 (Winter, 1984), Item 14.

CHRISTINE BROOKE-ROSE

"Go When You See the Green Man Walking"
Evans, Walter. "The English Short Story in the Seventies," in Vannatta, Dennis,
Ed. *The English Short Story, 1945–1980,* 165–166.

ALICE BROWN

"The Way of Peace"
Toth, Susan A. " 'The Rarest and Most Peculiar Grape': Versions of the New
England Woman in Nineteenth-Century Local Color Literature," in Toth,
Emily, Ed. *Regionalism . . . ,* 24–25.

ROSELLEN BROWN

"Good Housekeeping"
Suleiman, Susan R. "Writing and Motherhood," in Garner, Shirley N., Claire
Kahane, and Madelon Sprengnether, Eds. *The (M)other Tongue . . . ,* 372–
374.

MIKHAIL BULGAKOV

"The Adventures of Chichikov"
Fuhrhop, Doris, and W. Fousek. "Michail Bulgakovs Erzählung 'Pochoždenie
Čičikova' (Čičikovas Abenteur)," in Tretjakow, Pirjo, and Elisabeth Lübcke,
Eds. *Russische Autoren . . . ,* 11–17.
Natov, Nadine. *Mikhail Bulgakov,* 39–40.

"Diaboliad"
Natov, Nadine. *Mikhail Bulgakov,* 40–42.

"The Extraordinary Adventures of a Doctor"
Natov, Nadine. *Mikhail Bulgakov,* 26–27.

"Fatal Eggs"
Natov, Nadine. *Mikhail Bulgakov,* 42–44.

"I Killed"
Natov, Nadine. *Mikhail Bulgakov,* 48.

"Morphine"
Natov, Nadine. *Mikhail Bulgakov,* 24–26.

"Raid"
Natov, Nadine. *Mikhail Bulgakov,* 47–48.

"The Red Crown"
Natov, Nadine. *Mikhail Bulgakov,* 46–47.

EDWARD GEORGE BULWER-LYTTON

"The Haunted and the Haunters"
Bleiler, E. F. "Edward George Bulwer-Lytton," in Bleiler, E. F., Ed. *Supernatural Fiction Writers* . . . , I, 198–200.

IVAN BUNIN

"The Gentleman from San Francisco"
Moser, Charles A. *The Russian Short Story* . . . , 128–129.

"Light Breathing"
Moser, Charles A. *The Russian Short Story* . . . , 127–128.

H. C. BUNNER

"The Pettibone 'Brolly"
Gerlach, John. *Toward the End* . . . , 4–5.

DAVID BURN

"The Three Sisters"
Hadgraft, Cecil, Ed. *The Australian Short Story* . . . , 2–3.

EDWARD BURNE-JONES

"The Cousins"
Pfordresher, John. "'The Vocabulary of the Unconscious': Burne-Jones's First Story," *Mosaic*, 19, i (1986), 57–72.

"A Story of the North"
Pfordresher, John. "Edward Burne-Jones's Gothic Romance: 'A Story of the North,'" *Archiv*, 223 (1986), 283–296.

ROBERT WILSON BURTON

"Improvisatore: The Wonderful Shower of Frogs"
Hitchcock, Bert. "Rediscovering Alabama Literature: Three Writers of Lafayette," *Alabama R*, 36 (1983), 184–185.

JOHN K. BUTLER

"The Saint in Silver"
Geherin, David. *The American Private Eye* . . . , 48–49.

OCTAVIA E. BUTLER

"Bloodchild"
Salvaggio, Ruth. "Octavia E. Butler," in Barr, Marleen S., Ruth Salvaggio, and Richard Law. *Suzy McKee Charnas . . .* , 38–40.

"Crossover"
Salvaggio, Ruth. "Octavia E. Butler," 37.

"Near of Kin"
Salvaggio, Ruth. "Octavia E. Butler," 37–38.

JUAN DE LA CABADA

"El grillo crepuscular"
Barrientos, Juan J. "Encuentros cercanos: De Borges a Juan de la Cabada," *México en el arte*, 9 (June, 1985), 49–52.

LYDIA CABRERA

"Se hace ebó"
Montes-Huidobro, Matías. "Itinerario del ebó," *Stud Afro-Hispanic Lit*, 2–3 (1978–79), 1–13.

HORTENSE CALISHER

"If You Don't Want to Live I Can't Help You"
Shinn, Thelma J. *Radiant Daughters . . .* , 169–170.

"The Rabbi's Daughter"
Shinn, Thelma J. *Radiant Daughters . . .* , 169.

"Time, Gentlemen"
Shinn, Thelma J. *Radiant Daughters . . .* , 82–83.

"The Watchers"
Shinn, Thelma J. *Radiant Daughters . . .* , 84.

ITALO CALVINO

"The Adventure of a Photographer"
Pierce, Constance. "Calvino on Photography," *R Contemp Fiction*, 6, ii (1986), 130–137.

"The Baron in the Trees"
Byrne, Jack. "Calvino's Fantastic 'Ancestors': The Viscount, the Baron and the Knight," *R Contemp Fiction*, 6, ii (1986), 45–49.

"The Cloven Viscount"
Byrne, Jack. "Calvino's Fantastic 'Ancestors' . . . ," 42–45.

"How Much Should We Bet?"
Lucente, Gregory L. *Beautiful Fables* . . . , 283–287.

"Last Comes the Crow"
Carter, Albert H. "Calvino's 'Ultimo viene il corvo': Riflery as Realistic AND Fantastic," *Italian Q*, 22 (Spring, 1981), 61–67.

"The Nonexistent Knight"
Byrne, Jack. "Calvino's Fantastic 'Ancestors' . . . ," 49–52.
Schlobin, Roger C. "The Survival of the Fool in Modern Heroic Fantasy," in Coyle, William, Ed. *Aspects of Fantasy* . . . , 125.

"A Sign of Space"
Lucente, Gregory L. *Beautiful Fables* . . . , 277–283.

JOHN W. CAMPBELL

"The Invaders"
Clayton, David. "What Makes Hard Science Fiction 'Hard'?" in Slusser, George E., and Eric S. Rabkin, Eds. *Hard Science Fiction*, 61–65.

"Twilight"
Clareson, Thomas B. "Introduction," in Tymn, Marshall B., and Mike Ashley, Eds. *Science Fiction . . . Magazines*, xxiv–xxv.

RAMSEY CAMPBELL

"The Chimney"
Sullivan, Jack. "Ramsey Campbell: No Light Ahead," in Winter, Douglas E., Ed. *Shadowings* . . . , 82–83.

"Down There"
Sullivan, Jack. "Ramsey Campbell . . . ," 85–86.

"The Sneering"
Sullivan, Jack. "Ramsey Campbell . . . ," 83–84.

"The Trick"
Sullivan, Jack. "Ramsey Campbell . . . ," 82–83.

ALBERT CAMUS

"The Adulterous Woman"
LaVallee-Williams, Martha. "Arabs in 'La Femme adultère': From Faceless Other to Agent," *Celfan R*, 4, iii (1985), 6–10.
Tarrow, Susan. *Exile* . . . , 174–178.

"The Fall"
Clews, Hetty. *The Only Teller. . .*, 175–179.
Palumbo, Donald. "The Question of God's Existence, the Absurd, and Irony: Their Interconnection in the Philosophical Works of Sartre and Camus," *Lamar J Humanities*, 12, i (1986), 47–49.
Tarrow, Susan. *Exile . . .*, 156–158.
Viallaneix, Paul. "Jeux et enjeux de l'ironie dans 'La Chute,'" in Gay-Crosier, Raymond, and Jacqueline Lévi-Valensi, Eds. *Albert Camus . . .*, 187–200.
Witt, Mary A. F. *Existential Prisons . . .*, 102–107.

"The Growing Stone"
Tarrow, Susan. *Exile . . .*, 190–193.

"The Guest"
Kroker, Arthur, and David Cook. *The Postmodern Scene . . .*, 206–208.
McDermott, John V. "Camus' Daru: Just How Humane?" *Notes Contemp Lit*, 15, iii (1985), 11–12.
Storey, Michael L. "The Guests of Frank O'Connor and Albert Camus," *Comp Lit Stud*, 23 (1986), 250–262.
Tarrow, Susan. *Exile . . .*, 181–183.
Witt, Mary A. F. *Existential Prisons . . .*, 91–92.

"Jonas, or the Artist at Work"
Tarrow, Susan. *Exile . . .*, 188–189.

"The Renegade"
Hélein-Koss, Suzanne. "Une Relecture chiffrée du 'Renégat' d'Albert Camus," *R Lettres Modernes*, Nos. 715–719 (1985), 97–106.

"The Silent Men"
Tarrow, Susan. *Exile . . .*, 184–185.

"The Stranger"
Abbou, André. "Le Quitidien et le sacré: Introduction à une nouvelle lecture de 'L'Étranger,'" in Gay-Crosier, Raymond, and Jacqueline Lévi-Valensi, Eds. *Albert Camus . . .*, 231–265.
Adamson, Robin. "Speech Mannerisms in 'L'Étranger,'" *Lang & Style*, 17 (1984), 329–346.
Bohn, Willard. "The Trials and Tribulations of Josef K. and Meursault," *Orbis Litterarum*, 40 (1985), 145–158.
Canfield, Stephen A. "Plant Imagery in Camus' 'L'Étranger,'" *Pubs Missouri Philol Assoc*, 9 (1984), 14–21.
Cascardi, Anthony J. *The Bounds of Reason . . .*, 100–105.
Costes, Alain. "Le Double Meurtre de Meursault: Une Remarque préalable pour une lecture psychanalytique de 'L'Étranger,'" in Gay-Crosier, Raymond, and Jacqueline Lévi-Valensi, Eds. *Albert Camus . . .*, 55–76.
Gassin, Jean. "A propos de la femme 'Automate' de 'L'Étranger,'" in Gay-Crosier, Raymond, and Jacqueline Lévi-Valensi, Eds. *Albert Camus . . .*, 77–90.
Laurenson, Diana, and Alan Swingewood. *The Sociology . . .*, 227–236.
Palumbo, Donald. "The Question . . . ," 49.
Robbe-Grillet, Alain. "Monde trop plein, conscience vide," trans. Anaïk Hé-

chiche, in Gay-Crosier, Raymond, and Jacqueline Lévi-Valensi, Eds. *Albert Camus* . . . , 215–227.
Tarrow, Susan. *Exile* . . . , 75–88.

KAREL AND JOSEF ČAPEK

"The Living Flame"
Blackham, H. J. *The Fable* . . . , 233–234.

TRUMAN CAPOTE

"Miriam"
Gerlach, John. *Toward the End* . . . , 120–122.

WILLIAM CARLETON

"The Battle of the Factions"
Barbash, Nancy E. "Violence in the Fiction of William Carleton," *Carleton Newsletter*, 4, iii (1974), 21–22.
Sloan, Barry. *The Pioneers* . . . , 167–168.

"The Castle of Aughentain, or Legend of the Brown Goat"
Boué, André. *William Carleton* . . . , 200–201.

"Denis O'Shaughnessy Going to Maynooth"
Sloan, Barry. *The Pioneers* . . . , 153–160.

"Father Butler"
Sloan, Barry. *The Pioneers* . . . , 160–161.

"The Funeral and the Party Fight"
Barbash, Nancy E. "Violence in the Fiction . . . ," 22–23.
Boué, André. *William Carleton* . . . , 195–196.
Sloan, Barry. *The Pioneers* . . . , 168–170.

"The Hedge School"
Sloan, Barry. *The Pioneers* . . . , 151–152.

"Jane Sinclair, or the Fawn of Springvale"
Boué, André. *William Carleton* . . . , 84–85.

"A Legend of Knockmany"
Boué, André. *William Carleton* . . . , 200.
MacKillop, James. *Fionn mac Cumhaill* . . . , 128–133.

"The Lianhan Shee"
Dumbleton, William A. "Dramatic Qualities in Carleton's Fiction," *Carleton Newsletter*, 4, iv (1974), 30.
Sloan, Barry. *The Pioneers* . . . , 140–141.

"The Lough Derg Pilgrim"
Boué, André. *William Carleton* . . . , 157–158.
Sloan, Barry. *The Pioneers* . . . , 162–163.

"The Midnight Mass"
Sloan, Barry. *The Pioneers* . . . , 163–164.

"Ned M'Keown"
Orel, Harold. *The Victorian Short Story* . . . , 30–31.

"Phelim O'Toole's Courtship"
Sloan, Barry. *The Pioneers* . . . , 159–160.

"The Poor Scholar"
Orel, Harold. *The Victorian Short Story* . . . , 23–24.
Sloan, Barry. *The Pioneers* . . . , 147–154.

"The Rival Kempers"
Boué, André. *William Carleton* . . . , 203–204.

"Shane Fadh's Wedding"
Boué, André. *William Carleton* . . . , 189–190.
Sloan, Barry. *The Pioneers* . . . , 161–162.

"The Station"
Dumbleton, William A. "Dramatic Qualities . . . ," 29–30.

"The Three Tasks"
Boué, André. *William Carleton* . . . , 197–199.

"Wildgoose Lodge" [originally titled "Confessions of a Reformed Ribbonman"]
Barbash, Nancy E. "Violence in the Fiction . . . ," 20.
Boué, André. *William Carleton* . . . , 36–37.
Sloan, Barry. *The Pioneers* . . . , 165–166.

ALEJO CARPENTIER

"The Chosen"
Shaw, Donald L. *Alejo Carpentier,* 71–73.

"The Fugitives"
Escandell, Noemí. "Análisis de 'Los fugitivos' de Alejo Carpentier," *Folio,* 16 (December, 1984), 27–35.
LaRubia-Prado, Francisco. "'Los fugitivos' de Alejo Carpentier en su contexto: Convergencia de ideología y estructura," *Afro-Hispanic R,* 4, ii–iii (May–September, 1985), 17–21.
Shaw, Donald L. *Alejo Carpentier,* 38–42.

"The High Road of St. James"
Shaw, Donald L. *Alejo Carpentier,* 38–42.

"Journey to the Source"
Benitez Rojo, Antonio. "'Viaje a la semilla,' o el texto como espectáculo," *Discurso Literario*, 3, i (1985), 53–74.
Shaw, Donald L. *Alejo Carpentier*, 23–26.
Standish, Peter. "'Viaje a la semilla': Construction and Demolition," *Bull Hispanic Stud*, 63, ii (1986), 139–148.

"Like the Night"
Padura Fuentes, Leonardo. "'Semejante a la noche': El hombre, el tiempo y la revolución," *Casa de las Americas*, 25 (November–December, 1984), 37–43.
Shaw, Donald L. *Alejo Carpentier*, 35–38.

"Moonstruck"
Shaw, Donald L. *Alejo Carpentier*, 12–14.

"Morning Service"
Menéndez, Andrés. "La sombre de Agüero," *Plaza*, 9–10 (Autumn–Spring, 1985–1986), 23–27.
Shaw, Donald L. *Alejo Carpentier*, 18–19.

ROCH CARRIER

"The Nun Who Returned to Ireland"
Darling, Michael. "Reading Carrier's 'The Nun Who Returned to Ireland,'" *Canadian Lit*, 104 (Spring, 1985), 24–33.

ANGELA CARTER

"The Bloody Chamber"
Duncker, Patricia. "Re-examining the Fairy Tales: Angela Carter's Bloody Chamber," *Lit & Hist*, 10, i (1984), 10–12.
Evans, Walter. "The English Short Story in the Seventies," in Vannatta, Dennis, Ed. *The English Short Story, 1945–1980*, 154–156.

RAYMOND CARVER

"The Bath"
Stull, William L. "Beyond Hopelessville: Another Side of Raymond Carver," *Philol Q*, 64 (1985), 1–15.

"The Calm"
Facknitz, Mark A. R. "'The Calm,' 'A Small, Good Thing,' and 'Cathedral': Raymond Carver and the Rediscovery of Human Worth," *Stud Short Fiction*, 23 (1986), 288–290.

"Cathedral"
Bohner, Charles H. *Instructor's Manual . . .* , 19–20.
Facknitz, Mark A. R. ". . . Rediscovery of Human Worth," 292–295.

"A Small, Good Thing"
Facknitz, Mark A. R. ". . . Rediscovery of Human Worth," 290–292.
Stull, William L. "Beyond Hopelessville . . . ," 1–15.

"The Train"
Facknitz, Mark A. R. "Missing the Train: Raymond Carver's Sequel to John
    Cheever's 'The Five-Forty-Eight,'" *Stud Short Fiction,* 22 (1985), 345–347.

WILLA CATHER

"Before Breakfast"
Arnold, Marilyn. "Cather's Last Three Stories: A Testament of Life and En-
    durance," *Great Plains Q,* 4 (1984), 343–344.

"The Best Years"
Arnold, Marilyn. "Cather's Last Three Stories . . . ," 342–343.

"The Bohemian Girl"
Rosowski, Susan J. *The Voyage . . . ,* 39–42.

"The Burglar's Christmas"
O'Brien, Sharon. "Mothers, Daughters, and the 'Art Necessity': Willa Cather
    and the Creative Process," in Fleischmann, Fritz, Ed. *American Novelists
    Revisited . . . ,* 274–275.

"Coming, Aphrodite!"
Petry, Alice H. "Caesar and the Artist in Willa Cather's 'Coming, Aphrodite!'"
    Stud Short Fiction, 23 (1986), 307–314.
Sheehy, Donald G. "Aphrodite and the Factory: Commercialism and the Artist
    in Frost and Cather," *So Atlantic Q,* 51, ii (1986), 51–55.

"Consequences"
Oehlschlaeger, Fritz. "Willa Cather's 'Consequences' and *Alexander's Bridge:* An
    Approach Through R. D. Laing and Ernest Becker," *Mod Fiction Stud,* 32
    (1986), 191–202.

"The Fear That Walks by Noonday"
Rosowski, Susan J. *The Voyage . . . ,* 208–209.

"The Garden Lodge"
Rosowski, Susan J. *The Voyage . . . ,* 24–25.

"The Marriage of Phaedra"
Rosowski, Susan J. *The Voyage . . . ,* 25–26.

"Neighbour Rosicky"
Rosowski, Susan J. *The Voyage . . . ,* 190–195.

"The Old Beauty"
Arnold, Marilyn. "Cather's Last Three Stories . . . ," 240–242.

"On the Divide"
Rosowski, Susan J. *The Voyage* . . . , 16–18.

"Paul's Case"
Bohner, Charles H. *Instructor's Manual* . . . , 20–21.
Rosowski, Susan J. *The Voyage* . . . , 28–29.
Sheidley, William E., and Ann Charters. *Instructor's Manual* . . . , 54–56; rpt.
    Charters, Ann, William E. Sheidley, and Martha Ramsey. *Instructor's Man-
    ual* . . . , 2nd ed., 60–61.

"Two Friends"
Rosowski, Susan J. *The Voyage* . . . , 199–204.

"A Wagner Matinée"
Rosowski, Susan J. *The Voyage* . . . , 26–28.

MARY HARTWELL CATHERWOOD

"Career of a Prairie Farmer"
Fairbanks, Carol. *Prairie Women* . . . , 68–70.

"The Little Renault"
Fairbanks, Carol. *Prairie Women* . . . , 119–120.

"The Monument to the First Mrs. Smith"
Fairbanks, Carol. *Prairie Women* . . . , 107–108.

"The Spirit of an Illinois Town"
Fairbanks, Carol. *Prairie Women* . . . , 198–200.

ROBERT W. CHAMBERS

"The Demoiselle D'Ys"
Weinstein, Lee. "Robert W. Chambers," in Bleiler, E. F., Ed. *Supernatural Fiction
    Writers* . . . , II, 741–742.

"In the Court of the Dragon"
Weinstein, Lee. "Robert W. Chambers," 740.

"The Key to Grief"
Weinstein, Lee. "Robert W. Chambers," 743.

"The Mask"
Weinstein, Lee. "Robert W. Chambers," 740.

"The Messenger"
Weinstein, Lee. "Robert W. Chambers," 743.

The Repairer of Reputations"
Weinstein, Lee. "Robert W. Chambers," 740.

"The Silent Land"
Weinstein, Lee. "Robert W. Chambers," 742–743.

"The White Shadow"
Weinstein, Lee. "Robert W. Chambers," 743.

"The Yellow Sign"
Weinstein, Lee. "Robert W. Chambers," 740–741.

RAYMOND CHANDLER

"Bay City Blues"
Marling, William H. *Raymond Chandler*, 66–68.

"Blackmailers Don't Shoot"
Wolfe, Peter. *Something More . . .* , 96.

"English Summer"
Marling, William H. *Raymond Chandler*, 71–72.

"Goldfish"
Wolfe, Peter. *Something More . . .* , 113–115.

"Guns at Cyrano's"
Marling, William H. *Raymond Chandler*, 57–58.
Wolfe, Peter. *Something More . . .* , 97.

"I'll Be Waiting"
Wolfe, Peter. *Something More . . .* , 106–108.

"Killer in the Rain"
Marling, William H. *Raymond Chandler*, 53–55.

"The King in Yellow"
Marling, William H. *Raymond Chandler*, 66–67.
Wolfe, Peter. *Something More . . .* , 108–109.

"The Lady in the Lake"
Marling, William H. *Raymond Chandler*, 67–68.
Wolfe, Peter. *Something More . . .* , 109–110.

"Mandarin's Jade"
Marling, William H. *Raymond Chandler*, 64–65.

"Nevada Gas"
Marling, William H. *Raymond Chandler*, 55–56.

"No Crime"
Wolfe, Peter. *Something More . . .* , 110–112.

"Red Wind"
Marling, William H. *Raymond Chandler,* 55–56.
Wolfe, Peter. *Something More . . . ,* 92, 103–104.

"Spanish Blood"
Marling, William H. *Raymond Chandler,* 56–58.
Wolfe, Peter. *Something More . . . ,* 112–113.

"Try the Girl"
Marling, William H. *Raymond Chandler,* 62–64.

SUZY McKEE CHARNAS

"Scorched Supper on New Niger"
Barr, Marleen S. "Suzy McKee Charnas," in Barr, Marleen S., Ruth Salvaggio,
    and Richard Law. *Suzy McKee Charnas . . . ,* 45–48.

FRANÇOIS RENÉ DE CHATEAUBRIAND

"Atala"
Hamilton, James F. "The Ideology of Exoticism in Chateaubriand's 'Atala,' an
    Eighteenth-Century Perspective," *French Lit Series,* 13 (1986), 28–37.

"René"
Galand, René. "Chateaubriand: Le Rocher de René," *Romanic R,* 77 (1986),
    330–342.
Gourbin-Servenière, Malaka. "Le Désir de la mort dans 'René' et *Les Natchez:*
    Constantes du tourment romantique de l'âme," in Ernst, Gilles, Ed. *La
    Mort . . . ,* 109–120.

JOHN CHEEVER

"Artemis, the Honest Well Digger"
Gerlach, John. *Toward the End . . . ,* 152–159.

"The Brothers"
Coale, Samuel C. *In Hawthorne's Shadow . . . ,* 108–109.

"Chaste Clarissa"
Spacks, Patricia M. *Gossip,* 13–14.

"Clancy in the Tower"
Ahrens, Günter. "Adonis in Amerika: Zur Funktion transformierter Mythen in
    den Kurzegeschichten von John Cheever," *Anglia,* 103 (1985), 358–359.

"The Common Day"
Bidney, Martin. "'The Common Day' and the Immortality Ode: Cheever's
    Wordsworthian Craft," *Stud Short Fiction,* 23 (1986), 139–151.

"The Death of Justina"
Coale, Samuel C. *In Hawthorne's Shadow* . . . , 120.

"The Enormous Radio"
Ahrens, Günter. "Adonis in Amerika . . . ," 356–357.
Bohner, Charles H. *Instructor's Manual* . . . , 21–22.
Sheidley, William E., and Ann Charters. *Instructor's Manual* . . . , 136; rpt. Charters, Ann, William E. Sheidley, and Martha Ramsey. *Instructor's Manual* . . . , 2nd ed., 137–138.

"Goodbye, My Brother"
Ahrens, Günter. "Adonis in Amerika . . . ," 354–356.
Coale, Samuel C. *In Hawthorne's Shadow* . . . , 110–111.

"The Lowboy"
Coale, Samuel C. *In Hawthorne's Shadow* . . . , 109–110.

"The Scarlet Moving Van"
Ahrens, Günter. "Adonis in Amerika . . . ," 339–340.

"The Swimmer"
Bohner, Charles H. *Instructor's Manual* . . . , 23–24.
Byrne, Michael D. "The River of Names in 'The Swimmer,'" *Stud Short Fiction,* 23 (1986), 326–327.
Sheidley, Willlam E., and Ann Charters. *Instructor's Manual* . . . , 138–139; rpt. Charters, Ann, William E. Sheidley, and Martha Ramsey. *Instructor's Manual* . . . , 2nd ed., 139–140.

"Torch Song"
Ahrens, Günter. "Adonis in Amerika . . . ," 341–342.

ANTON CHEKHOV

"The Bishop"
Moser, Charles A. *The Russian Short Story* . . . , 121–122.

"The Black Monk"
Miller, Karl. *Doubles* . . . , 144–145.

"The Darling"
Bohner, Charles H. *Instructor's Manual* . . . , 24–25.

"The Daughter of Albion"
Pitcher, Harvey. "Chekhov's Humour," in Clyman, Toby W., Ed. *A Chekhov Companion,* 94–95.

"A Dreary Story" [same as "A Boring Story," "A Dull Story," or "A Tedious Story"]
Moser, Charles A. *The Russian Short Story* . . . , 114–115.

"The Duel"
Welty, Eudora. *The Eye of the Storm*, 69–74; rpt. McConkey, James, Ed. *Chekhov and Our Age . . .* , 112–117.

"Easter Eve"
May, Charles E. "Chekhov and the Modern Short Story," in Clyman, Toby W., Ed. *A Chekhov Companion*, 156–157.

"From the Diary of a Violent-Tempered Man"
Pitcher, Harvey. "Chekhov's Humour," 91–92.

"A Gentleman Friend"
Lantz, Kenneth A. "Chekhov's Cast of Characters," in Clyman, Toby W., Ed. *A Chekhov Companion*, 76–77.

"Gooseberries"
Bohner, Charles H. *Instructor's Manual . . .* , 25–26.
Slatoff, Walter J. *The Look of Distance . . .* , 29–31.
Welty, Eudora. *The Eye of the Storm*, 74–76; rpt. McConkey, James, Ed. *Chekhov and Our Age . . .* , 117–119.

"In the Ravine"
Welty, Eudora. *The Eye of the Storm*, 76–78; rpt. McConkey, James, Ed. *Chekhov and Our Age . . .* , 119–121.

"The Lady with the Dog" [same as "The Lady with the Lapdog," "The Lady with the Pet Dog," or "The Lady with the Small Dog"]
Bohner, Charles H. *Instructor's Manual . . .* , 26–27.
Cockrell, C. R. "Chekhov: 'The Lady with the Dog,'" in Cockrell, Roger, and David Richards, Eds. *The Voice of a Giant . . .* , 81–92.
Gerlach, John. *Toward the End . . .* , 131–132.
Miller, Karl. *Doubles . . .* , 151–152.
Winner, Thomas G. "The Poetry of Chekhov's Prose: Lyrical Structures in 'The Lady with the Dog,'" in Stolz, Benjamin A., I. R. Titunik, and Lubomír Doležel, Eds. *Language and Literary Theory*, 609–622.

"Misery" [same as "The Lament"]
Dessner, Lawrence J. "Head, Heart, and Snout: Narrative and Theme in Chekhov's 'Misery,'" *Coll Lit*, 12 (1985), 246–257.

"Neighbors"
Lindheim, Ralph. "Chekhov's Compassionate Irony in 'Neighbors,'" in McConkey, James, Ed. *Chekhov and Our Age . . .* , 213–237.

"The Party"
Miller, Karl. *Doubles . . .* , 145–146.

"Peasants"
Moser, Charles A. *The Russian Short Story . . .* , 118–119.
Welty, Eudora. *The Eye of the Storm*, 66–68; rpt. McConkey, James, Ed. *Chekhov and Our Age . . .* , 108–111.

"Rothschild's Fiddle"
Lantz, Kenneth A. "Chekhov's Cast of Characters," 73–74.

"The Steppe"
Miller, Karl. *Doubles . . .* , 146–148.
Moser, Charles A. *The Russian Short Story . . .* , 113–114.

"The Student"
Amsenga, B. J., and V. A. A. Bedaux. "Personendarstellung in Čechovs Erzäh-
    lung 'Student,'" trans. Waltraud Grübel-Stecklum, in Grübel, Rainer, Ed.
    Russische Erzählung . . . , 281–314.
May, Charles E. "Chekhov and the Modern Short Story," 157–158.
O'Toole, L. M. "Chekhov's 'The Student,'" in Andrew, Joe, and Christopher
    Pike, Eds. *The Structural Analysis . . .* , 1–25.
Slatoff, Walter J. *The Look of Distance . . .* , 24–29.

"Ward No. 6"
Moser, Charles A. *The Russian Short Story . . .* , 116–117.
Wexelblatt, Robert. "Chekhov, Salinger, and Epictetus," *Midwest Q,* 28, i (1986),
    52–63.

CHARLES W. CHESNUTT

"Baxter's Procrustes"
Chametzky, Jules. *Our Decentralized Literature . . .* , 40–41.

"Dave's Neckliss"
Christophersen, Bill. "Conjurin' the White Folks: Charles Chesnutt's Other
    'Julius' Tales," *Am Lit Realism,* 18 (1985), 212–214.

"The Dumb Witness"
Christophersen, Bill. "Conjurin' . . . ," 215–217.

"Her Virginia Mammy"
Fraiman, Susan. "Mother-Daughter Romance in Charles W. Chesnutt's 'Her
    Virginia Mammy,'" *Stud Short Fiction,* 22 (1985), 443–448.

"Lonesome Ben"
Christophersen, Bill. "Conjurin' . . . ," 214–215.

"The Marked Tree"
Christophersen, Bill. "Conjurin' . . . ," 209–210.

"A Victim of Heredity"
Christophersen, Bill. "Conjurin' . . . ," 211–212.

"The Wife of His Youth"
Sollors, Werner. *Beyond Ethnicity . . .* , 161–163.

GILBERT KEITH CHESTERTON

"The Chief Mourner of Marne"
Routley, Erik. *The Puritan Pleasures* . . . , 106–108.

"The Invisible Man"
Ffinch, Michael. *G. K. Chesterton,* 195–196.
Routley, Erik. *The Puritan Pleasures* . . . , 93–94.

"The Miracle of Moon Crescent"
Routley, Erik. *The Puritan Pleasures* . . . , 105–106.

"The Three Tools of Death"
Routley, Erik. *The Puritan Pleasures* . . . , 102–103.

LYDIA MARIA CHILD

"Chocorua's Curse"
Karcher, Carolyn L., Ed. *"Hobomok"* . . . [by Lydia Maria Child], 161.

"Hilda Silfverling"
Karcher, Carolyn L. "Patriarchal Society and Matriarchal Family in Irving's 'Rip Van Winkle' and Child's 'Hilda Silfverling,'" *Legacy,* 2, ii (1985), 35–41.

"Hobomok"
Karcher, Carolyn L., Ed. *"Hobomok"* . . . [by Lydia Maria Child], xxv–xxxiii.

"A Legend of the Falls of St. Anthony"
Karcher, Carolyn L., Ed. *"Hobomok"* . . . [by Lydia Maria Child], 202.

"She Waits in the Spirit Land"
Karcher, Carolyn L., Ed. *"Hobomok"* . . . [by Lydia Maria Child], 191.

KATE CHOPIN

"Alexander's Wonderful Experience"
Ewell, Barbara C. *Kate Chopin,* 176–177.

"At Chênière Caminada"
Ewell, Barbara C. *Kate Chopin,* 97–98.
Skaggs, Peggy. *Kate Chopin,* 34–35.

"At the 'Cadian Ball"
Ewell, Barbara C. *Kate Chopin,* 76–79.
Skaggs, Peggy. *Kate Chopin,* 22–25.

"Athénaïse"
Ewell, Barbara C. *Kate Chopin,* 108–112.

Newman, Judie. "Kate Chopin: Short Fiction and the Arts of Subversion," in
  Lee, A. Robert, Ed. . . . *American Short Story,* 159–160.
Skaggs, Peggy. *Kate Chopin,* 36–38.

"Azélie"
Ewell, Barbara C. *Kate Chopin,* 96–97.

"La Belle Zoraïde"
Ewell, Barbara C. *Kate Chopin,* 72–73.
Skaggs, Peggy. *Kate Chopin,* 19–21.

"Cavanelle"
Ewell, Barbara C. *Kate Chopin,* 101–102.

"Charlie"
Ewell, Barbara C. *Kate Chopin,* 77–80.
Newman, Judie. "Kate Chopin . . . ," 153–159.
Westling, Louise. *Sacred Groves . . . ,* 112–113.

"Désirée's Baby"
Ewell, Barbara C. *Kate Chopin,* 69–72.
Skaggs, Peggy. *Kate Chopin,* 25–26.

"An Egyptian Cigarette"
Ewell, Barbara C. *Kate Chopin,* 138–140.

"Elizabeth Stock's One Story"
Ewell, Barbara C. *Kate Chopin,* 165–168.

"A Family Affair"
Ewell, Barbara C. *Kate Chopin,* 164–165.

"Fedora"
Skaggs, Peggy. *Kate Chopin,* 47–48.

"The Gentleman from New Orleans"
Ewell, Barbara C. *Kate Chopin,* 177.

"A Gentleman of Bayou Têche"
Ewell, Barbara C. *Kate Chopin,* 60–62.

"The Godmother"
Ewell, Barbara C. *Kate Chopin,* 171–172.
Skaggs, Peggy. *Kate Chopin,* 48–49.

"The Haunted Chamber"
Ewell, Barbara C. *Kate Chopin,* 163–164.

"Her Letter"
Ewell, Barbara C. *Kate Chopin,* 105–107.

"In and Out of Old Natchitoches"
Ewell, Barbara C. *Kate Chopin*, 56–58.
Skaggs, Peggy. *Kate Chopin*, 18–19.

"In Sabine"
Ewell, Barbara C. *Kate Chopin*, 58–60.

"The Kiss"
Ewell, Barbara C. *Kate Chopin*, 103–104.

"A Lady of Bayou St. John"
Ewell, Barbara C. *Kate Chopin*, 73–74.
Skaggs, Peggy. *Kate Chopin*, 20–21.

"Lilacs"
Ewell, Barbara C. *Kate Chopin*, 91–92.
Skaggs, Peggy. *Kate Chopin*, 41–42.

"Loka"
Skaggs, Peggy. *Kate Chopin*, 13–14.

"Love on the Bon-Dieu"
Skaggs, Peggy. *Kate Chopin*, 17–18.

"Ma'ame Pélagie"
Ewell, Barbara C. *Kate Chopin*, 65–66.

"Madame Célestin's Divorce"
Ewell, Barbara C. *Kate Chopin*, 74–76.

"Madame Martel's Christmas Eve"
Skaggs, Peggy. *Kate Chopin*, 59.

"A Matter of Prejudice"
Ewell, Barbara C. *Kate Chopin*, 96.

"Miss McEnders"
Ewell, Barbara C. *Kate Chopin*, 82–84.

"Mrs. Mobry's Reason"
Skaggs, Peggy. *Kate Chopin*, 56–57.

"Nég Créol"
Ewell, Barbara C. *Kate Chopin*, 121–123.

"The Night Came Slowly"
Skaggs, Peggy. *Kate Chopin*, 39–40.

"A Night in Acadie"
Ewell, Barbara C. *Kate Chopin*, 117–118.
Skaggs, Peggy. *Kate Chopin*, 32–33.

"A No-Account Creole"
Ewell, Barbara C. *Kate Chopin*, 55–56.

"Ozème's Holiday"
Skaggs, Peggy. *Kate Chopin*, 30–31.

"A Pair of Silk Stockings"
Ewell, Barbara C. *Kate Chopin*, 118–120.

"A Point at Issue"
Skaggs, Peggy. *Kate Chopin*, 56.

"Polly"
Ewell, Barbara C. *Kate Chopin*, 181–182.

"Regret"
Ewell, Barbara C. *Kate Chopin*, 102–103.
Skaggs, Peggy. *Kate Chopin*, 28–29.

"A Respectable Woman"
Ewell, Barbara C. *Kate Chopin*, 98–99.
Skaggs, Peggy. *Kate Chopin*, 35–36.

"The Return of Alcibiade"
Ewell, Barbara C. *Kate Chopin*, 63–65.

"A Sentimental Soul"
Ewell, Barbara C. *Kate Chopin*, 104–105.
Skaggs, Peggy. *Kate Chopin*, 33–34.

"A Shameful Affair"
Simpson, Martin. "Chopin's 'A Shameful Affair,'" *Explicator*, 45, i (1986), 59–
    60.
Skaggs, Peggy. *Kate Chopin*, 57–58.

"The Storm"
Ewell, Barbara C. *Kate Chopin*, 168–171.
Skaggs, Peggy. *Kate Chopin*, 61–62.

"The Story of an Hour"
Bohner, Charles H. *Instructor's Manual . . .* , 27–28.
Ewell, Barbara C. *Kate Chopin*, 88–91.
Skaggs, Peggy. *Kate Chopin*, 52–53.

"Suzette"
Skaggs, Peggy. *Kate Chopin*, 46–47.

"Tante Cat'rinette"
Skaggs, Peggy. *Kate Chopin*, 29–30.

"Ti Démon"
Ewell, Barbara C. *Kate Chopin*, 175–176.
Skaggs, Peggy. *Kate Chopin*, 46.

"Two Portraits"
Ewell, Barbara C. *Kate Chopin*, 113–114.
Newman, Judie. "Kate Chopin . . . ," 161–162.

"Vagabonds"
Ewell, Barbara C. *Kate Chopin*, 115–116.
Skaggs, Peggy. *Kate Chopin*, 58–59.

"A Visit to Avoyelles"
Skaggs, Peggy. *Kate Chopin*, 21–22.

"A Vocation and a Voice"
Ewell, Barbara C. *Kate Chopin*, 127–131.
Skaggs, Peggy. *Kate Chopin*, 49–52.

"The White Eagle"
Ewell, Barbara C. *Kate Chopin*, 180–181.
Skaggs, Peggy. *Kate Chopin*, 44–45.

"Wiser Than a God"
Ewell, Barbara C. *Kate Chopin*, 45.
Skaggs, Peggy. *Kate Chopin*, 55–56.

AGATHA CHRISTIE

"Tragedy of Marsdon Manor"
Wagoner, Mary S. *Agatha Christie*, 16.

ARTHUR C. CLARKE

"The Star"
Bohner, Charles H. *Instructor's Manual . . .* , 28–29.
Quinn, William A. "Science Fiction's Harrowing of the Heavens," in Reilly,
    Robert, Ed. *The Transcendent Adventure . . .* , 45–46.

AUSTIN CLARKE

"They Heard a Ringing of Bells"
Minni, C. D. "The Short Story as an Ethnic Genre," in Pivato, Joseph, Ed.
    Contrasts . . . , 65–66.

HAL CLEMENT

"Fireproof"
Arbur, Rosemarie. "Ars Scientia = Ars Poetica," in Hassler, Donald M., Ed.
    Patterns . . . II, 19–21.

SIDONIE-GABRIELLE COLETTE

"The Cat"
Ford, Marianne. "Spatial Structures in 'La Chatte,'" *French R,* 58 (1985), 360–367.

"Chéri"
Fouchereaux, Jean. "Feminine Archetypes in Colette and Marie-Claire Blais," *J Midwest Mod Lang Assoc,* 19, i (1986), 43–46.

"Gigi"
Cohen, Susan D. "An Onomastic Double Bind: Colette's 'Gigi' and the Politics of Naming," *PMLA,* 100 (1985), 793–809.

JOHN COLLIER

"The Chaser"
Kessel, John J. "John Collier," in Bleiler, E. F., Ed. *Supernatural Fiction Writers . . . ,* II, 580.

"Three Bears Cottage"
Baldwin, Dean. "The English Short Story in the Fifties," in Vannatta, Dennis, Ed. *The English Short Story, 1945–1980,* 71–72.

"Thus I Refute Beelzy"
Kessel, John J. "John Collier," 580.

WILKIE COLLINS

"Brother Griffin's Story of Mad Monkton"
Donaldson, Norman. "Wilkie Collins," in Bleiler, E. F., Ed. *Supernatural Fiction Writers . . . ,* I, 235–236.

"Brother Morgan's Story of the Dead Hand"
Donaldson, Norman. "Wilkie Collins," 236.

"Miss Jéromette and the Clergyman"
Donaldson, Norman. "Wilkie Collins," 236–237.

"The Yellow Mask"
Donaldson, Norman. "Wilkie Collins," 235.

FRANK APPLETON COLLYMORE

"Mark Learns Another Lesson"
Baugh, Edward. "Frank Collymore," in Dance, Daryl C. *Fifty Caribbean Writers . . . ,* 126–127.

"Shadows"
Baugh, Edward. "Frank Collymore," 124–125.

"The Snag"
Baugh, Edward. "Frank Collymore," 125–126.

PADRAIC COLUM

"The Flute Player's Story"
Sternlicht, Sanford. *Padraic Colum*, 113.

RICHARD CONNELL

"The Most Dangerous Game"
Bohner, Charles H. *Instructor's Manual . . .*, 31–32.

JOSEPH CONRAD

"Amy Foster"
Fogel, Aaron. *Coercion . . .*, 171–172.
Milbauer, Asher Z. *Transcending Exile . . .*, 12–17.

"The Anarchist"
Weber, Horst. *Beiträge . . .*, 46–48.

"The Black Mate"
Fogel, Aaron. *Coercion . . .*, 250–257.

"The Duel"
Simons, Kenneth. *The Ludic Imagination . . .*, 18–19.
Stape, J. H. "Conrad's 'The Duel': A Reconsideration," *Conradiana*, 11 (1986),
    42–46.

"The End of the Tether"
Fogel, Aaron. *Coercion . . .*, 9–11.
Lombard, François. "Joseph Conrad et la mer dans 'The End of the Tether,'"
    Cahiers Victoriens et Edouardiens, 23 (1986), 147–155.
*Said, Edward W. "The Past and the Present: Conrad's Shorter Fiction," in
    Bloom, Harold, Ed. *Joseph Conrad*, 50–51.

"Falk"
Page, Norman. *A Conrad Companion*, 149–152.

"Gaspar Ruiz"
Weber, Horst. *Beiträge . . .*, 50–52.

"Heart of Darkness"
Alcorn, Marshall W. "Conrad and the Narcissistic Metaphysics of Morality,"
    Conradiana, 16 (1984), 107–120.

Bergstrom, Robert F. "Discovery of Meaning: Development of Formal Thought in the Teaching of Literature," *Coll Engl*, 45 (1983), 745–755.

Brantlinger, Patrick. "'Heart of Darkness': Anti-Imperialism, Racism, or Impressionism?" *Criticism*, 27 (1985), 363–385.

Cheatham, George. "The Absence of God in 'Heart of Darkness,'" *Stud Novel*, 18 (1986), 304–313.

Clews, Hetty. *The Only Teller*..., 132–141.

Clifford, James. "On Ethnographic Self-Fashioning: Conrad and Malinowski," in Heller, Thomas C., Morton Sosna, David E. Wellbery, Arnold I. Davidson, Ann Swidler, and Ian Watt, Eds. *Reconstructing Individualism*..., 140–161.

Day, William P. *In the Circles*..., 171–175.

DeMille, Barbara. "An Inquiry into Some Points of Seamanship: Narration As Preservation in 'Heart of Darkness,'" *Conradiana*, 18 (1986), 94–104.

Elliott, Dorice W. "'Hearing the Darkness': The Narrative Chain in Conrad's 'Heart of Darkness,'" *Engl Lit Transition*, 28 (1985), 162–181.

Firchow, Peter E. *The Death*..., 184–186.

Fogel, Aaron. *Coercion*..., 18–21.

Gribble, Jennifer. "The Fogginess of 'Heart of Darkness,'" *Sydney Stud Engl*, 11 (1985–1986), 83–94.

Hawkins, Hunt. "Conrad and the Psychology of Colonialism," in Murfin, Ross C., Ed. *Conrad Revisited*..., 80–82.

Hubbard, Francis A. *Theories of Action*..., 53–99.

Jones, Michael P. *Conrad's Heroism*..., 66–80.

Knox-Shaw, Peter. *The Explorer*..., 136–163.

Leverson, Michael. "The Value of Facts in 'The Heart of Darkness,'" *Nineteenth-Century Fiction*, 40 (1985), 261–280.

––––––. "On the Edge of the Heart of Darkness," *Stud Short Fiction*, 23 (1986), 153–157.

Littlewood, Ian. "Conrad's 'Heart of Darkness': From the Monstrous to the Commonplace," in Rigaud, Nadia, Ed. *Le Monstrueux*..., 159–170.

Lodigiani, Emilia. "Conrad e il mito: Un 'mistero' grottesco nel cuore dell'Africa," *Acme*, 38, iii (1985), 115–136.

McClure, John. "Problematic Presence: The Colonial Other in Kipling and Conrad," in Dabydeen, David, Ed. *The Black Presence*..., 159–162.

Madden, Fred. "Marlow and the Double Horror of 'Heart of Darkness,'" *Midwest Q*, 27 (1986), 504–517.

Melnick, Daniel. "The Morality of Conrad's Imagination: 'Heart of Darkness' and *Nostromo*," *Missouri R*, 5, ii (1982), 139–156; rpt. Bloom, Harold, Ed. *Joseph Conrad*, 113–130.

Milbauer, Asher Z. *Transcending Exile*..., 17–21.

Miller, Christopher L. *Blank Darkness*..., 169–183.

Miller, J. Hillis. "'Heart of Darkness' Revisited," in Murfin, Ross C., Ed. *Conrad Revisited*..., 31–50.

Miller, Karl. *Doubles*..., 260–265.

Orel, Harold. *The Victorian Short Story*..., 163–168.

Pecora, Vincent. "'Heart of Darkness' and the Phenomonology of Voice," *Engl Lit Hist*, 52 (1985), 993–1015.

Raval, Suresh. *The Art of Failure*..., 19–44.

Reeves, Charles E. "A Voice of Unrest: Conrad's Rhetoric of the Unspeakable," *Texas Stud Lit & Lang*, 27 (1985), 284–310.

Rose, Jonathan. *The Edwardian Temperament*..., 153–154.

Schwartz, Nina. "The Ideologies of Romanticism in 'Heart of Darkness,'" *New Orleans R*, 13 (1986), 84–95.
Seidel, Michael. *Exile...*, 44–70.
Staten, Henry. "Conrad's Mortal Word," *Critical I*, 12 (1986), 720–740.
Viola, André. "Conrad et les autres: Les Ecueils du langage dans 'Coeur des Ténèbres,'" *Cycnos*, 2 (Winter, 1985–1986), 91–101.
Watt, Ian. "Impressionism and Symbolism in 'Heart of Darkness,'" in Sherry, Norman, Ed. ... *A Commemoration*, 37–53; rpt. *Southern R*, 13 (1977), 96–113; Bloom, Harold, Ed. *Joseph Conrad*, 83–99.
Zhang, Weiwen. "A Tentative Comment on Conrad's 'Heart of Darkness,'" *Foreign Lit Stud*, 27, i (1985), 39–45.

"The Idiot"
Weber, Horst. *Beiträge...*, 63–65.

"The Informer"
Weber, Horst. *Beiträge...*, 48–49.

"The Inn of the Two Witches"
Barclay, Glen St. John. *Anatomy of Horror...*, 15.

"The Lagoon"
Bohner, Charles H. *Instructor's Manual...*, 32–33.

"An Outpost of Progress"
Black, Martha F. "Irony in Joseph Conrad's 'An Outpost of Progress,'" *Conradiana*, 10 (1985), 132–134.
Flora, Joseph M. *The English Short Story...*, 15–16.
*Said, Edward W. "The Past and the Present...," 37–38.
Weber, Horst. *Beiträge...*, 66–68.

"The Planter of Malata"
McLauchlan, Juliet. "Conrad's Heart of Emptiness: 'The Planter of Malata,'" *Conradiana*, 18 (1986), 180–192.
Weber, Horst. *Beiträge...*, 56–59.

"The Rescue"
Caserio, Robert. "'The Rescue' and the Ring of Meaning," in Murfin, Ross C., Ed. *Conrad Revisited...*, 125–149.

"The Return"
*Said, Edward W. "The Past and the Present...," 41–46.

"The Secret Sharer"
Abdoo, Sherlyn. "Ego Formation and the Land/Sea Metaphor in Conrad's 'Secret Sharer,'" in Tymieniecka, Anna-Teresa, Ed. *Poetics of the Elements...*, 67–76.
Bohner, Charles H. *Instructor's Manual...*, 33–34.
Dazey, Mary Ann. "Shared Secret or Secret Sharing in Conrad's 'The Secret Sharer,'" *Conradiana*, 18 (1986), 201–203.
Dobrinsky, Joseph. "The Two Lives of Conrad in 'The Secret Sharer,'" *Cahiers Victoriens et Edouardiens*, 21 (April, 1985), 33–49.

Jones, Michael P. *Conrad's Heroism* . . . , 101–112.
Miller, Karl. *Doubles* . . . , 255–257.
Milne, Fred L. "Conrad's 'The Secret Sharer,'" *Explicator*, 44, iii (1986), 38–39.
Murphy, Michael. "'The Secret Sharer': Conrad's Turn of the Winch," *Conradiana*, 18 (1986), 193–200.
Orel, Harold. *The Victorian Short Story* . . . , 168–172.
Page, Norman. *A Conrad Companion*, 156–159.
Simons, Kenneth. *The Ludic Imagination* . . . , 95–104.
Steiner, Joan E. "Conrad's 'The Secret Sharer': Complexities of the Doubling Relationship," *Conradiana*, 12 (1980), 173–186; rpt. Bloom, Harold, Ed. *Joseph Conrad*, 101–112.

"The Shadow Line"
Barclay, Glen St. John. *Anatomy of Horror* . . . , 13–14.
Miller, Karl. *Doubles* . . . , 257–259.

"A Smile of Fortune"
Armsby, Leslie. "Sujets et objets dans le roman post-symboliste: Gide, Alain-Fournier, et Conrad revisités," *Canadian R Comp Lit*, 13, i (1986), 64–75.
Watts, Cedric. "The Narrative Enigma of Conrad's 'A Smile of Fortune,'" *Conradiana*, 17 (1985), 131–136.
Weber, Horst. *Beiträge* . . . , 52–55.

"Typhoon"
Hubbard, Francis A. *Theories of Action* . . . , 1–22.
Page, Norman. *A Conrad Companion*, 146–148.
*Said, Edward W. "The Past and the Present . . . ," 48–50.

"Youth"
*Said, Edward W. "The Past and the Present . . . ," 30–32.

ROSE TERRY COOKE

"Dely's Cow"
Ammons, Elizabeth. "Introduction," in Cooke, Rose Terry. *"How Celia Changed Her Mind"* . . . , xxxii–xxxiii.

"Doom and Dan"
Kleitz, Katherine. "Essence of New England: The Portraits of Rose Terry Cooke," *Am Transcendental Q*, 47–48 (Summer–Fall, 1980), 130–131.

"Eben Jackson"
Newlyn, Evelyn. "Rose Terry Cooke and the Children of the Sphinx," *Regionalism & Female Imagination*, 4 (Winter, 1979), 6–7.

"Freedom Wheeler's Controversy with Providence"
Ammons, Elizabeth. "Introduction," xxx.
Kleitz, Katherine. "Essence of New England . . . ," 131–134.
Newlyn, Evelyn. ". . . Children of the Sphinx," 4–5.

"How Celia Changed Her Mind"
Ammons, Elizabeth. "Introduction," xxxi–xxxii.
Newlyn, Evelyn. ". . . Children of the Sphinx," 4.

"Maya the Princess"
Ammons, Elizabeth. "Introduction," xxvii.

"Miss Beulah's Bonnet"
Ammons, Elizabeth. "Introduction," xxxiii–xxxiv.

"Miss Lucinda"
Ammons, Elizabeth. "Introduction," xxxii.
Newlyn, Evelyn. ". . . Children of the Sphinx," 3.

"Mrs. Flint's Married Experience"
Ammons, Elizabeth. "Introduction," xxx–xxxi.
Newlyn, Evelyn. ". . . Children of the Sphinx," 5–6.
Toth, Susan A. "'The Rarest and Most Peculiar Grape': Versions of the New
    England Woman in Nineteenth-Century Local Color Literature," in Toth,
    Emily, Ed. *Regionalism . . .* , 22.

"My Visitation"
Ammons, Elizabeth. "Introduction," xxviii–xxix.

"Polly Mariner, Tailoress"
Newlyn, Evelyn. ". . . Children of the Sphinx," 3–4.

"The Ring Fetter"
Ammons, Elizabeth. "Introduction," xxix–xxx.
Toth, Susan A. "'The Rarest and Most Peculiar Grape' . . . ," 22–23.

"Some Account of Thomas Tucker"
Ammons, Elizabeth. "Introduction," xxxiv.

"Tenty Scran"
Buell, Lawrence. *New England . . .* , 298–300.

"Too Late"
Ammons, Elizabeth. "Introduction," xxxiv.
Kleitz, Katherine. "Essence of New England . . . ," 134–137.

"The Valley of Childish Things"
Ammons, Elizabeth. "Introduction," xxvii–xxviii.

ROBERT COOVER

"Aesop's Forest"
Cope, Jackson I. *Robert Coover's Fiction,* 26–33.

"The Babysitter"
Gerlach, John. *Toward the End . . .* , 145–148.

"A Brief Encounter"
Cope, Jackson I. *Robert Coover's Fiction,* 145–147.

"The Brother"
Cope, Jackson I. *Robert Coover's Fiction,* 20–22.

"The Dead Queen"
Cope, Jackson I. *Robert Coover's Fiction,* 16–19.

"The Door: A Prologue of Sorts"
Cope, Jackson I. *Robert Coover's Fiction,* 10–11.
Lee, L. L. "Robert Coover's Moral Vision: *Pricksongs & Descants,*" *Stud Short Fiction,* 23 (1986), 67–69.
Morris, Ann R. " 'Death-Cunt-and-Prick Songs,' Robert Coover, Prop.," in Hokenson, Jan, and Howard Pearce, Eds. *Forms of the Fantastic,* 211–212.

"The Elevator"
Morris, Ann R. " 'Death-Cunt-and-Prick Songs' . . . ," 212–213.

"The Gingerbread House"
Cope, Jackson I. *Robert Coover's Fiction,* 12–16.

"Gloomy Gus"
Cope, Jackson I. *Robert Coover's Fiction,* 59–65.

"J's Marriage"
Cope, Jackson I. *Robert Coover's Fiction,* 23–24.

"Leper's Helix"
Cope, Jackson I. *Robert Coover's Fiction,* 1–4.

"The Magic Poker"
Bohner, Charles H. *Instructor's Manual . . . ,* 35–36.

"The Marker"
Cope, Jackson I. *Robert Coover's Fiction,* 54.

"Morris in Chains"
Lee, L. L. "Robert Coover's Moral Vision . . . ," 65–67.

"Panel Game"
Cope, Jackson I. *Robert Coover's Fiction,* 125–126.

"Quenby and Ola, Swede and Karl"
Morris, Ann R. " 'Death-Cunt-and-Prick Songs' . . . ," 214.

"Spanking the Maid"
Cope, Jackson I. *Robert Coover's Fiction,* 55–58.
Gordon, Lois. *Robert Coover . . . ,* 163–166.
Ziegler, Heide. "A Room of One's Own: The Author and the Reader in the Text," in Chénetier, Marc, Ed. *Critical Angles . . . ,* 49–51.

"You Must Remember This"
Cope, Jackson I. *Robert Coover's Fiction*, 114–121.

DANIEL CORKERY

"Carrig-an-Afrinn"
Averill, Deborah M. *The Irish Short Story . . .* , 94–96.

"Joy"
Martin, Augustine. "Prose Fiction in the Irish Literary Renaissance," in Sekine,
Masaru, Ed. *Irish Writers . . .* , 158.

"On the Heights"
Averill, Deborah M. *The Irish Short Story . . .* , 92–93.

"The Ploughing of Leaca-Na-Naomh"
Averill, Deborah M. *The Irish Short Story . . .* , 89–92.
Martin, Augustine. "Prose Fiction . . . ," 160–161.

"Storm-Struck"
Averill, Deborah M. *The Irish Short Story . . .* , 87–89.

"The Wager"
Martin, Augustine. "Prose Fiction . . . ," 158–159.

JULIO CORTÁZAR

"Axolotl"
Bennett, Maurice J. "A Dialogue of Gazes: Metamorphosis and Epiphany in
Julio Cortázar's 'Axolotl,'" *Stud Short Fiction*, 23 (1986), 57–62.
Fuente, Bienvenido de la. "'Axolotl' de Julio Cortázar," *Explicación de Textos
Literarios*, 15, i (1986), 47–57.
Kauffmann, R. L. "J. C. y la narración del otro: 'Axolotl' como fábula etno-
gráfia," *Inti*, 22–23 (Fall, 1985–Spring, 1986), 317–326.
Malinow, Inéz. "Dos escritores y dos cuentos americanos: H. Quiroga y J. C.,
'Las moschas' y 'Axolotl'—Técnicas narrativas," *Inti*, 22–23 (Fall, 1985–
Spring, 1986), 385–389.
Yerlès, Pierre. "Un Fantastique intégral: 'Axolotl' de Julio Cortázar," *Les Lettres
Romanes*, 39, i–ii (1985), 139–150.

"Blow-Up"
Castro Lee, Cecilia. "Cortázar's 'Blow-Up': An Encounter with Reality," *Die-
ciocho*, 8 (1985), 181–186.
Cheever, Leonard A., and Leslie M. Thompson. "Meaning and Truth in Cor-
tázar's 'Blow-Up,'" *RE: Artes Liberales*, 12, i (1985), 1–17.
Linderman, Deborah. "Narrative Surplus: The 'Blow-Up' as Metarepresenta-
tion and Ideology," *Am J Semiotics*, 3, iv (1985), 99–118.
López, César G. "Strategies of Reading and Writing in Cortázar's 'Blow-Up,'"
Dieciocho, 8 (1985), 187–200.

Moon, Harold K. "Cortázar and Confusion: 'Las babas del diablo,'" *Dieciocho,* 8 (1985), 201–209.

Morón Arroyo, Ciriaco. "'Las babas del diablo': An Experiment on Reading," *Dieciocho,* 8 (1985), 139–146.

Padgett, Carmen H. A. "'Blow-Up' by Julio Cortázar: A Class Presentation," *Dieciocho,* 8 (1985), 210–214.

Parnell, Gary. "Fields of Interplay in Cortázar's 'Las babas del diablo,'" *Dieciocho,* 8 (1985), 213–219.

Sommer, Doris. "A Nowhere for Us: The Promising Pronouns in Cortázar's Utopian Stories," *Discurso Literario,* 4, i (1986), 241–242.

Urbina, Eduardo. "Beware: A Cautionary Reading of 'Las babas del diablo,'" *Dieciocho,* 8 (1985), 231–235.

"Cambio de luces"
Chanady, Amaryll B. "The Structure of the Fantastic in Cortázar's 'Cambio de luces,'" in Collins, Robert A., and Howard D. Pearce, Eds. *The Scope of the Fantastic . . . ,* 160–164.

"Cartas de Mamá"
Pucciarelli, Ana María. "Análisis de 'Cartas de Mamá,'" in Flores, Angel, Ed. *El realismo . . . ,* 259–274.

"Cefalea"
Aronne-Amestoy, Lida. *Utopía Paraíso . . . ,* 126–131.

"Circe"
Aronne-Amestoy, Lida. *Utopía Paraíso . . . ,* 131–133.

"Continuity of Parks"
Tyler, Joseph. "Möbius Strip and Other Designs within the Verbal Art of Julio Cortázar," in Paolini, Gilbert, Ed. *La Chispa '85 . . . ,* 361–368.

"Después del almuerzo"
Morell, Hortensia R. "Para una lectura psicoanalitica de 'Después del almuerzo,'" *Discurso Literario,* 2 (1985), 481–492.

"The Distances"
Aronne-Amestoy, Lida. *Utopía Paraíso . . . ,* 120–125.

Lavaud, Eliane. "Acercamiento a 'Lejana' de Julio Cortázar," *Co-textes,* 11 (April, 1986), 39–50.

"The Faces of the Medal"
Sommer, Doris. "A Nowhere . . . ," 248–249.

"The Gates of Heaven"
Aronne-Amestoy, Lida. *Utopía Paraíso . . . ,* 133–137.

"Graffiti"
Sommer, Doris. "A Nowhere . . . ," 256–258.

"House Taken Over"
Aronne-Amestoy, Lida. *Utopía Paraíso . . . ,* 114–117.

"Instructions for John Howell"
Troiano, James J. "Theatrical Techniques and the Fantastic in Cortázar's 'Instrucciónes para John Howell,'" *Hispanic J*, 6, i (1984), 111–119.

"Letter to a Girl in Paris"
Aronne-Amestoy, Lida. *Utopía Paraíso . . .*, 117–120.
Barrientos, Juan J. "Las palabras mágicas de Cortázar," in *Lo lúdico . . .*, 61–70.

"The Maenads"
Planells, Antonio. "Naración y musica en 'Las ménades' de Julio Cortázar," *Cahiers du Monde Hispanique*, 25 (1975), 31–36.

"Manuscript Found in a Pocket"
Bandini, Bruno. "Seduzioni trasversali: A proposito del 'Manoscritto trovato in una tasca' di Julio Cortázar," *Il Lettore di Provincia*, 16 (June–September, 1985), 49–53.
Sommer, Doris. "A Nowhere . . . ," 244.

"Moebius Strip"
Sommer, Doris. "A Nowhere . . . ," 253–256.

"Neck of the Black Kitten"
Sommer, Doris. "A Nowhere . . . ," 244–245.

"No se culpe a nadie"
Planells, Antonio. "Complicidad antropomórfica en 'No se culpe a nadie' de Julio Cortázar," *Cuadernos Americanos*, 262 (1985), 216–222.

"Omnibus"
Aronne-Amestoy, Lida. *Utopía Paraíso . . .*, 125–126.

"The Pursuer"
Fiddian, Robin W. "Religious Symbolism and the Ideological Critique in 'El perseguidor,' by Julio Cortázar," *Revista Canadiense de Estudios Hispánicos*, 9 (1985), 149–163.
Sommer, Doris. "A Nowhere . . . ," 239–241.

"Queremos tanto a Glenda"
Sommer, Doris. "A Nowhere . . . ," 251.

"Story with Spiders"
Sommer, Doris. "A Nowhere . . . ," 252–253.

"Trade Winds"
Sommer, Doris. "A Nowhere . . . ," 245–246.

STEPHEN CRANE

"The Blue Hotel"
Beaver, Harold. "Stephen Crane: Interpreting the Interpreter," in Lee, A. Robert, Ed. *. . . American Short Story*, 126–132.

Bohner, Charles H. *Instructor's Manual* . . . , 36–37.
Collins, Michael J. "Realism and Romance in the Western Stories of Stephen Crane," in Meldrum, Barbara H., Ed. *Under the Sun* . . . , 144–146.
Kent, Thomas. *Interpretation* . . . , 137–143.
Monteiro, George. "Crane's Coxcomb," *Mod Fiction Stud*, 31 (1985), 295–305.
Weiss, Daniel. *The Critical Agonistes* . . . , 100–101, 102–107.

"The Bride Comes to Yellow Sky"
Bohner, Charles H. *Instructor's Manual* . . . , 37–38.
Gerlach, John. *Toward the End* . . . , 70–73.
Sheidley, William E., and Ann Charters. *Instructor's Manual* . . . , 52–53; rpt. Charters, Ann, Willliam E. Sheidley, and Martha Ramsey. *Instructor's Manual* . . . , 2nd ed., 58–59.
Wolford, Chester L. *The Anger* . . . , 94–101; rpt. Meldrum, Barbara H., Ed. *Under the Sun* . . . , 129–136.

"The Clan of No-Name"
Rowe, Anne E. *The Idea of Florida* . . . , 54–55.

"The Five White Mice"
Collins, Michael J. "Realism and Romance . . . ," 141–142.

"Flanagan and His Short Filibustering Adventure"
Rowe, Anne E. *The Idea of Florida* . . . , 52–54.

"George's Mother"
Green, Carol H. "Stephen Crane and the Fallen Woman," in Fleischmann, Fritz, Ed. *American Novelists Revisited* . . . , 236–237.

"Maggie: A Girl of the Streets"
Baum, Rosalie M. "Alcoholism and Family Abuse in 'Maggie' and *The Bluest Eyes*," *Mosaic*, 19, iii (1986), 93–98.
Green, Carol H. ". . . Fallen Woman," 234–236.

"The Monster"
Green, Carol H. ". . . Fallen Woman," 237–238.
Warner, Michael D. "Value, Agency, and Stephen Crane's 'The Monster,'" *Nineteenth-Century Fiction*, 40 (1985), 76–93.

"The Open Boat"
Bohner, Charles H. *Instructor's Manual* . . . , 39–40.
Kazin, Alfred. *An American Procession*, 271–272.
Kent, Thomas. *Interpretation* . . . , 134–137.
Rowe, Anne E. *The Idea of Florida* . . . , 49–51.
Sheidley, William E., and Ann Charters. *Instructor's Manual* . . . , 48–50; rpt. Charters, Ann, William E. Sheidley, and Martha Ramsey. *Instructor's Manual* . . . , 2nd ed., 55–56.

FRANCIS MARION CRAWFORD

"The Dead Smile"
Morgan, Chris. "F. Marion Crawford," in Bleiler, E. F., Ed. *Supernatural Fiction Writers* . . . , II, 750–751.

"Man Overboard"
Morgan, Chris. "F. Marion Crawford," 750.

"The Screaming Skull"
Morgan, Chris. "F. Marion Crawford," 750.

"The Upper Berth"
Morgan, Chris. "F. Marion Crawford," 750.

CYRIL DABYDEEN

"Memphis"
Suganasiri, Suwanda. "Reality and Symbolism in the South Asian Canadian
Short Story," *World Lit Written Engl*, 26 (1986), 105.

ROALD DAHL

"Lamb to the Slaughter"
Warren, Alan. "Roald Dahl: Nasty, Nasty," in Schweitzer, Darrell, Ed. . . . *Horror
Fiction*, 123.

"Royal Jelly"
Warren, Alan. "Roald Dahl . . . ," 123.

"The Visitor"
Warren, Alan. "Roald Dahl . . . ," 125–126.

"The Wonderful World of Henry Sugar"
Warren, Alan. "Roald Dahl . . . ," 124.

VLADIMIR DAL [Pseudonym: COSSACK LUGANSKY]

"Vakkh Sidorov Chaikin"
Moser, Charles A. *The Russian Short Story* . . . , 31–32.

CARROLL JOHN DALY

"The False Burton Combs"
Geherin, David. *The American Private Eye* . . . , 8–9.

RUBÉNS DARÍO

"The Blue Bird"
Dixon, Paul B. "Rebirth Patterns in Several Short Stories by Rubéns Darío: A
Distinctive Feature," *Hispanic J*, 7, ii (1986), 88–89.

"The Death of the Empress of China"
Dixon, Paul B. "Rebirth Patterns . . . ," 88.

"El fardo"
Achugar, Hugo. " 'El fardo' de Rubéns Darío receptor armonioso y receptor
    heterogéneo," *Revista Iberoamericana*, 52 (1986), 857–874.

"The Ruby"
Dixon, Paul B. "Rebirth Patterns . . . ," 89–90.

"The Tree of King David"
Dixon, Paul B. "Rebirth Patterns . . . ," 90.

KAMALA DAS

"Sanatan Chaudhuri's Wife"
Elias, Mohamed. "The Short Stories of Kamala Das," *World Lit Written Engl*, 26
    (1985), 306–307.

"The Tattered Blanket"
Elias, Mohamed. "The Short Stories . . . ," 310–311.

AVRAM DAVIDSON

"Dagon"
Sanders, Joe. "Avram Davidson," in Bleiler, E. F., Ed. *Supernatural Fiction Writ-
    ers . . .* , II, 1004.

"Sacheverell"
Sanders, Joe. "Avram Davidson," 1003.

"What Strange Stars and Skies"
Sanders, Joe. "Avram Davidson," 1003.

RHYS DAVIES

"I Will Keep Her Company"
Baldwin, Dean. "The English Short Story in the Fifties," in Vannatta, Dennis,
    Ed. *The English Short Story, 1945–1980*, 37.

REBECCA HARDING DAVIS

"Life in the Iron Mills"
Malpezzi, Frances M. "Sisters in Protest: Rebecca Harding Davis and Tillie
    Olsen," *RE: Artes Liberales*, 12, ii (1986), 1–9.

"The Wife's Story"
DuPlessis, Rachel B. *Writing Beyond . . .* , 87–88.

JENNIFER DAWSON

"Hospital Wedding"
Evans, Walter. "The English Short Story in the Seventies," in Vannatta, Dennis,
   Ed. *The English Short Story, 1945–1980*, 147–148.

DAZAI OSAMU

"An Almanac of Pain"
Lyons, Phyllis I. *The Saga of Dazai . . .* , 152–153.

"Fifteen Years"
Lyons, Phyllis I. *The Saga of Dazai . . .* , 153–154.

"The Garden"
Lyons, Phyllis I. *The Saga of Dazai . . .* , 150–152.

"Going Home"
Lyons, Phyllis I. *The Saga of Dazai . . .* , 133–136.

"Hometown"
Lyons, Phyllis I. *The Saga of Dazai . . .* , 136–139.

"One Hundred Views of Mount Fuji"
Lyons, Phyllis I. *The Saga of Dazai . . .* , 119–124.

"Poor Mosquito"
Lyons, Phyllis I. *The Saga of Dazai . . .* , 93–94.

"A Record of the Autumn Wind"
Lyons, Phyllis I. *The Saga of Dazai . . .* , 99–100.

"Thinking of Zenzo"
Lyons, Phyllis I. *The Saga of Dazai . . .* , 129–132.

"Villon's Wife"
Lyons, Phyllis I. *The Saga of Dazai . . .* , 163–165.

M. DELAFIELD [EDMÉE ELIZABETH MONICA DE LA PASTURE]

"Appreciation"
McCullen, Maurice L. *E. M. Delafield*, 42–44.

"Not Yet"
McCullen, Maurice L. *E. M. Delafield*, 95–96.

"The Spoilers"
McCullen, Maurice L. *E. M. Delafield*, 47–48.

WALTER DE LA MARE

"The Creatures"
Clute, John. "Walter de la Mare," in Bleiler, E. F., Ed. *Supernatural Fiction Writers* . . . , I, 502.

"A Mote"
Clute, John. "Walter de la Mare," 502.

"The Riddle"
LeVay, John. "De la Mare's 'The Riddle,'" *Explicator,* 44, iii (1985), 23–24.

"Seaton's Aunt"
Clute, John. "Walter de la Mare," 500.

MARGARET DELAND

"The Eliots' Katy"
Reep, Diana C. *Margaret Deland,* 53–55.

"How COULD She!"
Reep, Diana C. *Margaret Deland,* 56–57.

"The Waiting Hand"
Reep, Diana C. *Margaret Deland,* 38–39.

SAMUEL DELANY

"The Tale of Dragons and Dreamers"
Spencer, Kathleen L. "Deconstructing *Tales of Nevèrÿon:* Delany, Derrida, and the 'Modular Calculus, Parts I–IV,'" *Essays Arts & Sciences,* 14 (May, 1985), 69–70.

"The Tale of Gorgik"
Spencer, Kathleen L. "Deconstructing *Tales* . . . ," 66–67.

"The Tale of Old Venn"
Spencer, Kathleen L. "Deconstructing *Tales* . . . ," 70–71.

"The Tale of Potters and Dragons"
Spencer, Kathleen L. "Deconstructing *Tales* . . . ," 67–69.

AUGUSTO MARIO DELFINO

"The Confidant"
Gai, Mijal. "Metonimia y Censura: Claves para un relato de Augusto Mario Delfino," *Hispamerica,* 14 (December, 1985), 3–27.

"The Telephone"
Zupanchih, Maria J. "Augusto Mario Delfino's 'El teléfono': Content in Har-
    mony with Stylistic Technique," *Romance Notes,* 26, ii (1985), 95–101.

ANTONIO DELGADO

"Continuous Time"
Duncan, L. Ann. *Voices, Visions . . .* , 156–158.

"José Destino"
Duncan, L. Ann. *Voices, Visions . . .* , 155.

"The Lost Space"
Duncan, L. Ann. *Voices, Visions . . .* , 149–151.

"The Luminous Scar"
Duncan, L. Ann. *Voices, Visions . . .* , 144–148.

"The Radiance of Fire"
Duncan, L. Ann. *Voices, Visions . . .* , 148–149.

LESTER DEL REY

"Helen O'Loy"
Goizet, Annette. "'Helen O'Loy' de Lester Del Rey: Helen est-elle femme ou
    robot?" in Société des Anglicistes de l'Enseignement Supérieur, Ed.
    Actes . . . , 579–586.

AUGUST DERLETH

"Alannah"
Tweet, Roald. "August Derleth," in Bleiler, E. F., Ed. *Supernatural Fiction Writ-
    ers . . .* , II, 887.

"The Dark Boy"
Tweet, Roald. "August Derleth," 888.

"The Extra Child"
Tweet, Roald. "August Derleth," 888.

SHASHI DESHPANDE

"The Intrusion"
Riemenschneider, Dieter. "Indian Women Writing in English: The Short Story,"
    World Lit Written Engl, 26 (1985), 312–314.

A. J. DEUTSCH

"A Subway Named Moebius"
Boyno, Edward A. "The Mathematics in Science Fiction: Of Measure Zero," in Hassler, Donald M., Ed. *Patterns . . . II*, 40.

PHILIP K. DICK

"The Defenders"
Christiansen, Peder. "The Classical Humanism of Philip K. Dick," in Weedman, Jane, Ed. *Women Worldwalkers . . .* , 72–73.

"Faith of Our Fathers"
Frisch, Adam J., and Joseph Martos. "Religious Imagination and Imagined Religion," in Reilly, Robert, Ed. *The Transcendent Adventure . . .* , 20–21.

"Jon's World"
Warrick, Patricia S. "Philip K. Dick's Answers to the Eternal Riddles," in Reilly, Robert, Ed. *The Transcendent Adventure . . .* , 108–109.

CHARLES DICKENS

"Main Line; The Boy at Mugby"
Orel, Harold. *The Victorian Short Story . . .* , 76–78.

"The Signalman"
Stableford, Brian M. "Charles Dickens," in Bleiler, E. F., Ed. *Supernatural Fiction Writers . . .* , I, 216–217.

"The Stroller's Tale"
Orel, Harold. *The Victorian Short Story . . .* , 66–69.

GORDON DICKSON

"Computers Don't Argue"
Berger, Harold L. *Science Fiction . . .* , 20–21.

ELMER DIKTONIUS

"The Boy and the Halter"
Schoolfield, George C. *Elmer Diktonius*, 159–160.

"Broad Back"
Schoolfield, George C. *Elmer Diktonius*, 156–157.

"The Child Killed the Knife"
Schoolfield, George C. *Elmer Diktonius*, 113–114.

"The Chimera" [originally titled "They and It"]
Schoolfield, George C. *Elmer Diktonius*, 87–89.

"The Elk Bullet"
Schoolfield, George C. *Elmer Diktonius*, 162–164.

"Hang Yourself, You Damned Kid!"
Schoolfield, George C. *Elmer Diktonius*, 109–111.

"Josef and Sussan"
Schoolfield, George C. *Elmer Diktonius*, 165–168.

"Mama"
Schoolfield, George C. *Elmer Diktonius*, 161–162.

"96%"
Schoolfield, George C. *Elmer Diktonius*, 158–159.

"Veikko, Little Slaughterer's Helper"
Schoolfield, George C. *Elmer Diktonius*, 164–165.

ISAK DINESEN [BARONESS KAREN BLIXEN]

"The Blank Page"
Greene, Gayle, and Coppélia Kahn. "Feminist Scholarship and the Social Contribution of Woman," in Greene, Gayle, and Coppélia Kahn, Eds. *Making a Difference* . . . , 5–6.

"The Cardinal's First Tale"
Aiken, Susan H. "The Use of Duplicity: Isak Dinesen and Questions of Feminist Criticism," *Scandinavian Stud*, 57 (1985), 400–411.

"Carnival"
Green, Martin, and John Swan. *The Triumph* . . . , 241–243.

"The Monkey"
Mishler, William. "Parents and Children, Brothers and Sisters in Isak Dinesen's 'The Monkey,'" *Scandinavian R*, 57 (1985), 412–451.

"The Roads Round Pisa"
Høyrup, Helene. "The Arabesque of Existence: Existential Focus and Aesthetic Form in Isak Dinesen's 'The Roads Round Pisa,'" *Scandinavica*, 24 (1985), 197–210.

DING LING

"In the Hospital"
Duke, Michael S. *Blooming* . . . , 82–84.

BIRAGO DIOP

"The Antelope and the Two Hunters"
Bourgeacq, Jacques. "The Cosmic Dimension of Diop's *Contes D'Amadou Koumba*," *Africana Journey*, 13, i–iv (1982), 55–58.

"Bad Company"
Bourgeacq, Jacques. "The Cosmic Dimension . . . ," 54–55.

"Sarzan"
Bourgeacq, Jacques. "The Cosmic Dimension . . . ," 58–61.

JAMES PATRICK DONLEAVY

"At Longitude and Latitude"
Sharma, R. K. *Isolation and Protest . . . ,* 74–75.

"Dear Hugo"
Sharma, R. K. *Isolation and Protest . . . ,* 75–76.

"Dear Sylvia"
Sharma, R. K. *Isolation and Protest . . . ,* 75–76.

"Franz F."
Sharma, R. K. *Isolation and Protest . . . ,* 77–80.

"Gustav G."
Sharma, R. K. *Isolation and Protest . . . ,* 83.

"It Was My Chimes"
Sharma, R. K. *Isolation and Protest . . . ,* 80–82.

"The Romantic Life of Alphonse A."
Sharma, R. K. *Isolation and Protest . . . ,* 72–74.

"The Saddest Summer of Samuel S."
Sharma, R. K. *Isolation and Protest . . . ,* 84–96.

"Whither Wigwams"
Sharma, R. K. *Isolation and Protest . . . ,* 76–77.

FYODOR DOSTOEVSKY

"The Double"
Anderson, Roger B. *Dostoevsky . . . ,* 12–26.
Miller, Karl. *Doubles . . . ,* 132–136.
Pekurovskaya, Asya. "The Nature of Referentiality in 'The Double,'" in Ugrimsky, Alexej, and Valija K. Ozolins, Eds. *Dostoevski and the Human Condition . . . ,* 41–51.

"The Dream of a Ridiculous Man"
Cox, Gary. *Tyrant and Victim* . . . , 32–33.
Holquist, Michael. *Dostoevsky* . . . , 155–164; rpt. Miller, Robin F. *Critical Essays on Dostoevsky*, 171–177.
Pike, Christopher. "Dostoevsky's 'Dream of a Ridiculous Man': Seeing Is Believing," in Andrew, Joe, and Christopher Pike, Eds. *The Structural Analysis* . . . , 26–63.

"The Eternal Husband"
Moser, Charles A. *The Russian Short Story* . . . , 72–73.

"A Gentle Creature"
Moser, Charles A. *The Russian Short Story* . . . , 71–72.

"The Grand Inquisitor"
Ward, Bruce K. *Dostoyevsky's Critique* . . . , 101–117.

"A Nasty Story"
Moser, Charles A. *The Russian Short Story* . . . , 70–71.

"Notes from Underground"
Behrendt, Patricia F. "The Russian Iconic Representation of the Christian Madonna: A Feminine Archetype in 'Notes from Underground,'" in Ugrimsky, Alexej, and Valija K. Ozolins, Eds. *Dostoevski and the Human Condition* . . . , 133–143.
Clews, Hetty. *The Only Teller* . . . , 171–174.
Coetzee, J. M. "Confession and Double Thoughts: Tolstoy, Rousseau, Dostoevsky," *Comp Lit*, 37 (1985), 216–228.
Cox, Gary. *Tyrant and Victim* . . . , 33–42.
*Frank, Joseph. "Nihilism and 'Notes from Underground,'" in Miller, Robin F., Ed. *Critical Essays on Dostoevsky*, 50–63.
———. *Dostoevsky: The Stir* . . . , 316–349.
Jones, Malcolm V. "Dostoevsky: 'Notes from Underground,'" in Cockrell, Roger, and David Richards, Eds. *The Voice of a Giant* . . . , 55–65.
Meyers, Jeffrey. *Disease* . . . , 27–47.
Nisula, Dasha C. "Dostoevsky and Richard Wright: From Petersburg to Chicago," in Ugrimsky, Alexej, and Valija K. Ozolins, Eds. *Dostoevski and the Human Condition* . . . , 163–170.
Sanborn, Pat. "Nasty Pleasures on 'Notes from Underground,'" *North Dakota Q*, 54 (1986), 200–211.

"The Peasant Marey"
Jackson, Robert L. "The Triple Vision: Dostoevsky's 'The Peasant Marey,'" *Yale R*, 67 (1978), 225–235; rpt. Miller, Robin F., Ed. *Critical Essays on Dostoevsky*, 177–188.
Rice, James L. *Dostoevsky* . . . , 46–48.

"White Nights"
Moser, Charles A. *The Russian Short Story* . . . , 40–41.

ARTHUR CONAN DOYLE

"The Adventure of Black Peter"
Cox, Don R. *Arthur Conan Doyle*, 105–108.
Wesson, Sheldon. "The Crimes of 'The Adventure of Black Peter,'" *Baker Street J*, 32 (1982), 153–155.

"The Adventure of Charles Augustus Milverton"
Cox, Don R. *Arthur Conan Doyle*, 108–111.
Harris, Bruce. "Did Sherlock Holmes Kill Charles Augustus Milverton?" *Baker Street J*, 32 (1982), 45–47.

"The Adventure of Silver Blaze"
Cox, Don R. *Arthur Conan Doyle*, 65–66.

"The Adventure of the Abbey Grange"
Cox, Don R. *Arthur Conan Doyle*, 118–120.

"The Adventure of the Beryl Coronet"
Cox, Don R. *Arthur Conan Doyle*, 61–63.

"The Adventure of the Blanched Soldier"
Cox, Don R. *Arthur Conan Doyle*, 155–157.

"The Adventure of the Blue Carbuncle"
Cox, Don R. *Arthur Conan Doyle*, 55–56.

"The Adventure of the Bruce-Partington Plan"
Cox, Don R. *Arthur Conan Doyle*, 142–144.

"The Adventure of the Cardboard Box"
Cox, Don R. *Arthur Conan Doyle*, 136–140.

"The Adventure of the Copper Beeches"
Cox, Don R. *Arthur Conan Doyle*, 63–64.

"The Adventure of the Creeping Man"
Cox, Don R. *Arthur Conan Doyle*, 167–170.

"The Adventure of the Crooked Man"
Cox, Don R. *Arthur Conan Doyle*, 73–74.

"The Adventure of the Dancing Men"
Cox, Don R. *Arthur Conan Doyle*, 98–101.

"The Adventure of the Devil's Foot"
Cox, Don R. *Arthur Conan Doyle*, 148–150.

"The Adventure of the Dying Detective"
Cox, Don R. *Arthur Conan Doyle*, 144–146.

"The Adventure of the Empty House"
Cox, Don R. *Arthur Conan Doyle*, 158–159.
Kamil, Irving. "Sherlock Holmes and the Locked-Room Mystery," *Baker Street J*, 32 (1982), 143–145.

"The Adventure of the Engineer's Thumb"
Cox, Don R. *Arthur Conan Doyle*, 60–61.

"The Adventure of the *Gloria Scott*"
Cox, Don R. *Arthur Conan Doyle*, 68–69.

"The Adventure of the Golden Pince-Nez"
Cox, Don R. *Arthur Conan Doyle*, 114–117.

"The Adventure of the Greek Interpreter"
Cox, Don R. *Arthur Conan Doyle*, 75–76.

"The Adventure of the Illustrious Client"
Cox, Don R. *Arthur Conan Doyle*, 153–155.

"The Adventure of the Lion's Mane"
Cox, Don R. *Arthur Conan Doyle*, 170–171.

"The Adventure of the Mazarin Stone"
Cox, Don R. *Arthur Conan Doyle*, 157–159.

"The Adventure of the Missing Three-Quarter"
Cox, Don R. *Arthur Conan Doyle*, 117–118.

"The Adventure of the Naval Treaty"
Cox, Don R. *Arthur Conan Doyle*, 76–79.

"The Adventure of the Noble Bachelor"
Cox, Don R. *Arthur Conan Doyle*, 61.

"The Adventure of the Norwood Builder"
Cox, Don R. *Arthur Conan Doyle*, 96–98.

"The Adventure of the Priory School"
Cox, Don R. *Arthur Conan Doyle*, 102–105.

"The Adventure of the Red Circle"
Cox, Don R. *Arthur Conan Doyle*, 140–142.

"The Adventure of the Reigate Squire"
Cox, Don R. *Arthur Conan Doyle*, 72–73.

"The Adventure of the Resident Patient"
Cox, Don R. *Arthur Conan Doyle*, 74–75.

"The Adventure of the Retired Colourman"
Cox, Don R. *Arthur Conan Doyle*, 175–176.

"The Adventure of the Second Stain"
Baum, Christopher F. "The Twice-Stained Treaty," *Baker Street J*, 32 (1982),
146–148.
Cox, Don R. *Arthur Conan Doyle*, 121–123.

"The Adventure of the Shoscombe Old Place"
Cox, Don R. *Arthur Conan Doyle*, 172–175.

"The Adventure of the Six Napoleons"
Cox, Don R. *Arthur Conan Doyle*, 111–112.

"The Adventure of the Solitary Cyclist"
Cox, Don R. *Arthur Conan Doyle*, 101–102.

"The Adventure of the Speckled Band"
Cox, Don R. *Arthur Conan Doyle*, 56–69.

"The Adventure of the Stockbroker's Clerk"
Cox, Don R. *Arthur Conan Doyle*, 67–68.

"The Adventure of the Sussex Vampire"
Cox, Don R. *Arthur Conan Doyle*, 161–163.

"The Adventure of the Three Gables"
Cox, Don R. *Arthur Conan Doyle*, 159–161.

"The Adventure of the Three Garridebs"
Cox, Don R. *Arthur Conan Doyle*, 163–165.

"The Adventure of the Three Students"
Cox, Don R. *Arthur Conan Doyle*, 112–114.

"The Adventure of the Veiled Lodger"
Cox, Don R. *Arthur Conan Doyle*, 171–172.

"The Adventure of the Yellow Face"
Cox, Don R. *Arthur Conan Doyle*, 66–67.

"The Adventure of Wisteria Lodge"
Cox, Don R. *Arthur Conan Doyle*, 132–136.

"The Boscombe Valley Mystery"
Cox, Don R. *Arthur Conan Doyle*, 51–52.

"The Brazilian Cat"
Cox, Don R. *Arthur Conan Doyle*, 202–203.

"A Case of Identity"
Cox, Don R. *Arthur Conan Doyle*, 50–51.

"Danger"
Cox, Don R. *Arthur Conan Doyle*, 208–209.

"The Disappearance of Lady Frances Carfax"
Cox, Don R. *Arthur Conan Doyle,* 146–148.

"The Disintegration Machine"
Cox, Don R. *Arthur Conan Doyle,* 194–195.

"The Final Problem"
Cox, Don R. *Arthur Conan Doyle,* 79–81.

"The Five Orange Pips"
Cox, Don R. *Arthur Conan Doyle,* 52–54.
Kalikoff, Beth. *Murder and Moral Decay . . . ,* 160.

"His Last Bow"
Cox, Don R. *Arthur Conan Doyle,* 150–153.

"The Horror of the Heights"
Cox, Don R. *Arthur Conan Doyle,* 200–201.

"The Hound of the Baskervilles"
Day, William P. *In the Circles . . . ,* 54–55.

"The Last Adventure of the Brigadier"
Cox, Don R. *Arthur Conan Doyle,* 31–32.

"The Man with the Twisted Lip"
Cox, Don R. *Arthur Conan Doyle,* 54–55.

"The Musgrave Ritual"
Cox, Don R. *Arthur Conan Doyle,* 69–72.

"The Problem at Thor Bridge"
Cox, Don R. *Arthur Conan Doyle,* 165–166.

"The Red-Headed League"
Bohner, Charles H. *Instructor's Manual . . . ,* 40–41.
Cox, Don R. *Arthur Conan Doyle,* 50.

"The Ring of Thoth"
Cox, Don R. *Arthur Conan Doyle,* 204–206.

"A Scandal in Bohemia"
Cox, Don R. *Arthur Conan Doyle,* 49–50.

"The Sign of Four"
Dahlinger, S. E. "In Search of the Agra Treasure (or Gelt by Association),"
    Baker Street J, 36 (1986), 217–219.
Kalikoff, Beth. *Murder and Moral Decay . . . ,* 159–160.

"A Study in Scarlet"
Umansky, Harlan L. "An Adventure in 'Wild Surmise,'" *Baker Street J,* 32
    (1982), 25–29.

"The Terror of Blue John Gap"
Cox, Don R. *Arthur Conan Doyle*, 201–202.

"When the World Screamed"
Cox, Don R. *Arthur Conan Doyle*, 195–196.

MARGARET DRABBLE

"Crossing the Alps"
Sadler, Lynn V. *Margaret Drabble*, 71–72.

"A Day in the Life of a Smiling Woman"
Sadler, Lynn V. *Margaret Drabble*, 38–40.

"The Gifts of War"
Sadler, Lynn V. *Margaret Drabble*, 63–65.

"Hassan's Tower"
Sadler, Lynn V. *Margaret Drabble*, 70–71.

"Homework"
Sadler, Lynn V. *Margaret Drabble*, 66–67.

"A Pyrrhic Victory"
Sadler, Lynn V. *Margaret Drabble*, 23–24.

"The Reunion"
Sadler, Lynn V. *Margaret Drabble*, 49–50.

"A Success Story"
Sadler, Lynn V. *Margaret Drabble*, 37–38.

"A Voyage to Cythera"
Sadler, Lynn V. *Margaret Drabble*, 50–51.

THEODORE DREISER

"Chains"
Griffin, Joseph. *The Small Canvas . . .* , 77–81.

"Convention"
Griffin, Joseph. *The Small Canvas . . .* , 96–100.

"The Cruise of the *Idlewild*"
Griffin, Joseph. *The Small Canvas . . .* , 38–40.

"Fine Furniture"
Griffin, Joseph. *The Small Canvas . . .* , 111–114.

"Free"
Griffin, Joseph. *The Small Canvas* . . . , 54–61.

"Fulfilment"
Griffin, Joseph. *The Small Canvas* . . . , 88–90.

"The Hand"
Griffin, Joseph. *The Small Canvas* . . . , 74–77.

"Khat"
Griffin, Joseph. *The Small Canvas* . . . , 107–108.

"The Lost Phoebe"
Griffin, Joseph. *The Small Canvas* . . . , 40–44.

"McEwen of the Shining Slave Makers"
Griffin, Joseph. *The Small Canvas* . . . , 29–31.
Howard, June. *Form and History* . . . , 106–107.

"Marriage—For One"
Griffin, Joseph. *The Small Canvas* . . . , 87–88.

"Married"
Griffin, Joseph. *The Small Canvas* . . . , 44–48.

"The Mercy of God"
Griffin, Joseph. *The Small Canvas* . . . , 91–93.

"Nigger Jeff"
Griffin, Joseph. *The Small Canvas* . . . , 31–36.
Howard, June. *Form and History* . . . , 102.

"The Old Neighborhood"
Griffin, Joseph. *The Small Canvas* . . . , 69–74.

"Old Rogaum and His Theresa"
Griffin, Joseph. *The Small Canvas* . . . , 36–38.

"The Prince Who Was a Thief"
Griffin, Joseph. *The Small Canvas* . . . , 108–109.

"St. Columbia and the River"
Griffin, Joseph. *The Small Canvas* . . . , 93–96.

"Sanctuary"
Griffin, Joseph. *The Small Canvas* . . . , 81–87.

"The Second Choice"
Griffin, Joseph. *The Small Canvas* . . . , 48–51.

"The Shadow"
Griffin, Joseph. *The Small Canvas* . . . , 90–91.

"Solution"
Griffin, Joseph. *The Small Canvas* . . . , 114–118.

"A Start in Life"
Griffin, Joseph. *The Small Canvas* . . . , 122–123.

"A Story of Stories"
Griffin, Joseph. *The Small Canvas* . . . , 61–64.

"Tabloid Tragedy"
Griffin, Joseph. *The Small Canvas* . . . , 118–121.

"The Tithe of the Lord"
Griffin, Joseph. *The Small Canvas* . . . , 123–127.

"Typhoon"
Griffin, Joseph. *The Small Canvas* . . . , 100–105.

"The Victor"
Griffin, Joseph. *The Small Canvas* . . . , 105–107.

"When the Old Century Was New"
Griffin, Joseph. *The Small Canvas* . . . , 25–28.

"Will You Walk into My Parlor?"
Griffin, Joseph. *The Small Canvas* . . . , 64–66.

ANNETTE VON DROSTE-HÜLSHOFF

"Die Judenbuche"
Paulin, Roger. *The Brief Compass* . . . , 64–67.
Wittkowski, Wolfgang. "Das Rätsel der 'Judenbuche' und seine Lösung: Religiöse Geheimsignale in Zeitangaben der literatur um 1840," *Sprachkunst*, 16 (1985), 175–192.

MAURICE DUGGAN

"Along Rideout Road That Summer"
Stead, C. K. *In the Glass Case* . . . , 111–115.

"The Deposition"
Stead, C. K. *In the Glass Case* . . . , 115–116.

"Riley's Handbook"
Stead, C. K. *In the Glass Case* . . . , 117–119.

ALICE DUNBAR-NELSON

"The Goodness of Saint Rocque"
Whitlow, Roger. "Alice Dunbar-Nelson, New Orleans Writer," in Toth, Emily, Ed. *Regionalism* . . . , 119–120.

"Little Miss Sophie"
Whitlow, Roger. "Alice Dunbar-Nelson . . . ," 113–115.

"Mr. Baptiste"
Whitlow, Roger. "Alice Dunbar-Nelson . . . ," 121–122.

"M'sieu Fortier's Violin"
Whitlow, Roger. "Alice Dunbar-Nelson . . . ," 120–121.

"A Story of Vengeance"
Whitlow, Roger. "Alice Dunbar-Nelson . . . ," 112–113.

"Titee"
Whitlow, Roger. "Alice Dunbar-Nelson . . . ," 115–116.

"Tony's Wife"
Whitlow, Roger. "Alice Dunbar-Nelson . . . ," 122–124.

"Violets"
Whitlow, Roger. "Alice Dunbar-Nelson . . . ," 110–112.

"The Woman"
Whitlow, Roger. "Alice Dunbar-Nelson . . . ," 117–118.

LORD DUNSANY [EDWARD JOHN MORETON DRAX PLUNKETT]

"Two Bottles of Relish"
Walker, Warren S. "'Tales That One Never Wants to Hear'—A Sample from
    Dunsany," *Stud Short Fiction*, 22 (1985), 449–454.

EDWARD DYSON

"A Golden Shanty"
Bennett, Bruce. "Asian Encounters in the Contemporary Australian Short
    Story," *World Lit Written Engl*, 26 (1986), 51–52.

MARIA VON EBNER-ESCHENBACH

"First Confession"
Thum, Reinhard. "Parental Authority and Childhood Trauma: An Analysis of
    Maria von Ebner-Eschenbach's 'Die erste Beichte,'" *Mod Austrian Lit*, 19, ii
    (1986), 15–32.

AMELIA B. EDWARDS

"The Eleventh of March"
Fisher, Benjamin F. "Amelia B. Edwards," in Bleiler, E. F., Ed. *Supernatural
    Fiction Writers . . .* , I, 257.

"A Night on the Border of the Black Forest"
Fisher, Benjamin F. "Amelia B. Edwards," 259.

"The Phantom Coach"
Fisher, Benjamin F. "Amelia B. Edwards," 258–259.

"The Professor's Story"
Fisher, Benjamin F. "Amelia B. Edwards," 256–257.

"The Story of a Clock"
Fisher, Benjamin F. "Amelia B. Edwards," 256.

"The Treasure Isle"
Fisher, Benjamin F. "Amelia B. Edwards," 257–258.

CATERINA EDWARDS

"The Last Young Man"
Minni, C. D. "The Short Story as an Ethnic Genre," in Pivato, Joseph, Ed. *Contrasts* . . . , 64–65.

GEORGE EGERTON [MARY CHAVELITA BRIGHT]

"A Lost Masterpiece: A City Mood, Aug. '93"
Hanson, Clare. *Short Stories* . . . , 15–17.

JOSEPH VON EICHENDORFF

"From the Life of a Good-for-Nothing"
Bohm, Arnd. "Competing Economies in Eichendorff's 'Aus dem Leben eines Taugenichts,'" *Germ Q*, 58 (1985), 540–553.

CYPRIAN O. D. EKWENSI

"Glittering City"
Grandsaigne, J. de. "A Narrative Grammar of Cyprian Ekwensi's Short Stories," *Research African Lit*, 16 (1985), 543–552.

"Lokotown" [same as "Loca Town"]
Grandsaigne, J. de. "A Narrative Grammar . . . ," 543–552.

"Stranger from Lagos"
Grandsaigne, J. de. "A Narrative Grammar . . . ," 543.

GEORGE ELIOT [MARY ANN EVANS]

"Brother Jacob"
Diedrick, James. "George Eliot's Experiments in Fiction: 'Brother Jacob' and the German *Novelle*," *Stud Short Fiction*, 22 (1985), 461–468.

Welsh, Alexander. *George Eliot . . . ,* 161–163.

"Janet's Repentance"
Ermarth, Elizabeth. *George Eliot,* 64–66.
Shaw, Sheila. "The Female Alcoholic in Victorian Fiction: George Eliot's Un-
poetic Heroine," in Nathan, Rhoda B., Ed. *Nineteenth-Century Woman Writers . . . ,* 173–176.

"The Lifted Veil"
Beet, Gilliam. *George Eliot,* 79–81.
Welsh, Alexander. *George Eliot . . . ,* 274–275.

"Mr. Gilfil's Love Story"
Ermarth, Elizabeth. *George Eliot,* 62–64.

"The Sad Fortunes of Amos Barton"
Ermarth, Elizabeth. *George Eliot,* 60–62.

SERGIO ELIZONDO

"Coyote, Tonight"
Miller, Yvette E. "Sergio Elizondo," in Martínez, Julio A., and Francisco A. Lomelí, Eds. *Chicano Literature . . . ,* 213–214.

"The Flowers"
Miller, Yvette E. "Sergio Elizondo," 214.

"I Shouldn't Have Danced That Night"
Miller, Yvette E. "Sergio Elizondo," 215–216.

"Lugar"
Miller, Yvette E. "Sergio Elizondo," 215.

"Quien le manda"
Miller, Yvette E. "Sergio Elizondo," 214.

"Rose, the Flute"
Miller, Yvette E. "Sergio Elizondo," 213.

"So Here I Am To Die"
Miller, Yvette E. "Sergio Elizondo," 216.

"Solitude with an Intruding Word"
Miller, Yvette E. "Sergio Elizondo," 216.

"Ur"
Miller, Yvette E. "Sergio Elizondo," 214–215.

STANLEY ELKIN

"Among the Witnesses"
Bailey, Peter. "Stanley Elkin's Tales of Last Resort," *Mid-American R*, 5, i (1985), 73–80.

"The Bailbondsman"
Bailey, Peter J. *Reading Stanley Elkin*, 153–164.

"The Condominium"
Bailey, Peter. "Stanley Elkin's Tales . . . ," 73–80; rpt. in his *Reading Stanley Elkin*, 144–153.

"The Making of Ashenden"
Abrioux, Yves. "Animal et être parlant: 'The Making of Ashenden,'" *Delta*, 20 (February, 1985), 149–180.
Bailey, Peter J. *Reading Stanley Elkin*, 139–1̞44.

"A Poetics for Bullies"
Bailey, Peter J. *Reading Stanley Elkin*, 1–20.

HARLAN ELLISON

"A Boy and His Dog"
Berger, Harold L. *Science Fiction . . .* , 143–145.

"The Deathbird"
Frisch, Adam J., and Joseph Martos. "Religious Imagination and Imagined Religion," in Reilly, Robert, Ed. *The Transcendent Adventure . . .* , 14.

RALPH ELLISON

"Battle Royal"
Sheidley, William E., and Ann Charters. *Instructor's Manual . . .* , 142–144; rpt. Charters, Ann, William E. Sheidley, and Martha Ramsey. *Instructor's Manual . . .* , 2nd ed., 143–144.
Spivey, Ted R. *Revival . . .* , 141–142.

"King of the Bingo Game"
Bohner, Charles H. *Instructor's Manual . . .* , 41–42.

MIRIAM ELSTON

"A Mess of Things"
Fairbanks, Carol. *Prairie Women . . .* , 115.

DENNIS ETCHISON

"The Dead Line"
Stamm, Michael E. "The Dark Side of the American Dream: Dennis Etchison,"
  in Schweiker, Darrell, Ed. . . . *Horror Fiction,* 51.

"Deathtracks"
Stamm, Michael E. "The Dark Side . . . ," 52.

"It Will Be Here Soon"
Stamm, Michael E. "The Dark Side . . . ," 52.

"The Late Shift"
Stamm, Michael E. "The Dark Side . . . ," 52.

"Sitting in the Corner, Whimpering Quietly"
Stamm, Michael E. "The Dark Side . . . ," 50–51.

"Wet Season"
Stamm, Michael E. "The Dark Side . . . ," 49–50.

CARADOC EVANS

"Be This Her Memorial"
Jones, Mary. "A Changing Myth: The Projection of the Welsh in the Short
  Stories of Caradoc Evans," *Anglo-Welsh R,* 81, i (1985), 92–93.

"A Father in Sion"
Davies, John, and John Harris. "Caradoc Evans and the Forcers of Conscience:
  A Reading of 'A Father in Sion,'" *Anglo-Welsh R,* 81, i (1985), 79–89.

"Taffy at Home"
Jones, Mary. "A Changing Myth . . . ," 92.

"The Woman Who Sowed Iniquity"
Jones, Mary. "A Changing Myth . . . ," 94.

PHILIP JOSÉ FARMER

"Father"
Chapman, Edgar L. "From Rebellious Rationalist to Mythmaker and Mystic:
  The Religious Quest of Philip José Farmer," in Reilly, Robert, Ed. *The
  Transcendent Adventure* . . . , 129–131.

WILLIAM FAULKNER

"Ad Astra"
Skei, Hans H. *William Faulkner* . . . , 130–131.

"Adolescence"
Skei, Hans H. *William Faulkner*... , 46–47.

"Afternoon of a Cow"
Carothers, James B. ... *Short Stories*, 127–128.

"All the Dead Pilots"
Skei, Hans H. *William Faulkner*... , 131–133.

"Artist at Home"
Carothers, James B. ... *Short Stories*, 72–75.
Skei, Hans H. *William Faulkner*... , 152–153.

"Barn Burning"
Carothers, James B. ... *Short Stories*, 60–64.
Hiles, Jane. "Kinship and Heredity in Faulkner's 'Barn Burning,'" *Mississippi Q*, 38 (1985), 329–337.

"The Bear"
Frazer, Winifred. "'Habet' in *The Bear*," *Notes Mississippi Writers*, 17, i (1985), 41–43.
Sederberg, Nancy B. "'A Momentary Anesthesia of the Heart': A Study of the Comic Elements in Faulkner's *Go Down, Moses*," in Fowler, Doreen, and Ann J. Abadie, Eds. *Faulkner and Women*... , 86–89.
Skei, Hans H. *William Faulkner*... , 249–252.
Waegner, Cathy. *Recollection and Discovery*... , 173–183.

"A Bear Hunt"
Skei, Hans H. *William Faulkner*... , 220–221.

"Beyond"
Skei, Hans H. *William Faulkner*... , 145–146.

"The Big Shot"
Putzel, Max. *Genius of Place*... , 245–247.
Skei, Hans H. *William Faulkner*... , 142–143.

"Black Music"
Skei, Hans H. *William Faulkner*... , 147–148.

"The Brooch"
Skei, Hans H. *William Faulkner*... , 118–119.

"By the People"
Skei, Hans H. *William Faulkner*... , 285–286.

"Carcassonne"
Carothers, James B. ... *Short Stories*, 81–83.
Skei, Hans H. *William Faulkner*... , 150–152.

"Centaur in Brass"
Carothers, James B. ... *Short Stories*, 118–122.

Skei, Hans H. *William Faulkner...*, 187–189.

"A Courtship"
Carothers, James B. *... Short Stories,* 77–79.
Skei, Hans H. *William Faulkner...*, 273–275.

"A Dangerous Man"
Skei, Hans H. *William Faulkner...*, 164–165.

"Death Drag"
Skei, Hans H. *William Faulkner...*, 140–141.

"Delta Autumn"
Sederberg, Nancy B. "'A Momentary Anesthesia...,'" 89–90.
Skei, Hans H. *William Faulkner...*, 252–253.
Vashchenko, Alexandre. "Woman and the Making of the New World: Faulkner's Short Stories," in Fowler, Doreen, and Ann J. Abadie, Eds. *Faulkner and Women...*, 214–218.

"Doctor Martino"
Skei, Hans H. *William Faulkner...*, 115–116, 125–126.

"Dry September"
Bohner, Charles H. *Instructor's Manual...*, 42–43.
Crane, John K. "But the Days Grow Short: A Reinterpretation of Faulkner's 'Dry September,'" *Twentieth Century Lit,* 31 (1985), 410–420.
Skei, Hans H. *William Faulkner...*, 112–114.
Weiss, Daniel. *The Critical Agonistes...*, 174–184.

"Elly"
Petry, Alice H. "Double Murder: The Women of Faulkner's 'Elly,'" in Fowler, Doreen, and Ann J. Abadie, Eds. *Faulkner and Women...*, 220–232.
Seidel, Kathryn L. *The Southern Belle...*, 103–104.
Skei, Hans H. *William Faulkner...*, 107–108.

"Evangeline"
Cornell, Brenda G. "Faulkner's 'Evangeline': A Preliminary Stage," *Southern Q,* 22, iv (1984), 22–41.
Skei, Hans H. *William Faulkner...*, 172–175.

"The Fire and the Hearth"
Sederberg, Nancy B. "'A Momentary Anesthesia...,'" 82–84.
Skei, Hans H. *William Faulkner...*, 245–247.
Waegner, Cathy. *Recollection and Discovery...*, 159–166.

"Fool About a Horse"
Carothers, James B. *... Short Stories,* 125–126.

"Fox Hunt"
Skei, Hans H. *William Faulkner...*, 116–117, 126–127.

"Go Down, Moses"
Donaldson, Susan V. "Isaac McCaslin and the Possibilities of Vision," *Southern R*, 22 (1986), 37–50.
Seizer, John L. "'Go Down, Moses' and *Go Down, Moses*," *Stud Am Fiction*, 13 (1985), 89–95.
Skei, Hans H. *William Faulkner...*, 254–255.
Waegner, Cathy. *Recollection and Discovery...*, 183–184.

"Hair"
Carothers, James B. ... *Short Stories*, 96–97.
Duvall, John N. "Faulkner's Critics and Women: The Voice of the Community," in Fowler, Doreen, and Ann J. Abadie, Eds. *Faulkner and Women...*, 42–43.
Skei, Hans H. *William Faulkner...*, 175–177.

"Hand Upon the Water"
Skei, Hans H. *William Faulkner...*, 256–257.

"The Hill"
Skei, Hans H. *William Faulkner...*, 41–45.

"The Hound"
Skei, Hans H. *William Faulkner...*, 166–169.

"Idyll in the Desert"
Díaz-Diocaretz, Myriam. "Faulkner's Hen-House: Woman as Bounded Text," in Fowler, Doreen, and Ann J. Abadie, Eds. *Faulkner and Women...*, 244–245.
Skei, Hans H. *William Faulkner...*, 162–164.

"A Justice"
Putzel, Max. *Genius of Place...*, 237–241.
Skei, Hans H. *William Faulkner...*, 189–194.

"The Kid Learns"
Skei, Hans H. *William Faulkner...*, 71–72.

"Knight's Gambit"
Carothers, James B. ... *Short Stories*, 99–100.
Schlepper, Wolfgang. "William Faulkner's Detective Stories," *Archiv*, 222, i (1985), 140–141.
Skei, Hans H. *William Faulkner...*, 259–261.

"Landing in Luck"
Carothers, James B. ... *Short Stories*, 51–53.
Skei, Hans H. *William Faulkner...*, 34–35.

"The Leg"
Skei, Hans H. *William Faulkner...*, 148–150.

"The Liar"
Skei, Hans H. *William Faulkner...*, 79–81.

"Lizards in Jamshyd's Courtyard"
Skei, Hans H. *William Faulkner*. . . , 185–187.

"Lo!"
Skei, Hans H. *William Faulkner*. . . , 221–222.

"Love"
Skei, Hans H. *William Faulkner*. . . , 38–40.

"Mirrors of Chartres Street"
Skei, Hans H. *William Faulkner*. . . , 56–59.

"Miss Zilphia Gant"
Carothers, James B. . . . *Short Stories*, 103–104.
Skei, Hans H. *William Faulkner*. . . , 104–107.

"Mr. Acarius"
Carothers, James B. . . . *Short Stories*, 105–106.
Skei, Hans H. *William Faulkner*. . . , 281–282.

"Monk"
Carothers, James B. . . . *Short Stories*, 97–98.
Schlepper, Wolfgang. ". . . Detective Stories," 138–139.

"Moonlight"
Skei, Hans H. *William Faulkner*. . . , 35–38.

"Mountain Victory"
Bomze, JoAnn. "Faulkner's 'Mountain Victory': The Triumph of 'The Middle Ground,'" *Coll Engl Assoc Critic*, 46 (1984), 9–11.
Vashchenko, Alexandre. "Woman and the Making . . . ," 211–214.

"Mule in the Yard"
Carothers, James B. . . . *Short Stories*, 122–123.
Skei, Hans H. *William Faulkner*. . . , 219–220.

"My Grandmother Millard"
Bungert, Hans. "Faulkner's Humor: A European View," in Fowler, Doreen, and Ann J. Abadie, Eds. *Faulkner and Women* . . . , 145–146.

"A Name for the City"
Skei, Hans H. *William Faulkner*. . . , 280–281.

"Notes on a Horsethief"
Skei, Hans H. *William Faulkner*. . . , 276–277.

"Nympholepsy"
Díaz-Diocaretz, Myriam. "Faulkner's Hen-House . . . ," 253–254.

"Odour of Verbena"
Gray, Richard. *Writing the South* . . . , 200–201.

"The Old People"
Harrison, James. "Faulkner's 'The Old People,'" *Explicator,* 44, ii (1986), 41.
Waegner, Cathy. *Recollection and Discovery* ... , 169–173.

"Out of Nazareth"
Skei, Hans H. *William Faulkner* ... , 76–77.

"Pantaloon in Black"
Sederberg, Nancy B. "'A Momentary Anesthesia ... ,'" 84–85.
Waegner, Cathy. *Recollection and Discovery* ... , 166–169.

"Pennsylvania Station"
Carothers, James B. ... *Short Stories,* 69–72.
Skei, Hans H. *William Faulkner* ... , 141–142.

"A Portrait of Elmer"
Skei, Hans H. *William Faulkner* ... , 85–86.

"The Priest"
Díaz-Diocaretz, Myriam. "Faulkner's Hen-House ... ," 251–253.

"Race at Morning"
Skei, Hans H. *William Faulkner* ... , 283–285.

"Red Leaves"
Carothers, James B. ... *Short Stories,* 75–77.
Skei, Hans H. *William Faulkner* ... , 194–198.

"A Return"
Skei, Hans H. *William Faulkner* ... , 143–144.

"A Rose for Emily"
Bohner, Charles H. *Instructor's Manual* ... , 43–44.
Hochman, Baruch. *Characters in Literature,* 149–152.
Kurtz, Elizabeth C. "Faulkner's 'A Rose for Emily,'" *Explicator,* 44, ii (1986), 40–41.
Petry, Alice H. "Faulkner's 'A Rose for Emily,'" *Explicator,* 44, iii (1986), 52–54.
Skei, Hans H. *William Faulkner* ... , 108–113.

"Sepulture South: Gaslight"
Skei, Hans H. *William Faulkner* ... , 286–287.

"Shall Not Perish"
Skei, Hans H. *William Faulkner* ... , 269–271.

"Shingles for the Lord"
Carothers, James B. ... *Short Stories,* 64–68.
Skei, Hans H. *William Faulkner* ... , 271–272.

"Smoke"
Carothers, James B. ... *Short Stories,* 95–96.

Schlepper, Wolfgang. ". . . Detective Stories," 137–138.

"Spotted Horses"
Skei, Hans H. *William Faulkner. . .* , 182–185.

"The Tall Men"
Carothers, James B. . . . *Short Stories,* 68–69.
Skei, Hans H. *William Faulkner. . .* , 265–267.

"That Evening Sun"
Bohner, Charles H. *Instructor's Manual . . .* , 45–46.
Gerlach, John. *Toward the End . . .* , 130–143.
Kuyk, Dirk and Betty M., and James A. Miller. "Black Culture in William
    Faulkner's 'That Evening Sun,'" *J Am Stud,* 20, i (1986), 33–50.
Perrine, Laurence. "'That Evening Sun': A Skein of Uncertainties," *Stud Short
    Fiction,* 22 (1985), 295–307.
Skei, Hans H. *William Faulkner. . .* , 198–200.

"That Will Be Fine"
Skei, Hans H. *William Faulkner. . .* , 225–226.

"There Was a Queen"
Skei, Hans H. *William Faulkner. . .* , 169–172.

"Thrift"
Skei, Hans H. *William Faulkner. . .* , 137–138.

"Tomorrow"
Skei, Hans H. *William Faulkner. . .* , 257–258.

"Turnabout"
Carothers, James B. . . . *Short Stories,* 79–80.
Skei, Hans H. *William Faulkner. . .* , 136–137.

"Two Soldiers"
Skei, Hans H. *William Faulkner. . .* , 268–269.

"Uncle Willy"
Skei, Hans H. *William Faulkner. . .* , 223–225.

"Victory"
Skei, Hans H. *William Faulkner. . .* , 133–134.

"Was"
Hoffman, Daniel. "Faulkner's 'Was' and Uncle Adam's Cow," in Fowler, Doreen,
    and Ann J. Abadie, Eds. *Faulkner and Humor . . .* , 57–78.
Waegner, Cathy. *Recollection and Discovery . . .* , 154–159.
Weiss, Daniel. *The Critical Agonistes . . .* , 174–184.

"Wash"
Skei, Hans H. *William Faulkner. . .* , 216–218.

"The Wild Palms"
Carothers, James B. . . . *Short Stories*, 30–31.

"The Wishing Tree"
Skei, Hans H. *William Faulkner*. . . , 88–89.

"Yo Ho and Two Bottles of Rum"
Skei, Hans H. *William Faulkner*. . . , 81–84.

JESSIE REDMON FAUSET

"The Sleeper Wakes"
McDowell, Deborah E. "The Neglected Dimension of Jessie Redmon Fauset,"
in Pryse, Marjorie, and Hortense J. Spillers, Eds. *Conjuring* . . . , 88–93.

MORDECAI ZEV FEIERBURG

"Whither"
Silberschlag, Eisig. *From Renaissance* . . . , 221–222.

BEPPE FENOGLIO

"The Whirlpool"
Di Paolo, Maria G. "Il 'gorgo' e la morte: Un simbolo di Beppe Fenoglio,"
Canadian J Italian Stud, 7, iii–iv (1985), 50–64.

ROSARIO FERRÉ

"Mercedes Benz 220SL"
Escalera Ortiz, Juan. "Perspectiva del cuento 'Mercedes Benz 220SL,'" *R Inter-
americana*, 12 (1982), 407–417.

"La muñeca menor"
Fernández Olmos, Margarita. "Desde una perspectiva feminina; La cuentística
de Rosario Ferré y Ana Lydia Vega," *Homines*, 8, ii (1984), 303–311.

"When Women Love Men"
Fernández Olmos, Margarita. "Sex, Color, and Class in Contemporary Puerto
Rican Women Authors," *Heresies*, 4, iii (1982), 46–47.

LESLIE FIEDLER

"The First Spade in the West"
Winchell, Mark R. *Leslie Fiedler*, 127–129.

"The Last Jew in America"
Winchell, Mark R. *Leslie Fiedler*, 125–126.

"The Last WASP in the World"
Winchell, Mark R. *Leslie Fiedler,* 126–127.

"Nobody Ever Dies from It"
Winchell, Mark R. *Leslie Fiedler,* 117–118.

"Nude Croquet"
Winchell, Mark R. *Leslie Fiedler,* 119–120.

"Pull Down Vanity"
Winchell, Mark R. *Leslie Fiedler,* 118–119.

AMANDA FINCH

"Back Trail: A Novella of Love in the South"
Watson, Carole M. *Prologue . . . ,* 133.

IAN HAMILTON FINLAY

"National Assistance Money"
Baldwin, Dean. "The English Short Story in the Fifties," in Vannatta, Dennis,
    Ed. *The English Short Story, 1945–1980,* 38.

CHARLES FINNEY

"The Captivity"
Smith, Curtis C. "Charles Finney," in Bleiler, E. F., Ed. *Supernatural Fiction
    Writers . . . ,* II, 824.

"The Door"
Smith, Curtis C. "Charles Finney," 822–823.

"The Life and Death of a Western Gladiator"
Smith, Curtis C. "Charles Finney," 823.

"The Magician Out of Manchuria"
Smith, Curtis C. "Charles Finney," 825.

F. SCOTT FITZGERALD

"Absolution"
Hagermann, E. P. "Should Scott Fitzgerald Be Absolved for the Sins of 'Ab-
    solution'?" *J Mod Lit,* 12 (1985), 169–174.

"Babylon Revisited"
Bohner, Charles H. *Instructor's Manual . . . ,* 46–47.
Sheidley, William E., and Ann Charters. *Instructor's Manual . . . ,* 102; rpt. Char-

ters, Ann, William E. Sheidley, and Martha Ramsey. *Instructor's Manual . . .*, 2nd ed., 103.

"Bernice Bobs Her Hair"
Cifelli, Edward. "Bernice's Liberation: Fitzgerald's 'Bernice Bobs Her Hair,'" *Notes Mod Am Lit*, 8, iii (1984), Item 19.

"O Russet Witch!"
Person, Leland S. "Fitzgerald's 'O Russet Witch!': Dangerous Women, Dangerous Art," *Stud Short Fiction*, 23 (1986), 443–448.

"The Rich Boy"
Fizer, John. "Indeterminancies as Structural Components in Semiotically Meaningful Wholes," in Köpeczi, Béla, and György Vajda, Eds. *Proceedings of the 8th Congress . . .*, 767–773.
Petry, Alice H. "The Picture(s) of Paula Legendre: Fitzgerald's 'The Rich Boy,'" *Stud Short Fiction*, 22 (1985), 232–234.

"Winter Dreams"
Pike, Gerald. "Four Voices in 'Winter Dreams,'" *Stud Short Fiction*, 23 (1986), 315–320.

GUSTAVE FLAUBERT

"Bouvard and Pécuchet"
Cascardi, Anthony J. *The Bounds of Reason . . .*, 225–237.
Donato, Eugenio. "The Museum's Furnace: Notes Toward a Contextual Reading of 'Bouvard and Pécuchet,'" in Harari, Jusué, Ed. *Textual Strategies*, 213–238; rpt. Porter, Laurence M., Ed. *Critical Essays . . .*, 207–222.
Galliard, Françoise. "The Great Illusion of Realism, or the Real as Representation," trans. Mya Weinberger, *Poetics Today*, 5 (1984), 753–766.
Ginsburg, Michal P. *Flaubert Writing . . .*, 154–164.
Humphries, Jefferson. "'Bouvard et Pécuchet' and the Fable of Stable Irony," *French Forum*, 10 (1985), 145–162.
Knight, Diana. *Flaubert's Characters . . .*, 42–44.

"Hérodias"
Ginsburg, Michal P. *Flaubert Writing . . .*, 175–177.
Leal, R. B. "Spatiality and Structure in Flaubert's 'Hérodias,'" *Mod Lang R*, 80 (1985), 810–816.
Reid, Ian. "The Death of the Implied Author? Voice, Sequence and Control in Flaubert's *Trois Contes*," *Australian J French Stud*, 23 (1986), 165–198, 206–209.

"St. Julien"
Bart, Benjamin F. "Psyche into Myth: Humanity and Animality in Flaubert's 'Saint Julien,'" *Kentucky Romance Q*, 20 (1973), 317–341; rpt. Porter, Laurence M., Ed. *Critical Essays . . .*, 186–205.
Biasi, Pierre-Marc de. "Le Palimpseste hagiographique: L'Appropriation ludique des sources édifiantes dans la redaction de 'La Légende de saint Julien l'Hospitalier,'" *R Lettres Modernes*, 777–781 (1986), 69–124.

Ginsburg, Michal P. *Flaubert Writing . . .* , 164–170.
Knight, Diana. *Flaubert's Characters . . .* , 70–73.
Marston, Jane E. "Narration as Subject in Flaubert's 'La Légende de Saint Julien
L'Hospitalier,'" *Nineteenth-Century French Stud*, 14 (1986), 341–345.
Reid, Ian. "The Death . . . ," 165–198, 203–206.

"A Simple Heart"
Debray-Genette, Raymonde. "Narrative Figures of Speech in 'A Simple Heart,'"
Poétique, 3 (1970), 348–364; rpt. Porter, Laurence M., Ed. *Critical Es-
says . . .* , 165–186.
Ginsburg, Michal P. *Flaubert Writing . . .* , 170–177.
Knight, Diana. *Flaubert's Characters . . .* , 61–65.
Marsh, Leonard. "Visual Perception in Flaubert's 'Un Coeur simple,'" *Stud Short
Fiction*, 23 (1986), 185–189.
Reid, Ian. "The Death . . . ," 165–203.
Sheidley, William E., and Ann Charters. *Instructor's Manual . . .* , 14–15; rpt.
Charters, Ann, William E. Sheidley, and Martha Ramsey. *Instructor's Man-
ual . . .* , 2nd ed., 14–16.

E. M. FORSTER

"The Celestial Omnibus"
Kessel, John J. "E. M. Forster," in Bleiler, E. F., Ed. *Supernatural Fiction Writers . . .* , I, 483–484.

"The Curate's Friend"
Kessel, John J. "E. M. Forster," 481–482.

"The Machine Stops"
Berger, Harold L. *Science Fiction . . .* , 25–26.

"The Other Boat"
Flora, Joseph M. *The English Short Story . . .* , 23–24.

"Other Kingdom"
Kessel, John J. "E. M. Forster," 481.

"The Point of It"
Kessel, John J. "E. M. Forster," 483.

"The Road from Colonus"
Kessel, John J. "E. M. Forster," 482–483.

"The Story of a Panic"
Kessel, John J. "E. M. Forster," 480–481.

JOHN FOWLES

"The Cloud"
Evans, Walter. "The English Short Story in the Seventies," in Vannatta, Dennis,
Ed. *The English Short Story, 1945–1980*, 171–172.

"The Ebony Tower"
Evans, Walter. "The English Short Story . . . ," 166–168.
Lemon, Lee T. *Portraits* . . . , 111–112.
Runyon, Randolph. *Fowles / Irving / Barthes* . . . , 26–27.

"Eliduc"
Evans, Walter. "The English Short Story . . . ," 168–169.
Runyon, Randolph. *Fowles / Irving / Barthes* . . . , 12–14.

"Poor Koko"
Evans, Walter. "The English Short Story . . . ," 169–170.

MARY E. WILKINS FREEMAN

"Evelina's Garden"
Donovan, Josephine. "Silence or Capitulation: Prepatriarchal 'Mothers' Gardens' in Jewett and Freeman," *Stud Short Fiction*, 23 (1986), 45–47.

"The Hall Bedroom"
Robillard, Douglas. "Mary Wilkins Freeman," in Bleiler, E. F., Ed. *Supernatural Fiction Writers* . . . , II, 772.

"The Lost Ghost"
Oaks, Susan. "The Haunted Will: The Ghost Stories of Mary Wilkins Freeman," *Colby Lib Q,* 21 (1985), 217–218.

"Luella Miller"
Oaks, Susan. "The Haunted Will . . . ," 214–215.
Robillard, Douglas. "Mary Wilkins Freeman," 771–772.

"A New England Nun"
Buell, Lawrence. *New England* . . . , 345–347.

"The Shadows on the Wall"
Oaks, Susan. "The Haunted Will . . . ," 213–214.

"The Southwest Chamber"
Oaks, Susan. "The Haunted Will . . . ," 215–217.

"The Vacant Lot"
Robillard, Douglas. "Mary Wilkins Freeman," 771.

"The Window in the Rose Bush"
Oaks, Susan. "The Haunted Will . . . ," 212–213.

ALICE FRENCH

"Mrs. Finlay's Elizabethan Chair"
Fairbanks, Carol. *Prairie Women* . . . , 195–197.

"Tommy and Thomas"
Fairbanks, Carol. *Prairie Women* . . . , 197–198.

CARLOS FUENTES

"In a Flemish Garden"
Knapp, Bettina L. *Archetype, Architecture* . . . , 125–146.

ERNEST J. GAINES

"Bloodline"
Byerman, Keith E. *Fingering the Jagged Grain* . . . , 83–85.
Callahan, John F. "Hearing Is Believing: The Landscape of Voice in Ernest
   Gaines's *Bloodline*," *Callaloo*, 7, i (1984), 104–107.

"Just Like a Tree"
Byerman, Keith E. *Fingering the Jagged Grain* . . . , 85–87.
Callahan, John F. "Hearing Is Believing . . . ," 107–110.

"A Long Day in November"
Byerman, Keith E. *Fingering the Jagged Grain* . . . , 74–76.
Callahan, John F. "Hearing Is Believing . . . ," 91–96.

"The Sky Is Gray"
Byerman, Keith E. *Fingering the Jagged Grain* . . . , 76–79.
Callahan, John F. "Hearing Is Believing . . . ," 96–99.

"Three Men"
Byerman, Keith E. *Fingering the Jagged Grain* . . . , 79–83.
Callahan, John F. "Hearing Is Believing . . . ," 99–104.

SERGIO GALINDO

"Heaven Knows"
Cluff, Russell M. "Iniciaciónes literarias del adolescente en Sergio Galindo y
   José Emilio Pachecos," *La Palabra y el Hombre*, 59–60 (July–December,
   1986), 17–28.

MAVIS GALLANT

"The Cost of Living"
Besner, Neil. "A Broken Dialogue: History and Memory in Mavis Gallant's
   Short Fiction," *Essays Canadian Writing*, 33 (Fall, 1986), 95–96.

"The Four Seasons"
Keefer, Janice K. "Mavis Gallant and the Angel of History," *Univ Toronto Q*, 55
   (1986), 298.

"In Youth Is Pleasure"
Besner, Neil. "A Broken Dialogue . . . ," 90–93.

"Its Image on the Mirror"
Besner, Neil. "A Broken Dialogue . . . ," 93–95.
Irvine, Lorna. *Sub/version* . . . , 75–89.

"Luk and His Father"
Fabre, Michel. " 'Orphans' Progress,' Reader's Progress: Voice and Understatement in Mavis Gallant's Stories," in Kroetsch, Robert, and Reingard M. Nischik, Eds. *Gaining Ground* . . . , 157–159.

"Malcolm and Bea"
Keefer, Janice K. "Mavis Gallant . . . ," 287–289.

"The Moslem Wife"
Besner, Neil. "A Broken Dialogue . . . ," 92–93.

"Orphans' Progress"
Fabre, Michel. " 'Orphans' Progress,' Reader's Progress . . . ," 150–157.

"The Other Paris"
Besner, Neil. "A Broken Dialogue . . . ," 90–93.

"The Pegnitz Junction"
Irvine, Lorna. *Sub-version* . . . , 135–139.
Keefer, Janice K. "Mavis Gallant . . . ," 291–296.

JOHN GALT

"The Seamstress"
Kestner, Joseph. *Protest and Reform* . . . , 83.

GAO XIAOSHENG

"Li Shunda Builds a House"
Duke, Michael S. *Blooming* . . . , 87–88.

YOLANDA A. GARCÍA

"Ellipses"
Lewis, Marvin A. "The Urban Experience in Selected Chicano Fiction," in Lattin, Vernon E., Ed. *Contemporary Chicano Fiction* . . . , 47–48.

GABRIEL GARCÍA MÁRQUEZ

"Big Mama's Funeral"
Paiewonsky-Conde, Edgar. "La escritura como acto revolucionario: *Los funerales de la Mamá Grande*," in Hernández de López, Ana María, Ed. *En el punto de mira* . . . , 33–53.

"Blacamán the Good, Vendor of Miracles"
Aronne-Amestoy, Lida. "Blacabunderías del método: El recurso al discurso en García Márquez," in Hernández de López, Ana María, Ed. *En el punto de mira . . .*, 55–62.

"The Handsomest Drowned Man in the World"
Aronne-Amestoy, Lida. *Utopía Paraíso . . .*, 31–35.
Gerlach, John. *Toward the End . . .*, 163–165.

"The Incredible and Sad Tale of the Innocent Eréndira and Her Heartless Grandmother"
Boo, Matilde L. "'La increíble y triste historia de la cándida Eréndira y de su abuela desalmada' de García Márquez y *Tormento* de Galdós: Significación irónica de la irrealidad," in Hernández de López, Ana María, Ed. *En el punto de mira . . .*, 71–82.
Burgos, Fernando. "El cuento como épica de la imaginación en García Márquez," in Hernández de López, Ana María, Ed. *En el punto de mira . . .*, 91–102.
Millington, Mark. "Actant and Character in García Márquez's 'La increíble y triste historia de la cándida Eréndira y de su abuela desalmada,'" in Cardwell, Richard A., Ed. *Essays in Honor of Robert Brian Tate . . .*, 83–90.

"Montiel's Widow"
Arrington, Melvin S. "'La viuda Montiel': Un retrato en miniatura de Macondo," in Hernández de López, Ana María, Ed. *En el punto de mira . . .*, 63–69.

"One of These Days"
Kason, Nancy M. "El arte del ambiente psicológico en 'Un día de éstos,'" in Hernández de López, Ana María, Ed. *En el punto de mira . . .*, 83–90.

"Tuesday Siesta"
Arango, Manuel A. "Tema y estructura en el cuento 'La siesta martes' de Gabriel García Márquez," *Thesaurus*, 40, iii (1985), 591–604.
Bohner, Charles H. *Instructor's Manual . . .*, 48.

"A Very Old Man with Enormous Wings"
Sheidley, William E., and Ann Charters. *Instructor's Manual . . .*, 165–166; rpt. Charters, Ann, William E. Sheidley, and Martha Ramsey. *Instructor's Manual . . .*, 2nd ed., 177–178.

JESÚS GARDEA

"The Sun You Are Watching"
Duncan, L. Ann. *Voices, Visions . . .*, 185–188.

JOHN GARDNER

"Redemption"
Howell, John M. "The Wound and the Albatross: John Gardner's Apprenticeship," in Henderson, Jeff, Ed. *Thor's Hammer . . .*, 4–6.

HAMLIN GARLAND

"Drifting Crane"
Meyer, R. W. "Hamlin Garland and the American Indian," *Western Am Lit,* 2
   (1967), 117; rpt. Silet, Charles L., Robert E. Welch, and Richard Boudreau, Eds. *The Critical Reception . . . ,* 305.

"The New Medicine House"
Meyer, R. W. "Hamlin Garland . . . ," 119–120; rpt. Silet, Charles L., Robert E.
   Welch, and Richard Boudreau, Eds. *The Critical Reception . . . ,* 306–307.

"The Silent Eaters"
Meyer, R. W. "Hamlin Garland . . . ," 121–122; rpt. Silet, Charles L., Robert E.
   Welch, and Richard Boudreau, Eds. *The Critical Reception . . . ,* 308–309.

RICHARD GARNETT

"The Demon Pope"
Clute, John. "Richard Garnett," in Bleiler, E. F., Ed. *Supernatural Fiction Writers . . . ,* I, 320.

"The Dumb Oracle"
Clute, John. "Richard Garnett," 319–320.

ELENA GARRO

"La culpa es de los tlaxcaltecas"
Duncan, Cynthia. " 'La culpa es de los tlaxcaltecas': A Reevaluation of Mexico's
   Past Through Myth," *Crítica Hispánica,* 7, ii (1985), 105–120.

ELIZABETH CLEGHORN GASKELL

"Cousin Phillis"
Brodetsky, Tessa. *Elizabeth Gaskell,* 86–87.

"French Life"
Nestor, Pauline. *Female Friendships . . . ,* 73–74.

"The Grey Woman"
Nestor, Pauline. *Female Friendships . . . ,* 76–78.
Reddy, Maureen T. "Gaskell's 'The Grey Woman': A Feminist Palimpsest," *J
   Narrative Technique,* 15 (1985), 183–193.

"Half a Life-Time Ago"
Brodetsky, Tessa. *Elizabeth Gaskell,* 81–82.
Nestor, Pauline. *Female Friendships . . . ,* 71–73.

"Libbie Marsh's Three Eras"
Kestner, Joseph. *Protest and Reform . . . ,* 117–119.

"Lizzie Leigh"
Homans, Margaret. *Bearing the Word* . . . , 226–235.
Nestor, Pauline. *Female Friendships* . . . , 67–68.

"Lois the Witch"
Brodetsky, Tessa. *Elizabeth Gaskell*, 84–86.
Homans, Margaret. *Bearing the Word* . . . , 238–248.
Nestor, Pauline. *Female Friendships* . . . , 61–62.

"The Manchester Marriage"
Nestor, Pauline. *Female Friendships* . . . , 59–60.

"Mr. Harrison's Confession"
Nestor, Pauline. *Female Friendships* . . . , 49–50.

"My Lady Ludlow"
Brodetsky, Tessa. *Elizabeth Gaskell*, 82–84.

"The Poor Clare"
Homans, Margaret. *Bearing the Word* . . . , 248–250.

WILLIAM GASS

"Icicles"
Saltzman, Arthur M. . . . *Consolation of Language*, 76–84.

"In the Heart of the Heart of the Country"
Gerlach, John. *Toward the End* . . . , 150–152.
Saltzman, Arthur M. . . . *Consolation of Language*, 90–101.

"Mrs. Mean"
Saltzman, Arthur M. . . . *Consolation of Language*, 70–76.

"Order of Insects"
Haley, Vanessa. "Egyptology and Entomology in William Gass's 'Order of Insects,'" *Notes Contemp Lit*, 16, iii (1986), 3–5.
Saltzman, Arthur M. . . . *Consolation of Language*, 84–89.
Shinn, Thelma J. *Radiant Daughters* . . . , 161–162.

"The Pedersen Kid"
Saltzman, Arthur M. . . . *Consolation of Language*, 59–69.

THÉOPHILE GAUTIER

"The Coffeepot"
Laszlo, Pierre. "Que la fête recommence!" *Stanford French R*, 9, i (1985), 47–59.

SALLY GEARHART

"Krueva and the Pony"
Caldwell, Patrice. "Earth Mothers or Male Memories: Wilhelm, Lem, and Future Women," in Weedman, Jane, Ed. *Women Worldwalkers* . . . , 67.

LEWIS GRASSIC GIBBON [JAMES LESLIE MITCHELL]

"Cartaphilus"
Malcolm, William K. *A Blasphemer* . . . , 62.

"Clay"
Campbell, Ian. *Lewis Grassic Gibbon*, 18–19.
Malcolm, William K. *A Blasphemer* . . . , 72–75.

"Dawn in Alarlu"
Malcolm, William K. *A Blasphemer* . . . , 62–63.

"Daybreak"
Malcolm, William K. *A Blasphemer* . . . , 54–56.

"Dieneke's Dream" [originally titled "Thermopylae"]
Malcolm, William K. *A Blasphemer* . . . , 58–60.

"The Floods of Spring"
Malcolm, William K. *A Blasphemer* . . . , 61–62.

"Forsaken"
Malcolm, William K. *A Blasphemer* . . . , 77–81.

"Gift of the River"
Malcolm, William K. *A Blasphemer* . . . , 54.

"Greenden"
Campbell, Ian. *Lewis Grassic Gibbon*, 17–18.
Malcolm, William K. *A Blasphemer* . . . , 65–69.

"If You Sleep in the Moonlight"
Malcolm, William K. *A Blasphemer* . . . , 45–46.

"It Is Written"
Malcolm, William K. *A Blasphemer* . . . , 51–52.

"The Lost Constituent"
Malcolm, William K. *A Blasphemer* . . . , 60–61.

"The Passage of the Dawn"
Malcolm, William K. *A Blasphemer* . . . , 52–54.

"Revolt" [originally titled "One Man with a Dream"]
Malcolm, William K. *A Blasphemer* . . . , 46–47.

"Road to Freedom"
Malcolm, William K. *A Blasphemer.* . . , 56–57.

"Smeddum"
Campbell, Ian. *Lewis Grassic Gibbon,* 21–22.
Malcolm, William K. *A Blasphemer.* . . , 69–71.

ANDRÉ GIDE

"The Immoralist"
Sacken, Jeanée P. *"A Certain Slant of Light".* . . , 98–167.

"Isabelle"
Armsby, Leslie. "Sujets et objets dans le roman post-symboliste: Gide, Alain-Fournier, et Conrad revisités," *Canadian R Comp Lit,* 13, i (1986), 64–75.

"The Pastoral Symphony"
O'Keefe, Charles. "Verbal-Erotic Anarchy in Gide's 'La Symphonie Pastorale,'" *French R,* 60 (1986), 20–29.

MARGARET GIBSON GILBOORD

"Considering Her Condition"
Davidson, Arnold E. "Regions of the Mind and Margaret Gibson Gilboord's *The Butterfly Ward,*" in Toth, Emily, Ed. *Regionalism* . . . , 173–174.

"Making It"
Davidson, Arnold E. "Regions of the Mind . . . ," 169–173.

ELLEN GILCHRIST

"Revenge"
Thompson, Jeanie, and Anita M. Gardner. "The Miracle of Realism: The Bid for Self Knowledge in the Fiction of Ellen Gilchrist," *Southern Q,* 22, i (1983), 103–104; rpt. Prenshaw, Peggy W., Ed. *Women Writers* . . . , 236–237.

"There's a Garden of Eden"
Thompson, Jeanie, and Anita M. Gardner. "The Miracle . . . ," 104; rpt. Prenshaw, Peggy W., Ed. *Women Writers* . . . , 237.

"Travelers"
Thompson, Jeanie, and Anita M. Gardner. "The Miracle . . . ," 102–103; rpt. Prenshaw, Peggy W., Ed. *Women Writers* . . . , 235–236.

PENELOPE GILLIATT

"Nobody's Business"
Evans, Walter. "The English Short Story in the Seventies," in Vannatta, Dennis, Ed. *The English Short Story, 1945–1980,* 133.

CHARLOTTE PERKINS GILMAN

"The Yellow Wallpaper"
Berman, Jeffrey. *The Talking Cure* . . . , 51–59.
Bohner, Charles H. *Instructor's Manual* . . . , 49.
DuPlessis, Rachel B. *Writing Beyond* . . . , 91–93.
Haney-Peritz, Janice. "Monumental Feminism and Literature's Ancestral House: Another Look at 'The Yellow Wallpaper,'" *Women's Stud*, 12 (1986), 113–128.

SUSAN GLASPELL

"A Jury of Her Peers"
Fairbanks, Carol. *Prairie Women* . . . , 114.
Hedges, Elaine. "Small Things Reconsidered: Susan Glaspell's 'A Jury of Her Peers,'" *Women's Stud*, 12, i (1986), 89–110.
Kolodny, Annette. "A Map for Rereading; or, Gender and the Interpretation of Literary Texts," in Garner, Shirley N., Claire Kahane, and Madelon Sprengnether, Eds. *The (M)other Tongue* . . . , 253–257.

"Pollen"
Fairbanks, Carol. *Prairie Women* . . . , 257–258.

PATRICIA GLYNN

"Bo and Be"
Klinkowitz, Jerome. *Literary Subversions* . . . , 169–170.

URI NISSAN GNESSIN

"Genia"
Silberschlag, Eisig. *From Renaissance* . . . , 223–224.

"In the Garden"
Silberschlag, Eisig. *From Renaissance* . . . , 224–225.

DAVID GODFREY

"River Two Blind Jacks"
York, Lorraine M. "'River Two Blind Jacks': Dave Godfrey's Chaucerian Allegory," *Stud Canadian Lit*, 9 (1984), 206–213.

TOM GODWIN

"The Cold Equation"
Huntington, John. "Hard-Core Science Fiction and the Illusion of Science," in Slusser, George E., and Eric S. Rabkin, Eds. *Hard Science Fiction*, 50–56.

NIKOLAI GOGOL

"The Carriage"
Gittin, Vladimir. "Toward a Poetics of the Gogolian Anecdote: 'The Carriage,'"
in Crone, Anna L., and Catherine V. Chvany, Eds. *New Studies*..., 132–
150.

"The Nevsky Prospect"
Höcherl, Alfons. "Naturalistiche Thematik bei Gogol und Kuprin," in Wedel,
Erwin, Ivan Galabov, and Herbert Schelesniker, Eds. *Symposium Slavicum
1977*..., 57–63.

"The Overcoat"
Bohner, Charles H. *Instructor's Manual*..., 50–51.
Moser, Charles A. *The Russian Short Story*..., 26–28.
Peace, R. A. "Gogol: 'The Greatcoat,'" in Cockrell, Roger, and David Richards,
Eds. *The Voice of a Giant*..., 27–40.
Rancour-Lafettiere, Daniel. *Out from Under Gogol's Overcoat*..., 188–222.
Sheidley, William E., and Ann Charters. *Instructor's Manual*..., 7–8; rpt. Char-
ters, Ann, William E. Sheidley, and Martha Ramsey. *Instructor's Man-
ual*..., 2nd ed., 11.

WILLIAM GOLDING

"Clonk Clonk"
Briggs, Julia. "*The Scorpion God*," in Crompton, Don, and Julia Briggs. *A View
from the Spire*..., 85–91.
Hodson, Leigh. "*The Scorpion God*...," 198–199.
Redpath, Philip. *William Golding*..., 116–118.

"Envoy Extraordinary"
Briggs, Julia. "*The Scorpion God*," 91–93.
Hodson, Leigh. "*The Scorpion God:* Clarity, Technique, and Communication,"
in Biles, Jack I., and Robert O. Evans, Eds. *William Golding*..., 199–200.
Redpath, Philip. *William Golding*..., 109–112.

"The Inheritors"
Hodson, Leigh. "*The Scorpion God*...," 200–201.

"The Scorpion God"
Briggs, Julia. "*The Scorpion God*," 72–85.
Hodson, Leigh. "*The Scorpion God*...," 193–198.
Redpath, Philip. *William Golding*..., 104–107.

DAVID J. GONZÁLEZ

"The Proletarian"
Lewis, Marvin A. "The Urban Experience in Selected Chicano Fiction," in
Lattin, Vernon E., Ed. *Contemporary Chicano Fiction*..., 49.

JOSÉ LUIS GONZALEZ

"La noche que volvimos a ser gente"
Falcón, Rafael. "'La noche que volvimos a ser gente': Una nueva y encantadora
visión de la emigración puertorriqueña," *Revista Chicano-Riquena,* 12, ii
(1984), 70–79.

NADINE GORDIMER

"A Chip of Glass Ruby"
Eckstein, Barbara. "Pleasure and Joy: Political Activism in Nadine Gordimer's
Short Stories," *World Lit Today,* 59 (1985), 345–346.

"Is There Nowhere Else Where We Can Meet?"
Cooke, John. . . . *Private Lives/Public Landscapes,* 128–129.
Eckstein, Barbara. "Pleasure and Joy . . . ," 343–344.

"Little Willie"
Cooke, John. . . . *Private Lives/Public Landscapes,* 125–126.

"The Smell of Death and Flowers"
Cooke, John. . . . *Private Lives/Public Landscapes,* 127–128.
Eckstein, Barbara. "Pleasure and Joy . . . ," 344–345.

"Something Out There"
Cooke, John. . . . *Private Lives/Public Landscapes,* 123–124.
Wieseltier, Leon. "Afterword," *Salmagundi,* 62 (1984), 193–196.

"The Train from Rhodesia"
Bohner, Charles H. *Instructor's Manual . . . ,* 51–52.

CAROLINE GORDON

"The Last Day in the Field"
Brinkmeyer, Robert H. *Three Catholic Writers . . . ,* 83–84.

"The Olive Garden"
Brinkmeyer, Robert H. *Three Catholic Writers . . . ,* 94–95.

"One Against Thebes"
Brinkmeyer, Robert H. *Three Catholic Writers . . . ,* 114–116.

"One More Time"
Brinkmeyer, Robert H. *Three Catholic Writers . . . ,* 84–85.

"The Presence"
Brinkmeyer, Robert H. *Three Catholic Writers . . . ,* 110–112.

MAXIM GORKY

"Chelkash"
Moser, Charles A. *The Russian Short Story* . . . , 123–124.

"Twenty-Six Men and a Girl"
Gutsche, George J. *Moral Apostasy* . . . , 99–116.

SHIRLEY ANN GRAU

"Fever Flower"
Shinn, Thelma J. *Radiant Daughters* . . . , 115–116.

"Joshua"
Shinn, Thelma J. *Radiant Daughters* . . . , 114–115.

"Miss Yellow Eyes"
Shinn, Thelma J. *Radiant Daughters* . . . , 114.

"White Girl, Fine Girl"
Shinn, Thelma J. *Radiant Daughters* . . . , 113–114.

ALVIN GREENBERG

"Delta q"
Davis, Robert M. "Ordinary Disorder: The Stories of Alvin Greenberg," *Int'l Fiction R*, 13, i (1986), 14.

"Disorder and Belated Sorrow: A Shadow Play"
Davis, Robert M. "Ordinary Disorder . . . ," 14–15.

GRAHAM GREENE

"Across the Bridge"
Flora, Joseph M. *The English Short Story* . . . , 29–30.

"The Basement Room"
Rai, Gangeshwar. *Graham Greene*, 110–112.

"A Chance for Mr. Lever"
Rai, Gangeshwar. *Graham Greene*, 108–109.

"Cheap in August"
Pickering, Jean. "The English Short Story in the Sixties," in Vannatta, Dennis, Ed. *The English Short Story, 1945–1980*, 97.

"The Destructors"
Clarke, Peter P. "Graham Greene's 'The Destructors': An Anarchist Parody," *Engl Lang Notes*, 23 (1986), 60–63.

Gorecki, J. "Graham Greene's 'The Destructors' and *Paradise Lost*," *Papers Lang & Lit,* 21 (1985), 336–340.

"Dream of Strange Land"
Rai, Gangeshwar. *Graham Greene,* 116–117.

"A Drive in the Country"
Rai, Gangeshwar. *Graham Greene,* 109–110.

"The End of the Party"
Rai, Gangeshwar. *Graham Greene,* 105–106.

"The Hint of an Explanation"
Rai, Gangeshwar. *Graham Greene,* 112–113.

"I Spy"
Rai, Gangeshwar. *Graham Greene,* 117–118.

"The Second Death"
Rai, Gangeshwar. *Graham Greene,* 106–107.

"Under the Garden"
Pickering, Jean. "The English Short Story . . . ," 113.
Rai, Gangeshwar. *Graham Greene,* 114–116.

"A Visit to Morin"
Rai, Gangeshwar. *Graham Greene,* 114.

GERALD GRIFFIN

"Card Drawing"
Sloan, Barry. *The Pioneers . . . ,* 65–68.

"The Half-Sir"
Sloan, Barry. *The Pioneers . . . ,* 65–72.

NEIL GUNN

"The Tax Gatherer"
Baldwin, Dean. "The English Short Story in the Fifties," in Vannatta, Dennis, Ed. *The English Short Story, 1945–1980,* 37–38.

ELENA GURO

"So Life Goes"
Banjanin, Milica. "Nature and the City in the Works of Elena Guro," *Slavonic & East European R,* 30 (1986), 239–241.

HUMBERTO GUZMÁN

"Ariel" [originally titled "Bad Dreams"]
Duncan, L. Ann. *Voices, Visions* . . . , 98–99.

"The Clock"
Duncan, L. Ann. *Voices, Visions* . . . , 98.

THOMAS CHANDLER HALIBURTON

"The Witch of Inky Dell"
Middlebro, Tom. "*Imitatio Inanitatis:* Literary Madness and the Canadian Short
Story," *Canadian Lit,* 107 (1985), 189–193.

MRS. S. C. HALL

"Kelly the Piper"
Sloan, Barry. *The Pioneers* . . . , 143–144.

DASHIELL HAMMETT

"The Big Knockover"
Dooley, Dennis. *Dashiell Hammett,* 66–69.
Naremore, James. "Dashiell Hammett and the Poetics of Hard-Boiled Detec-
tion," in Benstick, Bernard, Ed. *Art and Crime* . . . , 56.

"Corkscrew"
Dooley, Dennis. *Dashiell Hammett,* 62–65.
Naremore, James. "Dashiell Hammett . . . ," 55–56.

"Dead Yellow Women"
Dooley, Dennis. *Dashiell Hammett,* 60–61.

"The Farewell Murder"
Dooley, Dennis. *Dashiell Hammett,* 45–51.
Naremore, James. "Dashiell Hammett . . . ," 58–60.

"Fly Paper"
Dooley, Dennis. *Dashiell Hammett,* 53–54.

"The Gatewood Caper"
Dooley, Dennis. *Dashiell Hammett,* 46–48.

"The Golden Horseshoe"
Dooley, Dennis. *Dashiell Hammett,* 22–24.

"The Gutting of Couffignal"
Dooley, Dennis. *Dashiell Hammett,* 48–49.
Naremore, James. "Dashiell Hammett . . . ," 54–55.

"The House in Turk Street"
Dooley, Dennis. *Dashiell Hammett*, 24–27.

"The Main Death"
Dooley, Dennis. *Dashiell Hammett*, 39–42.

"The Man Who Killed Dan Odams"
Dooley, Dennis. *Dashiell Hammett*, 63–64.

"$106,000 Blood Money"
Dooley, Dennis. *Dashiell Hammett*, 69–71.

"The Scorched Face"
Dooley, Dennis. *Dashiell Hammett*, 51–53.

"The Tenth Clew"
Dooley, Dennis. *Dashiell Hammett*, 20–22.

"This King Business"
Dooley, Dennis. *Dashiell Hammett*, 54–47.

"The Whosis Kid"
Dooley, Dennis. *Dashiell Hammett*, 33–39.

THOMAS HARDY

"The Distracted Preacher"
Hasan, Noorul. *Thomas Hardy . . .* , 119–123.

"An Imaginative Woman"
Hasan, Noorul. *Thomas Hardy . . .* , 123–124.

"Our Exploits at West Poley"
Hasan, Noorul. *Thomas Hardy . . .* , 107–108.

"The Son's Veto"
Orel, Harold. *The Victorian Short Story . . .* , 112–113.

"A Tradition of Eighteen Hundred and Four"
Hasan, Noorul. *Thomas Hardy . . .* , 113–114.

"A Tragedy of Two Ambitions"
Alden, Patricia. *Social Mobility . . .* , 51–52.

"The Withered Arm"
Hasan, Noorul. *Thomas Hardy . . .* , 117–119.
Keys, Romey T. "Hardy's Uncanny Narrative: A Reading of 'The Withered Arm,'" *Texas Stud Lit & Lang*, 27 (1985), 106–123.

L[ESLIE] P[OLES] HARTLEY

"The Ghost Writer"
Pickering, Jean. "The English Short Story in the Sixties," in Vannatta, Dennis,
Ed. *The English Short Story, 1945–1980*, 81–82.

"The Shadow on the Wall"
Sullivan, Jack. "L. P. Hartley," in Bleiler, E. F., Ed. *Supernatural Fiction Writers . . .* , II, 643.

"The Visitor from Down Under"
Sullivan, Jack. "L. P. Hartley," 641.

"W.S."
Baldwin, Dean. "The English Short Story in the Fifties," in Vannatta, Dennis,
Ed. *The English Short Story, 1945–1980*, 40–41.

WILLIAM FRYER HARVEY

"The Arms of Mrs. Egan"
Dalby, Richard. "William Fryer Harvey," in Bleiler, E. F., Ed. *Supernatural Fiction Writers . . .* , II, 595.

"August Heat"
Dalby, Richard. "William Fryer Harvey," 593.

"The Beast with Five Fingers"
Dalby, Richard. "William Fryer Harvey," 593–594.

"The Clock"
Dalby, Richard. "William Fryer Harvey," 594.

"The Follower"
Dalby, Richard. "William Fryer Harvey," 594–595.

"Sambo"
Dalby, Richard. "William Fryer Harvey," 593.

JOHN HAWKES

"The Owl"
Greiner, Donald J. *Understanding John Hawkes*, 23–27.
Laing, Jeffrey. "The Dictatorial Voice in John Hawkes's *The Cannibal* and 'The Owl,'" *Notes Contemp Lit*, 16, iv (1986), 2–3.

NATHANIEL HAWTHORNE

"Alice Doane's Appeal"
Becker, Allienne R. "'Alice Doane's Appeal': A Literary Double of Hoffmann's
Die Elixiere des Teufels," *Comp Lit Stud*, 23, i (1986), 1–11.

Coale, Samuel C. *In Hawthorne's Shadow . . .* , 7–12.
Current-García, Eugene. *The American Short Story before 1850 . . .* , 51–52.
Timms, David. "Authorship and Authoritarianism in Hawthorne's Tales," in
 Lee, A. Robert, Ed. *. . . American Short Story*, 60–61.

"The Ambitious Guest"
Bush, Sargent. "Hawthorne's Domestic Quest: Narratives of the 1830s," *Books
 in Iowa*, 45 (November, 1986), 43–44.

"The Artist of the Beautiful"
Aldridge, A. Owen. *The Reemergence . . .* , 210–211.
Breinig, Helmbrecht. "Crushed Butterflies and Broken Fountains: Hawthorne
 Between Christian Idealism, Romanticism, and Modernism," in Herget,
 Winfried, Klaus P. Jochum, and Ingeborg Weber, Eds. *Theorie und
 Praxis . . .* , 233–248.
Fay, Stephanie. "Lights from Dark Corners: Works of Art in 'The Prophetic
 Pictures' and 'The Artist of the Beautiful,'" *Stud Am Fiction*, 13 (1985), 22–
 27.
Idol, John L. "A Show of Hands in 'The Artist of the Beautiful,'" *Stud Short
 Fiction*, 22 (1985), 455–460.
Liebman, Sheldon W. "Hawthorne's Romanticism: 'The Artist of the Beauti-
 ful,'" *ESQ: J Am Renaissance*, 22 (1976), 85–95; rpt. Bloom, Harold, Ed.
 Nathaniel Hawthorne, 127–140.
Marder, Daniel. *Exiles at Home . . .* , 154–155.
Von Frank, Albert J. *The Sacred Game . . .* , 85–87.

"The Birthmark"
Bohner, Charles H. *Instructor's Manual . . .* , 52–53.
Marder, Daniel. *Exiles at Home . . .* , 151–152.
Rupprecht, Erich S. "Nathaniel Hawthorne," in Bleiler, E. F., Ed. *Supernatural
 Fiction Writers . . .* , II, 713.
Youra, Steven J. "'The Fatal Hand': A Sign of Confusion in Hawthorne's 'The
 Birth-Mark,'" *Am Transcendental Q*, 60 (1986), 43–51.

"The Celestial Railroad"
Gerlach, John. *Toward the End . . .* , 35–36.

"The Devil in Manuscript"
Timms, David. "Authorship . . . ," 58–59.

"Earth's Holocaust"
Dunne, Michael. "Natural and Imposed Order in Two Sketches by Hawthorne,"
 Nathaniel Hawthorne J, 8 (1978), 199–200.

"Edward Randolph's Portrait"
Budick, E. Miller. "The World as Specter: Hawthorne's Historical Art," *PMLA*,
 101 (1986), 225–227.
Carton, Evan. *The Rhetoric . . .* , 175–180.

"Egotism; or, The Bosom Serpent"
Rupprecht, Erich S. "Nathaniel Hawthorne," 711–712.

Schechter, Harold. "The Bosom Serpent: Folklore and Popular Art," *Georgia R*, 39 (1985), 93–108.

"Endicott and the Red Cross"
Timms, David. "Authorship . . . ," 67–68.

"Ethan Brand"
Donohue, Agnes M. . . . *Calvin's Ironic Stepchild*, 211–216.

"The Gentle Boy"
Donohue, Agnes M. . . . *Calvin's Ironic Stepchild*, 142–149.

"Howe's Masquerade"
Carton, Evan. *The Rhetoric* . . . , 171–175.

"Lady Eleanore's Mantle"
Budick, E. Miller. "The World as Specter . . . ," 228–229.
Carton, Evan. *The Rhetoric* . . . , 180–184.

"Little Annie's Ramble"
Timms, David. "Authorship . . . ," 62–63.

"The Maypole of Merry Mount"
*Hoffman, Daniel G. " 'The Maypole of Merry Mount' and the Folklore of Love," in Bloom, Harold, Ed. *Nathaniel Hawthorne*, 41–58.
Marder, Daniel. *Exiles at Home* . . . , 147–148.
Pribek, Thomas. "The Conquest of Canaan: Suppression of Merry Mount," *Nineteenth-Century Fiction*, 40 (1985), 343–354.
Timms, David. "Authorship . . . ," 68–70.

"The Minister's Black Veil"
Budick, E. Miller. "The World as Specter . . . ," 227–228.
Davis, William V. "Hawthorne's 'The Minister's Black Veil': A Note on the Significance of the Subtitle," *Stud Short Fiction*, 23 (1986), 453–454.
Franklin, Rosemary F. " 'The Minister's Black Veil': A Parable," *Am Transcendental Q*, 56 (March, 1985), 55–63.
Marder, Daniel. *Exiles at Home* . . . , 149–150.
Slatoff, Walter J. *The Look of Distance* . . . , 174–185.

"Mr. Higginbotham's Catastrophe"
Von Frank, Albert J. *The Sacred Game* . . . , 84–85.

"Mrs. Bullfrog"
Gerlach, John. *Toward the End* . . . , 36–37.

"My Kinsman, Major Molineux"
Autrey, Max L. " 'My Kinsman, Major Molineux': Hawthorne's Allegory of the Urban Movement," *Coll Lit*, 12 (1985), 211–221.
Bohner, Charles H. *Instructor's Manual* . . . , 54–55.
Budick, E. Miller. "The World as Specter . . . ," 229–231.
Cohen, Hazel. "The Rupture of Relations: Revolution and Romance in Haw-

thorne's 'My Kinsman, Major Molineux,'" *Engl Stud Africa,* 29, i (1986), 19–30.

Current-García, Eugene. *The American Short Story before 1850* . . . , 53–54.

Donohue, Agnes M. . . . *Calvin's Ironic Stepchild,* 201–210.

Gerlach, John. *Toward the End* . . . , 106–107.

Mills, Nicolaus. *The Crowd* . . . , 49–51.

Reed, Michael D. "Robin and His Kinsman: A Psychoanalytic Re-Examination of 'My Kinsman, Major Molineux,'" *J Evolutionary Psych,* 40 (April, 1983), 94–103.

Von Frank, Albert J. *The Sacred Game* . . . , 89–91.

"The New Adam and Eve"
Dunne, Michael. "Natural and Imposed Order . . . ," 200–202.

"Old Esther Dudley"
Carton, Evan. *The Rhetoric* . . . , 184–191.

"The Paradise of Children"
Diudna, Martin K. "Hawthorne's Pandora, Milton's Eve, and the Fortunate Fall," *ESQ: J Am Renaissance,* 31, iii (1985), 164–172.

"The Prophetic Pictures"
Fay, Stephanie. "Lights from Dark Corners . . . ," 16–22.

Marder, Daniel. *Exiles at Home* . . . , 150–151.

"Rappaccini's Daughter"
Bensick, Carol M. *La Nouvelle Beatrice* . . . , 1–130.

Breinig, Helmbrecht. "Crushed Butterflies . . . ," 233–248.

Brenzo, Richard. "Beatrice Rappaccini: A Victim of Male Love and Horror," *Am Lit,* 48 (1976), 152–164: rpt. Bloom, Harold, Ed. *Nathaniel Hawthorne,* 141–152.

Gerlach, John. *Toward the End* . . . , 87–88.

Gilmore, Michael T. *American Romanticism* . . . , 62–70.

Kearney, Martin F. "Hawthorne's Beatrice Rappaccini: Unlocking Her Paradoxical Nature with a Shelleyean Key," *Coll Lang Assoc J,* 29 (1986), 309–317.

Marder, Daniel. *Exiles at Home* . . . , 152–154.

Rupprecht, Erich S. "Nathaniel Hawthorne," 713–714.

"Roger Malvin's Burial"
*Crews, Frederick C. "The Logic of Compulsion in 'Roger Malvin's Burial,'" in Bloom, Harold, Ed. *Nathaniel Hawthorne,* 71–83.

Donohue, Agnes M. . . . *Calvin's Ironic Stepchild,* 180–186.

Gerlach, John. *Toward the End* . . . , 37–41.

"The Snow Image"
Von Frank, Albert J. *The Sacred Game* . . . , 91–92.

"The Threefold Destiny"
Bush, Sargent. "Hawthorne's Domestic Quest . . . ," 39–43.

"Wakefield"
Donohue, Agnes M. . . . *Calvin's Ironic Stepchild,* 151–157.

"Young Goodman Brown"
Bohner, Charles H. *Instructor's Manual . . .* , 55–56.
Budick, E. Miller. "The World as Specter . . . ," 218–225.
Buell, Lawrence. *New England . . .* , 73–77.
Bush, Sargent. "Hawthorne's Domestic Quest . . . ," 43.
Christophersen, Bill. " 'Young Goodman Brown' As Historical Allegory: A Lexical Link," *Stud Short Fiction,* 23 (1986), 202–204.
Levy, Leo B. "The Problem of Faith in 'Young Goodman Brown,' " *J Engl & Germ Philol,* 74 (1975), 375–387; rpt. Bloom, Harold, Ed. *Nathaniel Hawthorne,* 115–126.
Marder, Daniel. *Exiles at Home . . .* , 148–149.
Rupprecht, Erich S. "Nathaniel Hawthorne," 712–713.
Shaw, Patrick W. "Checking Out Faith and Lust: Hawthorne's 'Young Goodman Brown' and Updike's 'A & P,' " *Stud Short Fiction,* 23 (1986), 321–323.
Smoot, Jeanne J. " 'Young Goodman Brown'—Puritan Don Juan: Faith in Tirso and Hawthorne," *Post Script,* 1 (1983), 42–48.
Timms, David. "Authorship . . . ," 64–66.
Tritt, Michael. " 'Young Goodman Brown' and the Psychology of Projection," *Stud Short Fiction,* 23 (1986), 113–117.

KATE SIMPSON HAYES

"Aweena"
Fairbanks, Carol. *Prairie Women . . .* , 149–150.

"The La-de-dah from London"
Fairbanks, Carol. *Prairie Women . . .* , 63.

HAIM HAZAZ

"Aristotle"
Nash, Stanley L. "Hazaz's 'Aristotle,' " *Mod Hebrew Lit,* 10, i–ii (1984), 20–23.

BESSIE HEAD

"The Collector of Treasures"
Taiwo, Oladele. *Female Novelists . . .* , 206–208.

"The Deep River"
Taiwo, Oladele. *Female Novelists . . .* , 198–201.

"Jacob"
Taiwo, Oladele. *Female Novelists . . .* , 201–203.

"Snapshots of a Wedding"
Taiwo, Oladele. *Female Novelists . . .* , 204–205.

"The Special One"
Taiwo, Oladele. *Female Novelists* . . . , 205–206.

"The Wind and a Boy"
Taiwo, Oladele. *Female Novelists* . . . , 203–204.

ANNE HÉBERT

"A Grand Marriage"
Minni, C. D. "The Short Story as an Ethnic Genre," in Pivato, Joseph, Ed. *Contrasts* . . . , 67.

ROBERT HEINLEIN

"They"
Berger, Harold L. *Science Fiction* . . . , 110–111.

ERNEST HEMINGWAY

"The Ash-Heels Tendon"
Nelson, Raymond. "Five Formerly Unpublished Hemingway Stories," *Int'l Fiction R*, 13 (1986), 88.
Reynolds, Michael. *The Young Hemingway*, 91–93.

"The Battler"
Dyer, Joyce. "Hemingway's Use of the Pejorative Term 'Nigger' in 'The Battler,'" *Notes Contemp Lit*, 16, v (1986), 5–10.
Jain, S. P. *Hemingway* . . . , 37–40.
Kobler, J. F. *Ernest Hemingway* . . . , 101–102.
Monteiro, George. "'This Is My Pal Bugs': Ernest Hemingway's 'The Battler,'" *Stud Short Fiction*, 23 (1986), 179–183.
Ward, J. A. *American Silences* . . . , 58–60.

"Big Two-Hearted River"
Jain, S. P. *Hemingway* . . . , 105–108.
Kobler, J. F. *Ernest Hemingway* . . . , 45–47.
Meyers, Jeffrey. *Hemingway*, 145.
Rovit, Earl, and Gerry Brenner. *Ernest Hemingway*, 2nd ed., 55–56.
Sojka, Gregory S. *Ernest Hemingway* . . . , 85–94.
Ward, J. A. *American Silences* . . . , 72–75.

"A Canary for One"
Jain, S. P. *Hemingway* . . . , 88–90.
Martin, W. R., and Warren U. Ober. "Hemingway and James: 'A Canary for One' and 'Daisy Miller,'" *Stud Short Fiction*, 22 (1985), 469–471.

"The Capital of the World"
Jain, S. P. *Hemingway* . . . , 28–31.
Meyers, Jeffrey. *Hemingway* . . . , 322.

"Cat in the Rain"
Gerlach, John. *Toward the End* . . . , 111–112.
Holmesland, Oddvar. "Structuralism and Interpretation: Ernest Hemingway's 'Cat in the Rain,'" *Engl Stud*, 67 (1986), 221–233.
Jain, S. P. *Hemingway* . . . , 80–84.

"Che Ti Dice La Patria"
Kobler, J. F. *Ernest Hemingway* . . . , 83.

"A Clean, Well-Lighted Place"
Grimes, Larry E. *The Religious Design* . . . , 74–75.
Hanson, Clare. *Short Stories* . . . , 75–77.
Jain, S. P. *Hemingway* . . . , 114–117.
Meyers, Jeffrey. *Hemingway* . . . , 258–259.
Rovit, Earl, and Gerry Brenner. *Ernest Hemingway*, 2nd ed., 93–94.

"The Current"
Nelson, Raymond. ". . . Hemingway Stories," 88–89.

"The Doctor and the Doctor's Wife"
Ward, J. A. *American Silences* . . . , 58.

"Fathers and Sons"
Grimes, Larry E. *The Religious Design* . . . , 69–71.
McCann, Richard. "To Embrace or Kill: 'Fathers and Sons,'" *Iowa J Lit Stud*, 3, i–ii (1981), 11–18.
Meyers, Jeffrey. *Hemingway* . . . , 16–17.

"Fifty Grand"
Grimes, Larry E. *The Religious Design* . . . , 77–78.
Rovit, Earl, and Gerry Brenner. *Ernest Hemingway*, 2nd ed., 44–45.

"The Gambler, the Nun, and the Radio"
Jain, S. P. *Hemingway* . . . , 108–113.

"Get a Seeing-Eye Dog"
Rovit, Earl, and Gerry Brenner. *Ernest Hemingway*, 2nd ed., 39–40.

"Hills Like White Elephants"
Bohner, Charles H. *Instructor's Manual* . . . , 56–57.
Gerlach, John. *Toward the End* . . . , 112–115.
Grimes, Larry E. *The Religious Design* . . . , 71–73.
Hughes, Kenneth J. *Signs of Literature* . . . , 157–166.
Jain, S. P. *Hemingway* . . . , 77–80.
Meyers, Jeffrey. *Hemingway* . . . , 196–197.

"In Another Country"
*Rovit, Earl, and Gerry Brenner. *Ernest Hemingway*, 2nd ed., 45–48.

"Indian Camp"
Grimes, Larry E. *The Religious Design* . . . , 55–58.
Jain, S. P. *Hemingway* . . . , 35–37.

Slatoff, Walter J. *The Look of Distance* . . . , 21–24.
Wainwright, J. Andrew. "The Far Shore: Gender Complexities in Hemingway's 'Indian Camp,'" *Dalhousie R*, 66 (1986), 181–187.

"The Killers"
Jain, S. P. *Hemingway* . . . , 40–44.
Meyers, Jeffrey. *Hemingway* . . . , 196.

"The Light of the World"
Collins, William J. "Taking on the Champion: Alice as Liar in 'The Light of the World,'" *Stud Am Fiction*, 14 (1986), 225–232.

"The Mercenaries"
Nelson, Raymond. ". . . Hemingway Stories," 86.

"Mr. and Mrs. Elliot"
Jain, S. P. *Hemingway* . . . , 84–87.
Ward, J. A. *American Silences* . . . , 68–70.

"My Old Man"
Grimes, Larry E. *The Religious Design* . . . , 28–33.
Jain, S. P. *Hemingway* . . . , 49–51.
Ward, J. A. *American Silences* . . . , 70–71.

"Natural History of the Dead"
Jain, S. P. *Hemingway* . . . , 68–70.

"Now I Lay Me"
Grimes, Larry E. *The Religious Design* . . . , 63–64.
Jain, S. P. *Hemingway* . . . , 64–67.
Scafella, Frank. "'I and the Abyss': Emerson, Hemingway, and the Modern Vision of Death," *Hemingway R*, 4, ii (1985), 2–6.

"The Old Man and the Sea"
Capellán, Angel. *Hemingway* . . . , 109–112.
Heaman, Robert J. and Patricia B. "Hemingway's Fabulous Fisherman," *Pennsylvania Engl*, 12, i (1985), 29–33.
Kinya, Tsuruta. "The Twilight Years, East and West: Hemingway's 'The Old Man and the Sea' and Kawabata's *The Sound of the Mountain*," in Ueda, Matoro, Ed. *Explorations* . . . , 87–99.
*Rovit, Earl, and Gerry Brenner. *Ernest Hemingway*, 2nd ed., 69–77.
Sojka, Gregory S. *Ernest Hemingway* . . . , 121–139.
Spilka, Mark. "Hemingway and Fauntleroy: An Androgynous Pursuit," in Fleischmann, Fritz, Ed. *American Novelists Revisited* . . . , 364–365.

"Old Man at the Bridge"
Jain, S. P. *Hemingway* . . . , 70–72.

"On the Quai at Smyrna"
Jain, S. P. *Hemingway* . . . , 59–61.
Meyers, Jeffrey. *Hemingway* . . . , 100–101.

"Out of Season"
Gerlach, John. *Toward the End* . . . , 109–110.

"A Pursuit Race"
Grimes, Larry E. *The Religious Design* . . . , 75–77.

"The Sea Change"
Fleming, Robert E. "Perversion and the Writer in 'The Sea Change,'" *Stud Am Fiction*, 14 (1986), 215–220.
Jain, S. P. *Hemingway* . . . , 90–93.

"The Short Happy Life of Francis Macomber"
Gerlach, John. *Toward the End* . . . , 116–118.
Gladstein, Mimi R. *The Indestructible Woman* . . . , 62–64.
Jain, S. P. *Hemingway* . . . , 127–133.
Moorhead, Michael. "Hemingway's 'The Short Happy Life of Francis Macomber,'" *Explicator*, 44, ii (1986), 41–43.
*Rovit, Earl, and Gerry Brenner. *Ernest Hemingway*, 2nd ed., 56–57.
Zapf, Hubert. "Die Leserrolle in Ernest Hemingways 'The Short Happy Life of Francis Macomber,'" *Arbeiten aus Anglistik und Amerikanistik*, 11, i (1986), 19–39.

"The Snows of Kilimanjaro"
Gladstein, Mimi R. *The Indestructible Woman* . . . , 64–65.
Herndon, Jerry A. "'The Snows of Kilimanjaro': Another Look at Theme and Point of View," *So Atlantic Q*, 85 (1986), 351–359.
Jain, S. P. *Hemingway* . . . , 122–127.
Meyers, Jeffrey. *Disease* . . . , 19–29.
*Rovit, Earl, and Gerry Brenner. *Ernest Hemingway*, 2nd ed., 19–22.
Sheidley, William E., and Ann Charters. *Instructor's Manual* . . . , 109–110; rpt. Charters, Ann, William E. Sheidley, and Martha Ramsey. *Instructor's Manual* . . . , 2nd ed., 109–110.
Yung-hsiao, Cheng. "Interior Monologue in Hemingway's Short Stories," *Stud Lang & Lit* (Taiwan), 1 (March, 1985), 88–92.

"Soldier's Home"
Jain, S. P. *Hemingway* . . . , 99–102.
Ward, J. A. *American Silences* . . . , 54–57.

"The Summer People"
Reynolds, Michael. *The Young Hemingway*, 123–124.

"Three Shots"
Grimes, Larry E. *The Religious Design* . . . , 55–56.

"Today Is Friday"
Jain, S. P. *Hemingway* . . . , 119–120.

"The Undefeated"
Rovit, Earl, and Gerry Brenner. *Ernest Hemingway*, 2nd ed., 43–44.

"Up in Michigan"
Grimes, Larry E. *The Religious Design* . . . , 25–27.
Jain, S. P. *Hemingway* . . . , 45–48.

"A Very Short Story"
Ward, J. A. *American Silences* . . . , 67–68.

"The Visiting Team"
Reynolds, Michael. *The Young Hemingway*, 178–179.

"A Way You'll Never Be"
Grimes, Larry E. *The Religious Design* . . . , 64–67.
Jain, S. P. *Hemingway* . . . , 61–64.
Johnston, Kenneth G. "'A Way You'll Never Be': A Mission of Morale," *Stud Short Fiction*, 23 (1986), 429–435.
Rovit, Earl, and Gerry Brenner. *Ernest Hemingway*, 2nd ed., 63–64.
Yung-hsiao, Cheng. "Interior Monologue . . . ," 82–85.

PEDRO HENRÍQUIZ UREÑA

"El peso falso"
Rosemberg, Fernando. "Dos cuentos poéticos de Pedro Henríquiz Ureña," *Sur*, 355 (July–December, 1984), 103–110.

"La sombra"
Rosemberg, Fernando. "Dos cuentos poéticos . . . ," 103–110.

JOSEPHINE HERBST

"As a Fair Young Girl"
Bevilacqua, Winifred F. *Josephine Herbst*, 88.

"Dry Sunday in Connecticut"
Bevilacqua, Winifred F. *Josephine Herbst*, 86.

"The Elegant M. Gason"
Bevilacqua, Winifred F. *Josephine Herbst*, 85–86.

"The Golden Egg"
Bevilacqua, Winifred F. *Josephine Herbst*, 87–88.

"Hunter of Doves"
Bevilacqua, Winifred F. *Josephine Herbst*, 77–84.

"The Last Word"
Bevilacqua, Winifred F. *Josephine Herbst*, 88–89.

"The Man of Steel"
Bevilacqua, Winifred F. *Josephine Herbst*, 86–87.

GYULA HERNÁDI

"Deszkakolostor"
Csúri, Károly. "Literary Coherence: How to Establish Possible Worlds (Demonstrated by an Analysis of Gyula Hernádi's *Plank Monastery*)," in Sözer, Emel, Ed. *Text Connexity . . .* , 439–485.

HERMANN HESSE

"The Poet"
Howard, Patricia J. "Hermann Hesse's 'Der Dichter': The Artist/Sage as Vessel Dissolving Paradox," *Comp Lit Stud*, 22 (1985), 110–120.

"Siddhartha"
Marret-Tising, Carlee. *The Reception of Hermann Hesse . . .* , 317–334.

ROBERT [SMYTHE] HICHENS

"How Love Came to Professor Guildea"
Stableford, Brian M. "Robert Hichens," in Bleiler, E. F., Ed. *Supernatural Fiction Writers . . .* , I, 417–418.

"The Lost Faith"
Stableford, Brian M. "Robert Hichens," 418.

"The Sin of Envy"
Stableford, Brian M. "Robert Hichens," 418.

HIGUCHI ICHIYŌ

"Separate Ways"
Mitsutani, Margaret. "Higuchi Ichiyō: A Literature of Her Own," *Comp Lit Stud*, 22 (1985), 57–62.

SUSAN HILL

"The Custodian"
Evans, Walter. "The English Short Story in the Seventies," in Vannatta, Dennis, Ed. *The English Short Story, 1945–1980*, 138–140.

CHESTER HIMES

"Prediction"
Davis, Ursula B. *Paris Without Regret . . .* , 94.

JACK HODGINS

"Ladies and Gentlemen, the Fabulous Barclay Sisters"
Delbaere-Garant, Jeanne. "Isolation and Community in Hodgins's Short Stories," *Recherches Anglaises et Américaines*, 16 (1983), 40–41.

"Separation"
Delbaere-Garant, Jeanne. "Isolation and Community . . . ," 35–37.

"Spit Delaney's Island"
Delbaere-Garant, Jeanne. "Isolation and Community . . . ," 37–39.

WILLIAM HOPE HODGSON

"The Baumoff Explosion" [originally titled "Eloi, Eloi, Lama Sabachthani"]
Stableford, Brian. *Scientific Romance* . . . , 100–101.

"The Hog"
Bleiler, E. F. "William Hope Hodgson," in Bleiler, E. F., Ed. *Supernatural Fiction Writers* . . . , I, 426.

E[RNEST] T[HEODOR] A[MADEUS] HOFFMANN

"Counselor Krespel"
Crisman, William. "E. T. A. Hoffmann's 'Ein siedler Serapion' and 'Rat Krespel' as Models of Reading," *J Engl & Germ Philol*, 85 (1986), 61–69.

"The Cousin's Corner Window"
Stadler, Ulrich. "Die Aussicht als Einblick: Zu E. T. A. Hoffmanns Erzählung 'Des Vetters Eckfenster' (1822)," *Zeitschrift für Deutsche Philologie*, 105 (1986), 498–515.

"The Enemy"
Terpstra, Jan U. "Hexenspruch Eierzauber und Feind-Komplex in E. T. A. Hoffmanns Fragment 'Der Feind,'" *Euphorion*, 80, i (1986), 26–45.

"The Entail"
Jennings, Lee B. "The Anatomy of *Spuk* in Two Tales of E. T. A. Hoffmann," *Colloquia Germanica*, 17, i–ii (1984), 64–68.

"A Fragment from the Life of Three Friends"
Jennings, Lee B. "The Anatomy of *Spuk* . . . ," 68–75.

"The Golden Pot"
Holzhausen, Hans-Dieter. "Die Palmen bibliothek in E. T. A. Hoffmanns Märchen 'Der Goldne Topf': Einige Randbemerkungen zu ihrem Vorbild im Dom zu Königsberg, Preussen," *Mitteilungen der E. T. A. Hoffmann*, 30 (1984), 34–41.

"The King's Bride"
Vitt-Maucher, Gisela. "E. T. A. Hoffmanns 'Die Königsbraut': Ein nach der Natur entworfenes Märchen," *Mitteilungen der E. T. A. Hoffmann*, 30 (1984), 34–41.

"The Mines of Falun"
Jennings, Lee B. "The Downward Transcendence: Hoffmann's 'Bergwerke zu Falun,'" *Deutsche Vierteljahrsschrift*, 59 (1985), 278–289.

"New Year's Eve Adventure"
Kontje, Todd. "Biography in Triplicate: E. T. A. Hoffmann's 'Die Abenteuer der Silvester-Nacht,'" *Germ Q*, 58 (1985), 348–360.

"The Sandman"
Charue, Jean. "Peut-on s'écrendre d'une femme-machine? Remarques à propos de *L'Homme au sable* d'E. T. A. Hoffmann," *Études Philosophiques*, 1 (1985), 57–75.
Jennings, Lee B. "Blood of the Android: A Post-Freudian Perspective on Hoffmann's 'Sandmann,'" *Seminar*, 22 (1986), 95–111.
Jones, Malcolm V. "'Der Sandmann' and 'the Uncanny': A Sketch for an Alternative Approach," *Paragraph*, 7 (March, 1986), 77–101.
Walter, Jürgen. "Das Unheimliche als Wirkungsfunktion: Eine Rezeptionsästhetische Analyse von E. T. A. Hoffmanns Erzählung 'Der Sandmann,'" *Mitteilungen der E. T. A. Hoffmann*, 30 (1984), 15–33.

"Serapion"
Crisman, William. ". . . Models of Reading," 50–61.

HUGH HOOD

"Around Theatres"
Struthers, J. R. "A Secular Liturgy: Hugh Hood's Aesthetics and *Around the Mountain*," *Stud Canadian Lit*, 10 (1985), 122–123.

"Bicultural Angela"
Struthers, J. R. "A Secular Liturgy . . . ," 121–122.

"Light Shining Out of Darkness"
Struthers, J. R. "A Secular Liturgy . . . ," 112–114.

"Looking Down from Above"
Struthers, J. R. "A Secular Liturgy . . . ," 125–126.

"One Way North and South"
Struthers, J. R. "A Secular Liturgy . . . ," 127–128.

"Predictions of Ice"
Struthers, J. R. "A Secular Liturgy . . . ," 133.

"The River Behind Things"
Struthers, J. R. "A Secular Liturgy . . . ," 134.

"The Sportive Centre of Saint Vincent de Paul"
Struthers, J. R. "A Secular Liturgy . . . ," 114–115.

"Starting Again on Sherbrooke Street"
Struthers, J. R. "A Secular Liturgy . . . ," 132–133.

"The Village Inside"
Struthers, J. R. "A Secular Liturgy . . . ," 128–130.

CLYDE HOSEIN

"I'm a Presbyterian, Mr. Kramer"
Suganasiri, Suwanda. "Reality and Symbolism in the South Asian Canadian
    Short Story," *World Lit Written Engl*, 26 (1986), 101.

ROBERT E. HOWARD

"The Hour of the Dragon"
Bleiler, E. F. "Robert E. Howard," in Bleiler, E. F., Ed. *Supernatural Fiction
    Writers . . .* , II, 866.

"The Phoenix on the Sword"
Bleiler, E. F. "Robert E. Howard," 865.

"The Valley of Worms"
Bleiler, E. F. "Robert E. Howard," 864.

WILLIAM DEAN HOWELLS

"How I Lost a Wife"
Crowley, John W. *The Black Heart's Truth . . .* , 24–25.

"Niagara Revisited"
Crowley, John W. *The Black Heart's Truth . . .* , 133–136.

MARY HOWITT

"The Lost White Woman"
Hadgraft, Cecil, Ed. *The Australian Short Story . . .* , 12.

W[ILLIAM] H[ENRY] HUDSON

"Marta Riquelme"
Hamilton, Robert. *W. H. Hudson . . .* , 62–64.

"El Ombú"
Hamilton, Robert. *W. H. Hudson . . .* , 60–62.

RICHARD HUGHES

"The Cart"
Poole, Richard. *Richard Hughes* . . . , 113–114.

"Jungle"
Poole, Richard. *Richard Hughes* . . . , 111.

"Llwyd"
Poole, Richard. *Richard Hughes* . . . , 112–113.

"Lochinvárovič"
Poole, Richard. *Richard Hughes* . . . , 115–116.

"Monoculism: A Fable"
Poole, Richard. *Richard Hughes* . . . , 111.

WILLIAM HUMPHREYS

"A Job of the Plains"
Grider, Sylvia, and Elizabeth Tebeaux. "Blessings into Curses: Sardonic Humor and Irony in 'A Job of the Plains,'" *Stud Short Fiction,* 23 (1986), 297–303.

T. A. G. HUNGERFORD

"Green Grow the Rushes"
Bennett, Bruce. "Asian Encounters in the Contemporary Australian Short Story," *World Lit Written Engl,* 26 (1986), 53.

"Wong Chu and the Queen's Letterbox"
Bennett, Bruce. "Asian Encounters . . . ," 52–53.

ZORA NEALE HURSTON

"Behold de Rib"
Wall, Cheryl A. "Zora Neale Hurston: Changing Her Own Words," in Fleischmann, Fritz, Ed. *American Novelists Revisited* . . . , 377–378.

YUSUF IDRIS

"The Journey"
Cohen, Dalya. " 'The Journey' by Yusuf Idris: Psychoanalysis and Interpretation," *J Arabic Lit,* 15 (1984), 135–138.

"The Omitted Letter"
Allen, Roger, Ed. *In the Eye of the Beholder* . . . , xxiii–xxiv.

WITI IHIMAERA

"Catching-Up"
Tiffin, Chris. "New Zealand and the Pacific," in Goodwin, K. L., Ed. *Common-wealth Literature* . . . , 129–130.

"Fire on Greenstone"
Simms, Norman. "Maori Literature in English: Prose Writing, Part Two—Witi Ihimaera," *Pacific Q* (Moana), 3 (1978), 339–340.

"The House with Sugarbag Windows"
Nightingale, Peggy. "All Any Man with a Club Can Do: Albert Wendt and Witi Ihimaera," in Sellick, Robert, Ed. *Myth and Metaphor,* 66.

"I, Ozymandias"
Nightingale, Peggy. "All Any Man . . . ," 66.

"Truth of the Matter"
Tiffin, Chris. "New Zealand and the Pacific," 130.

"The Whale"
Simms, Norman. "Maori Literature . . . ," 341–342.

EUGÈNE IONESCO

"The Colonel's Photograph"
Galli, Gemma M. "Edifying the Reader: Ionesco's 'The Colonel's Photograph,'" *Mod Fiction Stud,* 31 (1985), 645–657.

JOHN IRVING

"Lost in New York"
Budd, John. "The Inadequacy of Brevity: John Irving's Short Fiction," *Round Table,* 26 (Spring, 1985), 4–6.

"The Pension Grillparzer"
Runyon, Randolph. *Fowles / Irving / Barthes* . . . , 52–53.

"Vigilance"
Runyon, Randolph. *Fowles / Irving / Barthes* . . . , 55–60.

WASHINGTON IRVING

"The Adventure of the German Student"
Current-García, Eugene. *The American Short Story before 1850* . . . , 36.

"Annette Delarbe"
Current-García, Eugene. *The American Short Story before 1850* . . . , 31–32.

"Buckthorne and His Friends"
Current-García, Eugene. *The American Short Story before 1850* . . . , 38.

"The Devil and Tom Walker"
Current-García, Eugene. *The American Short Story before 1850* . . . , 40.

"Dolph Heyliger"
Current-García, Eugene. *The American Short Story before 1850* . . . , 32–33.

"The Italian Banditti"
Current-García, Eugene. *The American Short Story before 1850* . . . , 38–39.

"The Legend of Sleepy Hollow"
Current-García, Eugene. *The American Short Story before 1850* . . . , 26–28.
Fisher, Benjamin F. "Washington Irving," in Bleiler, E. F., Ed. *Supernatural Fiction Writers* . . . , II, 687.
Marder, Daniel. *Exiles at Home* . . . , 12–13.
Rubin-Dorsky, Jeffrey. "The Value of Storytelling: 'Rip Van Winkle' and 'The Legend of Sleepy Hollow' in the Context of *The Sketch Book*," *Mod Philol*, 82 (1985), 401–405.

"The Little Man in Black"
Papinchak, Robert A. "'The Little Man in Black': The Narrative Mode of America's First Short Story," *Stud Short Fiction*, 22 (1985), 195–201.

"Rip Van Winkle"
Current-García, Eugene. *The American Short Story before 1850* . . . , 26–28.
Daigrepont, Lloyd M. "'Rip Van Winkle' and the Gnostic Vision of History," *Clio*, 15, i (1985), 47–59.
Fisher, Benjamin F. "Washington Irving," 686–687.
Gerlach, John. *Toward the End* . . . , 41–47.
Karcher, Carolyn L. "Patriarchal Society and Matriarchal Family in Irving's 'Rip Van Winkle' and Child's 'Hilda Silfverling,'" *Legacy*, 2, ii (1985), 32–35.
Marder, Daniel. *Exiles at Home* . . . , 11–12.
Rubin-Dorsky, Jeffrey. "The Value of Storytelling . . . ," 398–401.

"The Spectre Bridegroom"
Fisher, Benjamin F. "Washington Irving," 687–688.

"The Story of the Young Italian"
Gerlach, John. *Toward the End* . . . , 27–29.

SHIRLEY JACKSON

"The Daemon Lover"
Sullivan, Jack. "Shirley Jackson," in Bleiler, E. F., Ed. *Supernatural Fiction Writers* . . . , II, 1032–1033.

"The Lottery"
Bohner, Charles H. *Instructor's Manual* . . . , 58–59.

Kittredge, Mary. "The Other Side of Magic: A Few Remarks About Shirley Jackson," in Schweitzer, Darrell, Ed. . . . *Horror Fiction*, 10–11.
Kosenko, Peter. "A Marxist/Feminist Reading of Shirley Jackson's 'The Lottery,'" *New Orleans R*, 12, i (1985), 27–32.
Sheidley, William E., and Ann Charters. *Instructor's Manual* . . . , 151–152; rpt. Charters, Ann, William E. Sheidley, and Martha Ramsey. *Instructor's Manual* . . . , 2nd ed., 156.

"The Visit"
Sullivan, Jack. "Shirley Jackson," 1033–1034.

W[ILLIAM] W[YMARK] JACOBS

"The Monkey's Paw"
Donaldson, Norman. "W. W. Jacobs," in Bleiler, E. F., Ed. *Supernatural Fiction Writers* . . . , I, 384–385.

"The Three Sisters"
Donaldson, Norman. "W. W. Jacobs," 385.

SAYYID MUHAMMAD ALI JAMAL-ZADEH

"The Bear Hug"
Mashiah, Yaakov. "Once Upon a Time: A Study of *Yeki Bud, Yeki Nabud,* the First Collection of Short Stories by Sayyid Muhammad Ali Jamal-Zadeh," *Acta Orientalia*, 33 (1971), 123–125.

"Every Man to His Deserts"
Mashiah, Yaakov. "Once Upon a Time . . . ," 131–134.

"Mulla Qurban-Ali's Confession"
Mashiah, Yaakov. "Once Upon a Time . . . ," 125–130.

"Persian Is Sugar"
Mashiah, Yaakov. "Once Upon a Time . . . ," 116–118.

"The Politician"
Mashiah, Yaakov. "Once Upon a Time . . . ," 119–122.

"Veylan Al-Dawleh"
Mashiah, Yaakov. "Once Upon a Time . . . ," 135–141.

C[YRIL] L[IONEL] R[OBERT] JAMES

"La Divina Pastora"
Collier, Eugenia. "C. L. R. James," in Dance, Daryl C., Ed. *Fifty Caribbean Writers* . . . , 232.

"Triumph"
Collier, Eugenia. "C. L. R. James," 233.
Whitlock, Gilliam. "The Bush, the Barrow-Yard and the Clearing: 'Colonial
 Realism' in the Sketches and Stories of Susan Moodie, C. L. R. James, and
 Henry Lawson," *J Commonwealth Lit*, 20, i (1985), 43–44.

HENRY JAMES

"The Abasement of the Northmores"
Wagenknecht, Edward. *The Tales of Henry James*, 126–127.

"The Altar of the Dead"
Burleson, Donald R. "Symmetry in Henry James's 'The Altar of the Dead,'"
 Stud Weird Fiction, 1, i (1986), 29–32.
Gerlach, John. *Toward the End . . .* , 83–85.
Layton, Lynne, and Barbara Ann Schapiro, Eds. *Narcissism . . .* , 221–226.
Mottram, Eric. "'The Infected Air' and 'The Guilt of Interference': Henry
 James's Short Stories," in Lee, A. Robert, Ed. *. . . American Short Story*, 181–
 182.
Tanner, Tony. *Henry James . . .* , 81–82.
Wagenknecht, Edward. *The Tales of Henry James*, 85–90.

"The Aspern Papers"
Person, Leland S. "Eroticism and Creativity in 'The Aspern Papers,'" *Lit &*
 Psych, 32, ii (1986), 20–31.
Putt, S. Gorley. *A Preface to Henry James*, 112–113.
Tanner, Tony. *Henry James . . .* , 76–79.
Wagenknecht, Edward. *The Tales of Henry James*, 36–44.

"At Isella"
Wagenknecht, Edward. *The Tales of Henry James*, 178–179.

"The Author of 'Beltraffio'"
Caws, Mary Ann. *Reading Frames . . .* , 131–132.
Wagenknecht, Edward. *The Tales of Henry James*, 132–135.

"The Beast in the Jungle"
Auchard, John. *Silence . . .* , 111–113.
Ellis, James. "The Archaeology of Ancient Rome: Sexual Metaphor in 'The
 Beast in the Jungle,'" *Henry James R*, 6, i (1984), 27–31.
Gargano, James W. "Imagery as Action in 'The Beast in the Jungle,'" *Arizona*
 Q, 42 (1986), 351–367.
Gerlach, John. *Toward the End . . .* , 82–83.
Goetz, William. *Henry James . . .* , 172–181.
Gutierrez, Donald. "The Self-Devouring Ego: Henry James' 'The Beast in the
 Jungle' as a Parable of Vanity," *Nassau R*, 5, ii (1986), 6–14.
Mottram, Eric. "'The Infected Air' . . . ," 185–186.
Przybylowicz, Donna. *Desire and Repression . . .* , 88–111.
Sedgwick, Eve K. "The Beast in the Closet: James and the Writing of Homo-
 sexual Panic," in Yeazell, Ruth B., Ed. *Sex, Politics . . .* , 168–186.
Wagenknecht, Edward. *The Tales of Henry James*, 145–150.
Wagner, Vern. "Henry James: Money and Sex," *Sewanee R*, 93 (1985), 223.

"The Beldonald Holbein"
Wagenknecht, Edward. *The Tales of Henry James*, 132–135.

"The Bench of Desolation"
Martin, W. R., and Warren U. Ober. "The Shaping Spirit in James's Last Tales,"
 Engl Stud Canada, 9, iii (1983), 345–349.
Mottram, Eric. "'The Infected Air'...," 184–185.
Wagenknecht, Edward. *The Tales of Henry James*, 170–173.

"The Birthplace"
Cowdery, Lauren T. *The Nouvelle*..., 95–112.
Martin, W. R., and Warren U. Ober. "Critical Responsibility in Henry James's
 'The Coxon Fund' and 'The Birthplace,'" *Engl Stud Canada*, 8, i (1982),
 66–74.
Wagenknecht, Edward. *The Tales of Henry James*, 140–143.

"Broken Wings"
Wagenknecht, Edward. *The Tales of Henry James*, 127–129.

"Brooksmith"
Wagenknecht, Edward. *The Tales of Henry James*, 61–62.

"A Bundle of Letters"
Gerlach, John. *Toward the End*..., 80–82.
Wagenknecht, Edward. *The Tales of Henry James*, 20–21.

"The Chaperon"
Wagenknecht, Edward. *The Tales of Henry James*, 63–64.

"Covering End"
Wagenknecht, Edward. *The Tales of Henry James*, 179–180.

"The Coxon Fund"
Cowdery, Lauren T. *The Nouvelle*..., 53–71.
Martin, W. R., and Warren U. Ober. "Critical Responsibility...," 62–66.
Wagenknecht, Edward. *The Tales of Henry James*, 79–82.

"Crapy Cornelia"
Przybylowicz, Donna. *Desire and Repression*..., 136–138.
Wagenknecht, Edward. *The Tales of Henry James*, 167–170.

"Crawford's Consistency"
Wagenknecht, Edward. *The Tales of Henry James*, 180–181.

"Daisy Miller"
Allen, Elizabeth. *A Woman's Place*..., 49–57.
Childress, Ron. "James's 'Daisy Miller,'" *Explicator*, 44, ii (1986), 24–25.
Cowdery, Lauren T. *The Nouvelle*..., 73–94.
Koprince, Susan. "The Clue from *Manfred* in 'Daisy Miller,'" *Arizona Q*, 42
 (1986), 293–304.
Putt, S. Gorley. *A Preface to Henry James*, 66–69.
Tanner, Tony. *Henry James*..., 30–32.

Wagenknecht, Edward. *The Tales of Henry James*, 12–18.
Yacobi, Tamar. "Hero or Heroine?" *Style*, 19 (1985), 1–35.

"The Death of the Lion"
Seltzer, Mark. *Henry James . . .* , 164–165.
Wagenknecht, Edward. *The Tales of Henry James*, 76–79.

"De Grey"
Elkins, Charles L. "Henry James," in Bleiler, E. F., Ed. *Supernatural Fiction Writers . . .* , I, 339.
Wagenknecht, Edward. *The Tales of Henry James*, 181–182.

"Eugene Pickering"
Wagenknecht, Edward. *The Tales of Henry James*, 182–183.

"Europe"
Wagenknecht, Edward. *The Tales of Henry James*, 117–118.

"The Figure in the Carpet"
Bales, Kent. "Intention and Readers' Response," *Neohelicon*, 13, i (1986), 177–194.
Caws, Mary Ann. *Reading Frames . . .* , 127–128.
Goetz, William. *Henry James . . .* , 166–172.
Halter, Peter. "Is Henry James's 'The Figure in the Carpet' 'Unreadable'?" *SPELL*, 1 (1984), 25–37.
Wagenknecht, Edward. *The Tales of Henry James*, 90–94.

"Flickerbridge"
Wagenknecht, Edward. *The Tales of Henry James*, 137–140.

"Fordham Castle"
Przybylowicz, Donna. *Desire and Repression . . .* , 90–92.
Wagenknecht, Edward. *The Tales of Henry James*, 143–144.

"Four Meetings"
Bohner, Charles H. *Instructor's Manual . . .* , 59–60.
Wagenknecht, Edward. *The Tales of Henry James*, 9–12.

"The Friends of the Friends" [originally titled "The Way It Came"]
Auchard, John. *Silence . . .* , 42–44.
Elkins, Charles L. "Henry James," 341.
Wagenknecht, Edward. *The Tales of Henry James*, 94–97.

"Gabrielle de Bergerac"
Wagenknecht, Edward. *The Tales of Henry James*, 183–184.

"The Ghostly Rental"
Elkins, Charles L. "Henry James," 339–340.
Wagenknecht, Edward. *The Tales of Henry James*, 184–185.

"Glasses"
Bishop, George. "Shattered Notions of Mastery: Henry James's 'Glasses,'" *Criticism*, 27 (1985), 347–362.
Wagenknecht, Edward. *The Tales of Henry James*, 185–186.

"The Great Condition"
Wagenknecht, Edward. *The Tales of Henry James*, 186–187.

"The Great Good Place"
Elkins, Charles L. "Henry James," 343.
Przybylowicz, Donna. *Desire and Repression* . . . , 40–48.
Wagenknecht, Edward. *The Tales of Henry James*, 121–123.

"Greville Fane"
Wagenknecht, Edward. *The Tales of Henry James*, 70–72.

"Guest's Confession"
Wagenknecht, Edward. *The Tales of Henry James*, 187–188.

"In the Cage"
Auchard, John. *Silence* . . . , 44–48.
Caws, Mary Ann. *Reading Frames* . . . , 128–131.
Mottram, Eric. "'The Infected Air' . . . ," 182–183.
Putt, S. Gorley. *A Preface to Henry James*, 108–110.
Wagenknecht, Edward. *The Tales of Henry James*, 113–117.

"An International Episode"
Putt, S. Gorley. *A Preface to Henry James*, 67–73.
Wagenknecht, Edward. *The Tales of Henry James*, 18–19.

"John Delavoy"
Wagenknecht, Edward. *The Tales of Henry James*, 188–189.

"The Jolly Corner"
Auchard, John. *Silence* . . . , 50–53.
Caws, Mary Ann. *Reading Frames* . . . , 134–136.
Chauchaix, Jacqueline, and Claudine Verley. "La Sémiotique de l'espace dans 'The Jolly Corner' de Henry James," *Licorne*, 10 (1986), 17–29.
Elkins, Charles L. "Henry James," 343–344.
Knapp, Bettina L. *Archetype, Architecture* . . . , 27–44.
Miller, Karl. *Doubles* . . . , 231–234.
Mottram, Eric. "'The Infected Air' . . . ," 186–188.
Przybylowicz, Donna. *Desire and Repression* . . . , 115–125.
Robinson, Douglas. *American Apocalypse* . . . , 184–186.
Wagenknecht, Edward. *The Tales of Henry James*, 155–160.

"Julia Bride"
Cowdery, Lauren T. *The Nouvelle* . . . , 35–51.
Wagenknecht, Edward. *The Tales of Henry James*, 150–155.

"Lady Barbarina"
Wagenknecht, Edward. *The Tales of Henry James*, 25–27.

"A Landscape Painter"
Wagenknecht, Edward. *The Tales of Henry James*, 189–190.

"The Last of the Valerii"
Elkins, Charles L. "Henry James," 339.

"The Lesson of the Master"
Putt, S. Gorley. *A Preface to Henry James*, 113–116.
Wagenknecht, Edward. *The Tales of Henry James*, 50–54.

"The Liar"
Ron, Moshe. "The Art of the Portrait According to James," *Yale French Stud*, 69 (1985), 222–237.
Wagenknecht, Edward. *The Tales of Henry James*, 44–46.

"A Light Man"
Martin, W. R., and Warren U. Ober. "Refurbishing James's 'A Light Man,'" *Arizona Q*, 42 (1986), 305–314.
Wagenknecht, Edward. *The Tales of Henry James*, 190–191.

"A London Life"
Greiner, Donald J. *Adultery . . .* , 80–83.
Wagenknecht, Edward. *The Tales of Henry James*, 46–50.

"Lord Beaupré"
Wagenknecht, Edward. *The Tales of Henry James*, 191–192.

"Louisa Pallant"
Tintner, Adeline R. "The Use of Stupidity as a Narrative Device: The Gullible Teller in James's 'Louisa Pallant,'" *J Narrative Technique*, 15 (1985), 70–74.
Wagenknecht, Edward. *The Tales of Henry James*, 33–36.

"Madame de Mauves"
Wagenknecht, Edward. *The Tales of Henry James*, 4–8.

"The Madonna of the Future"
Auchard, John. *Silence . . .* , 36–37.
Wagenknecht, Edward. *The Tales of Henry James*, 1–4.

"The Marriages"
Wagenknecht, Edward. *The Tales of Henry James*, 62–63.

"Maud-Evelyn"
Auchard, John. *Silence . . .* , 48–50.
Wagenknecht, Edward. *The Tales of Henry James*, 193–194.

"The Middle Years"
Mottram, Eric. "'The Infected Air' . . . ," 180–181.

"Miss Gunton of Poughkeepsie"
Wagenknecht, Edward. *The Tales of Henry James*, 123–124.

"Mrs. Medwin"
Wagenknecht, Edward. *The Tales of Henry James,* 132–133.

"Mora Montravers"
Wagenknecht, Edward. *The Tales of Henry James,* 164–167.

"A Most Extraordinary Case"
Wagenknecht, Edward. *The Tales of Henry James,* 194–195.

"My Friend Bingham"
Wagenknecht, Edward. *The Tales of Henry James,* 195–196.

"The Next Time"
Wagenknecht, Edward. *The Tales of Henry James,* 82–85.

"Nona Vincent"
Wagenknecht, Edward. *The Tales of Henry James,* 196–197.

"Owen Wingate"
Elkins, Charles L. "Henry James," 341.
Wagenknecht, Edward. *The Tales of Henry James,* 72–74.

"Pandora"
Wagenknecht, Edward. *The Tales of Henry James,* 31–32.

"Paste"
Wagenknecht, Edward. *The Tales of Henry James,* 118–119.

"Patagonia"
Wagenknecht, Edward. *The Tales of Henry James,* 54–58.

"The Pension Beaurepas"
Wagenknecht, Edward. *The Tales of Henry James,* 19–20.

"The Private Life"
Elkins, Charles L. "Henry James," 340–341.
Tanner, Tony. *Henry James . . . ,* 79–80.
Wagenknecht, Edward. *The Tales of Henry James,* 66–68.

"Professor Fargo"
Wagenknecht, Edward. *The Tales of Henry James,* 199–200.

"The Pupil"
Huss, Roy. *The Mindscapes . . . ,* 73–84.
Wagenknecht, Edward. *The Tales of Henry James,* 57–61.
Wagner, Vern. ". . . Money and Sex," 222.

"The Real Right Thing"
Wagenknecht, Edward. *The Tales of Henry James,* 119–120.

"The Real Thing"
Auchard, John. *Silence . . . ,* 37–39.

Beaver, Harold. "The Real Thing and Unreal Thing: Conflicts of Art and Society in Henry James," *Fabu,* 1 (March, 1983), 53–69.
Bohner, Charles H. *Instructor's Manual . . . ,* 60–61.
Sheidley, William E., and Ann Charters. *Instructor's Manual . . . ,* 22–23; rpt. Charters, Ann, William E. Sheidley, and Martha Ramsey. *Instructor's Manual . . . ,* 2nd ed., 25–26.
Telotte, J. P. "The Right Way with Reality: James's 'The Real Thing,'" *Henry James R,* 6, i (1984), 8–14.
Vieilledent, Catherine. "Representation and Reproduction: A Reading of Henry James's 'The Real Thing,'" in Royot, Daniel, Ed. *Interface . . . ,* 31–49.
Wagenknecht, Edward. *The Tales of Henry James,* 68–70.

"The Romance of Certain Old Clothes"
Elkins, Charles L. "Henry James," 338–339.

"A Round of Visits"
Wagenknecht, Edward. *The Tales of Henry James,* 173–177.

"The Siege of London"
Putt, S. Gorley. *A Preface to Henry James,* 77–80.
Wagenknecht, Edward. *The Tales of Henry James,* 23–25.

"Sir Edmund Orme"
Elkins, Charles L. "Henry James," 340.
Wagenknecht, Edward. *The Tales of Henry James,* 65–66.

"The Story in It"
Mottram, Eric. "'The Infected Air' . . . ," 178–179.
Wagenknecht, Edward. *The Tales of Henry James,* 135–137.

"The Story of a Masterpiece"
Wagenknecht, Edward. *The Tales of Henry James,* 203–204.

"The Third Person"
Wagenknecht, Edward. *The Tales of Henry James,* 205–206.

"The Tree of Knowledge"
Bohner, Charles H. *Instructor's Manual . . . ,* 61–62.
Wagenknecht, Edward. *The Tales of Henry James,* 124–126.

"The Turn of the Screw"
Auchard, John. *Silence . . . ,* 44–46.
Caws, Mary Ann. *Reading Frames . . . ,* 145–148.
Chase, Dennis. "The Ambiguity of Innocence: 'The Turn of the Screw,'" *Extrapolation,* 27 (1986), 197–202.
Clews, Hetty. *The Only Teller . . . ,* 154–166.
Cohen, Paula M. "Freud's *Dora* and James's 'Turn of the Screw': Two Treatments of the Female 'Case,'" *Criticism,* 28, i (1986), 73–87.
Day, William P. *In the Circles . . . ,* 114–119.
Elkins, Charles L. "Henry James," 342–343.
Goetz, William. *Henry James . . . ,* 111–149.

Horvath, Brooke K. "Henry James, E. D. Hirsch, and Relative Readability: A Note on the Style of 'The Turn of the Screw,'" *Hartford Stud Lit*, 17, iii (1985), 12–17.

Jones, Vivien. "Henry James's 'The Turn of the Screw,'" in Howard, Patricia, Ed. *Benjamin Britten* . . . , 11–22.

Mansell, Darrel. "The Ghost of Language in 'The Turn of the Screw,'" *Mod Lang Q*, 46, i (1985), 48–63.

Pecora, Vincent P. "Of Games and Governesses," *Perspectives Contemp Lit*, 11 (1985), 28–36.

Scott, Charles B. "How the Screw Is Turned: James's *Amusette*," *Univ Mississippi Stud Engl*, 4 (1983), 112–131.

Tanner, Tony. *Henry James* . . . , 91–95.

Wagenknecht, Edward. *The Tales of Henry James*, 98–113.

Wagner, Vern. ". . . Money and Sex," 222.

"The Two Faces"
Wagenknecht, Edward. *The Tales of Henry James*, 129–131.

"The Velvet Glove"
Martin, W. R., and Warren U. Ober. "The Shaping Spirit . . . ," 341–345.

Wagenknecht, Edward. *The Tales of Henry James*, 163–164.

"Washington Square"
Auchard, John. *Silence* . . . , 64–67.

Bell, Ian F. A. "'This Exchange of Epigrams': Commodity and Style in 'Washington Square,'" *J Am Stud*, 19, i (1985), 49–58.

Gargano, James W. "'Washington Square': A Study in the Growth of an Inner Self," *Stud Short Fiction*, 13 (1976), 355–362; rpt. Gargano, James W., Ed. *Critical Essays* . . . , 129–136.

Halperin, John. "Trollope, James, and 'The Retribution of Time,'" *Southern Hum R*, 19 (1985), 301–308.

Lucas, John. *Moderns and Contemporaries* . . . , 3–26.

Putt, S. Gorley. *A Preface to Henry James*, 24–33.

Tanner, Tony. *Henry James* . . . , 33–34.

"The Wheel of Time"
Wagenknecht, Edward. *The Tales of Henry James*, 207–208.

P. D. JAMES

"The Girl Who Loved Graveyards"
Gidez, Richard B. *P. D. James*, 121–122.

"Great-Aunt Allie's Flypapers"
Gidez, Richard B. *P. D. James*, 114–116.

"Moment of Power"
Gidez, Richard B. *P. D. James*, 122–124.

"Murder, 1986"
Gidez, Richard B. *P. D. James*, 116–117.

"The Murder of Santa Claus"
Gidez, Richard B. *P. D. James,* 117–118.

"A Very Desirable Residence"
Gidez, Richard B. *P. D. James,* 119.

"The Victim"
Gidez, Richard B. *P. D. James,* 119–121.

SARAH ORNE JEWETT

"A Born Farmer"
Nail, Rebecca W. "'Where Every Prospect Pleases': Sarah Orne Jewett, South
    Berwick, and the Importance of Place," in Nagel, Gwen L., Ed. *Critical
    Essays . . . ,* 190–191.

"The Courting of Sister Wisby"
Ammons, Elizabeth. "Jewett's Witches," in Nagel, Gwen L., Ed. *Critical Es-
    says . . . ,* 174–175.

"An Every-Day Girl"
Johns, Barbara A. "'Matchless and Appealing': Growing into Spinsterhood in
    Sarah Orne Jewett," in Nagel, Gwen L., Ed. *Critical Essays . . . ,* 157–158.

"Farmer Finch"
Johns, Barbara A. "'Matchless and Appealing' . . . ," 153–157.

"The Flight of Betsey Lane"
Johns, Barbara A. "'Matchless and Appealing' . . . ," 158.
Johnson, Robert. "Jewett's 'The Flight of Betsy Lane,'" *Explicator,* 43, iii (1985),
    22.

"The Foreigner"
Ammons, Elizabeth. "Jewett's Witches," 178–180.
Piacentino, Edward J. "Local Color and Beyond: The Artistic Dimension of
    Sarah Orne Jewett's 'The Foreigner,'" *Colby Lib Q,* 21, ii (1985), 92–98.

"The Garden Story"
Johns, Barbara A. "'Matchless and Appealing' . . . ," 159.

"The Green Bowl"
Ammons, Elizabeth. "Jewett's Witches," 180–182.

"A Guest at Home"
Johns, Barbara A. "'Matchless and Appealing' . . . ," 159.

"Lady Ferry"
Ammons, Elizabeth. "Jewett's Witches," 169–173.

"Luck of the Bogans"
Nail, Rebecca W. "'Where Every Prospect Pleases' . . . ," 191–192.

"Martha's Lady"
Hobbs, Glenda. "Pure and Passionate: Female Friendship in Sarah Orne Jewett's 'Martha's Lady,'" *Stud Short Fiction*, 17 (1980), 21–29; rpt. Nagel, Gwen L., Ed. *Critical Essays . . . ,*" 99–107.

"Miss Peck's Promotion"
Johns, Barbara A. "'Matchless and Appealing' . . . ," 160–161.

"Miss Sydney's Flowers"
Johns, Barbara A. "'Matchless and Appealing' . . . ," 158–159.

"Miss Tempy's Watchers"
Johns, Barbara A. "'Matchless and Appealing' . . . ," 157–158.

"A Player Queen"
Eppard, Philip B. "Two Lost Stories by Sarah Orne Jewett: 'A Player Queen' and 'Three Friends,'" in Nagel, Gwen L., Ed. *Critical Essays . . . ,* 225–227.

"The Queen's Twin"
Roman, Judith. "A Closer Look at the Jewett-Fields Relationship," in Nagel, Gwen L., Ed. *Critical Essays . . . ,* 130–132.

"Three Friends"
Eppard, Philip B. "Two Lost Stories . . . ," 227–229.

"A Village Shop"
Johns, Barbara A. "'Matchless and Appealing' . . . ," 159–161.

"A White Heron"
Ammons, Elizabeth. "The Shaping of Violence in Jewett's 'A White Heron,'" *Colby Lib Q,* 22 (1986), 6–16.
Bohner, Charles H. *Instructor's Manual . . . ,* 63.
Donovan, Josephine. "Silence or Capitulation: Prepatriarchal 'Mothers' Gardens' in Jewett and Freeman," *Stud Short Fiction,* 23 (1986), 43–45.
Gerlach, John. *Toward the End . . . ,* 66–69.
Griffith, Kelley. "Sylvia as Hero in Sarah Orne Jewett's 'A White Heron,'" *Colby Lib Q,* 21, i (1985), 22–27.
Held, George. "Heart of Hearts with Nature: Ways of Looking at 'A White Heron,'" *Colby Lib Q,* 18 (1982), 55–65; rpt. Nagel, Gwen L., Ed. *Critical Essays . . . ,* 58–68.
Johns, Barbara A. "'Matchless and Appealing' . . . ," 153–157.
Singley, Carol J. "Reaching Lonely Heights: Sarah Orne Jewett, Emily Dickinson, and Female Initiation," *Colby Lib Q,* 22 (1986), 76–80.

"William's Wedding"
Nail, Rebecca W. "'Where Every Prospect Pleases' . . . ," 193–194.

RUTH PRAWER JHABVALA

"How I Became a Holy Mother"
Evans, Walter. "The English Short Story in the Seventies," in Vannatta, Dennis, Ed. *The English Short Story, 1945–1980,* 128.

JIANG ZILONG

"A Factory Secretary's Diary"
Duke, Michael S. *Blooming* . . . , 91–93.

"Manager Qiao Assumes Office"
Duke, Michael S. *.Blooming* . . . , 89–92.

"More About Manager Qiao"
Duke, Michael S. *Blooming* . . . , 89–92.

JIBRAN KHALIL JIBRAN

"Martha of the Village of Ban"
Haywood, John A. *Modern Arabic Literature* . . . , 129–130.

"The Shout of Graves"
Haywood, John A. *Modern Arabic Literature* . . . , 130–131.

JIN HE

"Re-encounter"
Duke, Michael S. *Blooming* . . . , 79–80.

NICK JOAQUÍN

"Guardia de Honor"
Sharrad, Paul. "The Third Alternative: Nick Joaquín's Vision," in Amirthanayagam, Guy, and S. C. Harrex, Eds. *Only Connect* . . . , 244–258.

COLIN JOHNSON

"A Missionary Would I Have Been"
Bennett, Bruce. "Asian Encounters in the Contemporary Australian Short
Story," *World Lit Written Engl*, 26 (1986), 55–56.

ELIZABETH JOLLEY

"Grasshopper"
Daniel, Helen. "Elizabeth Jolley: Variations on a Theme," *Westerly*, 31, ii (1986),
52–53.

"Hilda's Wedding"
Daniel, Helen. "Elizabeth Jolley . . . ," 52.

"Liberation"
Daniel, Helen. "Elizabeth Jolley . . . ," 53.

"Paper Children"
Riemer, A. P. "Displaced Persons—Some Preoccupations in Elizabeth Jolley's
    Fiction," *Westerly*, 31, ii (1986), 66–68.

"Two Men Running"
Riemer, A. P. "Displaced Persons . . . ," 65–66.

GAYL JONES

"Asylum"
Byerman, Keith E. *Fingering the Jagged Grain* . . . , 176–177.

"White Rat"
Byerman, Keith E. *Fingering the Jagged Grain* . . . , 172–174.

"The Women"
Byerman, Keith E. *Fingering the Jagged Grain* . . . , 174–176.

GWYN JONES

"Bad Blood"
Price, Cecil. *Gwyn Jones*, 38.

"The Brute Creation"
Price, Cecil. *Gwyn Jones*, 37.

"The Green Island"
Stinson, John J. "The English Short Story, 1945–1950," in Vannatta, Dennis,
    Ed. *The English Short Story, 1945–1980*, 21–22.

"Where My Dark Lover Lies"
Baldwin, Dean. "The English Short Story in the Fifties," in Vannatta, Dennis,
    Ed. *The English Short Story, 1945–1980*, 54.

"A White Birthday"
Price, Cecil. *Gwyn Jones*, 38–39.

GABRIEL JOSIPOVICI

"Contiguities"
Evans, Walter. "The English Short Story in the Seventies," in Vannatta, Dennis,
    Ed. *The English Short Story, 1945–1980*, 159–161.

"Little Words"
Evans, Walter. "The English Short Story . . . ," 158–159.

"Second Person Looking Out"
Evans, Walter. "The English Short Story . . . ," 161.

JAMES JOYCE

"After the Race"
Torchiana, Donald T. . . . *Joyce's "Dubliners,"* 79–86.

"Araby"
Bohner, Charles H. *Instructor's Manual* . . . , 63–64.
Flynn, Elizabeth A. "Gender and Reading," in Flynn, Elizabeth A., and
Patrocinio P. Schweickart, Eds. *Gender and Reading* . . . , 267–288.
Hauge, Hans. "The Ambiguous Artistic Programme of 'Araby,'" in Westarp,
Karl-Heinz, Ed. *Joyce Centenary Offshoots* . . . , 47–52.
Henke, Suzette A. "Through a Cracked Looking-glass: Sex-role Stereotypes in
Dubliners," in Gaiser, Gottlieb, Ed. *International Perspectives* . . . , 6–8.
Torchiana, Donald T. . . . *Joyce's "Dubliners,"* 56–65.

"The Boarding House"
Henke, Suzette A. ". . . Sex-role Stereotypes in *Dubliners,"* 11–12.
Laroque, F. "'The Boarding House' as an Archetypal Story," *Mythes,* 4 (1986),
70–97.
Senn, Fritz. "'The Boarding House' Seen as a Tale of Misdirection," *James Joyce
Q,* 23 (1986), 405–413.
Torchiana, Donald T. . . . *Joyce's "Dubliners,"* 110–120.

"Clay"
Henke, Suzette A. ". . . Sex-role Stereotypes in *Dubliners,"* 16–18.
Torchiana, Donald T. . . . *Joyce's "Dubliners,"* 150–163.

"Counterparts"
Hansen, Erik A. "Joyce's Study in Wretched Wrath: Notes about 'Counter-
parts,'" in Westarp, Karl-Heinz, Ed. *Joyce Centenary Offshoots* . . . , 53–70.
Henke, Suzette A. ". . . Sex-role Stereotypes in *Dubliners,"* 15–16.
Torchiana, Donald T. . . . *Joyce's "Dubliners,"* 141–149.

"The Dead"
Averill, Deborah M. *The Irish Short Story* . . . , 59–65.
Benstock, Bernard. *James Joyce,* 32–33.
Bohner, Charles H. *Instructor's Manual* . . . , 65–66.
Brown, Richard. *James Joyce* . . . , 92–93.
Dilworth, Thomas. "Sex and Politics in 'The Dead,'" *James Joyce Q,* 23 (1986),
157–171.
Hanson, Clare. *Short Stories* . . . , 61–63.
Hedberg, Johannes. "On First Looking into a Long Short Story by James Joyce:
Reminiscences of a Once Young Man," *James Joyce Q,* 23 (1985), 84–86.
Henke, Suzette A. ". . . Sex-role Stereotypes in *Dubliners,"* 22–27.
Pecora, Vincent P. "'The Dead' and the Generosity of the Word," *PMLA,* 101
(1986), 233–234.
Sheidley, William E., and Ann Charters. *Instructor's Manual* . . . , 72–74; rpt.
Charters, Ann, William E. Sheidley, and Martha Ramsey. *Instructor's Man-
ual* . . . , 2nd ed., 78–79.
Shields, David. "A Note on the Conclusion of Joyce's 'The Dead,'" *James Joyce
Q,* 22 (1985), 427–428.
Torchiana, Donald T. . . . *Joyce's "Dubliners,"* 223–257.

"An Encounter"
Henke, Suzette A. ". . . Sex-role Stereotypes in *Dubliners,*" 6.

"Eveline"
Averill, Deborah M. *The Irish Short Story . . . ,* 54–56.
Henke, Suzette A. ". . . Sex-role Stereotypes in *Dubliners,*" 8–9.
Knapp, Bettina. "James Joyce's 'Eveline': An Auditory Experience," *Études Irlandaises,* 10 (December, 1985), 67–75.
Torchiana, Donald T. . . . *Joyce's "Dubliners,"* 71–76.

"Grace"
Henke, Suzette A. ". . . Sex-role Stereotypes in *Dubliners,*" 20–21.
Torchiana, Donald T. . . . *Joyce's "Dubliners,"* 205–216.

"Ivy Day in the Committee Room"
Torchiana, Donald T. . . . *Joyce's "Dubliners,"* 177–187.

"A Little Cloud"
Averill, Deborah M. *The Irish Short Story . . . ,* 56–59.
Henke, Suzette A. ". . . Sex-role Stereotypes in *Dubliners,*" 12–15.
Torchiana, Donald T. . . . *Joyce's "Dubliners,"* 126–140.

"A Mother"
Henke, Suzette A. ". . . Sex-role Stereotypes in *Dubliners,*" 21–22.
Torchiana, Donald T. . . . *Joyce's "Dubliners,"* 188–204.

"A Painful Case"
Benstock, Bernard. *James Joyce,* 45–47.
Henke, Suzette A. ". . . Sex-role Stereotypes in *Dubliners,*" 18–19.
Torchiana, Donald T. . . . *Joyce's "Dubliners,"* 165–175.

"The Sisters"
Averill, Deborah M. *The Irish Short Story . . . ,* 51–53.
Benstock, Bernard. *James Joyce,* 38–40.
Hanson, Clare. *Short Stories . . . ,* 60–61.
Henke, Suzette A. ". . . Sex-role Stereotypes in *Dubliners,*" 3–6.
Torchiana, Donald T. . . . *Joyce's "Dubliners,"* 21–35.

"Two Gallants"
Henke, Suzette A. ". . . Sex-role Stereotypes in *Dubliners,*" 10–11.
Torchiana, Donald T. . . . *Joyce's "Dubliners,"* 91–108.

FRANZ KAFKA

"Before the Law"
Steinberg, Erwin R. "Kafka's 'Before the Law'—A Reflection of Fear of Marriage, and Corroborating Language Patterns in the Diaries," *J Mod Lit,* 13 (1986), 129–148.

"Blumfeld, an Elderly Bachelor"
Goffman, Ethan. "Blumfeld's Balls: Notes on a Situation in a Kafka Short Story," *Neue Germanistik*, 4, i (1985), 3–6.
Quinney, Laura. "More Remote Than the Abyss," in Bloom, Harold, Ed. *Franz Kafka*, 225–226.
Robert, Marthe. *As Lonely As Franz Kafka*, 183–185.

"The Burrow"
Blackham, H. J. *The Fable . . .* , 133–134.
Henel, Heinrich. "'The Burrow,' or How to Escape from a Maze," in Bloom, Harold, Ed. *Franz Kafka*, 119–132.
Karl, Frederick R. *Modern and Modernism . . .* , 241–242.

"The Cares of a Family Man"
Robert, Marthe. *As Lonely As Franz Kafka*, 193–197.

"A Country Doctor"
Cohn, Dorrit. "Kafka's Eternal Present: Narrative Tense in 'A Country Doctor,'" in Bloom, Harold, Ed. *Franz Kafka*, 110–117.
Corngold, Stanley. *The Fate . . .* , 190–191.
Ray, Susan. "The Metaphysics of the *Doppelgänger* Motif in Kafka's 'Ein Landarzt,'" *Seminar*, 21 (1985), 123–138.
Robertson, Ritchie. *Kafka . . .* , 180–183.
Sussman, Henry. "Double Medicine: The Text That Was Never a Story," in Elling, Barbara, Ed. *Kafka-Studien*, 183–196.
Timms, Edward. "Kafka's Expanded Metaphors: A Freudian Approach to 'Ein Landarzt,'" in Stern, J. P., and J. J. White, Eds. *Paths and Labyrinths . . .* , 66–79.

"Description of a Struggle"
Karl, Frederick R. *Modern and Modernism . . .* , 250–254.
Robert, Marthe. *As Lonely As Franz Kafka*, 135–141.
Ternes, Hans. "The Fantastic in the Works of Franz Kafka," in Collins, Robert A., and Howard D. Pearce, Eds. *The Scope of the Fantastic . . .* , 223–225.

"A Fratricide"
Baum, Alwin L. "Parable as Paradox in Kafka's Stories," in Bloom, Harold, Ed. *Franz Kafka*, 161–162.

"The Great Wall of China"
Blackham, H. J. *The Fable . . .* , 135.
Norris, Margot. *Beasts . . .* , 65–66.
Rignall, J. M. "History and Consciousness in 'Beim Bau der Chinesischen Mauer,'" in Stern, J. P., and J. J. White, Eds. *Paths and Labyrinths . . .* , 111–126.
Robertson, Ritchie. *Kafka . . .* , 172–176.

"A Hunger Artist"
Bohner, Charles H. *Instructor's Manual . . .* , 66–67.
Neumann, Gerhard. "Hungerkünstler und Menschenfresser: Zum Verhältnis von Kunst und kulturellem Ritual im Werk Franz Kafkas," *Archiv für Kulturgeschichte*, 66 (1984), 347–388.

"The Hunter Gracchus"
Bloom, Harold. "Introduction," in Bloom, Harold, Ed. *Franz Kafka*, 5–7.
Corngold, Stanley. *The Fate . . .* , 188–189.

"A Hybrid" [same as "A Crossbreed"]
Robert, Marthe. *As Lonely As Franz Kafka*, 191–192.
Sussman, Henry. "Kafka in the Heart of the Twentieth Century: An Approach to Borges," in Udoff, Alan, Ed. *Kafka's Contextuality*, 181–185.

"In the Gallery"
Heller, Peter. " 'Up in the Gallery': Incongruity and Alienation," in Bloom, Harold, Ed. *Franz Kafka*, 86–93.

"In the Penal Colony"
Charue, Jeanine. "La Machine a tuer dans 'La Colonie penitentiaire' de Kafka," *Études Philosophiques*, 1 (1985), 101–112.
Koelb, Clayton. "The Text as Erotic/Auto-Erotic Device," *Midwest Q*, 26 (1985), 212–224.
Loeb, Ernst. "Kafkas 'In der Strafkolonie' im Spiegel 'klassischer' und 'romanischer' Religion," *Seminar*, 21 (1985), 139–149.
Norris, Margot. *Beasts . . .* , 111–117.
Pascal, Malcolm. "Kafka and the Theme of 'Berufung,' " *Oxford Germ Stud*, 11 (1980), 123–145.
Robertson, Ritchie. *Kafka . . .* , 152–155.

"Investigations of a Dog"
Blackham, H. J. *The Fable . . .* , 134–135.
Kluback, William. "A Few Thoughts on Franz Kafka," *J Evolutionary Psych*, 6 (1985), 261–267.
Robert, Marthe. *As Lonely As Franz Kafka*, 14–21.

"Josephine the Singer"
Gross, Ruth V. "Of Mice and Women: Reflections on Discourse in Kafka's 'Josefine, die Sängerin oder Das Volks der Mäuse,' " *Germ R*, 60 (1985), 59–68.
Norris, Margot. *Beasts . . .* , 118–133.
Robertson, Ritchie. *Kafka . . .* , 279–284.
Smock, Ann. *Double Dealing*, 93–117.
Stern, J. P. "Franz Kafka on Mice and Men," in Stern, J. P., and J. J. White, Eds. *Paths and Labyrinths . . .* , 141–155.

"The Judgment"
Sokel, Walter H. "Frozen Sea and River of Narration: The Poetics Behind Kafka's 'Breakthrough,' " *New Lit Hist*, 17 (1986), 357–363.

"Metamorphosis"
Anderson, Mark M. "Kafka and Sacher-Masoch," *J Kafka Soc Am*, 7, ii (1983), 4–19.
Blackham, H. J. *The Fable . . .* , 132–133.
Bouson, J. Brooks. "The Repressed Grandiosity of Gregor Samsa: A Kohutian Reading of Kafka's 'Metamorphosis,' " in Layton, Lynne, and Barbara Schapiro, Eds. *Narcissism . . .* , 192–215.

Brown, Russell E. "A Mistake in 'Die Verwandlung' of Kafka," *Germ Notes*, 16, ii (1985), 19–21.

Eggenschwiler, David. "'The Metamorphosis,' Freud, and the Chains of Odysseus," in Bloom, Harold, Ed. *Franz Kafka*, 204–219.

Goeppert, Herma C. "Sinn, Bedeutung, Bezeichnung: Zur Interpretation von Kafkas 'Verwandlung,'" in Geckeler, Horst, Ed. *Logos Semantikos* . . . , III, 71–79.

Hartman, Tom. "Kafka's 'The Metamorphosis,'" *Explicator*, 43, ii (1985), 32–34.

Kirby, David. *The Sun Rises* . . . , 56–57.

Layton, Lynne, and Barbara Ann Schapiro, Eds. *Narcissism* . . . , 192–212.

Leadbeater, Lewis W. "Aristophanes and Kafka: The Dung-Beetle Connection," *Stud Short Fiction*, 23 (1986), 169–178.

Quiquandon, Marianne, and Laure Malo. "Kafka et 'La Métamorphose,'" in *Littérature et psychanalyse* . . . , 54–69.

Sheidley, William E., and Ann Charters. *Instructor's Manual* . . . , 78–79; rpt. Charters, Ann, William E. Sheidley, and Martha Ramsey. *Instructor's Manual* . . . , 2nd ed., 81–82.

Sokel, Walter H. "From Marx to Myth: The Structure and Function of Self-Alienation in Kafka's 'Metamorphosis,'" in Elling, Barbara, Ed. *Kafka-Studien*, 153–167.

Ternes, Hans. "The Fantastic . . . ," 226–227.

"Poseidon"
Quinney, Laura. "More Remote . . . ," 226–227.

"Prometheus"
Robert, Marthe. *As Lonely As Franz Kafka*, 166–172.

"A Report to an Academy"
Norris, Margot. *Beasts* . . . , 66–72.

Reid, J. H. "Monkey Business in the GDR: Hermann Kant and Kafka," *Germ Life & Letters*, 38 (1985), 417–426.

Robertson, Ritchie. "Antizionismus, Zionismus': Kafka's Responses to Jewish Nationalism," in Stern, J. P., and J. J. White, Eds. *Paths and Labyrinths* . . . , 25–42.

———. *Kafka* . . . , 164–171.

"The Silence of the Sirens"
Eggenschwiler, David. ". . . Chains of Odysseus," 214.

"Unhappiness"
Cersowsky, Peter. "The Copernican Revolution in the History of Fantastic Literature at the Beginning of the Twentieth Century," in Collins, Robert A., and Howard D. Pearce, Eds. *The Scope of the Fantastic* . . . , 21–23.

NORMAN KAGAN

"The Mathenauts"
Boyno, Edward A. "The Mathematics in Science Fiction: Of Measure Zero," in Hassler, Donald A., Ed. *Patterns* . . . *II*, 42–43.

IVAN KATAEV [KATAYEV]

"Under Clear Skies"
Moser, Charles A. *The Russian Short Story* . . . , 169–170.

VALENTIN KATAEV [KATAYEV]

"Kranz's Experiment"
Moser, Charles A. *The Russian Short Story* . . . , 165–166.

KAWABATA YASUNORI

"The Moon on the Water"
Watanake, Nancy. "The Symbolism of Solar and Lunar Personas in the Vegetable Glass of Nature," in Ueda, Makoto, Ed. *Explorations* . . . , 65–67, 78.

WELDON KEES

"Applause"
Ross, William T. *Weldon Kees*, 23–24.

"The Ceremony"
Ross, William T. *Weldon Kees*, 33–34.

"Downward and Away"
Ross, William T. *Weldon Kees*, 32–33.

"Escape in Autumn"
Ross, William T. *Weldon Kees*, 34–35.

"The Evening of the Fourth of July"
Ross, William T. *Weldon Kees*, 36–39.

"Gents 50¢; Ladies 25¢"
Ross, William T. *Weldon Kees*, 24–26.

"I Should Worry"
Ross, William T. *Weldon Kees*, 28–31.

"The Life of the Mind"
Ross, William T. *Weldon Kees*, 18–20.

"A Man to Help"
Ross, William T. *Weldon Kees*, 28.

"Mrs. Lutz"
Ross, William T. *Weldon Kees*, 15–16.

"The Sign Painters"
Ross, William T. *Weldon Kees,* 26–28.

"So Cold Outside"
Ross, William T. *Weldon Kees,* 16–18.

"This Is Home"
Ross, William T. *Weldon Kees,* 31–32.

"Three Pretty Nifty Green Suits"
Ross, William T. *Weldon Kees,* 20–22.

"A Walk Home"
Ross, William T. *Weldon Kees,* 22–23.

GOTTFRIED KELLER

"Dietegen"
Schwarz, Peter P. "Zur Bedeutung der Kindheit in Kellers 'Dietegen,'" *Wirkendes Wort,* 35 (1985), 88–99.

"The Three Righteous Comb-Makers"
Siefken, Hinrich. "Kellers Novelle 'Die drei gerechten Kammacher': Vom Eigentum und den höheren Sphären der Meisterschaft," *Zeitschrift für Deutsche Philologie,* 104 (1985), 204–223.

"A Village Romeo and Juliet"
Holub, Robert C. "Realism, Repetition, Repression: The Nature of Desire in 'Romeo und Julia auf dem Dorfe,'" *Mod Lang Notes,* 100 (1985), 461–497.
Paulin, Roger. *The Brief Compass . . . ,* 85–87.
Swales, Martin. "Gottfried Kellers 'Romeo und Julia auf dem Dorfe,'" in Steinecke, Hartmut, Ed. *Zu Gottfried Keller,* 54–67.
————. "The Problem of Nineteenth-Century German Realism," in Boyle, Nicholas, and Martin Swales, Eds. *Realism . . . ,* 80–82.

SIEW YUE KILLINGLEY

"Everything's Arranged"
Gooneratne, Yasmine. "Lloyd Fernando's *Twenty-Two Malaysian Stories,*" in Goodwin, K. L., Ed. *Commonwealth Literature . . . ,* 122–123.

"A Question of Dowry"
Gooneratne, Yasmine. ". . . *Twenty-Two Malaysian Stories,*" 123.

JAMAICA KINCAID

"At the Bottom of the River"
Mangum, Bryant. "Jamaica Kincaid," in Dance, Daryl C., Ed. *Fifty Caribbean Writers . . . ,* 257–258, 260–261.

"In the Night"
Mangum, Bryant. "Jamaica Kincaid," 258.

"A Walk to the Jetty"
Mangum, Bryant. "Jamaica Kincaid," 261–262.

"What Have I Been Doing Lately?"
Mangum, Bryant. "Jamaica Kincaid," 258–259.

GRACE KING

"Joe"
Piacentino, Edward J. "The Enigma of Black Identity in Grace King's 'Joe,'"
    Southern Lit J, 9, i (1986), 56–67.

RUDYARD KIPLING

"At the End of the Passage"
Holt, Marilyn J. "Rudyard Kipling," in Bleiler, E. F., Ed. *Supernatural Fiction
    Writers . . . ,* I, 440.

"Beyond the Pale"
MacDonald, Robert H. "Discourse and Ideology in Kipling's 'Beyond the Pale,'"
    Stud Short Fiction, 23 (1986), 413–418.

"The Bridge-Builders"
Parry, Ann. "Imperialism in 'The Bridge-Builders,'" Part 1, *Kipling J*, 60
    (March, 1986), 12–22; Part 2, 60 (June, 1986), 9–16.

"The Brushwood Boy"
Holt, Marilyn J. "Rudyard Kipling," 440.

"The Bull That Thought"
Schaub, Danielle. "Kipling's Craftsmanship in 'The Bull That Thought,'" *Stud
    Short Fiction*, 22 (1985), 309–316.

"By Word of Mouth"
Holt, Marilyn J. "Rudyard Kipling," 438–439.

"The Captive"
Flora, Joseph M. *The English Short Story . . . ,* 11–12.

"Dayspring Mishandled"
Caesar, Terry. "Suppression, Textuality, Entanglement, and Revenge in Kip-
    ling's 'Dayspring Mishandled,'" *Engl Lit Transition*, 29 (1986), 34–63.
Hanson, Clare. *Short Stories . . . ,* 42–44.

"Debits and Credits"
Ricketts, Harry. "Kipling and the War: A Reading of 'Debits and Credits,'"
    Engl Lit Transition, 29 (1986), 29–39.

"The Enlightenment of Pagett, M.P."
McClure, John. "Problematic Presence: The Colonial Other in Kipling and
Conrad," in Dabydeen, David, Ed. *The Black Presence* . . . , 164–165.

"Haunted Subalterns"
Holt, Marilyn J. "Rudyard Kipling," 439.

"The Head of the District"
McClure, John. "Problematic Presence . . . ," 163.

"His Chance in Life"
McClure, John. "Problematic Presence . . . ," 164.

"The Killing of Hatim Tai"
Stewart, D. H. "Shooting Elephants Right," *Southern R,* 22, i (1986), 86–92.

"Little Foxes"
Flora, Joseph M. *The English Short Story* . . . , 13–14.

"The Man Who Would Be King"
Bohner, Charles H. *Instructor's Manual* . . . , 67–69.
Orel, Harold. *The Victorian Short Story* . . . , 156–158.

"The Mark of the Beast"
Holt, Marilyn J. "Rudyard Kipling," 439.

"Mary Postgate"
Firchow, Peter E. *The Death* . . . , 102–113.
Page, Norman. "What Happens in 'Mary Postgate'?" *Engl Lit Transition,* 29
(1986), 41–47.

"My Son's Wife"
Hanson, Clare. *Short Stories* . . . , 36–37.

"The Phantom Rickshaw"
Holt, Marilyn J. "Rudyard Kipling," 438.
Orel, Harold. *The Victorian Short Story* . . . , 154–155.
Scheick, William J. "Hesitation in Kipling's 'The Phantom Rickshaw,'" *Engl Lit
Transition,* 29 (1986), 48–53.

"The Return of Imray" [same as "The Recrudescence of Imray"]
Holt, Marilyn J. "Rudyard Kipling," 439.

"The Strange Ride of Morrowbie Jukes"
Crook, Nora. "The Even Stranger Ride of Morrowbie Jukes," *Kipling J,* 60
(June, 1986), 16–23.

"They"
Hanson, Clare. *Short Stories* . . . , 37–38.
Holt, Marilyn J. "Rudyard Kipling," 439.

"The Wish House"
Hanson, Clare. *Short Stories . . .* , 39–42.

"Without Benefit of Clergy"
Orel, Harold. *The Victorian Short Story . . .* , 146–149.

RUSSELL KIRK

"Ex Tenebris"
Herron, Don. "Russell Kirk: Ghost Master of Mecosta," in Schweitzer, Darrell, Ed. . . . *Horror Fiction,* 28–29.

"Lost Lake"
Herron, Don. "Russell Kirk . . . ," 25.

"The Princess of All Lands"
Herron, Don. "Russell Kirk . . . ," 33–34.

"The Reflex-Man of Whinnymuir Close"
Herron, Don. "Russell Kirk . . . ," 36–37.

"Saviorgate"
Herron, Don. "Russell Kirk . . . ," 34–35.

"Skyberia"
Herron, Don. "Russell Kirk . . . ," 44–45.

PERRI KLASS

"Not a Good Girl"
Bohner, Charles H. *Instructor's Manual . . .* , 69–70.

T. E. D. KLEIN

"Black Man with a Horn"
Price, Robert M. "T. E. D. Klein," in Schweitzer, Darrell, Ed. . . . *Horror Fiction,* 71–73.

"Children of the Kingdom"
Price, Robert M. "T. E. D. Klein," 73–75.

"Events at Poroth Farm"
Price, Robert M. "T. E. D. Klein," 68–70.

"Petey"
Price, Robert M. "T. E. D. Klein," 70–71.

HEINRICH VON KLEIST

"The Duel"
Fischer, Bernd. "Der Ernst des Scheins in der Prosa Heinrich von Kleists: Am
  Beispiel des 'Zweikampfs,'" *Zeitschrifte für Deutsche Philologie*, 105 (1986),
  213–234.
Paulin, Roger. *The Brief Compass* . . . , 38–40.

"The Earthquake in Chile"
Altenhofer, Norbert. "Der erschütterte Sinn Hermeneutische Überlegungen zu
  Kleists 'Das Erdbeben in Chili,'" in Wellbery, David E., Ed. *Positionen der
  Literaturwissenschaft* . . . , 39–53.
Bürger, Christa. "Statt einer Interpretation: Anmerkungen zu Kleists Erzäh-
  len," in Wellbery, David E., Ed. *Positionen der Literaturwissenschaft* . . . , 88–
  109.
Girard, René. "Mythos und Gegenmythos: Zu Kleists 'Das Erdbeben in Chili,'"
  in Wellbery, David E., Ed. *Positionen der Literaturwissenschaft* . . . , 130–148.
Hamacher, Werner. "Das Beben der Darstellung," in Wellbery, David E., Ed.
  Positionen der Literaturwissenschaft . . . , 149–173.
Kittler, Friedrich A. "Ein Erdbeben in Chili und Preussen," in Wellbery,
  David E., Ed. *Positionen der Literaturwissenschaft* . . . , 24–38.
Ledanff, Suzanne. "Kleist und die 'beste aller Welten': 'Das Erdbeben in
  Chili'—gesehen im Spiegel der philosophischen und literarischen Stellung-
  nahmen zur Theodizee im 18. Jahrhundert," *Kleist-Jahrbuch* [n.v.] (1986),
  125–155.
Paulin, Roger. *The Brief Compass* . . . , 45–48.
Schneider, Helmut J. "Der Zusammensturz des Allgemeinen," in Wellbery,
  David E., Ed. *Positionen der Literaturwissenschaft* . . . , 110–129.
Stierle, Karlheinz. "Das Beben des Bewusstseins: Die narrative Struktur von
  Kleists 'Das Erdbeben in Chili,'" in Wellbery, David E., Ed. *Positionen der
  Literaturwissenschaft* . . . , 54–68.
Wellbery, David E. "Semiotische Anmerkungen zu Kleists 'Das Erdbeben in
  Chili,'" in Wellbery, David E., Ed. *Positionen der Literaturwissenschaft* . . . ,
  69–87.

"The Engagement in Santo Domingo"
Kassé, Maguèye. "Heinrich von Kleist—Anna Seghers: La Révolution française
  et le thème de la révolte dans les Antilles françaises," *Études Germano-
  africaines*, 2 (1983), 57–71.
Musgrave, Marian E. "Literary Justifications of Slavery," in Grimm, Reinhold,
  and Jost Hermand, Eds. *Blacks and German Culture*, 17.
Paulin, Roger. *The Brief Compass* . . . , 38–40.

"The Foundling"
Behrens, Rudolf. "'Der Findling'—Heinrich von Kleists Erzählung von den
  'Infortunes de la vertu' im Spannungsfeld zwischen Helvétius und Rous-
  seau," in San Miguel, Angel, Richard Schwaderer, and Manfred Tietz, Eds.
  Romanische Literaturbeziehungen . . . , 9–28.
Schröder, Jürgen. "Kleists Novelle 'Der Findling': Ein Plädoyer für Nicolo,"
  Kleist-Jahrbuch, [n.v.] (1985), 109–127.

"The Marquise of O———"
Esch, Deborah. "Toward a Midwifery of Thought: Reading Kleist's 'Die Marquise von O———,'" in Caws, Mary A., Ed. *Textual Analysis*..., 144–155.
Krueger, Werner. "Rolle und Rollenwechsel: Überlegungen zu Kleists 'Marquise von O———,'" *Acta Germanica*, 17 (1984), 29–51.
Laurs, Axel. "Towards Idylls of Domesticity in Kleist's 'Die Marquise von O———,'" *J Australian Univs Lang & Lit Assoc*, 64 (1985), 175–189.
Paulin, Roger. *The Brief Compass*..., 51–57.
Schmidhäuser, Eberhard. "Das Verbrechen in Kleists 'Marquise von O———': Eine nur am Rande strafrechtliche Untersuchung," *Kleist-Jahrbuch*, [n.v.] (1986), 156–175.
Smith, John H. "Dialogic Midwifery in Kleist's 'Marquise von O' and the Hermeneutics of Telling the Untold in Kant and Plato," *PMLA*, 100 (1985), 203–219.

"Michael Kohlhaas"
Boockmann, Hartmut. "Mittelalterliches Recht bei Kleist: Ein Beitrag zum Verständnis des 'Michael Kohlhaas,'" *Kleist-Jahrbuch*, [n.v.] (1985), 84–108.

"St. Cecilia or the Power of Music"
Haase, Donald P., and Rachel Freudenburg. "Power, Truth, and Interpretation: The Hermeneutic Act and Kleist's 'Die heilige Cäcelie,'" *Deutsche Vierteljahrsschrift*, 60 (1986), 80–103.

V. KRESTOVSKY [NADEZHDA KHVOSCHIUSKAYA]

"Behind the Wall"
Moser, Charles A. *The Russian Short Story*..., 96–97.

"The Teacher"
Moser, Charles A. *The Russian Short Story*..., 97.

MILAN KUNDERA

"The Hitchhiking Game"
Sheidley, William E., and Ann Charters. *Instructor's Manual*..., 167–168; rpt. Charters, Ann, William E. Sheidley, and Martha Ramsey. *Instructor's Manual*..., 2nd ed., 181–182.

KUNIKIDA DOPPO

"Old Gen"
Chibbett, David G. "Introduction" to Kunikida Doppo, *River Mist*..., xxviii.
Mortimer, Maya. "Reflexivity in the Stories of Kunikida Doppo," *Japan Q,* 31 (1984), 159–160.

"Spring Birds"
Mortimer, Maya. "Reflexivity...," 160–163.

HAROLD SONNY LADOO

"The Quiet Peasant"
Suganasiri, Suwanda. "Reality and Symbolism in the South Asian Canadian Short Story," *World Lit Written Engl*, 26 (1986), 103.

R[APHAEL] A[LOYSIUS] LAFFERTY

"Among the Hairy Earthmen"
Morgan, Chris. "R. A. Lafferty," in Bleiler, E. F., Ed. *Supernatural Fiction Writers . . .* , II, 1047.

"The Six Fingers of Time"
Morgan, Chris. "R. A. Lafferty," 1046–1047.

"Slow Tuesday Night"
Morgan, Chris. "R. A. Lafferty," 1047.

ALEX LA GUMA

"At the Portagee's"
Abrahams, Cecil A. *Alex La Guma*, 38–40.

"Coffee for the Road"
Abrahams, Cecil A. *Alex La Guma*, 36–38.

"The Gladiators"
Abrahams, Cecil A. *Alex La Guma*, 32–33.

"A Glass of Wine"
Abrahams, Cecil A. *Alex La Guma*, 29–30.

"Late Edition"
Abrahams, Cecil A. *Alex La Guma*, 42–43.

"The Lemon Orchard"
Abrahams, Cecil A. *Alex La Guma*, 33–36.

"Nocturne" [originally titled "Étude"]
Abrahams, Cecil A. *Alex La Guma*, 25–26.

"Out of Darkness"
Abrahams, Cecil A. *Alex La Guma*, 22–25.

"Slipper Satin"
Abrahams, Cecil A. *Alex La Guma*, 30–32.

"Tattoo Marks and Nails"
Abrahams, Cecil A. *Alex La Guma*, 43–45.

"Thang's Bicycle"
Abrahams, Cecil A. *Alex La Guma,* 45.

RING LARDNER

"The Golden Honeymoon"
Rowe, Anne E. *The Idea of Florida . . . ,* 86–89.

"Haircut"
Blythe, Hal. "Lardner's 'Haircut,'" *Explicator,* 44, iii (1986), 48–49.
————, and Charlie Sweet. "The Barber of Civility: The Chief Conspirator of
    'Haircut,'" *Stud Short Fiction,* 23 (1986), 450–453.
Bohner, Charles H. *Instructor's Manual . . . ,* 70–71.
Gilead, Sarah. "Lardner's Discourses of Power," *Stud Short Fiction,* 22 (1985),
    332–333.

"The Maysville Minstrel"
Gilead, Sarah. "Lardner's Discourses . . . ," 335–337.

"Sun Cure"
Rowe, Anne E. *The Idea of Florida . . . ,* 89–90.

"Zone of Quiet"
Gilead, Sarah. "Lardner's Discourses . . . ," 333–335.

NELLA LARSEN

"Passing"
McDowell, Deborah. "Introduction," in Larsen, Nella. *"Quicksand" and "Passing,"*
    xxiii–xxxi.

"Quicksand"
McDowell, Deborah. "Introduction," xvii–xxii.

MARGARET LAURENCE

"The Drummer of All the World"
New, W. H. "The Other and I: Laurence's African Stories," in Woodcock,
    George, Ed. *A Place to Stand On . . . ,* 125–127.

"A Fetish for Love"
New, W. H. "The Other and I . . . ," 118–120.

"Godman's Master"
Kreisel, Henry. "The African Stories of Margaret Laurence," in Woodcock,
    George, Ed. *A Place to Stand On . . . ,* 106–107.

"Horses of the Night"
Middlebro, Tom. "*Imitatio Insanitatis:* Literary Madness and the Canadian Short
Story," *Canadian Lit,* 107 (1985), 189–193.

"Mask of the Bear"
Davidson, Cathy N. "Geography as Psychology in the Writings of Margaret
Laurence," in Toth, Emily, Ed. *Regionalism . . . ,* 135–136.

"The Perfume Sea"
New, W. H. "The Other and I . . . ," 120–121.

"To Set Our House in Order"
Capone, Giovanna. "*A Bird in the House:* Margaret Laurence on Order and the
Artist," in Kroetsch, Robert, and Reingard M. Nischik, Eds. *Gaining
Ground . . . ,* 161–170.

"The Tomorrow-Tamer"
New, W. H. "The Other and I . . . ," 121–125.

D. H. LAWRENCE

"The Blind Man"
Breen, Judith P. "D. H. Lawrence, World War I and the Battle Between the
Sexes: A Reading of 'The Blind Man' and 'Tickets, Please,'" in Gilbert,
Sandra M., and Susan Gubar, Eds. *The Female Imagination . . . ,* 64–65.

"The Captain's Doll"
Doherty, Gerald. "A 'Very Funny' Story: Figural Play in D. H. Lawrence's 'The
Captain's Doll,'" *D. H. Lawrence R,* 18 (1985–1986), 5–17.
Martin, W. R. "Hannele's 'Surrender': A Misreading of 'The Captain's Doll,'"
D. H. Lawrence R, 18 (1985–1986), 19–23.

"A Dream of Life"
Sagar, Keith. *D. H. Lawrence . . . ,* 315–316.

"The Fly in the Ointment"
Black, Michael. *D. H. Lawrence . . . ,* 113–114.

"The Fox"
Good, Jan. "Toward a Resolution of Gender Identity Confusion: The Relationship of Henry and March in 'The Fox,'" *D. H. Lawrence R,* 18 (1986), 217–
227.

"The Horse-Dealer's Daughter"
Bohner, Charles H. *Instructor's Manual . . . ,* 71–72.
Stewart, Jack F. "Eros and Thanatos in 'The Horse Dealer's Daughter,'" *Stud
Hum,* 12, i (1985), 11–19.

"The Ladybird" [originally titled "The Thimble"]
Gilbert, Sandra M. "Potent Griselda: 'The Ladybird' and the Great Mother," in
Balbert, Peter, and Phillip Marcus, Eds. *D. H. Lawrence . . . ,* 130–161.

Steven, Laurence. "From Thimble to Ladybird: D. H. Lawrence's Widening Vision?" *D. H. Lawrence R*, 18 (1986), 239–253.

"A Lesson on a Tortoise"
Black, Michael. *D. H. Lawrence . . .* , 113–114.

"Love Among the Haystacks"
Black, Michael. *D. H. Lawrence . . .* , 137–141.

"The Man Who Died"
Burgess, Anthony. *Flame into Being . . .* , 226–232.
Padhi, Bibhu. "Familiar and Unfamiliar Worlds: The Fabular Mode in Lawrence's Late Narratives," *Philol Q*, 64 (1985), 251–254.

"The Man Who Loved Islands"
Padhi, Bibhu. "Familiar and Unfamiliar . . . ," 248–251.
Sagar, Keith. *D. H. Lawrence . . .* , 290–291.

"A Modern Lover"
Alden, Patricia. *Social Mobility . . .* , 102–103.
Black, Michael. *D. H. Lawrence . . .* , 114–122.
Schneider, Daniel J. *The Consciousness . . .* , 39–40.

"Monkey Nuts"
Schneider, Daniel J. *The Consciousness . . .* , 135.

"New Eve and Old Adam"
Black, Michael. *D. H. Lawrence . . .* , 240–256.
Schneider, Daniel J. *The Consciousness . . .* , 110–112.

"Odour of Chrysanthemums"
Black, Michael. *D. H. Lawrence . . .* , 203–208.
Charters, Ann, William E. Sheidley, and Martha Ramsey. *Instructor's Manual . . .* , 2nd ed., 88–89.
Sagar, Keith. *D. H. Lawrence . . .* , 15–16.

"A Prelude"
Black, Michael. *D. H. Lawrence . . .* , 23–24.

"The Princess"
Schneider, Daniel J. *The Consciousness . . .* , 161–162.
Smalley, Barbara M. "Lawrence's 'The Princess' and Horney's 'Idealized Self,'" in Paris, Bernard J., Ed. *Third Force . . .* , 179–190.

"The Prussian Officer"
Anderson, Walter E. "'The Prussian Officer': Lawrence's Version of the Fall of Man Legend," *Essays Lit*, 12 (1985), 215–223.
Black, Michael. *D. H. Lawrence . . .* , 212–223.
Bohner, Charles H. *Instructor's Manual . . .* , 72–73.
Cowan, James C. "Lawrence and Touch," *D. H. Lawrence R*, 18 (1986), 121–132.
Huss, Roy. *The Mindscapes . . .* , 15–18.

Stewart, Jack. "Expressionism in 'The Prussian Officer,'" *D. H. Lawrence R*, 18 (1986), 275–289.

"The Rocking-Horse Winner"
Bohner, Charles H. *Instructor's Manual . . .* , 73–74.
Ingrasci, Hugh J. "Names as Symbolic Crowns Unifying Lawrence's 'The Rocking-Horse Winner,'" in Callary, Edward, Ed. *Festschrift . . . Virgil J. Vogel*, 1–22.
Padhi, Bibhu. "Familiar and Unfamiliar . . . ," 240–243.
Sheidley, William E., and Ann Charters. *Instructor's Manual . . .* , 83–84; rpt. Charters, Ann, William E. Sheidley, and Martha Ramsey. *Instructor's Manual . . .* , 2nd ed., 91–92.

"St. Mawr"
Fleishman, Avrom. "He Do the Polis in Different Voices: Lawrence's Later Style," in Balbert, Peter, and Phillip Marcus, Eds. *D. H. Lawrence . . .* , 169–179.
Norris, Margot. *Beasts . . .* , 170–194.
Rama Moorthy, Polanki. "'St. Mawr': The Third Eye," *Aligarh J Engl Stud*, 10 (1985), 188–204.
Sagar, Keith. *D. H. Lawrence . . .* , 246–277.
Schneider, Daniel J. *The Consciousness . . .* , 165–167.

"The Shades of Spring" [originally titled "The Soiled Rose"]
Alden, Patricia. *Social Mobility . . .* , 105–106.
Black, Michael. *D. H. Lawrence . . .* , 122–129.

"The Thorn in the Flesh"
Black, Michael. *D. H. Lawrence . . .* , 224–232.
Schneider, Daniel J. *The Consciousness . . .* , 71–72.

"Tickets, Please"
Breen, Judith P. "D. H. Lawrence, World War I . . . ," 68–72.

"The White Stocking"
Black, Michael. *D. H. Lawrence . . .* , 233–241.

"The Witch à la Mode"
Black, Michael. *D. H. Lawrence . . .* , 129–136.

"The Woman Who Rode Away"
Balbert, Peter. "Snake's Eyes and Obsidian Knife: Art, Ideology, and 'The Woman Who Rode Away,'" *D. H. Lawrence R*, 18 (1986), 255–273.
Padhi, Bibhu. "Familiar and Unfamiliar . . . ," 246–248.
Schneider, Daniel J. *The Consciousness . . .* , 163–164.

HENRY LAWSON

"Ah Soon"
Bennett, Bruce. "Asian Encounters in the Contemporary Australian Short Story," *World Lit Written Engl*, 26 (1986), 52.

"The Bush Undertaker"
Wieland, James. "Australian Literature and the Question of Historical Method: Reading Lawson and Furphy," *J Commonwealth Lit*, 20, i (1985), 27–29.

"The Drover's Wife"
Harrex, S. C., and Guy Amirthanayagam. "Introduction: Notes Towards a Comparative Cross-Cultural Criticism," in Amirthanayagam, Guy, and S. C. Harrex, Eds. *Only Connect...*, 1–29.

"The Loaded Dog"
Lawson, Alan. "The Framing of 'The Loaded Dog': The Story, Source, and Tradition," *Quadrant*, 29, v (1985), 63–65.

"Rats"
Wieland, James. "Australian Literature...," 22–23.

STEPHEN LEACOCK

"The Conjurer's Revenge"
Hughes, Kenneth J. *Signs of Literature...*, 179–186.

"L'Envoi: The Train to Mariposa"
El-Hassan, Karla. "Reflections on the Special Unity of Stephen Leacock's *Sunshine Sketches of a Little Town*," in Kroetsch, Robert, and Reingard M. Nischik, Eds. *Gaining Ground...*, 176–178.

JOHN LE CARRÉ [DAVID JOHN MOORE CORNWELL]

"Dare I Weep, Dare I Mourn?"
Lewis, Peter. *John Le Carré*, 111.

"What Ritual Is Being Observed Tonight?"
Lewis, Peter. *John Le Carré*, 111–112.

VERNON LEE [VIOLET PAGET]

"Amour Dure"
Clute, John. "Vernon Lee," in Bleiler, E. F., Ed. *Supernatural Fiction Writers...*, I, 332–333.

"Dionea"
Clute, John. "Vernon Lee," 333.

"Oke of Okehurst"
Clute, John. "Vernon Lee," 331–332.

"Prince Alberic and the Snake Lady"
Clute, John. "Vernon Lee," 333–334.

"A Wicked Voice"
Clute, John. "Vernon Lee," 333.

JOSEPH SHERIDAN LE FANU

"An Account of Some Strange Disturbances in Aungier Street"
Campbell, James L. "J. S. Le Fanu," in Bleiler, E. F., Ed. *Supernatural Fiction Writers* . . . , I, 224.

"Carmilla"
Barclay, Glen St. John. *Anatomy of Horror* . . . , 34–38.
Campbell, James L. "J. S. Le Fanu," 228–229.
Day, William P. *In the Circles* . . . , 86–89.
Foust, Ronald. "Rite of Passage: The Vampire Tale as Cosmogonic Myth," in Coyle, William, Ed. *Aspects of Fantasy* . . . , 75–76.
Orel, Harold. " 'Rigid Adherence to Facts': Le Fanu's *In a Glass Darkly*," *Éire*, 20, iv (1985), 85–87; rpt. in his *The Victorian Short Story* . . . , 49–52.

"A Chapter in the History of the Tyrone Family"
Orel, Harold. " 'Rigid Adherence . . . ,' " 68–69.

"The Dead Sexton"
Campbell, James L. "J. S. Le Fanu," 227.

"The Drunkard's Dream"
Campbell, James L. "J. S. Le Fanu," 221–222.

"The Fortunes of Sir Robert Ardagh"
Campbell, James L. "J. S. Le Fanu," 221.

"Green Tea"
Campbell, James L. "J. S. Le Fanu," 228.
Orel, Harold. " 'Rigid Adherence . . . ,' " 79–83; rpt. in his *The Victorian Short Story* . . . , 44–48.

"The Haunted Baronet"
Campbell, James L. "J. S. Le Fanu," 227–228.

"Madam Crowl's Ghost"
Campbell, James L. "J. S. Le Fanu," 226.

"Mr. Justice Harbottle"
Orel, Harold. " 'Rigid Adherence . . . ,' " 77–79.

"The Mysterious Lodge"
Campbell, James L. "J. S. Le Fanu," 223.

"The Room in the Dragon Volant"
Orel, Harold. " 'Rigid Adherence . . . ,' " 83–85; rpt. in his *The Victorian Short Story* . . . , 48–49.

"Sir Dominick's Bargain"
Campbell, James L. "J. S. Le Fanu," 227.

"Squire Toby's Will"
Campbell, James L. "J. S. Le Fanu," 226.

"Strange Event in the Life of Schalken the Painter"
Campbell, James L. "J. S. Le Fanu," 222.

"The Watcher"
Campbell, James L. "J. S. Le Fanu," 223–224.
Orel, Harold. "'Rigid Adherence . . . ,'" 72–77; rpt. in his *The Victorian Short Story . . .* , 38–42.

"The White Cat of Drumgunniol"
Campbell, James L. "J. S. Le Fanu," 226.

URSULA K. LE GUIN

"An die Musik"
Bittner, James W. "Persuading Us to Rejoice and Teaching Us How to Praise: Le Guin's 'Orsinian Tales,'" *Sci-Fiction Stud*, 5 (1978), 229–235; rpt. Bloom, Harold, Ed. *Ursula K. Le Guin*, 135–143.

"April in Paris"
Spivack, Charlotte. *Ursula K. Le Guin*, 94–95.

"The Author of the Acacia Seeds"
Spivack, Charlotte. *Ursula K. Le Guin*, 144.

"The Barrow"
Spivack, Charlotte. *Ursula K. Le Guin*, 102–103.

"The Child and the Shadow"
Spivack, Charlotte. *Ursula K. Le Guin*, 128.

"The Darkness Box"
Spivack, Charlotte. *Ursula K. Le Guin*, 95.

"The Day Before the Revolution"
Spivack, Charlotte. *Ursula K. Le Guin*, 84–85.

"The Diary of the Rose"
Spivack, Charlotte. *Ursula K. Le Guin*, 145–147.

"The Dowry of Angyar"
Bittner, James W. *Approaches . . .* , 91–93.

"The Eye Altering"
Spivack, Charlotte. *Ursula K. Le Guin*, 148–149.

"Field of Vision"
Spivack, Charlotte. *Ursula K. Le Guin,* 98–99.

"The Good Trip"
Spivack, Charlotte. *Ursula K. Le Guin,* 99–100.

"The House"
Spivack, Charlotte. *Ursula K. Le Guin,* 104–105.

"Imaginary Countries"
Bittner, James W. "Persuading Us . . . ," 225–229; rpt. in his *Approaches . . . ,*
    41–45; Bloom, Harold, Ed. *Ursula K. Le Guin,* 132–133.
Spivack, Charlotte. *Ursula K. Le Guin,* 101–102.

"The Lady of Moge"
Spivack, Charlotte. *Ursula K. Le Guin,* 102.

"The New Atlantis"
Spivack, Charlotte. *Ursula K. Le Guin,* 87–92.

"Nine Lives"
Spivack, Charlotte. *Ursula K. Le Guin,* 96.

"The Ones Who Walk Away from Omelas"
Bohner, Charles H. *Instructor's Manual . . . ,* 74–75.

"The Road East"
Spivack, Charlotte. *Ursula K. Le Guin,* 104.

"The Rule of Names"
Bittner, James W. *Approaches . . . ,* 60–62.

"Selection"
Spivack, Charlotte. *Ursula K. Le Guin,* 145.

"Semley's Necklace"
Bittner, James W. *Approaches . . . ,* 63–66.
Samuelson, David. "Ursula K. Le Guin," in Bleiler, E. F., Ed. *Supernatural Fiction
    Writers . . . ,* II, 1062.

"The Stars Beyond"
Spivack, Charlotte. *Ursula K. Le Guin,* 97–98.

"Vaster Than Empires and More Slow"
Spivack, Charlotte. *Ursula K. Le Guin,* 71–72.
Watson, Ian. "The Forest as Metaphor for Mind: 'The Word for World Is *Forest*'
    and 'Vaster Than Empires and More Slow,'" *Sci-Fiction Stud,* 2 (1975), 232–
    236; rpt. Bloom, Harold, Ed. *Ursula K. Le Guin,* 52–55.

"Winter's King"
Bittner, James W. *Approaches . . . ,* 103–109.
Spivack, Charlotte. *Ursula K. Le Guin,* 48–50.

"The Word for World is *Forest*"
Watson, Ian. "The Forest as Metaphor . . . ," 231–232; rpt. Bloom, Harold, Ed.
   Ursula K. Le Guin, 47–50.

"The Word of Unbinding"
Bittner, James W. *Approaches* . . . , 58–59.

FRITZ LEIBER

"Adept's Gambit"
Stableford, Brian M. "Fritz Leiber," in Bleiler, E. F., Ed. *Supernatural Fiction
   Writers* . . . , II, 936.

"Lean Times in Lankhmar"
Stableford, Brian M. "Fritz Leiber," 936.

"The Lords of Quarmall"
Stableford, Brian M. "Fritz Leiber," 936–937.

"The Man Who Never Grew Young"
O'Donohue, Nick. "Condemned to Life: 'The Mortal Immortal' and 'The Man
   Who Never Grew Young,'" in Yoke, Carl B., and Donald M. Hassler, Eds.
   Death and the Serpent . . . , 83–90.

"Scylla's Daughter"
Stableford, Brian M. "Fritz Leiber," 936.

"The Snow Women"
Stableford, Brian M. "Fritz Leiber," 937.

"You're All Alone"
Stableford, Brian M. "Fritz Leiber," 934.

STANISLAW LEM

"The Mask"
Philmus, Robert M. "The Cybernetic Paradigms of Stanislaw Lem," in Slusser,
   George E., and Eric S. Rabkin, Eds. *Hard Science Fiction*, 183–184.

"Professor A. Donda"
Jarzebski, Jerzy. "Stanislaw Lem's 'Star Diaries,'" *Sci-Fiction Stud*, 13 (1986), 369.

"Professor Corcoran"
Jarzebski, Jerzy. ". . . 'Star Diaries,'" 365–366.

"Rien du tout, ou la consequence"
Philmus, Robert M. "The Cybernetic Paradigms . . . ," 211–212.

"The Washing Machine Tragedy"
Jarzebski, Jerzy. ". . . 'Star Diaries,'" 363–364.

NIKOLAI LESKOV

"The Battle-Axe"
Moser, Charles A. *The Russian Short Story* . . . , 99–100.

"Iron Will"
Moser, Charles A. *The Russian Short Story* . . . , 101–102.

"The Sealed Angel"
Moser, Charles A. *The Russian Short Story* . . . , 100–101.

DORIS LESSING

"The Antheap"
Knapp, Mona. *Doris Lessing,* 33–34.

"Each Other"
Sprague, Claire. "The Politics of Sibling Incest in Doris Lessing's 'Each Other,'"
    San José Stud, 11, ii (1985), 42–49.

"The Eye of God in Paradise"
Knapp, Mona. *Doris Lessing,* 81–83.

"Flavours of Exile"
Allen, Orphia J. "Interpreting 'Flavours of Exile,'" *Doris Lessing Newsletter,* 7, i
    (1983), 8, 12.

"Getting Off the Altitude"
Knapp, Mona. *Doris Lessing,* 31–32.

"The Old Chief Mshlanga"
Baldwin, Dean. "The English Short Story in the Fifties," in Vannatta, Dennis,
    Ed. *The English Short Story, 1945–1980,* 59.
Smith, Angela. "In a Divided Mind," *Doris Lessing Newsletter,* 8, i (1984), 3–4,
    14.

"An Old Woman and Her Cat"
Knapp, Mona. *Doris Lessing,* 83–84.

"One Off the Short List"
Bohner, Charles H. *Instructor's Manual* . . . , 75–76.
Knapp, Mona. *Doris Lessing,* 77–78.
Pickering, Jean. "The English Short Story in the Sixties," in Vannatta, Dennis,
    Ed. *The English Short Story, 1945–1980,* 92.

"The Pig"
Hanson, Clare. "The Woman Writer as Exile: Gender and Possession in the
    African Stories of Doris Lessing," in Sprague, Claire, and Virginia Tiger,
    Eds. *Critical Essays* . . . , 109–112.

"The Second Hut"
Knapp, Mona. *Doris Lessing,* 30—31.

"The Story of a Non-Marrying Man"
Evans, Walter. "The English Short Story in the Seventies," in Vannatta, Dennis,
Ed. *The English Short Story, 1945–1980,* 126.

"Sunrise on the Veld"
Knapp, Mona. *Doris Lessing,* 34–35.

"The Temptation of Jack Orkney"
Knapp, Mona. *Doris Lessing,* 80–81.

"To Room Nineteen"
Bohner, Charles H. *Instructor's Manual . . . ,* 76–77.
Knapp, Mona. *Doris Lessing,* 78–81.
Sheidley, William E., and Ann Charters. *Instructor's Manual . . . ,* 148; rpt. Char-
ters, Ann, William E. Sheidley, and Martha Ramsey. *Instructor's Man-
ual . . . ,* 2nd ed., 154.

"The Trinket Box"
Hanson, Clare. "The Woman Writer as Exile . . . ," 112–113.

MERIDEL LE SUEUR

"Corn Village"
Fairbanks, Carol. *Prairie Women . . . ,* 223–224.

"Salute to Spring"
Fairbanks, Carol. *Prairie Women . . . ,* 224–225.

NORMAN LEVINE

"A Canadian Upbringing"
Minni, C. D. "The Short Story as an Ethnic Genre," in Pivato, Joseph, Ed.
Contrasts . . . , 70.

WYNDHAM LEWIS

"Cantleman's Spring Mate"
Materer, Timothy. "Wyndham Lewis the Soldier," in Cooney, Seamus, Bradford
Morrow, Bernard Lafourcade, and Hugh Kenner, Eds. *Blast 3,* 201–204.

"Creativity"
Lafourcade, Bernard. "Creativity en familie: A Study in Genetic Manipula-
tions," in Cooney, Seamus, Bradford Morrow, Bernard Lafourcade, and
Hugh Kenner, Eds. *Blast 3,* 201–204.

LEE KOK LIANG

"Return to Malaya"
Gooneratne, Yasmine. "Lloyd Fernando's *Twenty-Two Malaysian Stories*," in Goodwin, K. L., Ed. *Commonwealth Literature* . . . , 121–122.

ENRIQUE LIHN

"Huancho y Pochocha"
Hahn, Oscar. "Los efectos de irrealidad en un cuento de Enrique Lihn," *Revista Chilena de Literatura*, 22 (1983), 93–104.

JAKOV LIND

"Soul of Wood"
Rollfinke, Dieter and Jacqueline. *The Call of Human Nature* . . . , 123–127.

PAUL MYRON ANTHONY LINEBARGER
[pseudonym CORDWAINER SMITH]

"The Lady Who Sailed the Soul"
Suvin, Darko. "Science-Fiction: Metaphor, Parable and Chronotope," in Vos, Luk de, Ed. *Just the Other Day* . . . , 81–99.

ERIC LINKLATER

"The Abominable Imprecation of Shepherd Alken"
Parnell, Michael. *Eric Linklater* . . . , 184–185.

"Country-Born"
Parnell, Michael. *Eric Linklater* . . . , 179.

"The Crusader's Key"
Parnell, Michael. *Eric Linklater* . . . , 184.

"The Dancers"
Parnell, Michael. *Eric Linklater* . . . , 183.

"The Duke"
Parnell, Michael. *Eric Linklater* . . . , 181.

"Escape Forever"
Baldwin, Dean. "The English Short Story in the Fifties," in Vannatta, Dennis, Ed. *The English Short Story, 1945–1980*, 49.

"God Likes Them Plain"
Parnell, Michael. *Eric Linklater* . . . , 185–186.

"The Goose Girl"
Parnell, Michael. *Eric Linklater...*, 260–261.

"His Majesty the Dentist"
Parnell, Michael. *Eric Linklater...*, 182.

"Kind Kitty"
Parnell, Michael. *Eric Linklater...*, 183–184.

"The Masks of Purpose"
Baldwin, Dean. "The English Short Story...," 49–50.

"The Redundant Miracle"
Parnell, Michael. *Eric Linklater...*, 184–185.

"A Sociable Plover"
Parnell, Michael. *Eric Linklater...*, 303–306.

CLARICE LISPECTOR

"The Buffalo"
Fitz, Earl E. *Clarice Lispector,* 106–107.

"The Crime of the Mathematics Professor"
Anderson, Robert K. "Myth and Existentialism in Clarice Lispector's 'O Crime do Professor de Matemática,'" *Luso-Brazilian R,* 22, i (1985), 1–7.
DiAntonio, Robert E. "Myth as a Unifying Force in 'O Crime do Professor de Matemática,'" *Luso-Brazilian R,* 22, i (1985), 27–32.
Fitz, Earl E. *Clarice Lispector,* 105–106.

"Family Ties"
Fitz, Earl E. *Clarice Lispector,* 104–105.

"The Fifth Story"
Fitz, Earl E. *Clarice Lispector,* 108–109.

"Love"
Fitz, Earl E. *Clarice Lispector,* 97–105.

"Miss Ruth Algrave"
Fitz, Earl E. *Clarice Lispector,* 113–114.

LIU XINWU

"Black Wall"
Barme, Geremie. "'Black Wall,'" *Rendezvous* (China), 23 (Spring, 1985), 40–41.

"The Class Teacher" [same as "Class Counsellor"]
Duke, Michael S. *Blooming...*, 65–66.

SYLVIA LIZÁRRAGO

"El Don"
Sánchez, Rosauro. "Chicana Prose Writers: The Case of Gina Valdés and Sylvia
Lizárrago," in Herrera-Sobek, María, Ed. *Beyond Stereotypes* . . . , 69.

"Quinceañera"
Sánchez, Rosauro. "Chicana Prose Writers . . . ," 68–69.

TABAN LO LIYONG

"The Uniform Man"
Schulze, Frank. "Taban Lo Liyong's Short Stories: A Western Form of Art?"
World Lit Written Engl, 26 (1986), 230.

JACK LONDON

"The Call of the Wild"
Reed, A. Paul. "Running with the Pack: Jack London's 'The Call of the Wild'
and Jesse Stuart's *Mongrel Mettle*," *Jack London Newsletter*, 18, iii (1985), 94–
98.

"Chris Farrington, Able Seaman"
Perry, John. *Jack London* . . . , 32–34.

"Diable, A Dog"
Perry, John. *Jack London* . . . , 131–132.

"Kanaka Surf"
Perry, John. *Jack London* . . . , 287.

"The Red One"
Peterson, Per Serritslev. "Science-Fictionalizing the Paradox of Living: Jack
London's 'The Red One' and the Ecstasy of Regression," in Johansen, Ib,
and Peter Ronnon-Jessen, Eds. *Inventing the Future* . . . , 38–58.

"To Build a Fire"
Bohner, Charles H. *Instructor's Manual* . . . , 77–78.
Mitchell, Lee C. "'Keeping His Head': Repetition and Responsibility in Lon-
don's 'To Build a Fire,'" *J Mod Lit*, 13 (1986), 76–96.
Sheidley, William E., and Ann Charters. *Instructor's Manual* . . . , 60–61; rpt.
Charters, Ann, William E. Sheidley, and Martha Ramsey. *Instructor's Man-
ual* . . . , 2nd ed., 62–63.

FRANK BELKNAP LONG

"The Black Druid"
Daniels, Les. "Frank Belknap Long," in Bleiler, E. F., Ed. *Supernatural Fiction
Writers* . . . , II, 870–871.

"Dark Vision"
Daniels, Les. "Frank Belknap Long," 872.

"Second Night Out" [originally titled "The Black Dead Thing"]
Daniels, Les. "Frank Belknap Long," 871.

JESÚS LÓPEZ PACHECO

"Lucha contra el murciélago"
Sarfati-Arnaud, Monique. "El estilo circular en 'Lucha contra el murciélago' de
    Jesús López Pacheco," *Revista Canadiense de Estudios Hispánicos*, 10 (1985),
    133–140.

"Lucha por la respiración"
Rubio, Isaac. "'Lucha por la respiración' de Jesús López Pacheco," *Revista Cana-
    diense de Estudios Hispánicos*, 10 (1985), 121–131.

H. P. LOVECRAFT

"The Call of Cthulhu"
Barclay, Glen St. John. *Anatomy of Horror. . .* , 86–87.

"The Dunwich Horror"
Burleson, Donald R. "H. P. Lovecraft," in Bleiler, E. F., Ed. *Supernatural Fiction
    Writers . . .* , II, 856.
McInnis, John. "H. P. Lovecraft's Immortal Culture," in Yoke, Carl B., and
    Donald M. Hassler, Eds. *Death and the Serpent . . .* , 125–134.

SAMUEL LOVER

"Barney O'Reirdon"
Sloan, Barry. *The Pioneers . . .* , 177–178.

"The Burial of the Tithe"
Sloan, Barry. *The Pioneers . . .* , 178–179.

LU XINHUA

"The Wound"
Duke, Michael S. *Blooming . . .* , 64–65.

LU XUN [LU HSÜN or CHOU SHU-JEN]

"In the Wineshop"
Anderson, Marston. "The Morality of Form: Lu Xun and the Modern Chinese
    Short Story," in Lee, Leo Ou-fan, Ed. *Lu Xun . . .* , 42.

"New Year's Sacrifice"
Anderson, Marston. "The Morality of Form . . . ," 41–42.

"The True Story of Ah Q"
Lee, Leo Ou-fan. "Tradition and Modernity in the Writings of Lu Xun," in
Lee, Leo Ou-fan, Ed. *Lu Xun . . .* , 10.

LEOPOLDO LUGONES

"La lluvia de fuego"
Aguilar, Nadine M. de. "L'Homme face aux 'forces étranges' chez Poe et Lu-
gones," in Balakian, Anna, *et al.*, Eds. *Proceedings . . .* , III, 201–207.

"The Pillar of Salt"
Semilla, Maria A. "La organización narrativa de 'La estatua de sal,'" in Flores,
Angel, Ed. *El realismo . . .* , 86–98.

"Yzur"
Flores, Angel. "Antecedentes de 'Yzur,'" in Flores, Angel, Ed. *El realismo . . .* ,
54–58.

MARY McCARTHY

"The Man in the Brooks Brothers Suit"
Shinn, Thelma J. *Radiant Daughters . . .* , 91.

NELLIE McCLUNG

"The Way of the West"
Fairbanks, Carol. *Prairie Women . . .* , 194–195.

CARSON McCULLERS

"The Ballad of the Sad Café"
Dazey, Mary Ann. "Two Voices of the Single Narrator in 'The Ballad of the
Sad Café,'" *Southern Lit J*, 17, ii (1985), 33–40.
Kahane, Claire. "The Gothic Mirror," in Garner, Shirley N., Claire Kahane,
and Madelon Sprengnether, Eds. *The (M)other Tongue . . .* , 347–348.
Westling, Louise. *Sacred Groves . . .* , 122–126.

"Like That"
White, Barbara A. *Growing Up Female . . .* , 103–104.

"A Tree, A Rock, A Cloud"
Bohner, Charles H. *Instructor's Manual . . .* , 78–79.

ANSON MacDONALD [ROBERT HEINLEIN]

"Solution Unsatisfactory"
Berger, Albert I. *"Analog Science Fiction/Science Fact,"* in Tymn, Marshall B., and
  Mike Ashley, Eds. *Science Fiction . . . Magazines,* 72.

GEORGE MacDONALD

"The Golden Key"
Wolfe, Gary K. "George MacDonald," in Bleiler, E. F., Ed. *Supernatural Fiction
  Writers . . . ,* I, 242–243.

JOHN D. MacDONALD

"Interlude in India"
Hirshberg, Edgar W. *John D. MacDonald,* 11–12.

"Spectator Sport"
Hirshberg, Edgar W. *John D. MacDonald,* 38–39.

IAN McEWAN

"Dead As They Come"
Evans, Walter. "The English Short Story in the Seventies," in Vannatta, Dennis,
  Ed. *The English Short Story, 1945–1980,* 142.

"Disguise"
Evans, Walter. "The English Short Story . . . ," 141–142.
Hanson, Clare. *Short Stories . . . ,* 161–163.

"Homemade"
Evans, Walter. "The English Short Story . . . ," 140–141.

"Reflections of a Kept Ape"
Hanson, Clare. *Short Stories . . . ,* 163–164.

"Solid Geometry"
Hanson, Clare. *Short Stories . . . ,* 160–161.

GWENDOLYN MacEWEN

"The House of the Whale"
Minni, C. D. "The Short Story as an Ethnic Genre," in Pivato, Joseph, Ed.
  Contrasts . . . , 72–73.

ARTHUR MACHEN

"A Fragment of Life"
Bleiler, E. F. "Arthur Machen," in Bleiler, E. F., Ed. *Supernatural Fiction Writers . . .* , I, 355–356.

"The Great God Pan"
Bleiler, E. F. "Arthur Machen," 352–353.

"Novel of the Black Seal"
Bleiler, E. F. "Arthur Machen," 353.

"Novel of the White Powder"
Bleiler, E. F. "Arthur Machen," 353.

HUGH MacLENNAN

"So All Their Praises"
MacLulich, T. D. *Hugh MacLennan,* 17–22.

FIONA MACLEOD [WILLIAM SHARP]

"The Harping of Cravetheen"
Morgan, Chris. "Fiona Macleod," in Bleiler, E. F., Ed. *Supernatural Fiction Writers . . .* , I, 371.

"Honey of the Wild Bee"
Morgan, Chris. "Fiona Macleod," 371.

JAMES ALAN McPHERSON

"Elbow Room"
Byerman, Keith E. *Fingering the Jagged Grain . . .* , 62–66.

"The Faithful"
Domnarski, William. "The Voices of Misery and Despair in the Fiction of James Alan McPherson," *Arizona Q,* 42 (1986), 41–42.

"Gold Coast"
Byerman, Keith E. *Fingering the Jagged Grain . . .* , 51–55.

"A Loaf of Bread"
Domnarski, William. "The Voices . . . ," 42.

"A Matter of Vocabulary"
Byerman, Keith E. *Fingering the Jagged Grain . . .* , 42–47.
Domnarski, William. "The Voices . . . ," 38.

"Of Cabbages and Kings"
Domnarski, William. "The Voices . . . ," 41.

"On Trains"
Domnarski, William. "The Voices . . . ," 38–39.

"A Sense of Story"
Domnarski, William. "The Voices . . . ," 39–40.
Sheffey, Ruth T. "Antaeus Revisited: James A. McPherson and *Elbow Room*," in
   Hollis, Burney J., Ed. *Amid Visions* . . . , 129–130.

"The Silver Bullet"
Domnarski, William. "The Voices . . . ," 42.

"A Solo Song: For Doc"
Byerman, Keith E. *Fingering the Jagged Grain* . . . , 47–51.

"The Story of a Dead Man"
Byerman, Keith E. *Fingering the Jagged Grain* . . . , 55–59.
Sheffey, Ruth T. "Antaeus Revisited . . . ," 129–130.

"The Story of a Scar"
Byerman, Keith E. *Fingering the Jagged Grain* . . . , 59–62.
Domnarski, William. "The Voices . . . ," 40–41.

"Why I Like Country Music"
Sheffey, Ruth T. "Antaeus Revisited . . . ," 123–125.

NORMAN MAILER

"The Last Night"
Klinkowitz, Jerome. *The American 1960s* . . . , 11–12.

BERNARD MALAMUD

"The Bill"
Mortara di Veroli, Elèna. "Italian-Americans and Jews in Bernard Malamud's
   Fiction," *Revista di Studi Anglo-Americani*, 3, iv–v (1984–85), 198–199.

"The Cost of Living"
Mortara di Veroli, Elèna. "Italian-Americans and Jews . . . ," 199–200.

"The Death of Me"
Mortara di Veroli, Elèna. "Italian-Americans and Jews . . . ," 200–201.

"The German Refugee"
Berger, Alan L. *Crisis and Covenant* . . . , 95–96.

"Glass Blower of Vienna"
Malin, Irving. "Portrait of the Artist in Slapstick: Malamud's *Picture of Fidel-
   man*," *Lit R*, 24, i (1980), 136–138.

"Idiots First"
Gealy, Marcia. "Malamud's Short Stories: A Reshaping of Hasidic Tradition,"
    Judaism, 28, i (1979), 56–57.

"The Jewbird"
Gealy, Marcia. "Malamud's Short Stories . . . ," 57–58.
Gerlach, John. *Toward the End . . .* , 12–13.

"The Lady of the Lake"
Berger, Alan L. *Crisis and Covenant . . .* , 94–95.

"The Last Mohican"
Gealy, Marcia. "Malamud's Short Stories . . . ," 52–53.
Malin, Irving. "Portrait of the Artist . . . ," 121–126.

"The Magic Barrel"
Bohner, Charles H. *Instructor's Manual . . .* , 79–80.
Gealy, Marcia. "Malamud's Short Stories . . . ," 52–56.
Gerlach, John. *Toward the End . . .* , 128–130.
May, Charles E. "Something Fishy in 'The Magic Barrel,'" *Stud Am Fiction*, 14
    (1986), 93–98.

"Naked Nude"
Malin, Irving. "Portrait of the Artist . . . ," 130–132.

"A Pimp's Revenge"
Friedman, Edward H. "The Paradox of the Art Metaphor in Bernard Mala-
    mud's 'The Pimp's Revenge,'" *Notes Contemp Lit*, 9, ii (1979), 7–8.
Malin, Irving. "Portrait of the Artist . . . ," 132–136.

"The Silver Crown"
Gealy, Marcia. "Malamud's Short Stories . . . ," 59–60.

"Still Life"
Malin, Irving. "Portrait of the Artist . . . ," 126–130.

"Take Pity"
Salzberg, Joel. "Irremediable Suffering: A Reading of Malamud's 'Take Pity,'"
    Stud Short Fiction, 23 (1986), 19–24.

THOMAS MANN

"At the Prophet's"
McWilliams, James R. *Brother Artist . . .* , 115–118.

"The Black Swan"
McWilliams, James R. *Brother Artist . . .* , 363–370.
Meyers, Jeffrey. *Disease . . .* , 83–92.

"Blood of the Walsungs"
Kraske, Bernd M. "Thomas Manns 'Walsungenblut'—eine antisemitische No-
velle?" in Wolff, Rudolf, Ed. *Thomas Mann* . . . , 42–66.
McWilliams, James R. *Brother Artist* . . . , 120–128.

"Death"
McWilliams, James R. *Brother Artist* . . . , 78–80.

"Death in Venice"
Berman, Russell A. *The Rise of the Modern German Novel* . . . , 263–265.
Frank, Bernhard. "Mann's 'Death in Venice,'" *Explicator*, 45, i (1986), 31–32.
Gockel, Heinz. "Aschenbachs Tod in Venedig," in Wolff, Rudolf, Ed. *Thomas
Mann* . . . , 27–41.
Jofen, Jean. "A Freudian Commentary on Thomas Mann's 'Death in Venice,'"
J Evolutionary Psych, 6 (1985), 238–247.
Lubich, Frederick A. "Die Entfaltung der Dialektik von Logos und Eros in
Thomas Manns 'Tod in Venedig,'" *Colloquia Germanica*, 18 (1985), 140–
159.
McWilliams, James R. *Brother Artist* . . . , 147–158.

"The Dilettante" [same as "The Clown"]
McWilliams, James R. *Brother Artist* . . . , 80–82.

"Disillusionment"
McWilliams, James R. *Brother Artist* . . . , 72–74.

"Disorder and Early Sorrow"
McWilliams, James R. *Brother Artist* . . . , 194–198.

"Fallen"
McWilliams, James R. *Brother Artist* . . . , 68–72.

"The Fight Between Jappe and Do Escobar"
McWilliams, James R. *Brother Artist* . . . , 140–146.

"Gladius Dei"
McWilliams, James R. *Brother Artist* . . . , 52–54.

"A Gleam"
McWilliams, James R. *Brother Artist* . . . , 111–115.

"The Hungry"
McWilliams, James R. *Brother Artist* . . . , 94–96.

"The Infant Prodigy"
McWilliams, James R. *Brother Artist* . . . , 108–111.

"Little Herr Friedemann"
Bohner, Klaus. "Ein literarisches 'Muster' für Thomas Mann: J. P. Jacobsens
'Niels Lyhne' und 'Der kleine Friedemann,'" Goffin, Roger, Michel Van-
helleputte, and Monique Weyembergh-Boussart, Eds. *Littérature et cul-
ture* . . . , 197–215.
McWilliams, James R. *Brother Artist* . . . , 60–63.

"Little Lizzy"
McWilliams, James R. *Brother Artist . . .* , 74–76.

"A Man and His Dog"
McWilliams, James R. *Brother Artist . . .* , 184–193.
Rollfinke, Dieter and Jacqueline. *The Call of Human Nature . . .* , 70–76.

"Mario and the Magician"
Berman, Russell A. *The Rise of the Modern German Novel . . .* , 265–266.
Leneaux, Grant F. " 'Mario und der Zauberer': The Narration of Seduction or the Seduction of Narration?" *Orbis Litterarum,* 40 (1985), 327–347.
Lunn, Eugene. "Tales of Liberal Disquiet: Mann's 'Mario and the Magician' and Interpretations of Fascism," *Lit & Hist,* 11 (1985), 77–100.
McWilliams, James R. *Brother Artist . . .* , 241–247.
Meyers, Jeffrey. "Caligari and Cipolla: Mann's 'Mario and the Magician,'" *Mod Fiction Stud,* 32 (1986), 235–239.

"Railway Accident"
McWilliams, James R. *Brother Artist . . .* , 130–132.

"Revenge"
McWilliams, James R. *Brother Artist . . .* , 63–64.

"The Tables of the Law"
McWilliams, James R. *Brother Artist . . .* , 302–311.

"Tobias Mindernickel"
McWilliams, James R. *Brother Artist . . .* , 66–68.

"Tonio Kröger"
Fleissner, R. F. "The Balking Staircase and the Transparent Door: Prufrock and Kröger," *Comparatist,* 8 (1984), 21–32.
McWilliams, James R. *Brother Artist . . .* , 96–108.

"The Transposed Heads"
McWilliams, James R. *Brother Artist . . .* , 294–302.
Schulz, K. Lydia. "Thomas Manns Altersironie: *Etad vai tad* oder 'Die vertauschten Köpfe,'" *Selecta,* 5 (1984), 74–78.

"Tristan"
McWilliams, James R. *Brother Artist . . .* , 82–89.

"The Wardrobe"
McWilliams, James R. *Brother Artist . . .* , 76–78.

"The Way to the Churchyard" [same as "The Way to the Cemetery"]
McWilliams, James R. *Brother Artist . . .* , 57–60.

"A Weary Hour"
McWilliams, James R. *Brother Artist . . .* , 119–120.

"The Will to Happiness"
McWilliams, James R. *Brother Artist* . . . , 64–66.

KATHERINE MANSFIELD [KATHERINE BEAUCHAMP]

"An Advanced Lady"
Fullbrook, Kate. *Katherine Mansfield*, 60–61.

"At Lehmann's"
Fullbrook, Kate. *Katherine Mansfield*, 57–58.

"At the Bay"
Fullbrook, Kate. *Katherine Mansfield*, 106–114.
Stead, C. K. *In the Glass Case* . . . , 38–39.

"A Birthday"
Flora, Joseph M. *The English Short Story* . . . , 65–66.
Fullbrook, Kate. *Katherine Mansfield*, 58–60.

"Bliss"
Fullbrook, Kate. *Katherine Mansfield*, 95–102.
Sheidley, William E., and Ann Charters. *Instructor's Manual* . . . , 88–89; rpt.
    Charters, Ann, William E. Sheidley, and Martha Ramsey. *Instructor's Manual* . . . , 2nd ed., 94.

"The Child-Who-Was-Tired"
Fullbrook, Kate. *Katherine Mansfield*, 38–41.

"The Daughters of the Late Colonel"
Fullbrook, Kate. *Katherine Mansfield*, 124–126.

"A Dill Pickle"
Bohner, Charles H. *Instructor's Manual* . . . , 80–81.

"The Doll's House"
Fullbrook, Kate. *Katherine Mansfield*, 114–117.
Sheidley, William E., and Ann Charters. *Instructor's Manual* . . . , 90–91; rpt.
    Charters, Ann, William E. Sheidley, and Martha Ramsey. *Instructor's Manual* . . . , 2nd ed., 96.

"The Escape"
Hanson, Clare. *Short Stories* . . . , 78–81.

"Frau Brechenmacher Attends a Wedding"
Fullbrook, Kate. *Katherine Mansfield*, 53–57.

"The Garden Party"
Flora, Joseph M. *The English Short Story* . . . , 73–74.
Fullbrook, Kate. *Katherine Mansfield*, 117–123.

"Her First Ball"
Bohner, Charles H. *Instructor's Manual . . .* , 82.

"How Pearl Buttons Was Kidnapped"
Fullbrook, Kate. *Katherine Mansfield*, 41–42.

"Je ne parle pas français"
Fullbrook, Kate. *Katherine Mansfield*, 89–95.
Stead, C. K. *In the Glass Case . . .* , 41–42.

"The Life of Ma Parker"
Fullbrook, Kate. *Katherine Mansfield*, 126–127.

"The Little Girl"
Flora, Joseph M. *The English Short Story . . .* , 67–68.

"A Married Man's Story"
Stead, C. K. *In the Glass Case . . .* , 43–45.

"Miss Brill"
Bohner, Charles H. *Instructor's Manual . . .* , 82–83.
Fullbrook, Kate. *Katherine Mansfield*, 103–106.

"New Dresses"
Fullbrook, Kate. *Katherine Mansfield*, 44–49.

"Prelude"
Flora, Joseph M. *The English Short Story . . .* , 68–69.
Fullbrook, Kate. *Katherine Mansfield*, 63–85.

"The Tiredness of Rosabel"
Fullbrook, Kate. *Katherine Mansfield*, 36–41.

MAO TUN [same as MAO TUNG and MAO DUN]

"Autumn in Kuling"
Chen, Yo-shih. *Realism . . .* , 35–50.

"Haze"
Chen, Yo-shih. *Realism . . .* , 153–155.

"Lin Ch'ung the Leopard Head"
Chen, Yo-shih. *Realism . . .* , 168–172.

"Stone Tablet"
Chen, Yo-shih. *Realism . . .* , 176–178.

"Suicide"
Chen, Yo-shih. *Realism . . .* , 144–149.

"A Woman"
Chen, Yo-shih. *Realism . . .* , 149–153.

RENÉ MARAN

"Deux Amis"
Cameron, Keith. *René Maran*, 122–123.

"L'Homme qui attend"
Cameron, Keith. *René Maran*, 121–122.

"Peines de Coeur"
Cameron, Keith. *René Maran*, 120–121.

WILLIAM MARCH

"The Arrogant Shoat"
Simmonds, Roy S. *The Two Worlds* . . . , 109.

"Bill's Eyes"
Simmonds, Roy S. *The Two Worlds* . . . , 150.

"The Borax Bottle"
Simmonds, Roy S. *The Two Worlds* . . . , 201.

"Dirty Emma"
Simmonds, Roy S. *The Two Worlds* . . . , 206–208.

"The Female of the Fruit Fly"
Simmonds, Roy S. *The Two Worlds* . . . , 203.

"George and Charlie"
Simmonds, Roy S. *The Two Worlds* . . . , 110.

"A Great Town for Characters"
Simmonds, Roy S. *The Two Worlds* . . . , 194–195.

"A Haircut in Toulouse"
Simmonds, Roy S. *The Two Worlds* . . . , 146–147.

"Happy Jack"
Simmonds, Roy S. *The Two Worlds* . . . , 111–112.

"He Sits There All Day Long"
Simmonds, Roy S. *The Two Worlds* . . . , 104–105.

"The Holly Wreath"
Simmonds, Roy S. *The Two Worlds* . . . , 34–36.

"I'm Crying with Relief"
Simmonds, Roy S. *The Two Worlds* . . . , 201.

"The Last Meeting"
Simmonds, Roy S. *The Two Worlds* . . . , 150–151.

"The Little Wife"
Simmonds, Roy S. *The Two Worlds* . . . , 32–33.

"A Memorial to the Slain"
Simmonds, Roy S. *The Two Worlds* . . . , 153–155.

"Miss Daisy"
Simmonds, Roy S. *The Two Worlds* . . . , 105.

"Not Very—Subtle"
Simmonds, Roy S. *The Two Worlds* . . . , 202–203.

"October Island"
Simmonds, Roy S. *The Two Worlds* . . . , 246–250.

"One Way Ticket"
Simmonds, Roy S. *The Two Worlds* . . . , 195–196.

"The Patterns That Gulls Weave"
Simmonds, Roy S. *The Two Worlds* . . . , 108–109.

"Personal Letter"
Simmonds, Roy S. *The Two Worlds* . . . , 78–79.

"Runagate Niggers"
Simmonds, Roy S. *The Two Worlds* . . . , 148.

"She Talks Good Now"
Simmonds, Roy S. *The Two Worlds* . . . , 208–209.

"The Shoe Drummer"
Simmonds, Roy S. *The Two Worlds* . . . , 151–152.

"A Shop in St. Louis, Missouri"
Simmonds, Roy S. *The Two Worlds* . . . , 109–110.

"A Short History of England"
Simmonds, Roy S. *The Two Worlds* . . . , 149.

"The Slate"
Simmonds, Roy S. *The Two Worlds* . . . , 205.

"Snowstorm in the Alps"
Simmonds, Roy S. *The Two Worlds* . . . , 152–153.

"The Static Sisters"
Simmonds, Roy S. *The Two Worlds* . . . , 201–202.

"This Heavy Load"
Simmonds, Roy S. *The Two Worlds* . . . , 106–108.

"Time and Leigh Brothers"
Simmonds, Roy S. *The Two Worlds* . . . , 155.

"To the Rear"
Simmonds, Roy S. *The Two Worlds* . . . , 105–106.

"The Toy Bank"
Simmonds, Roy S. *The Two Worlds* . . . , 147–148.

"Transcribed Album of Familiar Music"
Simmonds, Roy S. *The Two Worlds* . . . , 200–201.

"The Tune the Old Cow Died To"
Simmonds, Roy S. *The Two Worlds* . . . , 149–150.

"The Unploughed Patch"
Simmonds, Roy S. *The Two Worlds* . . . , 121–132.

"Upon the Dull Earth Dwelling"
Simmonds, Roy S. *The Two Worlds* . . . , 151.

"Whistles"
Simmonds, Roy S. *The Two Worlds* . . . , 203–204.

"The Wood Nymph"
Simmonds, Roy S. *The Two Worlds* . . . , 202.

"Woolen Drawers" [same as "Woolen Underwear" or "Mrs. Joe Cotton"]
Simmonds, Roy S. *The Two Worlds* . . . , 110–111.

"You and Your Sister"
Simmonds, Roy S. *The Two Worlds* . . . , 204–205.

ROBERTO MARIANI

"Rillo"
Leland, Christopher T. *The Last Happy Men* . . . , 78–79.

"Riverita"
Leland, Christopher T. *The Last Happy Men* . . . , 79–82.

"Toulet"
Leland, Christopher T. *The Last Happy Men* . . . , 84–88.

"Uno"
Leland, Christopher T. *The Last Happy Men* . . . , 83–84.

JOSÉ MARÍN CAÑAS

"Coto"
Marín, Mario A. "Marín Cañas y el relato historico," *Revista Revenar,* 3 (January–
    March, 1983), 26–29.

RENÉ MARQUÉS

"Death"
Umpierre, Luz María. "Heidegger y Marqués: El ser-hacia-la muerte," *Revista de Estudios Hispanicos* (Puerto Rico), 11 (1984), 83–87.

"In the Stern There Lies a Body"
Ortiz Cardona, Evelyn. "Entrampamiento humano: Estructuras sociólogicas en 'Dos vueltas de llave y un arcángel' y 'En la popa hay un cuerpo reclinado,'" *Revista de Estudios Hispanicos* (Puerto Rico), 11 (1984), 89–98.

"Two Turns of the Key and an Archangel"
Ortiz Cardona, Evelyn. "Entrampamiento humano . . . ," 89–98.

PAULE MARSHALL

"Reena"
Christian, Barbara. *Black Feminist Criticism* . . . , 110–111.

"Some Get Wasted"
Christian, Barbara. *Black Feminist Criticism* . . . , 111–112.

"To da-duh in Memoriam"
Christian, Barbara. *Black Feminist Criticism* . . . , 111.

ADAM MARS-JONES

"Bathpool Park"
Hanson, Clare. *Short Stories* . . . , 170–172.

"Hooshi-mi"
Hanson, Clare. *Short Stories* . . . , 169–170.

"Lantern Lecture"
Hanson, Clare. *Short Stories* . . . , 168–169.

FRANCISCO MARTÍNEZ

"A Story"
Lewis, Marvin A. "The Urban Experience in Selected Chicano Fiction," in Lattin, Vernon E., Ed. *Contemporary Chicano Fiction* . . . , 48–49.

ANA MARÍA MATUTE

"The Dead Boys"
Myers, Eunice D. "'Los hijos muertos': The Spanish Civil War as a Perpetuator of Death," *Letras Femeninas*, 12, i–ii (1986), 85–93.

"A Few Kids"
Savariego, Berta. "La correspondencia entre el personaje y la naturaleza en obras representivas de Ana María Matute," *Explicación de Textos Literarios,* 13, i (1984–85), 63–64.

W. SOMERSET MAUGHAM

"The Colonel's Lady"
Hanson, Clare. *Short Stories . . . ,* 50–51.

"A Domiciliary Visit"
Burt, Forrest D. *W. Somerset Maugham,* 111–112.

"The Kite"
Hanson, Clare. *Short Stories . . . ,* 52–53.

"Mackintosh"
Flora, Joseph M. *The English Short Story . . . ,* 20–21.

"Miss King"
Burt, Forrest D. *W. Somerset Maugham,* 112–114.

"The Outstation"
Bohner, Charles H. *Instructor's Manual . . . ,* 83–84.

"Rain"
Burt, Forrest D. *W. Somerset Maugham,* 107–109.
Flora, Joseph M. *The English Short Story . . . ,* 18–19.

"The Unconquered"
Stinson, John J. "The English Short Story, 1945–1950," in Vannatta, Dennis, Ed. *The English Short Story, 1945–1980,* 7–8.

"Winter Cruise"
Stinson, John J. "The English Short Story . . . ," 7.

GUY DE MAUPASSANT

"The Chair Mender"
Moger, Angela S. "Narrative Structure in Maupassant: Frame of Desire," *PMLA,* 100 (1985), 315–317.

"Miss Harriet"
Fleming, John A. "The Structure of Textual Production in Maupassant's 'Miss Harriet,'" *Nineteenth-Century French Stud,* 13, ii–iii (1986), 85–98.

"The Necklace"
Bohner, Charles H. *Instructor's Manual . . . ,* 84–85.

"On the Journey"
Moger, Angela S. ". . . Frame of Desire," 317–323.

"The Rosebush of Madame Husson"
Nef, Frédéric. "Noms et échange dans 'Le Rosier de Madame Husson' de Maupassant," in Parret, Herman, and Hans-George Ruprecht, Eds. *Exigences et perspectives . . .* , 761–769.

"Who Knows?"
Kurk, Katherine C. "Maupassant and the Divided Self: 'Qui sait?'" *Nineteenth-Century French Stud*, 14 (1986), 284–294.

FRANÇOIS MAURIAC

"Thérèse Desqueyroux"
Gallagher, Edward J. "Sexual Ambiguity in Mauriac's 'Thérèse Desqueyroux,'" *Romance Notes*, 26 (1986), 215–221.
Monférier, Jacques. "L'Expression Littéraire de la norme et de la transgression chez François Mauriac: L'Exemple de 'Thérèse Desqueyroux,'" *Textes et Langages*, 12 (1986), 183–190.
Solomon, Philip H. "Symbolic Landscape and the Quest for Self in François Mauriac's 'Thérèse Desqueyroux,'" *Forum Mod Lang Stud*, 22, i (1986), 16–21.

HERMAN MELVILLE

"Bartleby the Scrivener"
Bohner, Charles H. *Instructor's Manual . . .* , 85–86.
Gilmore, Michael T. *American Romanticism . . .* , 132–145.
Kirby, David. *The Sun Rises . . .* , 57–64.
Lee, A. Robert. "Voices Off and On: Melville's Piazza and Other Stories," in Lee, A. Robert, Ed. *. . . American Short Story*, 82–85.
Marder, Daniel. *Exiles at Home . . .* , 255–257.
Murphy, Michael. "'Bartleby the Scrivener': A Simple Reading," *Arizona Q*, 41 (1985), 143–151.
Pribek, Thomas. "The Assumption of Naiveté: The Tone of Melville's Lawyer," *Arizona Q*, 41 (1985), 131–142.
———. "The 'Safe' Man of Wall Street: Characterizing Melville's Lawyer," *Stud Short Fiction*, 23 (1986), 191–192.
———. "Melville's Copyists: The 'Bar Tenders' of Wall Street," *Papers Lang & Lit*, 22 (1986), 176–186.
Riddle, Mary-Madeleine G. *. . . "Piazza Tales,"* 58–74.
Ross, Robert. "'Bartleby the Scrivener': An American Cousin," *Post Script*, 1 (1983), 27–33.

"The Bell Tower"
Goldoni, Annalisa. "Le (a)symmetrie in 'The Bell Tower,'" in Cabibbo, Paola, Ed. *Melvilliana*, 189–214.
Marder, Daniel. *Exiles at Home . . .* , 259–260.
Newman, Lea B. V. "Melville's 'Bell Tower' Revisited: A Story of Female Revenge," *Melville Soc Extracts*, 65 (February, 1986), 11–14.

Riddle, Mary-Madeleine G. . . . "*Piazza Tales*," 143–158.

"Benito Cereno"
Horsley-Meachum, Gloria. "Melville's Dark Satyr Unmasked," *Engl Lang Notes*, 23 (1986), 43–47.
Knafo-Sutton, Ruth. "Master and Slave in 'Benito Cereno,'" in Harkness, Don, Ed. *Ritual* . . . , 1–3.
Lee, A. Robert. "Voices . . . ," 93–96.
Marder, Daniel. *Exiles at Home* . . . , 260–261.
Riddle, Mary-Madeleine G. . . . "*Piazza Tales*," 75–98.
Rodgers, James. "Melville's Short Fiction: Many Voices, Many Modes," *SPELL*, 1 (1984), 44–50.
Sundquist, Eric J. "'Benito Cereno' and New World Slavery," in Bercovitch, Sacvan, Ed. *Reconstructing* . . . , 93–122.
Swann, Charles. "Whodunnit? Or Who Did What? 'Benito Cereno' and the Politics of Narrative Structure," in Nye, David E., and Kristen K. Thomsen, Eds. *American Studies in Transition*, 199–234.
———. "'Benito Cereno': Melville's De(con)struction of the Southern Reader," *Lit & Hist*, 12, i (1986), 3–15.
Zagarell, Sandra A. "Reenvisioning America: Melville's 'Benito Cereno,'" *ESQ: J Am Renaissance*, 30 (1984), 245–259.

"Billy Budd"
Baker, A. W. *Death Is a Good Solution* . . . , 125–127.
Dillingham, William B. *Melville's Later Novels*, 365–399.
Henderson, Eric. "Vices of the Intellect in 'Billy Budd,'" *Engl Stud Canada*, 11, i (1985), 40–52.
Marder, Daniel. *Exiles at Home* . . . , 270–275.
Martin, Robert K. *Hero, Captain, and Stranger* . . . , 107–124.
Srivastava, Ramesh K. "Malignant Trinity: A Study of Iago, Chillingworth, and Claggart as Villains," *Panjab Univ Research Bull*, 15, i (1984), 43–52.

"Cock-A-Doodle-Doo!"
Fisher, Martha A. "Massachusetts Choo-Choo and Cock-A-Doodle-Doo!: Two Devices for Humor in Hawthorne and Melville," *Pennsylvania Engl*, 11, ii (1985), 15–23.
Marder, Daniel. *Exiles at Home* . . . , 257–258.
Rosenblum, Joseph. "A Cock Fight Between Melville and Thoreau," *Stud Short Fiction*, 23 (1986), 159–167.

"The Encantadas"
Bercaw, Mary K. "The Crux of the Ass in 'The Encantadas,'" *Melville Soc Extracts*, 62 (May, 1985), 12.
Hattenhauer, Darryl. "Ambiguities of Time in Melville's 'The Encantadas,'" *Am Transcendental Q*, 56 (March, 1985), 5–17.
Lee, A. Robert. "Voices . . . ," 86–90.
Moses, Carole. "Hunilla and Oberlus: Ambiguous Companions," *Stud Short Fiction*, 22 (1985), 339–342.
Riddle, Mary-Madeleine G. . . . "*Piazza Tales*," 107–142.
Simard, Rodney. "More Black Than Bright: The Allegorical Structure of Melville's 'The Encantadas,'" *Melville Soc Extracts*, 66 (May, 1986), 10–12.

"The Lightning-Rod Man"
Riddle, Mary-Madeleine G. . . . "*Piazza Tales*," 99–106.

"The Paradise of Bachelors and the Tartarus of Maids"
Grover, Dorys C. "Melville's Mill 'Girls' and the Landscape," in Harkness, Don,
   Ed. *Design, Pattern, Style . . . ,* 36–37.
Hovanec, Carol P. "Melville as Artist of the Sublime: Design in 'The Tartarus
   of Maids,'" *Mid-Hudson Lang Stud,* 8 (1985), 41–51.
Martin, Robert K. *Hero, Captain, and Stranger . . . ,* 105–107.
Siegel, Adrienne. *The Image . . . ,* 94–95.

"The Piazza"
Lee, A. Robert. "Voices . . . ," 76–77.
Riddle, Mary-Madeleine G. . . . *"Piazza Tales,"* 32–57.
Rodgers, James. "Melville's Short Fiction . . . ," 41–43.
St. Armand, Barton L. "Melville, Malaise, and Mannerism: The Originality of
   'The Piazza,'" *Bucknell R,* 30, i (1986), 72–101.
Slouka, Mark Z. "Herman Melville's Journey to 'The Piazza,'" *Am Transcendental
   Q,* 61 (October, 1986), 3–14.

MIGUEL MÉNDEZ [same as C. MIGUEL MÉNDEZ
and M. MIGUEL MÉNDEZ]

"Estillo"
Lewis, Martin A. "The Urban Experience in Selected Chicano Fiction," in Lattin, Vernon E., Ed. *Contemporary Chicano Fiction . . . ,* 58–59.

"Tata Casehua"
Bruce-Novoa, Juan D. "Miguel Méndez: Voices of Silence," in Lattin,
   Vernon E., Ed. *Contemporary Chicano Fiction . . . ,* 206–214.
Urquídez-Somoza, Oscar, and Julio A. Martínez. "M. Miguel Méndez," in Mar-
   tínez, Julio A., and Francisco A. Lomelí, Eds. *Chicano Literature . . . ,* 271.
Vogt, Gregory M. "Archetypal Images of Apocalypse in Miguel Méndez's 'Tata
   Casehua,'" *Confluencia,* 1, ii (1986), 55–60.

PROSPER MÉRIMÉE

"The Capture of the Redoubt"
Sivert, Eileen B. "Fear and Confrontation in Prosper Mérimée's Narrative Fiction," *Nineteenth-Century French Stud,* 6 (1978), 222, 226–227.

"Colomba"
Crecelius, Kathryn J. "Narrative as Moral Action in Mérimée's 'Colomba,'"
   Nineteenth-Century French Stud, 14 (1986), 225–237.
Sivert, Eileen B. "Fear and Confrontation . . . ," 218–219.

"The Venus of Ille"
Sivert, Eileen B. "Fear and Confrontation . . . ," 217.

ABRAHAM MERRITT

"Burn, Witch, Burn!"
Bleiler, E. F. "A. Merritt," in Bleiler, E. F., Ed. *Supernatural Fiction Writers . . . ,*
   II, 840.

"The Conquest of the Moon Pool"
Bleiler, E. F. "A. Merritt," 837–838.

"The Face in the Abyss"
Bleiler, E. F. "A. Merritt," 839.

"The Metal Monster"
Bleiler, E. F. "A. Merritt," 838.

"The Moon Pool"
Bleiler, E. F. "A. Merritt," 837.

"The People of the Pit"
Bleiler, E. F. "A. Merritt," 835.

"The Ship of Ishtar"
Bleiler, E. F. "A. Merritt," 838–839.

"Three Lines of Old French"
Bleiler, E. F. "A. Merritt," 838.

"The Woman of the Wood"
Bleiler, E. F. "A. Merritt," 839.

JOHN METCALF

"A Bag of Cherries"
Cameron, Barry. *John Metcalf*, 54–56.

"The Beef Curry"
Cameron, Barry. *John Metcalf*, 15–17.

"Beryl"
Cameron, Barry. *John Metcalf*, 50–54.

"Biscuits"
Cameron, Barry. *John Metcalf*, 37–38.

"The Children Green and Golden"
Cameron, Barry. *John Metcalf*, 43–45.

"Dandelions"
Cameron, Barry. *John Metcalf*, 31–32.

"The Eastmill Reception Centre"
Cameron, Barry. *John Metcalf*, 122–125.

"The Estuary"
Cameron, Barry. *John Metcalf*, 32–35.
Vauthier, Simone. "Rambling Through John Metcalf's 'The Estuary,'" *Malahat R*, 70 (1985), 98–117.

"Gentle as Flowers Make the Stones"
Cameron, Barry. "An Approximation of Poetry: Three Stories by John Met-
    calf," in Struthers, J. R., Ed. *The Montreal Story Tellers* . . . , 160–163.

"Geography of the House"
Cameron, Barry. *John Metcalf*, 17–18.

"The Happiest Days"
Cameron, Barry. *John Metcalf*, 20–23.

"I've Got It Made"
Cameron, Barry. *John Metcalf*, 47–48.

"Keys and Watercress"
Cameron, Barry. *John Metcalf*, 41–43.

"The Lady Who Sold Furniture"
Rooke, Constance. "Pastoral Restraint: An Essay on John Metcalf's 'The Lady
    Who Sold Furniture,'" *Malahat R*, 70 (1985), 131–145.

"Our Mr. Benson"
Cameron, Barry. *John Metcalf*, 49–50.

"Playground"
Cameron, Barry. *John Metcalf*, 26–27.

"Polly Ongle"
Garebian, Keith. "In the End, a Beginning: The Montreal Story Tellers," in
    Struthers, J. R., Ed. *The Montreal Story Tellers* . . . , 201–203.

"The Practice of the Craft"
Cameron, Barry. *John Metcalf*, 63–66.

"Pretty Bay"
Cameron, Barry. *John Metcalf*, 48–49.

"A Process of Time"
Cameron, Barry. *John Metcalf*, 18–20.

"Single Gents Only"
Cameron, Barry. *John Metcalf*, 118–122.

"The Strange Aberration of Mr. Ken Smythe"
Cameron, Barry. *John Metcalf*, 58–66.

"The Teeth of My Father"
Cameron, Barry. "An Approximation . . . ," 165–167; rpt. in his *John Metcalf*,
    73–76.

"A Thing They Wear"
Cameron, Barry. *John Metcalf*, 45–47.

"The Tide Line"
Cameron, Barry. *John Metcalf*, 38–40.

"A Toy Called Peter Dog"
Cameron, Barry. *John Metcalf*, 24–26.

"Walking Around the City"
Cameron, Barry. *John Metcalf*, 27–30.

"The Years in Exile"
Cameron, Barry. "An Approximation . . . ," 163–165; rpt. in his *John Metcalf*, 70–73.
Minni, C. D. "The Short Story as an Ethnic Genre," in Pivato, Joseph, Ed. *Contrasts . . .* , 66.

JOHN METCALFE [WILLIAM JOHN METCALFE]

"The Feasting Dead"
Dalby, Richard. "John Metcalfe," in Bleiler, E. F., Ed. *Supernatural Fiction Writers . . .* , II, 600–601.

"The Firing-Chamber"
Dalby, Richard. "John Metcalfe," 601.

CONRAD FERDINAND MEYER

"The Amulet"
Brehmer, Karl. "Determination oder Freiheit: Zur Problematik der Prädestination in C. F. Meyers Novelle 'Das Amulett,'" *Wirkendes Wort*, 35 (1985), 18–38.
Crowhurst-Bond, Griseldis. "Conrad Ferdinand Meyer: 'Das Amulett,'" *Deutschunterricht in Südafrika*, 14, i (1983), 1–22.

"Plautus in the Convent"
Rowland, Herbert. "Conscience and the Aesthetic in Conrad Ferdinand Meyer's 'Plautus im Nonnenkloster,'" *Michigan Germ Stud*, 11 (1985), 159–181.

HENRY MILLER

"A Devil in Paradise"
Lewis, Leon. *Henry Miller . . .* , 157.

"Jabberwhorl Cronstadt"
Lewis, Leon. *Henry Miller . . .* , 116–121.

WALTER M. MILLER

"Blood Bank"
Ower, John. "Theology and Evolution in the Short Fiction of Walter M. Miller, Jr.," *Cithara*, 2, ii (1986), 62–70.

"Dark Benediction"
Ower, John. "Theology and Evolution . . . ," 70–71.

"Dumb Waiter"
Berger, Harold L. *Science Fiction* . . . , 154–155.

"You Triflin' Skunk"
Ower, John. "Theology and Evolution . . . ," 58–62.

MISHIMA YUKIO

"Patriotism"
Bohner, Charles H. *Instructor's Manual* . . . , 86–88.

DONALD G. MITCHELL

"Boldo's Story"
Kime, Wayne R. *Donald G. Mitchell*, 40–41.

"The Bride of the Ice-King"
Kime, Wayne R. *Donald G. Mitchell*, 84.

"The Petit Soulier"
Kime, Wayne R. *Donald G. Mitchell*, 81–82.

"Wet Day at an Irish Inn"
Kime, Wayne R. *Donald G. Mitchell*, 79–80.

JULIAN MITCHELL

"Can I Go Now?"
Pickering, Jean. "The English Short Story in the Sixties," in Vannatta, Dennis,
    Ed. *The English Short Story, 1945–1980*, 77–78.

W. O. MITCHELL

"The Liar Hunter"
Mitchell, O. S. "Tall Tales in the Fiction of W. O. Mitchell," *Canadian Lit*, 108
    (1986), 20–22.

NAOMI MITCHISON

"Round with the Boats"
Baldwin, Dean. "The English Short Story in the Fifties," in Vannatta, Dennis,
    Ed. *The English Short Story, 1945–1980*, 50.

N[AVARRO] SCOTT MOMADAY

"The Well"
Schubnell, Matthias. *N. Scott Momaday . . .* , 94–95.

NICHOLAS MONSARRAT

"Heavy Rescue"
Stinson, John J. "The English Short Story, 1945–1950," in Vannatta, Dennis,
Ed. *The English Short Story, 1945–1980,* 3–4.

CARLOS MONTEMAYOR

"Nora"
Duncan, L. Ann. *Voices, Visions . . .* , 73.

"Old Story"
Duncan, L. Ann. *Voices, Visions . . .* , 73–74.

C[ATHERINE] L[UCILLE] MOORE

"Black God's Kiss"
Letson, Russell. "C. L. Moore," in Bleiler, E. F., Ed. *Supernatural Fiction Writers . . .* , II, 894.

"Black God's Shadow"
Letson, Russell. "C. L. Moore," 894–895.

"The Bright Illusion"
Letson, Russell. "C. L. Moore," 895–896.

"Daemon"
Letson, Russell. "C. L. Moore," 896–897.

"Fruit of Knowledge"
Letson, Russell. "C. L. Moore," 896.

"Greater Glories"
Letson, Russell. "C. L. Moore," 896.

GEORGE MOORE

"Home Sickness"
Averill, Deborah M. *The Irish Short Story . . .* , 36–38.
Deane, Seamus. *. . . Irish Literature,* 170–171.

"The Window"
Averill, Deborah M. *The Irish Short Story . . .* , 38–39.

FRANK MOORHOUSE

"The Girl from the Family of Man"
Bennett, Bruce. "Asian Encounters in the Contemporary Australian Short
Story," *World Lit Written Engl*, 26 (1986), 57–58.

HANNAH MORE

"The History of Diligent Dick"
Gallagher, Catherine. *The Industrial Reformation* . . . , 39–40.

"The Lancashire Collier-Girl"
Gallagher, Catherine. *The Industrial Reformation* . . . , 38–39.

EDUARD MÖRIKE

"Mozart on the Way to Prague"
Paulin, Roger. *The Brief Compass* . . . , 59–62.

WILLIAM MORRIS

"Frank's Sealed Letter"
Pfeiffer, John R. "William Morris," in Bleiler, E. F., Ed. *Supernatural Fiction
Writers* . . . , I, 302.

"Gertha's Lovers"
Pfeiffer, John R. "William Morris," 301–302.

"The Hollow Land"
Pfeiffer, John R. "William Morris," 302.

"The Story of an Unknown Church"
Pfeiffer, John R. "William Morris," 301.

"Svend and His Brethren"
Pfeiffer, John R. "William Morris," 302.

EZEKIEL MPHAHLELE

"Mrs. Plum"
Tejani, Bahadur. "Christianity and Colonialism as Objects of Humour in East
and South Africa," *World Lit Written Engl*, 26 (1986), 237–238.

ALICE MUNRO

"Bardon Bus"
Irvine, Lorna. *Sub/version* . . . , 102–105.

"Boys and Girls"
Bohner, Charles H. *Instructor's Manual* . . . , 88–89.

"Connection"
Irvine, Lorna. *Sub/version* . . . , 95–97.

"Dulse"
Irvine, Lorna. *Sub/version* . . . , 100–102.

"Hard-Luck Stories"
Irvine, Lorna. *Sub/version* . . . , 105–108.

"Labour Day Dinner"
Irvine, Lorna. *Sub/version* . . . , 99–100.

"Marrakesh"
Martin, W. R. "Hanging Pictures Together: *Something I've Been Meaning to Tell You*," in Miller, Judith, Ed. *The Art of Alice Munro* . . . , 28–29.

"Material"
Gold, Joseph. "Our Feeling Exactly: The Writing of Alice Munro," in Miller, Judith, Ed. *The Art of Alice Munro* . . . , 17–18.
Martin, W. R. "Hanging Pictures . . . ," 22–24.

"The Moons of Jupiter"
Martin, W. R. "Hanging Pictures . . . ," 108–109.

"The Ottawa Valley"
Lamont-Stewart, Linda. "Order from Chaos: Writing as Self-Defense in the Fiction of Alice Munro and Clark Blaise," in Miller, Judith, Ed. *The Art of Alice Munro* . . . , 119–120.
Martin, W. R. "Hanging Pictures . . . ," 30–32.

"Something I've Been Meaning to Tell You"
Gold, Joseph. "Our Feeling Exactly . . . ," 17.
Struthers, J. R. "Alice Munro's Fictive Imagination," in Miller, Judith, Ed. *The Art of Alice Munro* . . . , 104–107.

"The Spanish Lady"
Gold, Joseph. "Our Feeling Exactly . . . ," 18–19.

"Spelling"
Struthers, J. R. ". . . Fictive Imagination," 111–112.

"The Stone in the Field"
Irvine, Lorna. *Sub/version* . . . , 97–98.

"Walking on the Water"
Martin, W. R. "Hanging Pictures . . . ," 24–26.

"Winter Wind"
Lamont-Stewart, Linda. "Order from Chaos . . . ," 120.

AMADO JESÚS MURO [CHESTER E. SELZER]

"Ay, Chihuahua"
Chavarría, Mary. "Amado Jesús Muro," in Martínez, Julio A., and Francisco A.
Lomelí, Eds. *Chicano Literature* . . . , 450.

"Cecilia Rosas"
Chavarría, Mary. "Amado Jesús Muro," 453–454.

"María Tepache"
Chavarría, Mary. "Amado Jesús Muro," 452–453.

"My Aunt Dominga"
Chavarría, Mary. "Amado Jesús Muro," 451.

"My Grandfather's Brave Songs"
Chavarría, Mary. "Amado Jesús Muro," 450–451.

"Street of the Crazy Women"
Chavarría, Mary. "Amado Jesús Muro," 452.

"Sunday in Little Chihuahua"
Chavarría, Mary. "Amado Jesús Muro," 452.

ROBERT MUSIL

"The Blackbird"
Hoppler, Rudolf. "Musils 'Amsel': Paradiesvogel des Narziss," in Sturtz, Josef
and Johann, Eds. *Robert Musil* . . . , 187–202.

"Grigia"
Hickman, Hannah. *Robert Musil* . . . , 83–86.
Strelka, Joseph. "Musils Novelle 'Grigia' als Gegenstück der 'Vollendung der
Liebe,'" in Goffin, Roger, Michel Vanhelleputte, and Monique Weyem-
bergh-Boussart, Eds. *Littérature et culture* . . . , 335–343.

"The Perfection of Love"
Hickman, Hannah. *Robert Musil* . . . , 58–61.
Strelka, Joseph. "Musils Novelle . . . ," 335–343.
Wilson, Catherine. "Morality and the Self in Robert Musil's 'The Perfection of
Love,'" *Philosophy & Lit*, 8 (1984), 222–235.

"The Portuguese Lady"
Erickson, Susan. "The Psychopoetics of Narrative in Musil's 'Die Portugiesin,'"
Monatshefte, 78 (1986), 167–181.
Hickman, Hannah. *Robert Musil* . . . , 86–90.

"The Temptation of Silent Veronica"
Hickman, Hannah. *Robert Musil* . . . , 61–65.

"Tonka"
Hickman, Hannah. *Robert Musil* . . . , 90–92.
Homann, Renate. "Literatur und Erkenntnis: Robert Musils Erzählung
'Tonka,'" *Deutsche Vierteljahrsschrift*, 50 (1985), 497–518.

VLADIMIR NABOKOV

"The Leonardo"
Green, Martin, and John Swan. *The Triumph* . . . , 238.

"Signs and Symbols"
Lane, John B. "A Funny Thing about Nabokov's 'Signs and Symbols,'" *Russian
Lang J*, 40 (1986), 147–160.

"Spring in Fialta"
Green, Martin, and John Swan. *The Triumph* . . . , 238–239.
White, Edmund. "Nabokov: Beyond Parody," in Gibian, George, and Stephen
Jan Parker, Eds. *The Achievement* . . . , 5–9.

"Terror"
Aikhenval'd, Iulii I. "'Terror,'" trans. Marina T. Naumann, in Roth, Phyllis A.,
Ed. *Critical Essays* . . . , 45–46.

MIKHAIL NAIMY [or NUAYMA]

"Her New Year"
Naimy, Nadim. *Mikhail Naimy* . . . , 155–156.

R. K. NARAYAN

"Dodu"
Trivedi, H. C., and N. C. Soni. "Short Stories of R. K. Narayan: An Estimate,"
in Ram, Atma, Ed. *Perspectives* . . . , 186.

"A Horse and Two Goats"
Trivedi, H. C., and N. C. Soni. "Short Stories . . . ," 191.

"Ranga"
Trivedi, H. C., and N. C. Soni. "Short Stories . . . ," 186.

"Uncle"
Trivedi, H. C., and N. C. Soni. "Short Stories . . . ," 191–192.

J. L. NAVARRO

"Blue Day on Main Street"
Lewis, Marvin A. "The Urban Experience in Selected Chicano Fiction," in
Lattin, Vernon E., Ed. *Contemporary Chicano Fiction* . . . , 51.

"Cutting Mirrors"
Lewis, Marvin A. "The Urban Experience . . . ," 50.

"Frankie's Last Wish"
Lewis, Marvin A. "The Urban Experience . . . ," 51–52.

"Weekend"
Lewis, Marvin A. "The Urban Experience . . . ," 49–50.

JOHN NEAL

"Otter-Bag, the Oneida Chief"
Gerlach, John. *Toward the End* . . . , 24–27.

GÉRARD DE NERVAL

"Sylvie"
Bonnet, Henri. "Idyllique 'Sylvie' ou 'l'astre trompeur d'Aldebaran,'" *Cahiers Gérard de Nerval*, 6 (1983), 2–7.
Tristman, Bruno. "Système et jeu dans 'Sylvie,'" *Poétique*, 17 (February, 1986), 77–89.

MARTIN ANDERSEN NEXØ

"An' Mari's Journey"
Ingwersen, Faith and Niels. *Quest* . . . , 98–99.

"Awash"
Ingwersen, Faith and Niels. *Quest* . . . , 95–96.

"Fate"
Ingwersen, Faith and Niels. *Quest* . . . , 38.

"Fraenke"
Ingwersen, Faith and Niels. *Quest* . . . , 37–38.

"Good Fortune"
Ingwersen, Faith and Niels. *Quest* . . . , 25.

"Gossamer"
Ingwersen, Faith and Niels. *Quest* . . . , 99–100.

"The Idiot"
Ingwersen, Faith and Niels. *Quest* . . . , 96–97.

"The Lottery-Swede"
Ingwersen, Faith and Niels. *Quest* . . . , 39–41.

"The Musical Pig"
Ingwersen, Faith and Niels. *Quest* . . . , 35.

"The Old Bachelor's Story"
Ingwersen, Faith and Niels. *Quest* . . . , 37.

"Paradise"
Ingwersen, Faith and Niels. *Quest* . . . , 97–98.

"Passengers for Empty Seats"
Ingwersen, Faith and Niels. *Quest* . . . , 101.

"Payday"
Ingwersen, Faith and Niels. *Quest* . . . , 41.

"The Smith from Dyndeby"
Ingwersen, Faith and Niels. *Quest* . . . , 39.

"The Walls"
Ingwersen, Faith and Niels. *Quest* . . . , 100–101.

HUGH NISSENSON

"The Blessing"
Berger, Alan L. *Crisis and Covenant* . . . , 61.

"The Crazy Old Man"
Berger, Alan L. *Crisis and Covenant* . . . , 214–215.

"The Law"
Berger, Alan L. *Crisis and Covenant* . . . , 61–65.

"The Prisoner"
Berger, Alan L. *Crisis and Covenant* . . . , 60–61.

DER NISTER [PINKHES KAHANOVITSH]

"Under the Fence"
Shmeruk, Kh. "Der Nister's 'Under the Fence': Tribulations of a Soviet Yiddish
 Symbolist," in Weinreich, Uriel, Ed. *The Field of Yiddish* . . . , 263–285.

FRANK NORRIS

"A Case for Lombroso"
Howard, June. *Form and History* . . . , 93–93.

"A Reversion to Type"
Howard, June. *Form and History* . . . , 91–92.

LINO NOVÁS CALVO

"'Allies' and 'Germans'"
Roses, Lorraine E. *Voices* . . . , 102–106.

"A Bad Man"
Lichblau, Myron I. "Visión irónica en tres cuentos de Lino Novás Calvo," *Caribe*,
1, ii (1976), 25–26.
Roses, Lorraine E. *Voices* . . . , 102–103.

"A Bum"
Lichblau, Myron I. "Visión irónica . . . ," 24–25.

"Can't Really Say"
Roses, Lorraine E. *Voices* . . . , 100–102.

"Cayo Canas"
Roses, Lorraine E. *Voices* . . . , 88–93.

"The Dark Night of Ramón Yendía"
Roses, Lorraine E. *Voices* . . . , 75–79.

"The Execution of Fernández"
Roses, Lorraine E. *Voices* . . . , 127–130.

"A Finger on Him"
Roses, Lorraine E. *Voices* . . . , 95–100.

"The First Lesson"
Roses, Lorraine E. *Voices* . . . , 82–83.

"The Flutist"
Roses, Lorraine E. *Voices* . . . , 53–54.

"The Grandmother Queen and Her Nephew Delfín"
Roses, Lorraine E. *Voices* . . . , 123–127.

"Hold That Man Down!"
Roses, Lorraine E. *Voices* . . . , 108.

"The Invisible Husband"
Lichblau, Myron I. "Visión irónica . . . ," 23–24.
Roses, Lorraine E. *Voices* . . . , 121.

"Long Island"
Roses, Lorraine E. *Voices* . . . , 79–82.

"The Moon Ceremony"
Roses, Lorraine E. *Voices* . . . , 58–64.

"My Uncle Antón Luna"
Roses, Lorraine E. *Voices* . . . , 133–136.

"The Night the Dead Came Forth"
Roses, Lorraine E. *Voices* . . . , 67–70.

"On the Island" [same as "On the Key"]
Roses, Lorraine E. *Voices* . . . , 64–67.

"The Place That Called Me"
Roses, Lorraine E. *Voices* . . . , 110–113.

"The Reed: A Cuban Story"
Roses, Lorraine E. *Voices* . . . , 57.

"The Room for Dying"
Roses, Lorraine E. *Voices* . . . , 108–110.

"The Secret of Narciso Campana"
Roses, Lorraine E. *Voices* . . . , 130–133.

"A Singular Encounter"
Roses, Lorraine E. *Voices* . . . , 54–56.

"A Sip of Coffee"
Roses, Lorraine E. *Voices* . . . , 130.

"The Spider Man"
Roses, Lorraine E. *Voices* . . . , 121–122.

"The Thinking Head"
Roses, Lorraine E. *Voices* . . . , 47–51.

"The Vision of Tamaria"
Roses, Lorraine E. *Voices* . . . , 93–95.

"Worse Than a Hell"
Roses, Lorraine E. *Voices* . . . , 118–121.

FLORA NWAPA

"The Chief's Daughter"
Taiwo, Oladele. *Female Novelists* . . . , 81–82.

"Daddy, Don't Strike the Match"
Taiwo, Oladele. *Female Novelists* . . . , 79–80.

"The Delinquent Adults"
Taiwo, Oladele. *Female Novelists* . . . , 73–75.

"The Loss of Eze"
Taiwo, Oladele. *Female Novelists* . . . , 75–78.

"The Road to Benin"
Taiwo, Oladele. *Female Novelists . . .* , 71–73.

"This Is Lagos"
Taiwo, Oladele. *Female Novelists . . .* , 69–71.

"The Traveller"
Taiwo, Oladele. *Female Novelists . . .* , 68–69.

"A Wife's Dilemma"
Taiwo, Oladele. *Female Novelists . . .* , 80–81.

"Wives at War"
Taiwo, Oladele. *Female Novelists . . .* , 78–79.

JOYCE CAROL OATES

"Accomplished Desires"
Norman, Torborg. *Isolation and Contact . . .* , 178–183.

"All the Good People I've Left Behind"
Bastian, Katherine. *Joyce Carol Oates's Short Stories . . .* , 148–150.

"An American Adventure"
Bastian, Katherine. *Joyce Carol Oates's Short Stories . . .* , 70–71.

"An American Dream"
Bastian, Katherine. *Joyce Carol Oates's Short Stories . . .* , 68–70.

". . . & Answers"
Bastian, Katherine. *Joyce Carol Oates's Short Stories . . .* , 114–115.
Norman, Torborg. *Isolation and Contact . . .* , 106–107.

"Archways"
Norman, Torborg. *Isolation and Contact . . .* , 163–165.

"The Assailant"
Norman, Torborg. *Isolation and Contact . . .* , 171.

"Assault"
Bastian, Katherine. *Joyce Carol Oates's Short Stories . . .* , 92–97.

"At the Seminary"
Norman, Torborg. *Isolation and Contact . . .* , 85–87.

"The Blessing"
Norman, Torborg. *Isolation and Contact . . .* , 96–99.

"Bloodstains"
Norman, Torborg. *Isolation and Contact . . .* , 150–151.

"Blood-Swollen Landscape"
Bastian, Katherine. *Joyce Carol Oates's Short Stories* . . . , 86–87.

"Bodies"
Bastian, Katherine. *Joyce Carol Oates's Short Stories* . . . , 65–68.

"Boy and Girl"
Norman, Torborg. *Isolation and Contact* . . . , 145–146.

"Boys at a Picnic"
Norman, Torborg. *Isolation and Contact* . . . , 63–64.

"The Census Taker"
Norman, Torborg. *Isolation and Contact* . . . , 58–62.

"Ceremonies"
Norman, Torborg. *Isolation and Contact* . . . , 124–125.

"The Children"
Norman, Torborg. *Isolation and Contact* . . . , 136–137.

"Convalescing"
Norman, Torborg. *Isolation and Contact* . . . , 64–65, 175–178.

"Crossing the Border"
Norman, Torborg. *Isolation and Contact* . . . , 204–205.

"Customs"
Norman, Torborg. *Isolation and Contact* . . . , 65–67, 207–208.

"The Daughter"
Norman, Torborg. *Isolation and Contact* . . . , 146–147.

"The Dead"
Bastian, Katherine. *Joyce Carol Oates's Short Stories* . . . , 47–51.
Norman, Torborg. *Isolation and Contact* . . . , 194–195.

"DOUBLE TRAGEDY STRIKES TENNESSEE HILL FAMILY"
Norman, Torborg. *Isolation and Contact* . . . , 154–155.

"The Dreaming Woman"
Norman, Torborg. *Isolation and Contact* . . . , 155–156.

"The Dungeon"
Bastian, Katherine. *Joyce Carol Oates's Short Stories* . . . , 112–113.

"Dying"
Norman, Torborg. *Isolation and Contact* . . . , 165–167.

"The Dying Child"
Norman, Torborg. *Isolation and Contact* . . . , 147–148.

"Edge of the World"
Norman, Torborg. *Isolation and Contact* . . . , 125–126.

"Images"
Norman, Torborg. *Isolation and Contact* . . . , 143–144.

"In the Old World"
Norman, Torborg. *Isolation and Contact* . . . , 68–71.

"In the Region of Ice"
Norman, Torborg. *Isolation and Contact* . . . , 90–92.

"An Incident in the Park"
Bastian, Katherine. *Joyce Carol Oates's Short Stories* . . . , 139.
Norman, Torborg. *Isolation and Contact* . . . , 210.

"The Lady with the Pet Dog"
Bastian, Katherine. *Joyce Carol Oates's Short Stories* . . . , 52–55.
Brennan, Matthew C. "Plotting Against Chekhov: Joyce Carol Oates and 'The Lady with the Dog,'" *Notes Mod Am Lit*, 9 (1985), Item 13.
Norman, Torborg. *Isolation and Contact* . . . , 195–198.
Sheidley, William E., and Ann Charters. *Instructor's Manual* . . . , 188–189; rpt. Charters, Ann, William E. Sheidley, and Martha Ramsey. *Instructor's Manual* . . . , 2nd ed., 213–214.

"Landscape of Neutral Colors"
Norman, Torborg. *Isolation and Contact* . . . , 184–185.

"The Leap"
Bastian, Katherine. *Joyce Carol Oates's Short Stories* . . . , 143–144.
Norman, Torborg. *Isolation and Contact* . . . , 216–217.

"Loving/Losing/Loving a Man"
Norman, Torborg. *Isolation and Contact* . . . , 193.

"The Madwoman"
Bastian, Katherine. *Joyce Carol Oates's Short Stories* . . . , 74–75.
Norman, Torborg. *Isolation and Contact* . . . , 147.

"Magna Mater"
Bastian, Katherine. *Joyce Carol Oates's Short Stories* . . . , 82–84.
Norman, Torborg. *Isolation and Contact* . . . , 139–140.

"The Man That Turned into a Statue"
Norman, Torborg. *Isolation and Contact* . . . , 161–162.

"The Maniac"
Bastian, Katherine. *Joyce Carol Oates's Short Stories* . . . , 79–80.

"Matter and Energy"
Norman, Torborg. *Isolation and Contact* . . . , 171–172.

"The Metamorphosis"
Bastian, Katherine. *Joyce Carol Oates's Short Stories* . . . , 27–36.

"Wednesday's Child"
Norman, Torborg. *Isolation and Contact* . . . , 137–139.

"What Death with Love Should Have to Do"
Norman, Torborg. *Isolation and Contact* . . . , 161.

"What Is the Connection Between Men and Women?"
Norman, Torborg. *Isolation and Contact* . . . , 183–184.

"Where Are You Going, Where Have You Been?"
Bastian, Katherine. *Joyce Carol Oates's Short Stories* . . . , 99.
Bohner, Charles H. *Instructor's Manual* . . . , 90–91.
Gerlach, John. *Toward the End* . . . , 120–122.
Norman, Torborg. *Isolation and Contact* . . . , 168–169.
Sheidley, William E., and Ann Charters. *Instructor's Manual* . . . , 184–185; rpt.
    Charters, Ann, William E. Sheidley, and Martha Ramsey. *Instructor's Manual* . . . , 2nd ed., 209–211.
Tierce, Mike, and John M. Crafton. "Connie's Tambourine Man: A New Reading of Arnold Friend," *Stud Short Fiction*, 22 (1985), 216–224.

"Wild Saturday"
Norman, Torborg. *Isolation and Contact* . . . , 133–135.

"Year of Wonders"
Bastian, Katherine. *Joyce Carol Oates's Short Stories* . . . , 100–102.

"You"
Norman, Torborg. *Isolation and Contact* . . . , 144–145.

FITZ-JAMES O'BRIEN

"The Diamond Lens"
Clareson, Thomas D. "Fitz-James O'Brien," in Bleiler, E. F., Ed. *Supernatural Fiction Writers* . . . , II, 720.

"From Hand to Mouth"
Clareson, Thomas D. "Fitz-James O'Brien," 720–722.

"A Terrible Night"
Clareson, Thomas D. "Fitz-James O'Brien," 719.

"What Was It?—A Mystery"
Clareson, Thomas D. "Fitz-James O'Brien," 720.

"The Wondersmith"
Clareson, Thomas D. "Fitz-James O'Brien," 719–720.

SILVINA OCAMPO

"La fotografias"
Perassi, Emilia. "Ratratto e fotografia: Note per due racconti di Silvina Ocampo," *Quaderni Ibero-Americani*, 55–56 (1982–83), 387–390.

"La paciente y el médico"
Perassi, Emilia. "Ratratto e fotografia . . . ," 387–390.

FLANNERY O'CONNOR

"The Artificial Nigger"
Cheatham, George. "Jesus, O'Connor's Artificial Nigger," *Stud Short Fiction*, 22 (1985), 475–479.
Gentry, Marshall B. *Flannery O'Connor's Religion* . . . , 81–87.
Kessler, Edward. *Flannery O'Connor* . . . , 22–23.
Yukima, Hashizume. "Urban Experience in Flannery O'Connor's 'The Artificial Nigger,'" *Sophia Engl Stud*, 11 (1986), 41–58.

"The Barber"
Dunleavy, Janet E. "A Particular History: Black and White in Flannery O'Connor's Short Fiction," in Friedman, Melvin J., and Beverly L. Clark, Eds. *Critical Essays* . . . , 195–196.

"A Circle in the Fire"
Cleary, Michael. "Environmental Influences in Flannery O'Connor's Fiction," *Flannery O'Connor Bull*, 8 (Autumn, 1979), 23–24.
Desmond, John. "Flannery O'Connor, Henry James, and the International Theme," *Flannery O'Connor Bull*, 9 (Autumn, 1980), 7–8.
Ettin, Andrew V. *Literature and the Pastoral*, 67–69.
Gentry, Marshall B. *Flannery O'Connor's Religion* . . . , 54–57.
Kessler, Edward. *Flannery O'Connor* . . . , 30–33.
Morton, Mary L. "Doubling in Flannery O'Connor's Female Characters: Animus and Anima," *Southern Q*, 23, iv (1985), 57–59.
Westling, Louise. *Sacred Groves* . . . , 166–171.

"The Comforts of Home"
Asals, Frederick. "The Double in Flannery O'Connor's Stories," *Flannery O'Connor Bull*, 9 (Autumn, 1980), 67–77.
Murphy, George D., and Caroline L. Cherry. "Flannery O'Connor and the Integration of Personality," *Flannery O'Connor Bull*, 7 (Autumn, 1978), 91–94.
Nisly, Paul W. "The Mystery of Evil: Flannery O'Connor's Gothic Power," *Flannery O'Connor Bull*, 11 (Autumn, 1982), 25–26.
Shinn, Thelma J. *Radiant Daughters* . . . , 88–89.

"The Displaced Person"
Burke, William. "Displaced Communities and Literary Form in Flannery O'Connor's 'The Displaced Person,'" *Mod Fiction Stud*, 32 (1986), 219–227.
Desmond, John. "Flannery O'Connor . . . ," 9–14.
Fickett, Harold, and Douglas R. Gilbert. *Flannery O'Connor* . . . , 57–66.
Gentry, Marshall B. *Flannery O'Connor's Religion* . . . , 21–31, 102–108.
Humphries, Jefferson. *Metamorphoses* . . . , 167–172.
Kessler, Edward. *Flannery O'Connor* . . . , 38–39.
McMillan, Norman R. "Mrs. McIntyre, Mrs. Shortley, and the Priest: Empathetic Understanding in Flannery O'Connor's 'The Displaced Person,'" *West Virginia Univ Philol Papers*, 31 (1986), 97–103.

Morton, Mary L. "Doubling . . . ," 61–62.
*Rubin, Louis D. "Two Ladies of the South," in Friedman, Melvin J., and
   Beverly L. Clark, Eds. *Critical Essays . . . ,* 27–28.

"The Enduring Chill"
Dunleavy, Janet E. "A Particular History . . . ," 196–197.
Gentry, Marshall B. *Flannery O'Connor's Religion . . . ,* 49–54.
Kessler, Edward. *Flannery O'Connor . . . ,* 126–132.

"Everything That Rises Must Converge"
Denham, Robert. "The World of Guilt and Sorrow: Flannery O'Connor's
   'Everything That Rises Must Converge,'" *Flannery O'Connor Bull,* 4 (Au-
   tumn, 1975), 42–51.
Bohner, Charles H. *Instructor's Manual . . . ,* 91–92.
Dunleavy, Janet E. "A Particular History . . . ," 197–199.
Gentry, Marshall B. *Flannery O'Connor's Religion . . . ,* 97–100.
Hopkins, Mary F. "Julian's Mother," *Flannery O'Connor Bull,* 7 (Autumn, 1978),
   114–115.
Kessler, Edward. *Flannery O'Connor . . . ,* 42–44, 123–126.
Ower, John. "The Penny and the Nickel in 'Everything That Rises Must Con-
   verge,'" *Stud Short Fiction,* 23 (1986), 107–110.

"The Geranium"
Dunleavy, Janet E. "A Particular History . . . ," 187–192.
Wood, Ralph C. "From Fashionable Tolerance to Redemption: A Reading of
   Flannery O'Connor's First and Last Stories," *Flannery O'Connor Bull,* 7 (Au-
   tumn, 1978), 13–14.

"Good Country People"
Asals, Frederick. "The Double . . . ," 58–64.
Bowen, Rose. "Baptism by Inversion," *Flannery O'Connor Bull,* 14 (1985), 94–
   98.
Gentry, Marshall B. *Flannery O'Connor's Religion . . . ,* 115–118.
Kessler, Edward. *Flannery O'Connor . . . ,* 105–106.
Scouten, Kenneth. "The Mythological Dimensions of Five of Flannery O'Con-
   nor's Works," *Flannery O'Connor Bull,* 2 (Autumn, 1973), 69–70.
Shinn, Thelma J. *Radiant Daughters . . . ,* 87, 89.
Westling, Louise. *Sacred Groves . . . ,* 146–153.

"A Good Man Is Hard to Find"
Bellamy, Michael O. "Everything Off Balance: Protestant Election in Flannery
   O'Connor's 'A Good Man Is Hard to Find,'" *Flannery O'Connor Bull,* 8
   (Autumn, 1979), 116–124.
Bohner, Charles H. *Instructor's Manual . . . ,* 92–94.
Coulthard, A. R. "Flannery O'Connor's Deadly Conversions," *Flannery O'Connor
   Bull,* 13 (1984), 93–97.
Gentry, Marshall B. *Flannery O'Connor's Religion . . . ,* 31–39, 108–112.
Kessler, Edward. *Flannery O'Connor . . . ,* 60–63.
Montgomery, Marion. "Grace: A Tricky Fictional Agent," *Flannery O'Connor
   Bull,* 9 (Autumn, 1980), 19–29.
Nisly, Paul W. "The Mystery of Evil . . . ," 27–30.
Scouten, Kenneth. "The Mythological Dimensions . . . ," 63–64.

Sheidley, William E., and Ann Charters. *Instructor's Manual . . .* , 158–159; rpt.
Charters, Ann, William E. Sheidley, and Martha Ramsey. *Instructor's Manual . . .* , 2nd ed., 167–168.
Thompson, Terry. "The Killer in O'Connor's 'A Good Man Is Hard to Find,'"
Notes Contemp Lit, 16, iv (1986), 4.

"Greenleaf"
Coulthard, A. R. ". . . Deadly Conversions," 90–93.
Desmond, John. "Flannery O'Connor . . . ," 14–17.
Gentry, Marshall B. *Flannery O'Connor's Religion . . .* , 57–62.
Giannone, Richard. "'Greenleaf': A Story of Lent," *Stud Short Fiction,* 22 (1985),
421–429.
Gidden, Nancy A. "Classical Agents of Christian Grace in Flannery O'Connor's
'Greenleaf,'" *Stud Short Fiction,* 23 (1986), 201–202.
Kessler, Edward. *Flannery O'Connor . . .* , 113–121.
Morton, Mary L. "Doubling . . . ," 59–61.
Westling, Louise. *Sacred Groves . . .* , 161–166.

"Judgement Day"
Gentry, Marshall B. *Flannery O'Connor's Religion . . .* , 87–89.
Wood, Ralph C. "From Fashionable Tolerance . . . ," 14–24.

"The Lame Shall Enter First"
Gentry, Marshall B. *Flannery O'Connor's Religion . . .* , 155–159.
Kessler, Edward. *Flannery O'Connor . . .* , 96–97.
Nisly, Paul W. "The Mystery of Evil . . . ," 30–33.

"A Late Encounter with the Enemy"
Gentry, Marshall B. *Flannery O'Connor's Religion . . .* , 91–92.
Kessler, Edward. *Flannery O'Connor . . .* , 36–37.

"The Life You Save May Be Your Own"
Gentry, Marshall B. *Flannery O'Connor's Religion . . .* , 113–115.
Kessler, Edward. *Flannery O'Connor . . .* , 141–147.
Westling, Louise. *Sacred Groves . . .* , 153–155.

"Parker's Back"
Gentry, Marshall B. *Flannery O'Connor's Religion . . .* , 77–81.
Gerlach, John. *Toward the End . . .* , 122–124.
Kessler, Edward. *Flannery O'Connor . . .* , 77–83.

"The Partridge Festival"
Gentry, Marshall B. *Flannery O'Connor's Religion . . .* , 70–74.
Malin, Irving. "Singular Vision: 'The Partridge Festival,'" in Friedman,
Melvin J., and Beverly L. Clark, Eds. *Critical Essays . . .* , 180–186.
Murphy, George D., and Caroline L. Cherry. "Flannery O'Connor . . . ," 87–
91.
Scouten, Kenneth. "The Mythological Dimensions . . . ," 70–71.

"Revelation"
Fickett, Harold, and Douglas R. Gilbert. *Flannery O'Connor . . .* , 99–106.
Gentry, Marshall B. *Flannery O'Connor's Religion . . .* , 42–49.

Kessler, Edward. *Flannery O'Connor...* , 106–108.

"The River"
Coulthard, A. R. "... Deadly Conversions," 87–90.
Gentry, Marshall B. *Flannery O'Connor's Religion...* , 94–97.
Greiff, Louis K. "J. D. Salinger's 'Teddy' and Flannery O'Connor's 'The River':
    A Comparative Analysis," *Flannery O'Connor Bull,* 9 (Autumn, 1980), 104–
    111.
Kessler, Edward. *Flannery O'Connor...* , 55–57.

"A Stroke of Good Fortune"
Gentry, Marshall B. *Flannery O'Connor's Religion...* , 92–94.
Kahane, Claire. "The Gothic Mirror," in Garner, Shirley N., Claire Kahane,
    and Madelon Sprengnether, Eds. *The (M)other Tongue...* , 345–346.
Westling, Louise. *Sacred Groves...* , 148–149.

"A Temple of the Holy Ghost"
Gentry, Marshall B. *Flannery O'Connor's Religion...* , 64–70.
Kahane, Claire. "The Gothic Mirror," 348–350.
Kessler, Edward. *Flannery O'Connor...* , 101–105.
Michaels, J. Ramsey. "'The Oldest Nun at the Sisters of Mercy': O'Connor's
    Saints and Martyrs," *Flannery O'Connor Bull,* 13 (1984), 80–86.
Westling, Louise. "The Perils of Adolescence in Flannery O'Connor and Carson
    McCullers," *Flannery O'Connor Bull,* 8 (Autumn, 1979), 94–97.
————. *Sacred Groves...* , 138–143.

"The Train"
Dunleavy, Janet E. "A Particular History...," 192–193.

"A View of the Woods"
Asals, Frederick. "The Double...," 54–58.
Kessler, Edward. *Flannery O'Connor...* , 109–111.
Murphy, George D., and Caroline L. Cherry. "Flannery O'Connor...," 94–
    98.

"The Wildcat"
Dunleavy, Janet E. "A Particular History...," 193–194.

FRANK O'CONNOR [MICHAEL O'DONOVAN]

"After Fourteen Years"
Bordewyk, Gordon. "Quest for Meaning: The Stories of Frank O'Connor,"
    Illinois Q, 14, ii (1978), 46.

"The Babes in the Wood"
Averill, Deborah M. *The Irish Short Story...* , 277–279.
Hanson, Clare. *Short Stories...* , 92–94.

"The Custom of the Country"
Averill, Deborah M. *The Irish Short Story...* , 283–285.

Thompson, Richard J. "A Kingdom of Commoners: The Moral Art of Frank O'Connor," *Éire*, 13, iv (1978), 79–80.

"The Frying Pan"
Averill, Deborah M. *The Irish Short Story . . . ,* 274–276.

"Guests of the Nation"
Averill, Deborah M. *The Irish Short Story . . . ,* 249–253.
Bohner, Charles H. *Instructor's Manual . . . ,* 94–95.
Crider, J[ohn] R[ichard]. "Jupiter Pluvius in 'Guests of the Nation,'" *Stud Short Fiction*, 23 (1986), 407–411.
Robinson, Patricia. "O'Connor's 'Guests of the Nation,'" *Explicator*, 45, i (1986), 58.
Sheidley, William E., and Ann Charters. *Instructor's Manual . . . ,* 122–123; rpt. Charters, Ann, William E. Sheidley, and Martha Ramsey. *Instructor's Manual . . . ,* 2nd ed., 122–123.
Storey, Michael L. "The Guests of Frank O'Connor and Albert Camus," *Comp Lit Stud*, 23 (1986), 250–262.

"The Holy Door"
Averill, Deborah M. *The Irish Short Story . . . ,* 285–287.

"The House That Johnny Built"
Averill, Deborah M. *The Irish Short Story . . . ,* 272–273.

"The Idealist"
Bordewyk, Gordon. "Quest for Meaning . . . ," 44.

"In the Train"
Averill, Deborah M. *The Irish Short Story . . . ,* 258–261.

"Jerome"
Bordewyk, Gordon. "Quest for Meaning . . . ," 47.

"The Little Mother"
Averill, Deborah M. *The Irish Short Story . . . ,* 299–300.

"Lost Fatherland"
Averill, Deborah M. *The Irish Short Story . . . ,* 291–294.

"The Luceys"
Averill, Deborah M. *The Irish Short Story . . . ,* 268–269.

"The Majesty of the Law"
Hanson, Clare. *Short Stories . . . ,* 87–88.

"The Man of the World"
Bordewyk, Gordon. "Quest for Meaning . . . ," 44.

"My Da"
Hanson, Clare. *Short Stories . . . ,* 90–91.

"My First Protestant"
Bordewyk, Gordon. "Quest for Meaning . . . ," 42–43.

"My Oedipus Complex"
Averill, Deborah M. *The Irish Short Story* . . . , 281–282.
Bohner, Charles H. *Instructor's Manual* . . . , 95–96.
Hanson, Clare. *Short Stories* . . . , 90.

"Nightpiece with Figures"
Bordewyk, Gordon. "Quest for Meaning . . . ," 39.

"The Old Faith"
Bordewyk, Gordon. "Quest for Meaning . . . ," 41.

"Peasants"
Averill, Deborah M. *The Irish Short Story* . . . , 255–257.

"September Dawn"
Averill, Deborah M. *The Irish Short Story* . . . , 247–249.
Bordewyk, Gordon. "Quest for Meaning . . . ," 39–40.

"A Set of Variations"
Averill, Deborah M. *The Irish Short Story* . . . , 297–298.

"Song Without Words"
Averill, Deborah M. *The Irish Short Story* . . . , 261–262.

"The Star That Bids the Shepherd Fold"
Bordewyk, Gordon. "Quest for Meaning . . . ," 41–42.

"A Torrent Damned"
Bordewyk, Gordon. "Quest for Meaning . . . ," 46.

"The Ugly Duckling"
Averill, Deborah M. *The Irish Short Story* . . . , 301–304.

"Uprooted"
Averill, Deborah M. *The Irish Short Story* . . . , 293–294.
Hanson, Clare. *Short Stories* . . . , 86–87.

JULIA O'FAOLAIN

"Daughters of Passion"
Burleigh, David. "Dead and Gone: The Fiction of Jennifer Johnston and Julia O'Faolain," in Sekine, Masaru, Ed. *Irish Writers* . . . , 13.

"Melancholy Baby"
Burleigh, David. "Dead and Gone . . . ," 8–9.

"We Might See Sights"
Burleigh, David. "Dead and Gone . . . ," 8.

SEAN O'FAOLAIN

"Angels and Ministers of Grace"
Hanson, Clare. *Short Stories* . . . , 102–104.

"A Born Genius"
Averill, Deborah M. *The Irish Short Story* . . . , 184–186.

"A Broken World"
Averill, Deborah M. *The Irish Short Story* . . . , 178–179.

"Feed My Lambs"
Averill, Deborah M. *The Irish Short Story* . . . , 211–213.

"Fugue"
Averill, Deborah M. *The Irish Short Story* . . . , 169–172.

"The Human Thing"
Averill, Deborah M. *The Irish Short Story* . . . , 200–201.

"I Remember! I Remember!"
Averill, Deborah M. *The Irish Short Story* . . . , 201–204.

"In the Bosom of the Country"
Averill, Deborah M. *The Irish Short Story* . . . , 207–210.

"An Inside-Outside Complex"
Averill, Deborah M. *The Irish Short Story* . . . , 219–220.

"The Kitchen"
Averill, Deborah M. *The Irish Short Story* . . . , 214–216.

"Lovers of the Lake"
Averill, Deborah M. *The Irish Short Story* . . . , 189–195.
Deane, Seamus. . . . *Irish Literature*, 213.

"The Man Who Invented Sin"
Averill, Deborah M. *The Irish Short Story* . . . , 182–184.

"Midsummer Night Madness"
Hanson, Clare. *Short Stories* . . . , 96–98.

"No Country for Old Men"
Hanson, Clare. *Short Stories* . . . , 98–99.

"One Night in Turin"
Averill, Deborah M. *The Irish Short Story* . . . , 206–207.

"Our Fearful Innocence"
Averill, Deborah M. *The Irish Short Story* . . . , 217–219.

"The Patriot"
Averill, Deborah M. *The Irish Short Story* . . . , 172–174.

"The Silence of the Valley"
Averill, Deborah M. *The Irish Short Story* . . . , 181–182.
Hanson, Clare. *Short Stories* . . . , 100–102.

"Two of a Kind"
Averill, Deborah M. *The Irish Short Story* . . . , 204–205.

"Up the Bare Stairs"
Averill, Deborah M. *The Irish Short Story* . . . , 186–188.

"The Younger Generation"
Averill, Deborah M. *The Irish Short Story* . . . , 198–200.

LIAM O'FLAHERTY

"The Caress"
Averill, Deborah M. *The Irish Short Story* . . . , 139–142.

"The Child of God"
Averill, Deborah M. *The Irish Short Story* . . . , 136–139.

"The Fairy Goose"
Averill, Deborah M. *The Irish Short Story* . . . , 134–135.

"Galway Bay"
Averill, Deborah M. *The Irish Short Story* . . . , 147–148.

"Going into Exile"
Averill, Deborah M. *The Irish Short Story* . . . , 122–124.

"The Landing"
Averill, Deborah M. *The Irish Short Story* . . . , 126–128.

"The Oar"
Averill, Deborah M. *The Irish Short Story* . . . , 132–133.

"Trapped"
Averill, Deborah M. *The Irish Short Story* . . . , 128–129.

"Two Lovely Beasts"
Averill, Deborah M. *The Irish Short Story* . . . , 144–145.

"The Wild Goat's Kid"
Averill, Deborah M. *The Irish Short Story* . . . , 130–131.

GRACE OGOT

"The Family Doctor"
Taiwo, Oladele. *Female Novelists* . . . , 155–156.

"Fishing Village"
Taiwo, Oladele. *Female Novelists* . . . , 156–157.

"The Honourable Minister"
Taiwo, Oladele. *Female Novelists* . . . , 153–155.

"The Island of Tears"
Taiwo, Oladele. *Female Novelists* . . . , 159–160.

"Karatina"
Taiwo, Oladele. *Female Novelists* . . . , 147–148.

"Land Without Thunder"
Taiwo, Oladele. *Female Novelists* . . . , 142–143.

"The Middle Door"
Taiwo, Oladele. *Female Novelists* . . . , 150–152.

"The Old White Witch"
Taiwo, Oladele. *Female Novelists* . . . , 143–145.

"The Other Woman"
Taiwo, Oladele. *Female Novelists* . . . , 152–153.

"The Rain Came"
Taiwo, Oladele. *Female Novelists* . . . , 140–142.

"Tekayo"
Taiwo, Oladele. *Female Novelists* . . . , 145–147.

"The Wayward Father"
Taiwo, Oladele. *Female Novelists* . . . , 157–159.

"The White Veil"
Taiwo, Oladele. *Female Novelists* . . . , 148–150.

JOHN O'HARA

"Do You Like It Here?"
Bohner, Charles H. *Instructor's Manual* . . . , 96–97.

O. HENRY [WILLIAM SYDNEY PORTER]

"The Cop and the Anthem"
Bohner, Charles H. *Instructor's Manual* . . . , 57–58.

SEUMAS O'KELLY

"Both Sides of the Pond"
Averill, Deborah M. *The Irish Short Story* . . . , 76–77.

"Nan Hogan's House"
Averill, Deborah M. *The Irish Short Story* . . . , 72–75.

"The Prodigal Daughter"
Martin, Augustine. "Prose Fiction in the Irish Literary Renaissance," in Sekine,
    Masaru, Ed. *Irish Writers* . . . , 156–157.

"The Rector"
Averill, Deborah M. *The Irish Short Story* . . . , 75–76.

"The Story of a Spell"
Martin, Augustine. "Prose Fiction . . . ," 155–156.

"The Weaver's Grave"
Averill, Deborah M. *The Irish Short Story* . . . , 78–81.
Martin, Augustine. "Prose Fiction . . . ," 157.

IURIĬ [JURY] MARLOVICH OLESHA

"The Cherry Pit" [same as "The Cherry Stone"]
Russell, Robert. "Olesha's 'The Cherry Stone,'" in Andrew, Joe, and Christo-
    pher Pike, Eds. *The Structural Analysis* . . . , 82–95.

MARGARET OLIPHANT

"A Christmas Tale"
Clute, John. "Mrs. Oliphant," in Bleiler, E. F., Ed. *Supernatural Fiction Writ-
    ers* . . . , I, 262–263.

"The Land of Darkness"
Clute, John. "Mrs. Oliphant," 265.

"The Land of Suspense"
Clute, John. "Mrs. Oliphant," 265.

"The Library Window"
Clute, John. "Mrs. Oliphant," 267.

TILLIE OLSEN

"Hey Sailor, What Ship?"
Shinn, Thelma J. *Radiant Daughters* . . . , 176.

"I Stand Here Ironing"
Bohner, Charles H. *Instructor's Manual* . . . , 97–98.
Sheidley, William E., and Ann Charters. *Instructor's Manual* . . . , 140–141; rpt.
    Charters, Ann, William E. Sheidley, and Martha Ramsey. *Instructor's Man-
    ual* . . . , 2nd ed., 141–142.

"O Yes"
Jacobs, N[aomi] M. "Olsen's 'O Yes': Akva's Vision as Childbirth Account," *Notes Contemp Lit,* 16, i (1986), 7–8.
Shinn, Thelma J. *Radiant Daughters . . . ,* 176–177.

"Tell Me a Riddle"
DuPlessis, Rachel B. *Writing Beyond . . . ,* 99–100.
Jacobs, Naomi. "Earth, Air, Fire and Water in 'Tell Me a Riddle,'" *Stud Short Fiction,* 23 (1986), 401–406.
Shinn, Thelma J. *Radiant Daughters . . . ,* 177.

JUAN CARLOS ONETTI

"A Dream Come True"
Puccini, Dario. "Vida y muerte como representación en 'Un sueño realizado' de Onetti," *Hispamerica,* 13 (August, 1984), 19–26.
Ruffinelli, Jorge. "Análisis de 'Un sueño realizado,'" in Flores, Angel, Ed. *El realismo . . . ,* 167–177.

OLIVER ONIONS

"The Beckoning Fair One"
Donaldson, Norman. "Oliver Onions," in Bleiler, E. F., Ed. *Supernatural Fiction Writers . . . ,* I, 507–508.

"The Honey in the Wall"
Donaldson, Norman. "Oliver Onions," 509.

"The Master of the House"
Donaldson, Norman. "Oliver Onions," 509.

"The Rosewood Door"
Donaldson, Norman. "Oliver Onions," 509.

"The Woman in the Way"
Donaldson, Norman. "Oliver Onions," 509.

GEORGE ORWELL

"Animal Farm"
Blackham, H. J. *The Fable . . . ,* 135–137.
*Lee, Robert A., Ed. "The Use of Form: A Reading of 'Animal Farm,'" in Oldsey, Bernard, and Joseph Browne, Eds. *Critical Essays on George Orwell,* 39–53.
Reilly, Patrick. *George Orwell . . . ,* 251–268.

CAROLYN OSBORN

"A Horse of Another Color"
Clayton, Lawrence. "The Fiction of Carolyn Osborn," *RE: Artes Liberales*, 12, ii (1986), 12–13.

"Reversals"
Clayton, Lawrence. "The Fiction . . . ," 13.

AMOS OZ

"Longing"
Gilman, Sander L. "Black Sexuality and Modern Consciousness," in Grimm, Reinhold, and Jost Hermand, Eds. *Blacks and German Culture*, 35–36.

CYNTHIA OZICK

"Bloodshed"
Berger, Alan L. *Crisis and Covenant* . . . , 49–52.
Harap, Louis. "The Religious Art of Cynthia Ozick," *Judaism*, 33 (1984), 362.

"Envy; or, Yiddish in America"
Harap, Louis. "The Religious Art . . . ," 358–359.

"Levitation"
Berger, Alan L. *Crisis and Covenant* . . . , 54–58.

"A Mercenary"
Harap, Louis. "The Religious Art . . . ," 361–362.

"Rose"
Berger, Alan L. *Crisis and Covenant* . . . , 120–126.

"The Shawl"
Berger, Alan L. *Crisis and Covenant* . . . , 52–54.

"The Suitcase"
Harap, Louis. "The Religious Art . . . ," 357.

"Usurpation (Other People's Stories)"
Harap, Louis. "The Religious Art . . . ," 362–363.

"Virility"
Harap, Louis. "The Religious Art . . . ," 359–360.

JOSÉ EMILIO PACHECO

"August Afternoon"
Cluff, Russell M. "Iniciaciónes literarias del adolescente en Sergio Galindo y José Emilio Pacheco," *La Palabra y el Hombre*, 59–60 (July–December, 1986), 17–28.

"The Bullfight"
Duncan, L. Ann. *Voices, Visions . . .* , 38–39.

"Cuando sali de La Habana, válgame Dios"
Cluff, Russell M. "'Lo absurdo' en dos cuentos José Emilio Pacheco," *Hispano,*
    28, iii (1985), 103–116.

"La fiesta brava"
Díaz, Nancy G. "El mexicano naufragado y la literatura 'pop': 'La fiesta brava'
    de José Emilio Pacheco," *Hispanic J,* 6 (1984), 131–139.
Duncan, Cynthia. "The Fantastic as a Vehicle of Social Criticism in José Emilio
    Pacheco's 'La fiesta brava,'" *Chasqui,* 14, ii–iii (1985), 3–13.

"Parque de diversiones"
Cluff, Russell M. "'Lo absurdo' en dos cuentos . . . , 103–116.

LEWIS PADGETT [CATHERINE L. MOORE and HENRY KUTTNER]

"Minsy [sic] Were the Borogroves [sic]"
Boyno, Edward A. "The Mathematics in Science Fiction: Of Measure Zero," in
    Hassler, Donald M., Ed. *Patterns . . . II,* 40–41.

THOMAS NELSON PAGE

"Marse Chan"
Gerlach, John. *Toward the End . . .* , 52–53.

BARRY PAIN [BARRY ERIC ODELL PAIN]

"The Diary of a God"
Clute, John. "Barry Pain," in Bleiler, E. F., Ed. *Supernatural Fiction Writers . . .* ,
    I, 445.

"The Glass of Supreme Moments"
Clute, John. "Barry Pain," 446.

"The Moon-Slave"
Clute, John. "Barry Pain," 444–445, 445–446.

"The Tree of Death"
Clute, John. "Barry Pain," 446.

RALPH PAINE

"The Freshman Fullback"
Graber, Ralph S. "A Goal-Line Tackle with a Broken Shoulder Blade: Early
    Football Fiction," *Markham R,* 9 (1979), 2–3.

GRACE PALEY

"A Conversation with My Father"
Bohner, Charles H. *Instructor's Manual* . . . , 98.
Klinkowitz, Jerome. *Literary Subversions* . . . , 71–72.
Sheidley, William E., and Ann Charters. *Instructor's Manual* . . . , 154–155; rpt.
    Charters, Ann, William E. Sheidley, and Martha Ramsey. *Instructor's Manual* . . . , 2nd ed., 159–160.

"An Interest in Life"
Shinn, Thelma J. *Radiant Daughters* . . . , 162–164.

"An Irrevocable Diameter"
Klinkowitz, Jerome. *Literary Subversions* . . . , 73–74.

"The Pale Pink Roast"
Schleifer, Ronald. "Grace Paley: Chaste Compactness," in Rainwater, Catherine,
    and William J. Scheick, Eds. . . . *Narrative Strategies*, 33–35.

IVAN I. PANAEV

"Actaeon"
Moser, Charles A. *The Russian Short Story* . . . , 34–35.

BREECE D'J PANCAKE

"Hollow"
Wilhelm, Albert E. "Poverty of Spirit in Breece Pancake's Short Fiction," *Critique*, 28, i (1986), 40–41.

"The Honored Dead"
Harpham, Geoffrey G. "Short Stack: The Stories of Breece D'J Pancake," *Stud Short Fiction*, 23 (1986), 266–267.

"The Scrapper"
Wilhelm, Albert E. "Poverty of Spirit . . . ," 41–42.

"Trilobites"
Harpham, Geoffrey G. "Short Stack . . . ," 266.
Wilhelm, Albert E. "Poverty of Spirit . . . ," 42–44.

DOROTHY PARKER

"Big Blonde"
Bohner, Charles H. *Instructor's Manual* . . . , 99.

"Iseult of Brittany"
Mitsch, Ruthmarie H. "Parker's 'Iseult of Brittany,'" *Explicator*, 44, ii (1986), 37–40.

MARIANO PASCUAL

"The Major's Story"
Gonzalez, N. V. M. *Mindoro and Beyond* . . . , 231–232.

WALTER PATER

"Child in the House"
Monsman, Gerald. "Pater's 'Child in the House' and the Renovation of the Self,"
Texas Stud Lit & Lang, 28 (1986), 281–295.

NIKOLAI PAVLOV

"The Nameday Party"
Moser, Charles A. *The Russian Short Story* . . . , 28–29.

MARTIN PEARSON [DONALD A. WOLLHEIM]

"Private World"
Bousfield, Wendy. *"Ten Story Fantasy,"* in Tymn, Marshall B., and Mike Ashley,
Eds. *Science Fiction . . . Magazines,* 627.

RAYMOND PILLAI

"Muni Deo's Devil"
Shameem, Shaista. "The Art of Raymond Pillai, Subramani, and Prem Banfal:
A Feminist Critique of the Indo-Fijian Short Story," *SPAN,* 20 (April, 1985),
32–36.

"To Market, To Market"
Shameem, Shaista. "The Art . . . ," 36–38.

VIRGILIO PIÑERA

"Allegations Against the Uninstalled Bathtub"
Koch, Dolores M. "Virgilio Piñera, Short-Fiction Writer," *Folio,* 16 (December,
1984), 85–87.

H. BEAM PIPER

"Omnilingual"
Sefler, George F. "Science, Science Fiction, and Possible World Semantics," in
Coyle, William, Ed. *Aspects of Fantasy* . . . , 213–219.

228 LUIGI PIRANDELLO

LUIGI PIRANDELLO

"War"
Bohner, Charles H. *Instructor's Manual* . . . , 99–100.

"The Wheelbarrow"
Moraldo, Sandro. "Identität als Ekstrase in Pirandellos Novelle 'La carriola,'"
Germanisch-Romanische Monatsschrift, 35 (1985), 57–68.

SYLVIA PLATH

"The Brink"
Wagner, Linda W. "Sylvia Plath's Specialness in Her Short Stories," *J Narrative Technique*, 15, i (1985), 3.

"In the Mountains"
Zajdel, Melody. "Apprenticed in a Bible of Dreams: Sylvia Plath's Short Stories," in Wagner, Linda W., Ed. *Critical Essays* . . . , 188–189.

"Johnny Panic and the Bible of Dreams"
Zajdel, Melody. "Apprenticed in a Bible . . . ," 190–191.

"Stone Boy with Dolphin"
Wagner, Linda W. "Sylvia Plath's Specialness . . . ," 9–11.

"Sunday at the Mintons'"
Wagner, Linda W. "Sylvia Plath's Specialness . . . ," 6–9.
Zajdel, Melody. "Apprenticed in a Bible . . . ," 191–192.

"Sweetie-Pie and the Gutter Men"
Zajdel, Melody. "Apprenticed in a Bible . . . ," 189–190.

"Tongues of Stone"
Zajdel, Melody. "Apprenticed in a Bible . . . ," 182–188.

"The Wishing Box"
Zajdel, Melody. "Apprenticed in a Bible . . . ," 192.

ANDREI PLATONOV

"Makar the Doubtful"
Moser, Charles A. *The Russian Short Story* . . . , 168–169.

EDGAR ALLAN POE

"The Assignation"
Fisher, Benjamin F. "The Flight of a Good Man's Mind: Gothic Fantasy in Poe's 'The Assignation,'" *Mod Lang Stud*, 16, iii (1986), 27–34.

Pitcher, Edward W. R. "'To Die Laughing': Poe's Allusion to Sir Thomas More in 'The Assignation,'" *Stud Short Fiction*, 23 (1986), 197–200.

"Berenice"
Current-García, Eugene. *The American Short Story before 1850* . . . , 63–64.
Zanger, Jules. "Poe's 'Berenice': Philosophical Fantasy and Its Pitfalls," in Collins, Robert A., and Howard D. Pearce, Eds. *The Scope of the Fantastic* . . . , 135–141.

"The Black Cat"
Frieden, Ken. *Genius and Monologue*, 161–162.
*Hoffman, Daniel. "The Marriage Group," in Bloom, Harold, Ed. *Edgar Allan Poe*, 82–84.
Matheson, T. J. "Poe's 'The Black Cat' as a Critique of Temperance Literature," *Mosaic*, 19, iii (1986), 69–81.

"The Cask of Amontillado"
Bohner, Charles H. *Instructor's Manual* . . . , 100–101.
Current-García, Eugene. *The American Short Story before 1850* . . . , 77–78.
Frieden, Ken. *Genius and Monologue*, 166–168.

"The Colloquy of Monos and Una"
*Tate, Allen. "The Angelic Imagination," in Bloom, Harold, Ed. *Edgar Allan Poe*, 42–44.

"The Conversation of Eiros and Charmion"
Koch, Christian. "The Irony of Oxygen in Poe's 'Eiros and Charmion,'" *Stud Short Fiction*, 22 (1985), 317–321.
*Tate, Allen. "The Angelic Imagination," 39–42.

"A Descent into the Maelström"
Carton, Evan. *The Rhetoric* . . . , 70–72.
Clifton, Michael. "Down Hecate's Chain: Infernal Inspiration in Three of Poe's Tales," *Nineteenth-Century Fiction*, 41 (1986), 220–224.
Ljungquist, Kent. *The Grand and the Fair* . . . , 72–80.
Odin, Jaishree. "Suggestiveness—Poe's Writing from the Perspective of Indian *Rasa* Theory," *Comp Lit Stud*, 23 (1986), 304–306.
Robinson, Douglas. *American Apocalypse* . . . , 139–142.

"The Domain of Arnheim"
Carton, Evan. *The Rhetoric* . . . , 94–95.
Ljungquist, Kent. *The Grand and the Fair* . . . , 129–134.

"The Duc de L'Omelette"
Clifton, Michael. "Down Hecate's Chain . . . ," 218–220.

"Eleonora"
Ljungquist, Kent. *The Grand and the Fair* . . . , 119–124.

"The Facts in the Case of M. Valdemar"
Wood, Michael. "Poe's Tales: The Art of the Impossible," in Lee, A. Robert, Ed. . . . *American Short Story*, 15–16.

"The Fall of the House of Usher"
Bleiler, E. F. "Edgar Allan Poe," in Bleiler, E. F., Ed. *Supernatural Fiction Writers* . . . , II, 701–702.
Bohner, Charles H. *Instructor's Manual* . . . , 101–102.
Carton, Evan. *The Rhetoric* . . . , 72–76.
Caws, Mary Ann. *Reading Frames* . . . , 109–118.
Clifton, Michael. "Down Hecate's Chain . . . ," 224–227.
Day, William P. *In the Circles* . . . , 129–131.
Engel, Leonard W. "The Journey from Reason to Madness: Edgar Allan Poe's 'The Fall of the House of Usher,'" *Essays Arts & Sciences*, 14 (May, 1985), 23–31.
Gerlach, John. *Toward the End* . . . , 30–35.
Howes, Craig. " 'The Fall of the House of Usher' and Elegiac Romance," *Southern Lit J*, 19, i (1986), 68–78.
Hughes, Kenneth J. *Signs of Literature* . . . , 167–169.
Kent, Thomas. *Interpretation* . . . , 50–53.
*Lawrence, D. H. "Edgar Allan Poe," in Bloom, Harold, Ed. *Edgar Allan Poe*, 30–31.
Ljungquist, Kent. *The Grand and the Fair* . . . , 100–106.
Marder, Daniel. *Exiles at Home* . . . , 89–93.
Odin, Jaishree. "Suggestiveness . . . , " 306–308.
Robinson, Douglas. *American Apocalypse* . . . , 174–177.
Shackelford, Lynne. "Poe's 'The Fall of the House of Usher,'" *Explicator*, 45, i (1986), 18–19.
Voloshin, Beverly R. "Explanation in 'The Fall of the House of Usher,'" *Stud Short Fiction*, 23 (1986), 419–428.
Wilbur, Richard. "The House of Poe," in Hillyer, Robert, Richard Wilbur, and Cleanth Brooks. *Anniversary Lectures*, 25–31; rpt. Carlson, Eric W., Ed. . . . *Edgar Allan Poe*, 264–268; Regan, Robert, Ed. *Poe* . . . , 104–111; Basler, Roy, Ed. *Literary Lectures* . . . , 331–342; Bloom, Harold, Ed. *Edgar Allan Poe*, 56–62; Barbour, James, and Thomas Quirk, Eds. *Romanticism* . . . , 150–155.
Wood, Michael. "Poe's Tales . . . ," 25–26.

"The Gold Bug"
Goldhurst, William. "Self-Reflective Fiction by Poe: Three Tales," *Mod Lang Stud*, 16, iii (1986), 8–10.
Phillips, Elizabeth C. " 'His Right of Attendance': The Image of the Black Man in Poe and Two of His Contemporaries," in Dameron, J. Lasley, and James W. Mathews, Eds. *No Fairer Land* . . . , 172–184.

"The Imp of the Perverse"
Frieden, Ken. *Genius and Monologue*, 162–164.

"The Island of the Fay"
Ljungquist, Kent. *The Grand and the Fair* . . . , 110–119.

"Landor's Cottage"
Carton, Evan. *The Rhetoric* . . . , 95–97.

"Ligeia"
Bleiler, E. F. "Edgar Allan Poe," 699–700.

Carton, Evan. *The Rhetoric* . . . , 98–105.
*Griffith, Clark. "Poe's 'Ligeia' and the English Romantics," in Bloom, Harold, Ed. *Edgar Allan Poe*, 71–80.
*Hoffman, Daniel. "The Marriage Group," 89–102.
*————. "Poe's 'Ligeia': I Have Been Faithful to You in My Fashion," in Barbour, James, and Thomas Quirk, Eds. *Romanticism* . . . , 165–178.
*Lawrence, D. H. *Edgar Allan Poe*, 22–29.
Ljungquist, Kent. *The Grand and the Fair* . . . , 203–209.
Marder, Daniel. *Exiles at Home* . . . , 86–89.
Robinson, Douglas. *American Apocalypse* . . . , 234–240.

"Loss of Breath"
Carton, Evan. *The Rhetoric* . . . , 91–93.

"The Man of the Crowd"
Marder, Daniel. *Exiles at Home* . . . , 66–68.
Robinson, Douglas. *American Apocalypse* . . . , 240–242.

"The Man That Was Used Up"
Carton, Evan. *The Rhetoric* . . . , 144–145.
Rougé, Bertrand. "La Pratique des corps limites chez Poe: La Vérité sur le cas de 'The Man That Was Used Up,'" *Poétique*, 15 (1984), 473–488.

"MS. Found in a Bottle"
Carton, Evan. *The Rhetoric* . . . , 67–71.
Frieden, Ken. *Genius and Monologue*, 164–166.
Ljungquist, Kent. *The Grand and the Fair* . . . , 53–56.
Scharnhorst, Gary. "Another Night-Sea Journey: Poe's 'MS. Found in a Bottle,'" *Stud Short Fiction*, 22 (1985), 203–208.

"The Masque of the Red Death"
Robinson, Douglas. *American Apocalypse* . . . , 201–204.
Ruddick, Nicholas. "The Hoax of the Red Death: Poe as Allegorist," *Sphinx*, 4 (1985), 268–276.
Wilbur, Richard. "The House of Poe," 37–38; rpt. Regan, Robert, Ed. *Poe* . . . , 118–119; Bloom, Harold, Ed. *Edgar Allan Poe*, 68–69; Barbour, James, and Thomas Quirk, Eds. *Romanticism* . . . , 162–163.

"Mesmeric Revelation"
Carton, Evan. *The Rhetoric* . . . , 62–67.

"Metzengerstein"
Bleiler, E. F. "Edgar Allan Poe," 698–699.

"The Murders in the Rue Morgue"
Lemay, J. A. Leo. "The Psychology of 'The Murders in the Rue Morgue,'" *Am Lit*, 54 (1982), 165–188; rpt. Barbour, James, and Thomas Quirk, Eds. *Romanticism* . . . , 179–200.
Pollin, Burton R. "Poe's 'Murders in the Rue Morgue': The Ingenious Web Unravelled," *Stud Am Renaissance*, [I] (1977), 235–259; rpt. in his *Insights and Outlooks* . . . , 101–129.
Ruehlmann, William. *Saint with a Gun* . . . , 32–34.

"The Narrative of Arthur Gordon Pym"
Carton, Evan. *The Rhetoric* . . . , 137–138.
Caws, Mary Ann. *Reading Frames* . . . , 114–120.
Irwin, John T. *American Hieroglyphics* . . . , 188–205; rpt. Bloom, Harold, Ed. *Edgar Allan Poe*, 103–118.
Kazin, Alfred. *An American Procession*, 95–100.
Ljungquist, Kent. *The Grand and the Fair* . . . , 56–72.
Robinson, Douglas. *American Apocalypse* . . . , 111–122.
Zanger, Jules. "Poe's Endless Voyage: 'The Narrative of Arthur Gordon Pym,'" *Papers Lang & Lit*, 22 (1986), 276–283.

"The Oblong Box"
Goldhurst, William. "Self-Reflective Fiction . . . ," 5–8.

"The Oval Portrait"
Carton, Evan. *The Rhetoric* . . . , 138–144.
Caws, Mary Ann. *Reading Frames* . . . , 89–100.
Current-García, Eugene. *The American Short Story before 1850* . . . , 75–76.
Gerlach, John. *Toward the End* . . . , 85–86.

"The Pit and the Pendulum"
Ljungquist, Kent. *The Grand and the Fair* . . . , 195–203.

"The Power of Words"
*Tate, Allen. "The Angelic Imagination," 44–47.

"The Premature Burial"
Carton, Evan. *The Rhetoric* . . . , 145–147.

"The Purloined Letter"
Bohner, Charles H. *Instructor's Manual* . . . , 102–103.
Irwin, John T. "Mysteries We Reread, Mysteries of Rereading: Poe, Borges, and the Analytic Detective Story; Also Lacan, Derrida, and Johnson," *Mod Lang Notes*, 101 (1986), 1170–1188.
Ponzio, Augusto. "Dupin e i giochi," *Il Lettore di Provincia*, 16 (March, 1985), 19–27.

"The Spectacles"
*Hoffman, Daniel. "The Marriage Group," 87–88.

"The Sphinx"
Elmar, Schenkel. "Disease and Vision: Perspectives on Poe's 'The Sphinx,'" *Stud Am Fiction*, 13 (1985), 97–102.
Goldhurst, William. "Self-Reflective Fiction . . . ," 10–13.

"The System of Doctor Tarr and Professor Fether"
Carton, Evan. *The Rhetoric* . . . , 135–137.

"The Tell-Tale Heart"
Frieden, Ken. *Genius and Monologue*, 160–161.
Witherington, Paul. "The Accomplice in 'The Tell-Tale Heart,'" *Stud Short Fiction*, 22 (1985), 471–475.

"Thou Art the Man"
Rougé, Bertrand. "Irony and Ventriloquism: Notes Toward an Interpretation of Edgar Allan Poe's 'Thou Art the Man,'" in Royot, Daniel, Ed. *Interface . . .* , 21–30.

"Three Sundays in a Week"
Roth, Martin. "Poe's 'Three Sundays in a Week,'" *Sphinx*, 4 (1985), 258–267.

"The Unparalleled Adventures of One Hans Pfaall"
Miller, Karl. *Doubles . . .* , 160–163.

"Von Kempelen and His Discovery"
McGann, Jerome J. *The Beauty of Inflection . . .* , 102–107.

"William Wilson"
Carton, Evan. *The Rhetoric . . .* , 36–41.
Engel, Leonard W. "Identity and Enclosure in Edgar Allan Poe's 'William Wilson,'" *Coll Lang Assoc J*, 29 (1985), 91–99.
Robinson, Douglas. *American Apocalypse . . .* , 207–211.

FREDERIK POHL

"Let the Ants Try"
Manlove, C. N. *Science Fiction . . .* , 40.

"Pythians"
Manlove, C. N. *Science Fiction . . .* , 40–41.

"Rafferty's Reasons"
Manlove, C. N. *Science Fiction . . .* , 48–52.

"The Tunnel Under the World"
Berger, Harold L. *Science Fiction . . .* , 117.

"What to Do Till the Analyst Comes"
Berger, Harold L. *Science Fiction . . .* , 42.
Manlove, C. N. *Science Fiction . . .* , 38–39.

"The Wizard of Pung's Corner"
Berger, Harold L. *Science Fiction . . .* , 117–118.

RENÉ POPPE

"Una mita más mi General"
Prada, Ana R. "El cuento contemporáneo de la represión en Bolivia," in Sanjinés C., Javier, Ed. *Tendencias actuales . . .* , 68–71.

HAL PORTER

"A Double Because It's Snowing"
Hawley-Crowcroft, Jean. "Hal Porter's Asian Stories: The Writer as Watcher," *Quadrant*, 28, vii–viii (1984), 42–43.

"The Housegirl"
Hawley-Crowcroft, Jean. "Hal Porter's Asian Stories . . . ," 43.

"Say to Me Ronald"
Hawley-Crowcroft, Jean. "Hal Porter's Asian Stories . . . ," 41–42.

"They're Funny People"
Bennett, Bruce. "Asian Encounters in the Contemporary Australian Short
    Story," *World Lit Written Engl*, 26 (1986), 55.
Hawley-Crowcroft, Jean. "Hal Porter's Asian Stories . . . ," 44–45.

KATHERINE ANNE PORTER

"The Circus"
Malik, Meera. "Use of Animal Imagery in the Work of Katherine Anne Porter,"
    Panjab Univ Research Bull, 16, i (1985), 32–33.
Teixeira, Cristina M. "Fiction As an Outlet for Problems of Identity: Analysis
    of Some of Katherine Anne Porter's Stories," *Estudos Anglo-Americanos*, 7–
    8 (1983–84), 51–52.
Unrue, Darlene H. *Truth and Vision . . . ,* 30–33.

"The Cracked Looking-Glass"
Unrue, Darlene H. *Truth and Vision . . . ,* 122–124.

"The Downward Path to Wisdom"
Unrue, Darlene H. *Truth and Vision . . . ,* 36–39.

"The Fig Tree"
Teixeira, Cristina M. "Fiction As an Outlet . . . ," 50–51.
Unrue, Darlene H. *Truth and Vision . . . ,* 45–48.

"Flowering Judas"
Bohner, Charles H. *Instructor's Manual . . . ,* 103–104.
Gerlach, John. *Toward the End . . . ,* 100–107.
Sheidley, William E., and Ann Charters. *Instructor's Manual . . . ,* 94–95; rpt.
    Charters, Ann, William E. Sheidley, and Martha Ramsey. *Instructor's Man-
    ual . . . ,* 2nd ed., 97–99.
Teixeira, Cristina M. "Fiction As an Outlet . . . ," 47–49.
Unrue, Darlene H. *Truth and Vision . . . ,* 52–59.
Walsh, Thomas F. "Braggioni's Songs in 'Flowering Judas,'" *Coll Lit*, 12 (1985),
    147–152.
Walter, James. "Revolution and Time: Laura in 'Flowering Judas,'" *Renascence*,
    38, i (1985), 26–38.
Welty, Eudora. *The Eye of the Storm*, 37–38.

"The Grave"
Bohner, Charles H. *Instructor's Manual . . . ,* 104–105.
Teixeira, Cristina M. "Fiction As an Outlet . . . ," 52–53.
Unrue, Darlene H. *Truth and Vision . . . ,* 48–53.

"Hacienda"
Malik, Meera. "Use of Animal Imagery . . . ," 33.
Unrue, Darlene H. *Truth and Vision* . . . , 26–29.

"He"
Unrue, Darlene H. *Truth and Vision* . . . , 33–35.

"Holiday"
Unrue, Darlene H. *Truth and Vision* . . . , 147–149.

"The Jilting of Granny Weatherall"
Estes, David C. "Granny Weatherall's Dying Moment: Katherine Anne Porter's
    Allusion to Emily Dickinson," *Stud Short Fiction*, 22 (1985), 437–442.
Meyers, Robert. "Porter's 'The Jilting of Granny Weatherall,'" *Explicator*, 44, ii
    (1986), 37.
Timson, Stephen. "Katherine Anne Porter and the Essential Spirit: The Pursuit
    and Discovery of Truth in 'The Jilting of Granny Weatherall,'" *Kyushu Am
    Lit*, 27 (1986), 71–80.
Unrue, Darlene H. *Truth and Vision* . . . , 98–101.

"The Leaning Tower"
Jones, Annie G. "Gender and the Great War: The Case of Faulkner and Porter,"
    in Gilbert, Sandra M., and Susan Gubar, Eds. *The Female Imagination* . . . ,
    145–146.
Unrue, Darlene H. *Truth and Vision* . . . , 139–145.

"Magic"
Leath, Helen L. "Washing the Dirty Linen in Private: An Analysis of Katherine
    Anne Porter's 'Magic,'" *Conference Coll Teachers Engl*, 50 (September, 1985),
    51–58.

"Maria Concepción"
Teixeira, Cristina M. "Fiction As an Outlet . . . ," 45–46.
Unrue, Darlene H. *Truth and Vision* . . . , 16–25.

"The Martyr"
Unrue, Darlene H. *Truth and Vision* . . . , 107–115.

"Noon Wine"
Stout, Janis P. "Mr. Hatch's Volubility and Miss Porter's Reserve," *Essays Lit*, 12
    (1985), 285–293.
Unrue, Darlene H. *Truth and Vision* . . . , 40–45.

"Old Mortality"
Teixeira, Cristina M. "Fiction As an Outlet . . . ," 53–55.
Unrue, Darlene H. *Truth and Vision* . . . , 124–131.
White, Barbara A. *Growing Up Female* . . . , 141–142.

"The Old Order"
Hankins, Leslie K. "Ritual: Representation and Reversal in Katherine Anne
    Porter's 'The Old Order,'" in Harkness, Don, Ed. *Ritual* . . . , 20–23.
Teixeira, Cristina M. "Fiction As an Outlet . . . ," 49–50.

ESTELA PORTILLO TRAMBLEY

"The Secret Room"
Martínez, Eliud. "Personal Vision . . . ," 85.

"The Trees"
Martínez, Eliud. "Personal Vision . . . ," 74–78.
Salazar Parr, Carmen, and Genevieve M. Ramírez. "The Female Hero . . . ,"
    52–53.
Vallejos, Tomás. ". . . Search for Paradise," 270–272.

J. F. POWERS

"The Valiant Woman"
Bohner, Charles H. *Instructor's Manual* . . . , 105–106.

T. F. POWYS

"The Bucket and the Rope"
Hanson, Clare. *Short Stories* . . . , 105–106.

"Darkness and Nathaniel"
Hanson, Clare. *Short Stories* . . . , 106–107.

"The Only Penitent"
Hanson, Clare. *Short Stories* . . . , 109–110.

"The Stone and Mr. Thomas"
Hanson, Clare. *Short Stories* . . . , 107–108.

MUNSHI PREM CHAND [MUNSHI DHANPAT RAI]

"Kafan"
Mukerjee, Meenakshi. *Realism and Reality* . . . , 46.

V. S. PRITCHETT

"Blind Love"
Hanson, Clare. *Short Stories* . . . , 131–132.

"The Camberwell Beauty"
Evans, Walter. "The English Short Story in the Seventies," in Vannatta, Dennis,
    Ed. *The English Short Story, 1945–1980,* 130–131.

"The Corsican Inn"
Flora, Joseph M. *The English Short Story* . . . , 143–144.

"Handsome Is as Handsome Does"
Hanson, Clare. *Short Stories* . . . , 129–131.

"The Sailor"
Flora, Joseph M. *The English Short Story* . . . , 147–148.
Hanson, Clare. *Short Stories* . . . , 126–129.

"The Saint"
Stinson, John J. "The English Short Story, 1945–1950," in Vannatta, Dennis,
    Ed. *The English Short Story, 1945–1980,* 11–12.

"The Speech"
Pickering, Jean. "The English Short Story in the Sixties," in Vannatta, Dennis,
    Ed. *The English Short Story, 1945–1980,* 100–101.

JAMES PURDY

"Color of Darkness"
Miller, Paul W. "James Purdy's Early Years in Ohio and His Early Short Stories,"
    Midamerica, 11 (1984), 113–114.

"Cutting Edge"
Miller, Paul W. "James Purdy's Early Years . . . ," 115–116.

"Don't Call Me by My Right Name"
Miller, Paul W. "James Purdy's Early Years . . . ," 112.

"Man and Wife"
Miller, Paul W. "James Purdy's Early Years . . . ," 110.

"Why Can't They Tell You Why?"
Renner, Stanley. " 'Why Can't They Tell You Why?': A Clarifying Echo of 'The
    Turn of the Screw,' " *Stud Am Fiction,* 14 (1986), 205–213.

"You Reach for Your Hat"
Miller, Paul W. "James Purdy's Early Years . . . ," 112–113.

ALEXANDER PUSHKIN

"The Blizzard"
Moser, Charles A. *The Russian Short Story* . . . , 6–7.

"Egyptian Nights"
Todd, William M. *Fiction and Society* . . . , 108.

"The Queen of Spades"
Leatherbarrow, W. J. "Pushkin: 'The Queen of Spades,' " in Cockrell, Roger,
    and David Richards, Eds. *The Voice of a Giant* . . . , 1–14.
Moser, Charles A. *The Russian Short Story* . . . , 8–9.
Pursglove, Michael. "Chronology in Pushkin's 'Pikovaia dama,' " *Irish Slavonic
    Stud,* 6 (1985), 11–18.
Simpson, Mark S. *The Officer* . . . , 70–74.

"The Shot"
Bohner, Charles H. *Instructor's Manual* . . . , 106–107.
Simpson, Mark S. *The Officer* . . . , 63–70.

BARBARA PYM

"Across the Crowded Room"
Kaufman, Anthony. "The Short Fiction of Barbara Pym," *Twentieth Century Lit,*
    32 (1986), 62–66.

"The Day the Music Came"
Kaufman, Anthony. "The Short Fiction . . . ," 54–57.

"English Ladies"
Kaufman, Anthony. "The Short Fiction . . . ," 59–62.

"Goodbye, Balkan Capital!"
Kaufman, Anthony. "The Short Fiction . . . ," 57.

"So Some Tempestuous Morn . . ."
Kaufman, Anthony. "The Short Fiction . . . ," 69–72.

"The White Elephant"
Kaufman, Anthony. "The Short Fiction . . . ," 66–68.

THOMAS PYNCHON

"Entropy"
Newman, Robert D. *Understanding Thomas Pynchon,* 22–25.
Tabbi, Joseph. "Merging Orders: The Shaping Influence of Science on 'Entropy,'" *Pynchon Notes,* 15 (Fall, 1984), 58–68.

"Low-Lands"
Newman, Robert D. *Understanding Thomas Pynchon,* 15–22.

"Mortality and Mercy in Vienna"
Smetak, Jacqueline. "Thomas Pynchon's 'Mortality and Mercy in Vienna': Major
    Themes in an Early Work," *Iowa J Lit Stud,* 4, i (1983), 65–76.
Tylee, Claire M. "'Spot This Mumbo Jumbo': Thomas Pynchon's Emblems for
    American Culture in 'Mortality and Mercy in Vienna,'" *Revista Canaria,* 10
    (1985), 141–156.

"The Secret Integration"
Newman, Robert D. *Understanding Thomas Pynchon,* 29–32.

"The Small Rain"
Newman, Robert D. *Understanding Thomas Pynchon,* 13–15.

"Under the Rose"
Newman, Robert D. *Understanding Thomas Pynchon,* 25–29.

QIAO SHI

"Providing a Meal"
Duke, Michael S. *Blooming . . .* , 76–79.

RAYMOND QUENEAU

"A la limite de la forêt"
Shorley, Christopher. *Queneau's Fiction . . .* , 140–141.

ARTHUR QUILLER-COUCH

"The Mystery of Joseph Laquedem"
Elkins, Charles L. "Arthur Quiller-Couch," in Bleiler, E. F., Ed. *Supernatural Fiction Writers . . .* , I, 394.

"The Room of Mirrors"
Elkins, Charles L. "Arthur Quiller-Couch," 392.

HORACIO QUIROGA

"A la deriva"
Yurkievich, Saul. "Análisis de 'A la deriva,'" in Flores, Angel, Ed. *El realismo . . .* , 115–121.

"El crimen del otro"
Gambarini, Elsa K. "La escritura como lectura: La parodia en 'El crimen del otro,' de Horacio Quiroga," *Revista Iberoamericana*, 52 (1986), 475–488.

"The Dead Man"
Etcheverry, José E. "Análisis de 'El hombre muerto,'" in Flores, Angel, Ed. *El realismo . . .* , 126–131.

"The Decapitated Chicken"
Pearson, Lon. "Horacio Quiroga's Obsessions with Abnormal Psychology and Medicine as Reflected in 'La Gallina Degollada,'" *Lit & Psych*, 22, ii (1986), 32–46.

"The Flies"
Malinow, Inéz. "Dos escritores y dos cuentos americanos: H. Quiroga y J. C., 'Las moschas' y 'Axolotl'—Técnicas narrativas," *Inti*, 22–23 (Fall, 1985– Spring, 1986), 385–389.

"La insolación"
Köner, K. H. "Horacio Quiroga, écologiste hispanamércain et sémiologue avant la lettre," *Bull Hispanique*, 87 (1985), 387–409.

"Juan Darién"
Porras Collantes, Ernesto. "Estructura del personaje central en 'Juan Darién' de Horacio Quiroga," *Thesaurus*, 40 (1985), 579.

"The Spectre"
Gambarini, Elsa K. "Horacio Quiroga: Un cambio de codigo y su descodificacion," *Acta Literaria*, 10–11 (1985–1986), 155–165.

ESTHER RAAB

"The Days of *Hedim*"
Melamed, David. "Requiem for a Landscape," *Mod Hebrew Lit*, 9, iii–iv (1984), 71–72.

RAJA RAO

"The Cow of the Barricades"
Kalinnikova, Elena J. *Indian-English Literature* . . . , 136–137.

"Javni"
Kalinnikova, Elena J. *Indian-English Literature* . . . , 138.

VALENTIN GRIGOREVICH RASPUTIN

"Parting with Matera"
Marsh, Rosalind J. *Soviet Fiction Since Stalin* . . . , 183–184.

"Vasily and Vasilisa"
Moser, Charles A. *The Russian Short Story* . . . , 188–189.

ISHMAEL REED

"Cab Calloway Stands in for Moon"
Bamberger, W. C. "The Waxing and Waning of Cab Calloway," *R Contemp Fiction*, 4 (1984), 202–204.

JEAN RHYS [ELLA GWENDOLEN REES WILLIAMS]

"Fishy Waters"
Davidson, Arnold E. *Jean Rhys*, 128–129.

"Goodbye Marcus, Goodbye Rose"
Davidson, Arnold E. *Jean Rhys*, 129–133.

"La Gross Fifi"
Davidson, Arnold E. *Jean Rhys*, 117–120.

"I Spy a Stranger"
Angier, Carole. *Jean Rhys,* 72–73.

"Illusion"
Davidson, Arnold E. *Jean Rhys,* 114.

"Let Them Call It Jazz"
Angier, Carole. *Jean Rhys,* 80–81.
Wilson, Lucy. "'Women Must Have Spunk': Jean Rhys's West Indian Outcasts,"
    Mod Fiction Stud, 32 (1986), 442–443.

"The Lotus"
Davidson, Arnold E. *Jean Rhys,* 123.

"Outside the Machine"
Davidson, Arnold E. *Jean Rhys,* 125–128.

"Sleep It Off, Lady"
Davidson, Arnold E. *Jean Rhys,* 120–123.

"A Solid House"
Davidson, Arnold E. *Jean Rhys,* 123–124.

"Tea with an Artist"
Flora, Joseph M. *The English Short Story . . . ,* 26–27.

"Tigers Are Better Looking"
Davidson, Arnold E. *Jean Rhys,* 129.

"Vienna"
Davidson, Arnold E. *Jean Rhys,* 116–117.

J. H. RIDDELL

"Forewarned, Forearmed"
Campbell, James L. "Mrs. J. H. Riddell," in Bleiler, E. F., Ed. *Supernatural Fiction Writers . . . ,* I, 272–273.

"Hertford O'Donnell's Warning"
Campbell, James L. "Mrs. J. H. Riddell," 271–272.

"Nut Bush Farm"
Campbell, James L. "Mrs. J. H. Riddell," 273–274.

"The Old House in Vauxhall Walk"
Campbell, James L. "Mrs. J. H. Riddell," 274.

"Old Mrs. Jones"
Campbell, James L. "Mrs. J. H. Riddell," 275.

"The Open Door"
Campbell, James L. "Mrs. J. H. Riddell," 273.

"Sandy the Tinker"
Campbell, James L. "Mrs. J. H. Riddell," 274–275.

"A Strange Christmas Game"
Campbell, James L. "Mrs. J. H. Riddell," 272.

"Walnut-Tree House"
Campbell, James L. "Mrs. J. H. Riddell," 273.

TOMÁS RIVERA

". . . And the Earth Did Not Part"
Urquídez-Somoza, Oscar. "Tomás Rivera," in Martínez, Julio A., and
Francisco A. Lomelí, Eds. *Chicano Literature* . . . , 338–339.

"The Children Were Victims"
Urquídez-Somoza, Oscar. "Tomás Rivera," 337.

"Christmas Eve"
Urquídez-Somoza, Oscar. "Tomás Rivera," 340–341.

"First Holy Communion"
Urquídez-Somoza, Oscar. "Tomás Rivera," 339.

"His Hands in His Pockets"
Urquídez-Somoza, Oscar. "Tomás Rivera," 338.

"It Is Painful"
Urquídez-Somoza, Oscar. "Tomás Rivera," 337–338.

"It Was a Silvery Night"
Saldívar, Ramón. "A Dialectic of Difference: Toward a Theory of the Chicano
Novel," in Lattin, Vernon E., Ed. *Contemporary Chicano Fiction* . . . , 21–22.
Urquídez-Somoza, Oscar. "Tomás Rivera," 338.

"Little Children Burned"
Urquídez-Somoza, Oscar. "Tomás Rivera," 339–340.

"The Lost Year"
Urquídez-Somoza, Oscar. "Tomás Rivera," 336–337.

"The Night of the Blackout"
Lizáragga, Sylvia S. "The Patriarchal Ideology in 'La noche que se apagaron
las luces,'" *Revista Chicano-Riqueña*, 13, iii–iv (1985), 90–95.
Urquídez-Somoza, Oscar. "Tomás Rivera," 340.

"On the Way to Texas"
Urquídez-Somoza, Oscar. "Tomás Rivera," 343.

"A Prayer"
Urquídez-Somoza, Oscar. "Tomás Rivera," 337.

"The Salamander"
Urquídez-Somoza, Oscar. "Tomás Rivera," 343.

"Under the House"
Urquídez-Somoza, Oscar. "Tomás Rivera," 341–342.

"When We Arrive"
Urquídez-Somoza, Oscar. "Tomás Rivera," 341.

AUGUSTO ROA BASTOS

"Brothers"
Scroggins, Daniel S. "Brotherhood and Fratricide in the Early Fiction of Augusto Roa Bastos," *Hispanic J*, 6, ii (1985), 142–143.

"The Excavation"
Scroggins, Daniel S. "Brotherhood and Fratricide . . . ," 139–141.

"The Prisoner"
Scroggins, Daniel S. "Brotherhood and Fratricide . . . ," 141–142.

RAMÓN ROCHA MONROY

"Hora cero"
Prada, Ana R. "El cuento contemporanéo de la represión en Bolivia," in Sanjinés C., Javier, Ed. *Tendencias actuales . . .* , 64–68.

EDWARD PAYSON ROE

"Gentle Woman Roused"
Carey, Glenn O. *Edward Payson Roe*, 85–86.

OCTAVIO ROMANO

"One More Rosary for Doña Marina"
Bruce-Novoa, Juan. "'One More Rosary for Doña Marina,'" *Confluencia*, 1, ii (1986), 73–84.

LEON ROOKE

"The End of the Revolution"
Vauthier, Simone. "'Entering Other Skins'; Or, Leon Rooke's 'The End of the Revolution,'" *Lit R*, 28 (1985), 456–479.

JOÃO GUIMARÃES ROSA

"The Time and Turn of Augusto Matraga"
Andrade, Ana L. "The Carnivalization of the Holy Sinner: An Intertextual Dialogue between Thomas Mann and João Guimarães Rosa," *Latin Am Lit R*, 14 (January–June, 1986), 136–144.

SINCLAIR ROSS

"The Lamp at Noon"
Hughes, Kenneth J. *Signs of Literature . . .* , 170–174.

PHILIP ROTH

"The Conversion of the Jews"
Bohner, Charles H. *Instructor's Manual . . .* , 108.
Searles, George J. *The Fiction . . .* , 92–94.
Tippens, Darryl. "The *Shechinah* Theme in Roth's 'Conversion of the Jews,'" *Christianity & Lit*, 35, iii (1986), 13–20.

"Eli the Fanatic"
Berger, Alan L. *Crisis and Covenant . . .* , 153–157.

"Epstein"
Searles, George J. *The Fiction . . .* , 131–133.

"On the Air"
Searles, George J. *The Fiction . . .* , 143–144.

GABRIELLE ROY

"The Garden in the Wind"
Fairbanks, Carol. *Prairie Women . . .* , 64–65.

"Hoodoo Valley"
Fairbanks, Carol. *Prairie Women . . .* , 171–172.

RU ZHIJUAN

"A Mis-edited Story"
Duke, Michael S. *Blooming . . .* , 73–74.

HENRY RUFFNER

"Arnheim"
Bakker, Jan. "Some Other Versions of Pastoral: The Disturbed Landscape in Tales of the Antebellum South," in Dameron, J. Lasley, and James W. Mathews, Eds. *No Fairer Land . . .* , 73–74.

"Judith Bensaddi"
Bakker, Jan. "Some Other Versions . . . ," 72.

"Seclusaval"
Bakker, Jan. "Some Other Versions . . . ," 72–73.

JUAN RULFO

"The Burning Plain"
Boldy, Steven. "Authority and Identity in 'El llano en llamas,'" *Mod Lang Notes,*
    101 (1986), 395–404.
Peavler, Terry J. "Perspectiva, voz y distancia en 'El llano en llamas,'" *Hispania,*
    69 (1986), 845–852.

"Es que somos muy pobres"
Lagmanovich, David. "Vox y verboen 'Es que somos muy pobres,' cuento de
    Juan Rulfo," *Hispamerica,* 14 (August, 1985), 3–15.

"The Heritage of Matilde Archangel"
Ortega, José. "Una lectura de 'La herencia de Matilde Arcángel,'" *Cuadernos
    Hispanoamericanos,* 421–423 (July–September, 1985), 277–282.

"The Hill of the *Comadres*"
Semilla, María A. "Análisis de 'La cuesta de las comadres,'" in Flores, Angel,
    Ed. *El realismo . . . ,* 226–241.

"Luvina"
Megged, Nahum. "Juan Rulfo: Mitología y dolor existencial," *Boletín Editorial,*
    4 (November–December, 1985), 7–16.
Rodríguez Padrón, Jorge. "El 'más allá' de Juan Rulfo: Algunas notas en torno
    a 'Luvina,'" *Cuadernos Hispanoamericanos,* 421–423 (July–September,
    1985), 249–259.
Varela Jácombe, Benito. "Discurso narrativo de 'Luvina,'" *Cuadernos Hispa-
    noamericanos,* 421–423 (July–September, 1985), 261–275.

"The Man"
Poeta, Salvatore J. "Aproximación alegórica a 'El hombre' de Jaun Rulfo: Ven-
    ganza trágica o tragedia vengativa?" *Cuadernos Hispanoamericanos,* 421–423
    (July–September, 1985), 283–302.

"Tell Them Not To Kill Me!"
Manning, Raquel T. "En torno a la muerte en el cuento 'Díles que no me maten!'
    de Juan Rulfo," *Pubs Missouri Philol Assoc,* 9 (1984), 72–77.
Pennington, Eric. "Freud's Death Instinct as Seen in Rulfo's 'Díles que no me
    maten!'" *Quaderni Ibero-Americani,* 57–58 (1984–1985), 50–52.

RURICOLLA [identity unknown]

"The Captain's Wife"
Current-García, Eugene. *The American Short Story before 1850 . . . ,* 13.

GARTH ST. OMER

"Another Place, Another Time"
Bush, Roland E. "Garth St. Omer," in Dance, Daryl C., Ed. *Fifty Caribbean Writers* . . . , 412.

"Light on the Hill"
Bush, Roland E. "Garth St. Omer," 411–412.

SAKI [HECTOR HUGH MUNRO]

"Esmé"
Flora, Joseph M. *The English Short Story* . . . , 93–94.

"The Music on the Hill"
Hanson, Clare. *Short Stories* . . . , 45.
Jurkiewicz, Kenneth. "Saki," in Bleiler, E. F., Ed. *Supernatural Fiction Writers* . . . ,
    I, 452.

"The Open Window"
Hanson, Clare. *Short Stories* . . . , 47–48.

"Reginald on House Parties"
Flora, Joseph M. *The English Short Story* . . . , 85–86.

"The Scharz-Metterklume Method"
Flora, Joseph M. *The English Short Story* . . . , 90–92.

"The She-Wolf"
Jurkiewicz, Kenneth. "Saki," 451–452.

"Sredni Vashtar"
Flora, Joseph M. *The English Short Story* . . . , 95.
Hanson, Clare. *Short Stories* . . . , 44–45.
Jurkiewicz, Kenneth. "Saki," 453.

"The Story-Teller"
Hanson, Clare. *Short Stories* . . . , 46–47.

"Tobermory"
Jurkiewicz, Kenneth. "Saki," 452.

J. D. SALINGER

"De Daumier-Smith's Blue Period"
Piwinsky, David J. "Salinger's 'De Daumier-Smith's Blue Period': Pseudonym
    as Cryptogram," *Notes Contemp Lit,* 15, v (1985), 3–4.

"For Esmé—with Love and Squalor"
Emerson, Gloria. "The Children in the Field," *TriQuarterly,* 65 (1986), 221–228.

"Franny"
Alsen, Eberhard. *Salinger's Glass Stories . . .* , 21–32.
Kirby, David. *The Sun Rises . . .* , 123–126.

"Hapworth 16, 1924"
Alsen, Eberhard. *Salinger's Glass Stories . . .* , 78–96.
Keymer, Stefan, and Reinhard Markner. "Zwei Jahrzehnte Schweigen: Jerome David Salingers 'Hapworth 16, 1924,'" *Horen*, 31, ii (1986), 161–165.

"The Laughing Man"
Strong, Paul. "Black Wing, Black Heart—Betrayal in J. D. Salinger's 'The Laughing Man,'" *West Virginia Univ Philol Papers*, 31 (1986), 91–96.

"A Perfect Day for Bananafish"
Alsen, Eberhard. *Salinger's Glass Stories . . .* , 9–20.

"Raise High the Roofbeam, Carpenters"
Alsen, Eberhard. *Salinger's Glass Stories . . .* , 33–47.
Tae, Yasuhiro. "Between Suicide and Enlightenment," *Kyushu Am Lit*, 26 (October, 1985), 21–27.

"Seymour—An Introduction"
Alsen, Eberhard. *Salinger's Glass Stories . . .* , 63–77.

"Teddy"
Greiff, Louis K. "J. D. Salinger's 'Teddy' and Flannery O'Connor's 'The River': A Comparative Analysis," *Flannery O'Connor Bull*, 9 (Autumn, 1980), 104–111.
Wexelblatt, Robert. "Chekhov, Salinger, and Epictetus," *Midwest Q*, 28, i (1986), 63–73.

"Zooey"
Alsen, Eberhard. *Salinger's Glass Stories . . .* , 48–62.
Kirby, David. *The Sun Rises . . .* , 123–126.

ANDREW SALKEY

"How Anancy Became a Spider Individual Person"
Dance, Daryl C. "Andrew Salkey," in Dance, Daryl C., Ed. *Fifty Caribbean Writers . . .* , 423.

WILLIAM SANSOM

"A Country Walk"
Pickering, Jean. "The English Short Story in the Sixties," in Vannatta, Dennis, Ed. *The English Short Story, 1945–1980*, 87–88.

"Fireman Flower"
Hanson, Clare. *Short Stories . . .* , 133–136.

"Gliding Gulls and Going People"
Hanson, Clare. *Short Stories . . .* , 137–139.

"Life, Death"
Baldwin, Dean. "The English Short Story in the Fifties," in Vannatta, Dennis,
    Ed. *The English Short Story, 1945–1980,* 67–68.

"The Wall"
Hanson, Clare. *Short Stories . . .* , 136–137.

"A Waning Moon"
Baldwin, Dean. "The English Short Story in the Fifties," 67.

SARBAN [JOHN W. WALL]

"Capra"
Nicholls, Peter. "Sarban," in Bleiler, E. F., Ed. *Supernatural Fiction Writers . . .* ,
    II, 670–671.

"The Doll Maker"
Nicholls, Peter. "Sarban," 672.

"A House of Call"
Nicholls, Peter. "Sarban," 673.

"The Khan"
Nicholls, Peter. "Sarban," 669–670.

"Ringstone"
Nicholls, Peter. "Sarban," 668–669.

"The Trespassers"
Nicholls, Peter. "Sarban," 673.

FRANK SARGESON

"City and Suburban"
Stead, C. K. *In the Glass Case . . .* , 17–18.

"The Hole That Jack Dug"
During, Simon. "Reading New Zealand Literature," *Southern R* (Adelaide), 18,
    i (1985), 65–85.

WILLIAM SAROYAN

"Laughter"
Petite, Joseph. "Saroyan's 'Laughter,' " *Explicator,* 43, iii (1985), 41–42.

JEAN-PAUL SARTRE

"The Childhood of a Leader"
Green, Mary J. *Fiction* . . . , 204–212.

"Erostratus"
Aldridge, A. Owen. *The Reemergence* . . . , 213–220.

"Intimacy"
Witt, Mary A. F. *Existential Prisons* . . . , 115–116.

"The Wall"
Green, Mary J. *Fiction* . . . , 243–257.
Harvey, Carol J. " 'Le Mur' de Jean-Paul Sartre: Techniques et philosophie de la caractérisation," *Canadian Mod Lang R*, 43, i (1986), 79–86.
Sweeney, Kevin W. "Lying to the Murderer: Sartre's Use of Kant in 'The Wall,' " *Mosaic*, 18, ii (1985), 1–16.

DOROTHY L. SAYERS

"The Man Who Knew How"
Merry, Bruce. "Dorothy L. Sayers: Mystery and Demystification," in Benstock, Bernard, Ed. *Art and Crime* . . . , 22–23.

"The Queen's Square"
Merry, Bruce. "Dorothy L. Sayers . . . ," 20–21.

JOHN SAYLES

"I-80 Nebraska, M. 490—M. 205"
Bohner, Charles H. *Instructor's Manual* . . . , 109.

BERND SCHIRMER

"Sindbad's Cap"
Mieth, Annemarie. "Jugundliche Leser auf der Spur von Schuffenhauers 'Irritationen': Erkundigungen zu Bernd Schirmers 'Sindbads Mütze,' " *Weimarer Beiträge*, 31 (1985), 252–266.

ARTHUR SCHNITZLER

"The Diary of Redegonda"
Beharriell, Frederick J. "Arthur Schnitzler and the Fantastic," in Collins, Robert A., and Howard D. Pearce, Eds. *The Scope of the Fantastic* . . . , 209–210.

"Lieutenant Gustl"
Vanhelleputte, Michel. "Der Leutnant und der Tod: Betrachtungen zu einem

Schnitzlerschen Thema," in Goffin, Roger, Michel Vanhelleputte, and Monique Weyembergh-Boussart, Eds. *Littérature et culture* . . . , 217–236.

"The Prophecy"
Beharriell, Frederick J. "Arthur Schnitzler . . . ," 210–213.

"Rhapsody"
Sebald, W. G. "Das Schrecknis der Liebe: Überlegungen zu Schnitzlers 'Traumnovelle,'" *Merkur*, 39 (1985), 120–131.

BRUNO SCHULZ

"August"
Ravichandra, C. P. "The Febrile World of Bruno Schulz: An Analysis of 'August,'" *Lit Criterion*, 20, i (1985), 1–6.

WALTER SCOTT

"The Highland Widow"
Campbell, James L. "Sir Walter Scott," in Bleiler, E. F., Ed. *Supernatural Fiction Writers* . . . , I, 174.

"My Aunt Margaret's Mirror"
Campbell, James L. "Sir Walter Scott," 173–174.

"The Tapestried Chamber" [originally titled "Story of an Apparition"]
Campbell, James L. "Sir Walter Scott," 172–173.

"The Two Drovers"
Campbell, James L. "Sir Walter Scott," 174.

"Wandering Willie's Tale"
Campbell, James L. "Sir Walter Scott," 174–176.

ANNA SEGHERS

"The Light on the Gallows"
Grimm, Reinhold. "Germans, Blacks, and Jews; or, Is There a German Blackness of Its Own?" in Grimm, Reinhold, and Jost Hermand, Eds. *Blacks and German Culture*, 160–161.

"The Wedding in Haiti"
Grimm, Reinhold. "Germans, Blacks, and Jews . . . ," 160–161.

HUBERT SELBY

"Double Feature"
Stephens, Michael. *The Dramaturgy of Style* . . . , 114–115.

ESTHER SELIGSON

"Distinto mundo habitual"
Duncan, L. Ann. *Voices, Visions* . . . , 123–124.

"Por el monte hacia le mar"
Duncan, L. Ann. *Voices, Visions* . . . , 122–123.

"Un viento de hojas secas"
Duncan, L. Ann. *Voices, Visions* . . . , 124–125.

IRWIN SHAW

"The Girls in Their Summer Dresses"
Gerlach, John. *Toward the End* . . . , 124–125.

RACCOONA SHELDON [ALICE HASTINGS SHELDON]

"The Screwfly Solution"
Siegel, Mark. *James Tiptree, Jr.*, 54–56.

"Your Faces, O My Sisters! Your Faces Filled of Light"
Siegel, Mark. *James Tiptree, Jr.*, 52–53.

MARY WOLLSTONECRAFT SHELLEY

"The Mortal Immortal"
O'Donohue, Nick. "Condemned to Life: 'The Mortal Immortal' and 'The Man
    Who Never Grew Young,'" in Yoke, Carl B., and Donald M. Hassler, Eds.
    Death and the Serpent . . . , 83–90.

SHI MO [ZHAO ZHENKAI]

"On the Ruins"
Duke, Michael S. *Blooming* . . . , 69–71.

SHI TIESHENG

"Blacky"
Duke, Michael S. *Blooming* . . . , 74–76.

M. P. SHIEL [MATTHEW PHIPPS SHIELL]

"The Bride"
Bleiler, E. F. "M. P. Shiel," in Bleiler, E. F., Ed. *Supernatural Fiction Writers* . . . ,
    I, 364–365.

"Xélucha"
Bleiler, E. F. "M. P. Shiel," 362.

ALAN SILLITOE

"The Loneliness of the Long-Distance Runner"
Baldwin, Dean. "The English Short Story in the Fifties," in Vannatta, Dennis,
    Ed. *The English Short Story, 1945–1980,* 61–62.
Spacks, Patricia M. *The Adolescent Idea . . . ,* 269–275.

ROBERT SILVERBERG

"Passengers"
Berger, Harold L. *Science Fiction . . . ,* 109–110.

WILLIAM GILMORE SIMMS

"Bald-Head Bill Baulby"
Meriwether, James B. "Simms's 'Sharp Snaffles' and 'Bald-Head Bill Baulby':
    Two Views of Men—and of Women," *So Carolina R,* 16, ii (1984), 66–71.

"How Sharp Snaffles Got His Capital and Wife"
Current-García, Eugene. *The American Short Story before 1850 . . . ,* 97–98.
Marshall, Ian. "The American Dream of Sam Snaffles," *Southern Lit J,* 18, ii
    (1986), 96–107.
Meriwether, James B. "Simms's 'Sharp Snaffles' . . . ," 66–71.

"Oakatibbe"
Shillingburg, Miriam. "The Maturing of Simms's Short Fiction: The Example
    of 'Oakatibbe,'" *Mississippi Q,* 38 (1985), 99–117.

CLIVE SINCLAIR

"Genesis"
Hanson, Clare. *Short Stories . . . ,* 167–168.

"A Moment of Happiness"
Hanson, Clare. *Short Stories . . . ,* 166–167.

MAY SINCLAIR

"The Finding of the Absolute"
Hatfield, Len. "May Sinclair," in Bleiler, E. F., Ed. *Supernatural Fiction Writ-*
    ers . . . , I, 517–518.

"The Flaw in the Crystal"
Hatfield, Len. "May Sinclair," 515.

"The Intercessor"
Hatfield, Len. "May Sinclair," 517.

"The Mahatma's Story"
Hatfield, Len. "May Sinclair," 517.

"The Nature of the Evidence"
Hatfield, Len. "May Sinclair," 516.

"The Villa Desirée"
Hatfield, Len. "May Sinclair," 516.

"When Their Fire Is Not Quenched"
Hatfield, Len. "May Sinclair," 515–516.

ISAAC BASHEVIS SINGER

"Aunt Yentl"
Miller, David N. *Fear of Fiction* . . . , 79–81.

"The Ball"
Liptzin, Sol. *The Maturing* . . . , 166.

"Blood"
Alexander, Edward. *Isaac Bashevis Singer,* 135–137.

"A Crown of Feathers"
Sheidley, William E., and Ann Charters. *Instructor's Manual* . . . , 126–127; rpt.
    Charters, Ann, William E. Sheidley, and Martha Ramsey. *Instructor's Man-
    ual* . . . , 2nd ed., 125–126.

"A Day in Coney Island"
Alexander, Edward. *Isaac Bashevis Singer,* 139–140.

"The Destruction of Kreshev"
Alexander, Edward. *Isaac Bashevis Singer,* 128–130.

"The Fire"
Miller, David N. *Fear of Fiction* . . . , 75–76.

"The Gentleman from Cracow"
Alexander, Edward. *Isaac Bashevis Singer,* 126–128.

"Gimpel the Fool"
Alexander, Edward. *Isaac Bashevis Singer,* 143–146.
Bohner, Charles H. *Instructor's Manual* . . . , 110–111.
Liptzin, Sol. *The Maturing* . . . , 168.
Miller, David N. *Fear of Fiction* . . . , 75–76.

"Hanka"
Miller, David N. *Fear of Fiction* . . . , 95–101.

"Jachid and Jechidah"
Bernheim, Mark. "I. B. Singer's *Yenne Velt*," in Collins, Robert A., and Howard D. Pearce, Eds. *The Scope of the Fantastic* . . . , 199–200.

"The Lantuck"
Miller, David N. *Fear of Fiction* . . . , 89–93.

"The Last Demon"
Alexander, Edward. *Isaac Bashevis Singer,* 142–143.

"The Lecture"
Alexander, Edward. *Isaac Bashevis Singer,* 140–142.
Milbauer, Asher Z. *Transcending Exile* . . . , 73–77.

"The Man Who Was Called Back"
Miller, David N. *Fear of Fiction* . . . , 76–78.

"The Needle"
Miller, David N. *Fear of Fiction* . . . , 82–83.

"Old Love"
Lee, Grace F. "Isaac Bashevis Singer: Mediating Between the Biblical and the Modern," *Mod Lang Stud,* 15, iv (1985), 117–123.

"An Old Man: A Chronicle"
Miller, David N. *Fear of Fiction* . . . , 16–23.

"On the Sidewalk"
Miller, David N. *Fear of Fiction* . . . , 84–85.

"Sale"
Miller, David N. *Fear of Fiction* . . . , 12–15.

"Shiddah and Kuziba"
Bernheim, Mark. "I. B. Singer's *Yenne Velt,*" 199.

"Short Friday"
Liptzin, Sol. *The Maturing* . . . , 167–168.

"Something Is There"
Milbauer, Asher Z. *Transcending Exile* . . . , 108–109.

"The Spinoza of Market Street"
Liptzin, Sol. *The Maturing* . . . , 168–169.

"The Wife Killer: An Old Wives' Tale"
Miller, David N. *Fear of Fiction* . . . , 72–77.

"Woman Trusts Editor with Important Secret"
Miller, David N. *Fear of Fiction* . . . , 63–65, 68–69.

"Yentl the Yeshiva Boy"
Alexander, Edward. *Isaac Bashevis Singer,* 137–139.

"Zlateh the Goat"
Bernheim, Mark. "I. B. Singer's *Yenne Velt,*" 198–199.

MIKHAIL SLONIMSKY

"The Emery Machine"
Moser, Charles A. *The Russian Short Story . . . ,* 151–152.

CLARK ASHTON SMITH

"The Empire of the Necromancers"
Robillard, Douglas. "Clark Ashton Smith," in Bleiler, E. F., Ed. *Supernatural Fiction Writers . . . ,* II, 878–879.

"The Master of the Asteroid"
Robillard, Douglas. "Clark Ashton Smith," 880.

E[DWARD] E[LMER] "DOC" SMITH

"Imperial Stars"
Sanders, Joseph. *E. E. "Doc" Smith,* 80.

LEE SMITH

"All the Days of our Lives"
Goodwyn, Anne J. "The World of Lee Smith," *Southern Q,* 22, i (1983), 131–132; rpt. Prenshaw, Peggy W., Ed. *Women Writers . . . ,* 264.

"Artists"
Goodwyn, Anne J. "The World . . . ," 130; rpt. Prenshaw, Peggy W., Ed. *Women Writers . . . ,* 263.

"Between the Lines"
Goodwyn, Anne J. "The World . . . ," 130–131; rpt. Prenshaw, Peggy W., Ed. *Women Writers . . . ,* 263–264.

"Cakewalk"
Goodwyn, Anne J. "The World . . . ," 117–119; rpt. Prenshaw, Peggy W., Ed. *Women Writers . . . ,* 250–251.

"Mrs. Darcy Meets the Blue-Eyed Stranger at the Beach"
Goodwyn, Anne J. "The World . . . ," 117; rpt. Prenshaw, Peggy W., Ed. *Women Writers . . . ,* 250.

"Saint Paul"
Goodwyn, Anne J. "The World . . . ," 115; rpt. Prenshaw, Peggy W., Ed. *Women Writers . . .* , 249.

VLADIMIR ALEXANDROVICH SOLLOGUB

"The Snowstorm"
Simpson, Mark S. *The Officer. . .* , 87–93.

VLADIMIR SOLOUKHIN

"Pasha"
Moser, Charles A. *The Russian Short Story . . .* , 189–190.

ALEXANDER SOLZHENITSYN

"Matryona's House"
Marsh, Rosalind J. *Soviet Fiction Since Stalin . . .* , 257–258.

ARMONÍA SOMERS

"The Cave-In"
Garfield, Evelyn P. *Women's Voices . . .* , 34–35.

OREST MIKHAILOVICH SOMOV

"Mommy and Sonny"
Mersereau, John. "Orest Somov," in Proffer, Carl R., Ed. *Russian Romantic Prose . . .* , 211.

MURIEL SPARK

"Black Madonna"
Pickering, Jean. "The English Short Story in the Sixties," in Vannatta, Dennis, Ed. *The English Short Story, 1945–1980,* 113–114.

"The Portobello Road"
Bold, Alan N. *Muriel Spark,* 26–27.

"The Seraph and the Zambesi"
Bold, Alan N. *Muriel Spark,* 20–21.

ELIZABETH SPENCER

"The Day Before"
Prenshaw, Peggy W. *Elizabeth Spencer,* 136–137.

"The Eclipse"
Prenshaw, Peggy W. *Elizabeth Spencer,* 133–134.

"The Finder"
Prenshaw, Peggy W. *Elizabeth Spencer,* 146–147.

"The Girl Who Loved Horses"
Prenshaw, Peggy W. *Elizabeth Spencer,* 148–149.

"I, Maureen"
Prenshaw, Peggy W. *Elizabeth Spencer,* 143–145.

"Indian Summer"
Prenshaw, Peggy W. *Elizabeth Spencer,* 140–141.

"Instrument of Destruction"
Prenshaw, Peggy W. *Elizabeth Spencer,* 141–142.

"Judith Kane"
Prenshaw, Peggy W. *Elizabeth Spencer,* 145–146.

"A Kiss at the Door"
Prenshaw, Peggy W. *Elizabeth Spencer,* 142.

"Knights and Dragons"
Anderson, Hilton. "Elizabeth Spencer's Two Italian Novellas," *Notes Mississippi Writers,* 13, i (1981), 26–32.
Prenshaw, Peggy W. *Elizabeth Spencer,* 83–90.

"The Light in the Piazza"
Anderson, Hilton. ". . . Two Italian Novellas," 18–25.
Prenshaw, Peggy W. *Elizabeth Spencer,* 68–77.

"The Little Brown Girl"
Prenshaw, Peggy W. *Elizabeth Spencer,* 133.

"Mr. McMillan"
Prenshaw, Peggy W. *Elizabeth Spencer,* 142–143.

"On the Gulf"
Prenshaw, Peggy W. *Elizabeth Spencer,* 135–136.

"Sharon"
Prenshaw, Peggy W. *Elizabeth Spencer,* 140.

"Ship Island: The Story of a Mermaid"
Prenshaw, Peggy W. "Mermaids, Angels and Free Women: The Heroines of Elizabeth Spencer's Fiction," *Southern Q,* 22, i (1983), 18–22; rpt. Prenshaw, Peggy W., Ed. *Women Writers . . . ,* 152–154; and in her *Elizabeth Spencer,* 78–83.

"The Visit"
Prenshaw, Peggy W. *Elizabeth Spencer,* 147–148.

MICKEY SPILLANE

"The Affair with the Dragon Lady"
Collins, Max A., and James L. Traylor. *One Lonely Knight* . . . , 127–128.

"The Bastard Bannerman"
Collins, Max A., and James L. Traylor. *One Lonely Knight* . . . , 125.

"The Big Bang" [originally titled "Return of the Hood"]
Collins, Max A., and James L. Traylor. *One Lonely Knight* . . . , 125–126.

"Everybody's Watching Me"
Collins, Max A., and James L. Traylor. *One Lonely Knight* . . . , 120.

"The Flier" [originally titled "Hot Cat"]
Collins, Max A., and James L. Traylor. *One Lonely Knight* . . . , 124–125.

"The Girl Behind the Hedge"
Collins, Max A., and James L. Traylor. *One Lonely Knight* . . . , 120–121.

"The Gold Fever Tapes"
Collins, Max A., and James L. Traylor. *One Lonely Knight* . . . , 126–127.

"I'll Die Tomorrow"
Collins, Max A., and James L. Traylor. *One Lonely Knight* . . . , 122–123.

"Kick It or Kill"
Collins, Max A., and James L. Traylor. *One Lonely Knight* . . . , 123–124.

"Killer Mine"
Collins, Max A., and James L. Traylor. *One Lonely Knight* . . . , 124.

"Me, Hood!"
Collins, Max A., and James L. Traylor. *One Lonely Knight* . . . , 122.

"The Seven-Year Kill"
Collins, Max A., and James L. Traylor. *One Lonely Knight* . . . , 123.

"Stand Up and Die"
Collins, Max A., and James L. Traylor. *One Lonely Knight* . . . , 121–122.

"Tomorrow I Die"
Collins, Max A., and James L. Traylor. *One Lonely Knight* . . . , 121.

"The Veiled Woman"
Collins, Max A., and James L. Traylor. *One Lonely Knight* . . . , 128.

HARRIET PRESCOTT SPOFFORD

"Circumstance"
Dalke, Anne. "'Circumstance' and the Creative Woman: Harriet Prescott Spofford," *Arizona Q,* 41 (1985), 73–80.

JEAN STAFFORD

"And Lots of Solid Color"
Walsh, Mary E. W. *Jean Stafford,* 45–46.

"Bad Characters"
Walsh, Mary E. W. *Jean Stafford,* 20–21.

"Beatrice Trueblood's Story"
Walsh, Mary E. W. *Jean Stafford,* 67–68.

"The Bleeding Heart"
Walsh, Mary E. W. *Jean Stafford,* 49–50.

"The Captain's Gift"
Walsh, Mary E. W. *Jean Stafford,* 73–74.

"The Cavalier"
Walsh, Mary E. W. *Jean Stafford,* 14–15.

"Caveat Emptor"
Walsh, Mary E. W. *Jean Stafford,* 47–48.

"Children Are Bored on Sunday"
Walsh, Mary E. W. *Jean Stafford,* 53–54.

"The Children's Game"
Walsh, Mary E. W. *Jean Stafford,* 71–72.

"The Connoisseurs"
Walsh, Mary E. W. *Jean Stafford,* 66–67.

"Cops and Robbers"
Walsh, Mary E. W. *Jean Stafford,* 28–29.

"A Country Love Story"
Walsh, Mary E. W. *Jean Stafford,* 63–64.

"The Darkening Moon"
Walsh, Mary E. W. "The Young Girl in the West: Disenchantment in Jean Stafford's Short Fiction," in Stauffer, Helen W., and Susan J. Rosowski, Eds. . . . *Western American Literature,* 240–241; rpt. Walsh, Mary E. W. *Jean Stafford,* 26–27.

"The Echo and the Nemesis"
Walsh, Mary E. W. *Jean Stafford*, 43–45.

"The End of a Career"
Walsh, Mary E. W. *Jean Stafford*, 72–73.
White, Barbara A. *Growing Up Female . . .* , 129.

"The Healthiest Girl in Town"
Walsh, Mary E. W. *Jean Stafford*, 23.

"The Home Front"
Walsh, Mary E. W. *Jean Stafford*, 16.

"The Hope Chest"
Walsh, Mary E. W. *Jean Stafford*, 74–75.

"I Love Someone"
Walsh, Mary E. W. *Jean Stafford*, 73.

"In the Zoo"
Walsh, Mary E. W. *Jean Stafford*, 24–25.

"An Influx of Poets"
Walsh, Mary E. W. *Jean Stafford*, 65–66.

"The Interior Castle"
Walsh, Mary E. W. *Jean Stafford*, 52–53.

"The Liberation"
Walsh, Mary E. W. *Jean Stafford*, 41–42.

"Life Is No Abyss"
Walsh, Mary E. W. *Jean Stafford*, 75–76.

"The Lippia Lawn"
Walsh, Mary E. W. *Jean Stafford*, 61–62.

"Maggie Meriwether's Rich Experience"
Walsh, Mary E. W. *Jean Stafford*, 45.

"A Modest Proposal"
Walsh, Mary E. W. *Jean Stafford*, 69.

"The Mountain Day"
Walsh, Mary E. W. "The Young Girl . . . ," 239–240; rpt. in her *Jean Stafford*, 42–43.

"Mountain Jim"
Walsh, Mary E. W. *Jean Stafford*, 27–28.

"My Blithe, Sad Bird"
Walsh, Mary E. W. *Jean Stafford*, 15.

"Old Flaming Youth"
Walsh, Mary E. W. *Jean Stafford*, 25–26.

"The Ordeal of Conrad Pardee"
Walsh, Mary E. W. *Jean Stafford*, 16–17.

"The Philosophy Lesson"
Walsh, Mary E. W. *Jean Stafford*, 40–41.

"Polite Conversation"
Walsh, Mary E. W. *Jean Stafford*, 62–63.

"Reading Problems"
Walsh, Mary E. W. *Jean Stafford*, 21–22.

"A Reasonable Facsimile"
Walsh, Mary E. W. *Jean Stafford*, 17.

"A Reunion"
Walsh, Mary E. W. *Jean Stafford*, 46–47.

"A Slight Maneuver"
Leary, William G. "Checkmate: Jean Stafford's 'A Slight Maneuver,'" *Western Am Lit*, 21 (1986), 99–109.
Walsh, Mary E. W. *Jean Stafford*, 14.

"A Summer Day"
Walsh, Mary E. W. "The Young Girl . . . ," 239; rpt. in her *Jean Stafford*, 14.

"The Tea Time of Stouthearted Ladies"
Walsh, Mary E. W. *Jean Stafford*, 39–40.

"The Violet Rock"
Walsh, Mary E. W. *Jean Stafford*, 20.

"The Warlock"
Walsh, Mary E. W. *Jean Stafford*, 69–70.

"A Winter's Tale"
Walsh, Mary E. W. *Jean Stafford*, 76–78.

"Woden's Day"
Walsh, Mary E. W. *Jean Stafford*, 50–51.

OLAF STAPLEDON

"Arms Out of Hand"
Kinnaird, John. *Olaf Stapledon*, 93.

"A Modern Magician"
Kinnaird, John. *Olaf Stapledon*, 95.

GERTRUDE STEIN

"Melanctha"
Saunders, Judith P. "Bipolar Conflict in Stein's 'Melanctha,'" *Mod Lang Stud,*
    15, ii (1985), 55–64.

JOHN STEINBECK

"The Affair at 7, Rue de M———"
Hughes, Robert S. "Steinbeck's Uncollected Stories," *Steinbeck Q,* 18 (1985), 86–
    87.

"The Case of the Hotel Ghost . . ." [same as "A Reunion at the Quiet Hotel"]
Hughes, Robert S. ". . . Uncollected Stories," 90–91.

"The Chrysanthemums"
Bohner, Charles H. *Instructor's Manual . . . ,* 111–112.
Matsumoto, Fusae. "Steinbeck's Women in *The Long Valley,*" in Hayashi, Tet-
    sumaro, Yasuo Hashiguchi, and Richard F. Peterson, Eds. *John Stein-
    beck . . . ,* 50–52.
Mitchell, Marilyn. "Steinbeck's Strong Women: Feminine Identity in the Short
    Stories," *Southwest R,* 61 (1976), 304–315; rpt. Hayashi, Tetsumaro, Ed.
    Steinbeck's Women . . . , 26–35.
Owens, Louis. . . . *Re-Vision of America,* 108–113.
Renner, Stanley. "The Real Woman Inside the Fence in 'The Chrysanthe-
    mums,'" *Mod Fiction Stud,* 31 (1985), 305–317.
Timmerman, John H. *John Steinbeck . . . ,* 63–68.

"Flight"
Gladstein, Mimi R. "Female Characters in Steinbeck: Minor Characters of Ma-
    jor Importance," in Hayashi, Tetsumaro, Ed. *Steinbeck's Women . . . ,* 22–23;
    rpt. in her *The Indestructible Woman . . . ,* 95–96.
Owens, Louis. . . . *Re-Vision of America,* 29–35.

"The Gift"
Owens, Louis. . . . *Re-Vision of America,* 48–50.

"The Great Mountains"
Owens, Louis. . . . *Re-Vision of America,* 50–53.

"The Harness"
Owens, Louis. . . . *Re-Vision of America,* 116–118.
Timmerman, John H. *John Steinbeck . . . ,* 69–71.

"Helen Van Deventer"
Gladstein, Mimi R. "Female Characters . . . ," 19–20.

"His Father"
Hughes, Robert S. ". . . Uncollected Stories," 85.

"How Edith McGillcuddy Met R. L. Stevenson"
Hughes, Robert S. ". . . Uncollected Stories," 80–82.

"How Mr. Hogan Robbed a Bank"
Hughes, Robert S. ". . . Uncollected Stories," 89–90.

"Johnny Bear"
Owens, Louis. . . . *Re-Vision of America*, 118–120.

"The Lopez Sisters"
Gladstein, Mimi R. "Female Characters . . . ," 18.

"The Miracle of Tepayac"
Hughes, Robert S. ". . . Uncollected Stories," 83–84.

"The Murder"
Owens, Louis. . . . *Re-Vision of America*, 121–126.

"The Promise"
Owens, Louis. . . . *Re-Vision of America*, 54–55.

"The Raid"
Owens, Louis. . . . *Re-Vision of America*, 126.

"The Short-Short Story of Mankind" [same as "We're Holding Our Own"]
Hughes, Robert S. ". . . Uncollected Stories," 88–89.

"The Snake"
Owens, Louis. . . . *Re-Vision of America*, 161–163.

"The Summer Before"
Hughes, Robert S. ". . . Uncollected Stories," 87–88.

"The Time the Wolves Ate the Vice-Principal"
Hughes, Robert S. ". . . Uncollected Stories," 82–83.

"Tularecito"
Timmerman, John H. *John Steinbeck . . .* , 60–62.

"The Vigilante"
Owens, Louis. . . . *Re-Vision of America*, 127–128.

"The White Quail"
Matsumoto, Fusae. "Steinbeck's Women in *The Long Valley*," 49–50.
Mitchell, Marilyn. "Steinbeck's Strong Women . . . ," 304–315; rpt. Hayashi,
    Tetsumaro, Ed. *Steinbeck's Women . . .* , 26–35.
Owens, Louis. . . . *Re-Vision of America*, 113–116.

"The Whiteside Family" [same as "The Whitesides"]
Gladstein, Mimi R. "Female Characters . . . ," 20–21.

"The Wicks Family" [same as "Shark Wicks"]
Gladstein, Mimi R. "Female Characters . . . ," 21–22.

JAMES STEPHENS

"Etched in Moonlight"
Douglas, Aileen. "James Stephens," in Bleiler, E. F., Ed. *Supernatural Fiction Writers* . . . , I, 488–489.

"The Threepenny Piece"
Douglas, Aileen. "James Stephens," 487.

CARL STERNHEIM

"Busekow"
Williams, Rhys W. *Carl Sternheim* . . . , 186–189.

"Heidenstam"
Williams, Rhys W. *Carl Sternheim* . . . , 198–199.

"Die Laus"
Williams, Rhys W. *Carl Sternheim* . . . , 200–201.

"Meta"
Williams, Rhys W. *Carl Sternheim* . . . , 194–195.

"Napoleon"
Williams, Rhys W. *Carl Sternheim* . . . , 189–190.

"Posinsky"
Williams, Rhys W. *Carl Sternheim* . . . , 201–203.

"Schuhlin"
Williams, Rhys W. *Carl Sternheim* . . . , 190–194.

"Die Schwestern Stork"
Williams, Rhys W. *Carl Sternheim* . . . , 195–197.

"Ulrike"
Williams, Rhys W. *Carl Sternheim* . . . , 197–198.

ROBERT LOUIS STEVENSON

"The Beach of Falesá"
Hanson, Clare. *Short Stories* . . . , 26–28.

"The Body Snatcher"
Orel, Harold. *The Victorian Short Story* . . . , 133–134.
Smith, Curtis C. "Robert Louis Stevenson," in Bleiler, E. F., Ed. *Supernatural Fiction Writers* . . . , I, 309–310.

"The Bottle Imp"
Smith, Curtis C. "Robert Louis Stevenson," 310.

"The Merry Men"
Shearer, Tom. "A Strange Judgement of God's?: Stevenson's 'The Merry Men,'"
    Stud Scottish Lit, 20 (1985), 71–87.
Smith, Curtis C. "Robert Louis Stevenson," 309.

"The Sinking Ship"
Orel, Harold. The Victorian Short Story . . . , 119–120.

"The Sire de Maletroit's Door"
Hanson, Clare. Short Stories . . . , 21–23.

"The Strange Case of Dr. Jekyll and Mr. Hyde"
Day, William P. In the Circles . . . , 89–92.
Hanson, Clare. Short Stories . . . , 23–25.
Kalikoff, Beth. Murder and Moral Decay . . . , 166–168.
Miller, Karl. Doubles . . . , 213–214.
*Miyoshi, Masao. The Divided Self . . . , 296–301; rpt. in part Geduld, Harry M.,
    Ed. The Definitive . . . Companion, 104–105.
Orel, Harold. The Victorian Short Story . . . , 123–127.
Showalter, Elaine. "Syphilis, Sexuality, and the Fiction of the Fin de Siècle," in
    Yeazell, Ruth B., Ed. Sex, Politics . . . , 100–103.
Thomas, Ronald R. "In the Company of Strangers: Absent Voices in Steven-
    son's 'Dr. Jekyll and Mr. Hyde' and Beckett's Company," Mod Fiction Stud,
    32 (1986), 157–164.
Watson, Roderick. "Introduction," The Strange Case . . . , [vii–xvi].

"The Suicide Club"
Orel, Harold. The Victorian Short Story . . . , 120–122.

"Thrawn Janet"
Orel, Harold. The Victorian Short Story . . . , 125–126.
Smith, Curtis C. "Robert Louis Stevenson," 308–309.

"Will o' the Mill"
Orel, Harold. The Victorian Short Story . . . , 118–120.
Smith, Curtis C. "Robert Louis Stevenson," 308.

ROBERT LOUIS STEVENSON and FANNY STEVENSON

"The Squire of Dames"
Melchiori, Barbara A. Terrorism . . . , 63–64.

"The Superfluous Mansion"
Melchiori, Barbara A. Terrorism . . . , 65–67.

"Zero's Tale of the Explosive Bomb"
Melchiori, Barbara A. Terrorism . . . , 68–69.

ADALBERT STIFTER

"Aragonite"
Mason, Eve. *Stifter,* 78–80.

"The Elderly Bachelor"
Helmetag, Charles H. "The Gentle Law in Adalbert Stifter's 'Der Hagestolz,'"
   Mod Lang Stud, 16 (1986), 183–188.

"The Fountain in the Woods"
Sjogren, Christine O. "The Frame of 'Der Waldbrunnen' Reconsidered: A Note
   on Adalbert Stifter's Aesthetics," *Mod Austrian Lit,* 19, i (1986), 9–25.

"Granite"
Mason, Eve. *Stifter,* 22–34.

"Limestone"
Iehl, Dominique. "Réalité et pénurie dans l'oeuvre littéraire et picturale de
   Stifter: A partir de la nouvelle 'Kalkstein' et des tableaux de l'époque des
   Bunte Steine," *Études Germaniques,* 40, iii (1985), 297–310.
Mason, Eve. *Stifter,* 43–60.

"Mica"
Mason, Eve. *Stifter,* 69–77.

"The Pitch-Burner"
Cimaz, Pierre. "Unheil und Ordnung in Stifters Erzählung 'Die Pechbrenner'
   im Vergleich mit Gotthelfs *Schwarzer Spinne,*" *Études Germaniques,* 40, iii
   (1985), 374–386.

"The Primeval Forest"
Steffan, Hans. "Traumbedürfnis und Traumanalyse: Stifters 'Hochwald' als
   ästhetisches Bedeutungsspiel über die Innerlichkeit des modernen
   Menschen," *Études Germaniques,* 40, iii (1985), 311–334.

"Rock Crystal"
Mason, Eve. *Stifter,* 35–42.

"Tourmaline"
Esselborn, Hans. "Adalbert Stifters 'Turmalin': Die Absage an den Subjektiv-
   ismus durch das naturgesetzliche Erzählen," *Adalbert Stifter Institut,* 34, i–ii
   (1983), 3–26.
Mason, Eve. *Stifter,* 61–68.

FRANK R. STOCKTON

"Amos Kilbright: His Adscititious Experiences"
Butrym, Alexander J. "For Suffering Humanity: The Ethics of Science in Science Fiction," in Reilly, Robert, Ed. *The Transcendent Adventure . . . ,* 59.

"The Griffin and the Minor Canon"
Waggoner, Diana. "Frank R. Stockton," in Bleiler, E. F., Ed. *Supernatural Fiction Writers* . . . , II, 755–756.

"The Knife That Killed Po' Hancy"
Waggoner, Diana. "Frank R. Stockton," 756–757.

"A Tale of Negative Gravity"
Butrym, Alexander J. "For Suffering Humanity . . . ," 58–59.

BRAM STOKER [ABRAHAM STOKER]

"The Judge's House"
Daniels, Les. "Bram Stoker," in Bleiler, E. F., Ed. *Supernatural Fiction Writers* . . . , I, 379.

"The Secret of the Growing Gold"
Daniels, Les. "Bram Stoker," 379–380.

ELIZABETH WHEELER STONE

"The Widow's Son"
Kestner, Joseph. *Protest and Reform* . . . , 75.

TOM STOPPARD [TOMAS STRAUSSLER]

"Life, Times: Fragments"
Brassell, Tim. *Tom Stoppard* . . . , 10–11.

"Reunion"
Brassell, Tim. *Tom Stoppard* . . . , 8–9.

"The Story"
Brassell, Tim. *Tom Stoppard* . . . , 7–8.

THEODOR STORM

"Aquis Submersus"
Holub, Robert C. "Realism and Recollection: The Commemoration of Art and the Aesthetics of Abnegation in 'Aquis Submersus,'" *Colloquia Germanica*, 18, ii (1985), 120–139.
Ward, Mark G. "Narrative and Ideological Tension in the Works of Theodor Storm: A Comparative Study of 'Aquis Submersus' and *Pole Poppenspäler*," *Deutsche Vierteljahrsschrift*, 50 (1985), 445–473.

"Auf dem Staatshof"
Paulin, Roger. *The Brief Compass* . . . , 120–122.

"Immensee"
Brülls, Holger. "Der Künstler als Biedermann: Zum Problem der 'Bürger-lichkeit' in Theodor Storms 'Immensee,'" *Wirkendes Wort,* 35 (1985), 184–202.
Paulin, Roger. *The Brief Compass . . . ,* 116–119.

"Die Regentrude"
Freund, Winfried. "Rückkehr zum Mythos: Mythisches und symbolisches Er-zählen in Theodor Storms Märchen 'Die Regentrude,'" *Schriften der Theo-dor-Storm-Gesellschaft,* 35 (1986), 38–47.
Roebling, Irmgard. "Prinzip Heimat eine regressive Utopie? Zur Interpretation von Theodor Storms 'Regentrude,'" *Schriften der Theodor-Storm-Gesellschaft,* 34 (1985), 55–66.

"The Rider of the White Horse"
Paulin, Roger. *The Brief Compass . . . ,* 71–75.
Peischl, Margaret T. "The Persistent Pagan in Theodor Storm's 'Der Schim-melreiter,'" *Seminar,* 22, ii (1986), 112–125.
White, Alfred D. "Society, Progress and Reaction in 'Der Schimmelreiter,'" *New Germ Stud,* 12 (1984), 151–173.

RANDOLPH STOW

"The Arrival at the Homestead: A Mind-Film"
Hassall, Anthony J. *Strange Country . . . ,* 125–126.

"Dokonikan"
Hassall, Anthony J. *Strange Country . . . ,* 124–125.

"Magic"
Hassall, Anthony J. *Strange Country . . . ,* 124–125.

AUGUST STRINDBERG

"Above the Clouds"
Berendsohn, Walter A. *August Strindberg . . . ,* 337–338.

"The Conquering Hero and the Fool"
Berendsohn, Walter A. *August Strindberg . . . ,* 371–372.

"A Criminal"
Berendsohn, Walter A. *August Strindberg . . . ,* 349–350.

"The Criminal Disposition"
Berendsohn, Walter A. *August Strindberg . . . ,* 330.

"The Customs Agent"
Berendsohn, Walter A. *August Strindberg . . . ,* 353–354.

"A Doll's House"
Berendsohn, Walter A. *August Strindberg . . . ,* 328–329.

ARKADY STRUGATSKY

THEODORE STURGEON

"Baby Is Three"
Stableford, Brian M. "Theodore Sturgeon," in Bleiler, E. F., Ed. *Supernatural Fiction Writers* . . . , II, 944.

"Bianca's Hands"
Stableford, Brian M. "Theodore Sturgeon," 941–942.

"Need"
Stableford, Brian M. "Theodore Sturgeon," 943–944.

JORGE SUÁREZ

"El llanto del impuesto"
Prada, Ana R. "El cuento contemporáneo de la represión en Bolivia," in Sanjinés C., Javier, Ed. *Tendencias actuales* . . . , 71–73.

SUBRAMANI

"Marigolds"
Shameem, Shaista. "The Art of Raymond Pillai, Subramani, and Prem Banfal: A Feminist Critique of the Indo-Fijian Short Story," *SPAN*, 20 (April, 1985), 39–40.

"Tell Me Where the Train Goes"
Shameem, Shaista. "The Art . . . ," 38–39.

RUTH SUCKOW

"The Best of the Lot"
White, Barbara A. *Growing Up Female* . . . , 67–68.

RONALD SUKENICK

"The Birds"
Kutnik, Jerzy. *The Novel As Performance* . . . , 86–88.

"The Death of the Novel"
Kutnik, Jerzy. *The Novel As Performance* . . . , 78–85.

"Momentum"
Kutnik, Jerzy. *The Novel As Performance* . . . , 75–78.

"The Permanent Crisis"
Kutnik, Jerzy. *The Novel As Performance* . . . , 74–75.

"The Sleeping Gypsy"
Kutnik, Jerzy. *The Novel As Performance* . . . , 94.

"What's Your Story?"
Kutnik, Jerzy. *The Novel As Performance* . . . , 85–86.

JULES SUPERVIELLE

"The Minotaur"
Harrison, Regina. "Mythopoesis: The Monster in the Labyrinth According to Supervielle, Gide, Borges, and Cortázar," *Kentucky Romance Q*, 32, ii (1985), 127–137.

ARTHUR SYMONS

"The Life and Adventures of Lucy Newcome"
Johnson, Alan. "Arthur Symons's 'The Life and Adventures of Lucy Newcome': Preface and Text," *Engl Lit Transition*, 28 (1985), 332–335.

JOHN TAINE [ERIC TEMPLE BELL]

"Black Goldfish"
Bousfield, Wendy. "*Fantasy Book*," in Tymn, Marshall B., and Mike Ashley, Eds. *Science Fiction . . . Magazines*, 262.

TANIZAKI JUN'ICHIRŌ

"A Matter of Taste"
Morrison, John W. *Modern Japanese Fiction*, 71–72.

"Tattoo"
Morrison, John W. *Modern Japanese Fiction*, 70.

AHMET HAMDI TANPINAR

"The Dream of Abdullah Efendi"
Atiş, Sarah M. *Semantic Structuring* . . . , 92–101.

"Master of the House"
Atiş, Sarah M. *Semantic Structuring* . . . , 130–139.

"Old-Fashioned Clothes"
Atiş, Sarah M. *Semantic Structuring* . . . , 101–123.

"A Road"
Atiş, Sarah M. *Semantic Structuring* . . . , 123–130.

"Tahsin of Erzurum"
Atiş, Sarah M. *Semantic Structuring . . .* , 89–92.

VALERY TARSIS

"Ward No. 7"
Marsh, Rosalind J. *Soviet Fiction Since Stalin . . .* , 208–209.

ELIZABETH TAYLOR

"The Blush"
Leclerq, Florence. *Elizabeth Taylor,* 116.

"A Dedicated Man"
Leclerq, Florence. *Elizabeth Taylor,* 117–118.

"Girl Reading"
Leclerq, Florence. *Elizabeth Taylor,* 118.

"Hester Lilly"
Leclerq, Florence. *Elizabeth Taylor,* 113–114.

"The Letter Writers"
Leclerq, Florence. *Elizabeth Taylor,* 116.

"Swan Moving"
Leclerq, Florence. *Elizabeth Taylor,* 114–115.

VLADIMIR FËDOROVICH TENDRIAKOV

"An Exceptional Event"
Marsh, Rosalind J. *Soviet Fiction Since Stalin . . .* , 244–245.

"The Trial"
Marsh, Rosalind J. *Soviet Fiction Since Stalin . . .* , 187–188.

AUDREY THOMAS

"Déjeuner sur l'Herbe"
Davey, Frank. "Alternate Stories: The Short Fiction of Audrey Thomas and
    Margaret Atwood," *Canadian Lit,* 109 (1986), 9–10.

"Out in the Midday"
Davey, Frank. "Alternate Stories . . . ," 7–8.

"Two in the Bush"
Davey, Frank. "Alternate Stories . . . ," 9.

"A Winter's Tale"
Davey, Frank. "Alternate Stories . . . ," 7.

JAMES THURBER

"The Catbird Seat"
Bohner, Charles H. *Instructor's Manual . . .* , 112.

"The Secret Life of Walter Mitty"
Blythe, Hal, and Charles S. Sweet. "Coitus Interruptus: Sexual Symbolism in
  'The Secret Life of Walter Mitty,'" *Stud Short Fiction*, 23 (1986), 110–113.
Hughes, Kenneth J. *Signs of Literature . . .* , 175–178.
Rupprecht, Erich S. "James Thurber," in Bleiler, E. F., Ed. *Supernatural Fiction
  Writers . . .* , II, 830.
Sheidley, William E., and Ann Charters. *Instructor's Manual . . .* , 97; rpt. Char-
  ters, Ann, William E. Sheidley, and Martha Ramsey. *Instructor's Man-
  ual . . .* , 2nd ed., 101–102.
Thompson, Terry. "'Look Out for That Buick!': Mitty vs. Machine," *Notes Con-
  temp Lit*, 16, ii (1986), 11–12.

JAMES TIPTREE, JR. [ALICE HASTINGS SHELDON]

"All the Kinds of Yes"
Siegel, Mark. *James Tiptree, Jr.*, 28–29.

"Amberjack"
Siegel, Mark. *James Tiptree, Jr.*, 31.

"And I Awoke and Found Me Here on the Cold Hill's Side"
Siegel, Mark. *James Tiptree, Jr.*, 18–19.

"And I Have Come upon This Place by Lost Ways"
Siegel, Mark. *James Tiptree, Jr.*, 29–30.

"And So On, And So On"
Siegel, Mark. *James Tiptree, Jr.*, 39.

"Beam Us Home"
Siegel, Mark. *James Tiptree, Jr.*, 26–27.

"Beyond the Dead Reef"
Siegel, Mark. *James Tiptree, Jr.*, 66.

"The Boy Who Waterskied to Forever"
Siegel, Mark. *James Tiptree, Jr.*, 66–67.

"Excursion Fare"
Siegel, Mark. *James Tiptree, Jr.*, 68–69.

"Faithful to Thee, Terra, in Our Fashion"
Siegel, Mark. "Double-Souled Man: Immortality and Transcendence in the Fiction of James Tiptree, Jr.," in Yoke, Carl B., and Donald M. Hassler, Eds. *Death and the Serpent* . . . , 165.

"Forever to a Hudson Bay Blanket"
Siegel, Mark. *James Tiptree, Jr.,* 23.

"The Girl Who Was Plugged In"
Siegel, Mark. *James Tiptree, Jr.,* 32–33.

"Her Smoke Rose Up Forever"
Siegel, Mark. "Double-Souled Man . . . ," 167–168.

"Houston, Houston, Do You Read?"
Barr, Marleen. "Immortal Feminist Communities of Women: A Recent Idea in Science Fiction," in Yoke, Carl B., and Donald M. Hassler, Eds. *Death and the Serpent* . . . , 39–47.
Siegel, Mark. *James Tiptree, Jr.,* 41–43.

"I'll Be Waiting for You When the Swimming Pool Is Empty"
Siegel, Mark. *James Tiptree, Jr.,* 24.

"I'm Too Big But I Love to Play"
Siegel, Mark. *James Tiptree, Jr.,* 24–25.

"The Last Flight of Dr. Ain"
Siegel, Mark. *James Tiptree, Jr.,* 30–31.

"Lirios: A Tale of the Quintana Roo"
Siegel, Mark. *James Tiptree, Jr.,* 65–66.

"Love Is the Plan, the Plan Is Death"
Barr, Marleen. "'The *Females* Do the Fathering!': James Tiptree's Male Matriarchs and Adult Human Gametes," *Sci-Fiction Stud,* 13 (1986), 46–47.
Siegel, Mark. *James Tiptree, Jr.,* 33–34.

"Mama Comes Home" [originally titled "The Mother Ship"]
Siegel, Mark. *James Tiptree, Jr.,* 20–21.

"The Milk of Paradise"
Siegel, Mark. *James Tiptree, Jr.,* 29.

"A Momentary Taste of Being"
Siegel, Mark. *James Tiptree, Jr.,* 37–39; rpt. Yoke, Carl B., and Donald M. Hassler, Eds. *Death and the Serpent* . . . , 168.

"Mother in the Sky with Diamonds"
Siegel, Mark. *James Tiptree, Jr.,* 25–26; rpt. Yoke, Carl B., and Donald M. Hassler, Eds. *Death and the Serpent* . . . , 165–166.

"On the Last Afternoon"
Siegel, Mark. *James Tiptree, Jr.*, 34–35; rpt. Yoke, Carl B., and Donald M. Hassler, Eds. *Death and the Serpent . . .* , 166–167.

"Out of the Everywhere"
Siegel, Mark. *James Tiptree, Jr.*, 60–61.

"The Peacefulness of Vivyan"
Siegel, Mark. *James Tiptree, Jr.*, 19–20.

"She Waits for All Men Born"
Siegel, Mark. *James Tiptree, Jr.*, 39–40.

"Slow Music"
Siegel, Mark. *James Tiptree, Jr.*, 57–59; rpt. Yoke, Carl B., and Donald M. Hassler, Eds. *Death and the Serpent . . .* , 171–172.

"The Snows Are Melting, the Snows Are Gone"
Siegel, Mark. *James Tiptree, Jr.*, 44.

"A Source of Innocent Merriment"
Siegel, Mark. *James Tiptree, Jr.*, 59–60.

"We Who Stole the Dream"
Siegel, Mark. *James Tiptree, Jr.*, 55–56.

"With Delicate Mad Hands"
Siegel, Mark. *James Tiptree, Jr.*, 61–63.

"The Women Men Don't See"
Siegel, Mark. *James Tiptree, Jr.*, 31–32.

"Your Haploid Heart"
Siegel, Mark. *James Tiptree, Jr.*, 36–37.

ALEKSEY KONSTANTINOVICH TOLSTOY

"The Russian Character"
Moser, Charles A. *The Russian Short Story . . .* , 97–98.

LEO TOLSTOY

"Albert"
Moser, Charles A. *The Russian Short Story . . .* , 67–68.

"The Death of Ivan Ilych"
Bohner, Charles H. *Instructor's Manual . . .* , 113.
Comstock, Gary. "Face to Face with *It:* The Naive Reader's Moral Response to 'Ivan Ilych,'" *Neophilologus*, 70 (1986), 321–333.
Green, Mary J. *Fiction in the Historical Present . . .* , 99–101.

Gustafson, Richard F. *Leo Tolstoy . . .* , 155–160.
Gutsche, George J. *Moral Apostasy . . .* , 70–98.
Hajnády, Zoltán. "Ivan Ilych and Existence Compared to Death: Lev Tolstoy and Martin Heidegger," *Acta Litteraria*, 27, i–ii (1985), 3–15.
Lisker, Sheldon A. "Literature and the Dying Patient," *Pennsylvania Engl*, 12, i (1985), 5–9.
Meyers, Jeffrey. *Disease . . .* , 19–29.
Parthe, Kathleen. "The Metamorphosis of Death in Tolstoy," *Lang Sci*, 18 (1985), 205–214.
Rajakrishnan, V. "Tolstoy's 'The Death of Ivan Ilych': Illness as Motif and Metaphor," in Paul, J. V., Ed. *Studies in Russian Literature*, 28–35.
Salys, Rima. "Signs on the Road of Life: 'The Death of Ivan Il'ič,' " *Slavic & East European J*, 30 (1986), 18–28.
Sheidley, William E., and Ann Charters. *Instructor's Manual . . .* , 16–18; rpt. Charters, Ann, William E. Sheidley, and Martha Ramsey. *Instructor's Manual . . .* , 2nd ed., 17–18.

"The Devil"
Gustafson, Richard F. *Leo Tolstoy . . .* , 346–347.

"Family Happiness"
Gustafson, Richard F. *Leo Tolstoy . . .* , 110–117.

"Hadji Murat"
Bloom, Harold. "Homer, Virgil, Tolstoy: The Epic Hero," *Raritan*, 6, i (1986), 1–25.
Layton, Susan. "Imagining the Caucasian Hero: Tolstoj vs. Mordovcev," *Slavic & Eastern European J*, 30, i (1986), 1–17.

"The Kreutzer Sonata"
Gustafson, Richard F. *Leo Tolstoy . . .* , 352–355.
Moser, Charles A. *The Russian Short Story . . .* , 109–110.

"Lucerne"
Gustafson, Richard F. *Leo Tolstoy . . .* , 22–26.

"Sevastopol in December, 1854"
Moser, Charles A. *The Russian Short Story . . .* , 65–66.

"Sevastopol in May"
Gustafson, Richard F. *Leo Tolstoy . . .* , 293–297.

"The Snowstorm"
Haard, Eric de. "L. N. Tolstoj's 'Metel' ('The Snowstorm')," in Grübel, Rainer, Ed. *Russische Erzählung . . .* , 239–259.

"Two Hussars"
Simpson, Mark S. *The Officer . . .* , 103–107.

JEAN TOOMER

"Blood-Burning Moon"
Solard, Alain. "Myth and Narrative Fiction in *Cane*: 'Blood-Burning Moon,' " *Callaloo*, 8, iii (1985), 551–560.

"York Beach"
Noyes, Sylvia G. "A Particular Patriotism in Jean Toomer's 'York Beach,'" *Coll Lang Assoc J*, 29 (1986), 288–294.

MICHEL TOURNIER

"L'Aire du Muguet"
Cloonan, William. *Michel Tournier*, 83–86.

"Le Coq de bruyère"
Cloonan, William. *Michel Tournier*, 82–83.

"La Fugue du Poucet"
Cloonan, William. *Michel Tournier*, 79–81.

"La Mère Noël"
Cloonan, William. *Michel Tournier*, 77–78.

"Tristan Vox"
Cloonan, William. *Michel Tournier*, 76–77.

CATHERINE WEBB TOWLES

"The Orphan's Miniature"
Hitchcock, Bert. "Rediscovering Alabama Literature: Three Writers of Lafayette," *Alabama R*, 36 (1983), 179–180.

MICHEL TREMBLAY

"Gentle Warmth"
Antosh, Ruth B. "Michel Tremblay and the Fantastic of Violence," in Coyle, William, Ed. *Aspects of Fantasy . . .* , 19.

"Lady Barbara's Last Outing"
Antosh, Ruth B. "Michel Tremblay . . . ," 21.

"The Thirteenth Wife of Baron Klugg"
Antosh, Ruth B. "Michel Tremblay . . . ," 19.

WILLIAM TREVOR [TREVOR COX]

"An Evening with John Joe Dempsey"
Stinson, John J. "Replicas, Foils, and Revelation in Some 'Irish' Short Stories of William Trevor," *Canadian J Irish Stud*, 11, ii (1985), 20–21.

"The Paradise Lounge"
Stinson, John J. "Replicas, Foils . . . ," 21–22.

"Teresa's Wedding"
Stinson, John J. "Replicas, Foils . . . ," 22–24.

IURII TRIFONOV

"The House on the Embankment"
Marsh, Rosalind J. *Soviet Fiction Since Stalin* . . . , 59–60.

ANTHONY TROLLOPE

"The Panjandrum"
Orel, Harold. *The Victorian Short Story* . . . , 79–80.

"The Spotted Dog"
Orel, Harold. *The Victorian Short Story* . . . , 87–88.

FRANK TUOHY

"The Admiral and the Nuns"
Pickering, Jean. "The English Short Story in the Sixties," in Vannatta, Dennis,
   Ed. *The English Short Story, 1945–1980*, 85.

"Two Private Lives"
Pickering, Jean. "The English Short Story . . . ," 85–86.

IVAN SERGEEVICH TURGENEV

"The Brigadier"
Simpson, Mark S. *The Officer* . . . , 95–98.

"Faust"
Moser, Charles A. *The Russian Short Story* . . . , 59–60.

"The Tryst"
Bohner, Charles H. *Instructor's Manual* . . . , 114–115.

"The Unfortunate Girl"
Moser, Charles A. *The Russian Short Story* . . . , 61–62.

HENRY GILES TURNER

"The Confessions of a Loafer"
Hadgraft, Cecil, Ed. *The Australian Short Story* . . . , 4–5.

MARK TWAIN [SAMUEL L. CLEMENS]

"The Celebrated Jumping Frog from Calaveras County"
Bohner, Charles H. *Instructor's Manual* . . . , 29–30.
Gerlach, John. *Toward the End* . . . , 60–65.

"The Facts Concerning the Recent Carnival of Crime in Connecticut"
Clareson, Thomas D. "Mark Twain," in Bleiler, E. F., Ed. *Supernatural Fiction Writers* . . . , II, 763–764.

"The Golden Arm"
Hook, Andrew. "Reporting Reality: Mark Twain's Short Stories," in Lee, A. Robert, Ed. . . . *American Short Story,* 109–110.

"The Great Dark"
Clareson, Thomas D. "Mark Twain," 767.

"The Mysterious Stranger"
Coyle, William. "Mark Twain as Fantasist," in Coyle, William, Ed. *Aspects of Fantasy* . . . , 176–177.
Hook, Andrew. "Reporting Reality . . . ," 114–115.

"The Stolen White Elephant"
Baetzhold, Howard G. "Of Detectives and Their Derring-Do: The Genesis of Mark Twain's 'The Stolen White Elephant,'" *Stud Am Humor,* 2 (1976), 183–195.

"A True Story"
Hook, Andrew. "Reporting Reality . . . ," 117–118.

SABINE ULIBARRÍ

"Brujerías o tonterías"
Tatum, Charles M. "Sabine Ulibarrí," in Martínez, Julio A., and Francisco A. Lomelí, Eds. *Chicano Literature* . . . , 393.

"Mi abuela fumaba puros"
Tatum, Charles M. "Sabine Ulibarrí," 392–393.

"My Magic Horse"
Tatum, Charles M. "Sabine Ulibarrí," 389–390.

"Sábelo"
Tatum, Charles M. "Sabine Ulibarrí," 390–391.

MIGUEL DE UNAMUNO

"Abel Sanchez"
Marcone, Rose M. "Internal Conflict in 'Abel Sanchez,'" *Lang Q,* 25, i–ii (1986), 54–56.

"Aunt Tula"

Montes-Huidobro, Matías. "Un retrato femenino: 'La tía Tula,'" *Káñina*, 8, i–ii (1984), 83–95.

————. "'La tía Tula': Matrimonio en el cosmos," in González-del-Valle, Luis T., and Darío Villanueva, Eds. *Estudios en honor a Ricardo Gullón*, 229–248.

————. "'La tía Tula': Credo de la abejidad y erótica de Dios," *Discurso Literario*, 2 (1985), 457–479.

Reiff, Catherine M. "Maternidad y soledad en 'La tía Tula,'" *Insula*, 40 (June, 1985), 14–15.

"Saint Manuel the Good, Martyr"

Gordon, M. "The Elusive Self: Narrative Method and Its Implications in 'San Manuel Bueno, mártir,'" *Hispanic R*, 54 (1986), 147–161.

Hammitt, Gene M. "Unamuno's Peña del Buitre and Valverde de Lucerna," *Romance Notes*, 25, i (1984), 30–34.

King, Shirley. "'San Manuel Bueno' and Unamuno's Reading of Hauptmann," *Revista de Estudios Hispánicos* (Univ. Alabama), 19 (1985), 39–54.

Nepaulsingh, Colbert I. "In Search of a Tradition, Not a Source, for 'San Manuel Bueno,'" Goertz, R. O. W., Ed. *Iberia . . .* , 127–140.

Orringer, Nelson R. "Saintliness and Its Unstudied Sources in 'San Manuel Bueno, mártir,'" in Boudreau, H. L., and Luis T. González-del-Valle, Eds. *Studies in Honor . . .* , 173–185.

Sesler, Gregorio. "Unamuno y los militares: 'Venceréis pero no convenceréis,'" *Cuadernos Americanos*, 6 (November–December, 1984), 103–119.

Summerhill, Stephen J. "'San Manuel Bueno, mártir' and the Reader," *Anales de la Literatura Espanola*, 10, i–iii (1985), 61–79.

JOHN UPDIKE

"A & P"

Bohner, Charles H. *Instructor's Manual . . .* , 115–116.

Emmett, Paul J. "A Slip That Shows: Updike's 'A & P,'" *Notes Contemp Lit*, 15, ii (1985), 9–11.

Petry, Alice H. "The Dress Code in Updike's 'A & P,'" *Notes Contemp Lit*, 16, i (1986), 8–10.

Shaw, Patrick W. "Checking Out Faith and Lust: Hawthorne's 'Young Goodman Brown' and Updike's 'A & P,'" *Stud Short Fiction*, 23 (1986), 321–323.

"Ace in the Hole"

Gerlach, John. *Toward the End . . .* , 125–128.

"Domestic Life in America"

Greiner, Donald J. *Adultery . . .* , 108–109.

"The Music School"

Bohner, Charles H. *Instructor's Manual . . .* , 116–117.

"Packed Dirt, Churchgoing, A Dying Cat, A Traded Car"

Conn, Saundra M. "Do Not Go Gentle: Visions of Death and Immortality in John Updike's 'Pigeon Feathers' and 'Packed Dirt, Churchgoing, A Dying Cat, A Traded Car,'" *Pubs Mississippi Philol Assoc*, [n.v.] (1985), 29–31.

"Pigeon Feathers"
Conn, Saundra M. "Do Not Go Gentle . . . ," 25–28.
Klinkowitz, Jerome. *Literary Subversions* . . . , 62–63.

"Toward Evening"
Searles, George J. *The Fiction* . . . , 21.

"Wife-Wooing"
Bohner, Charles H. *Instructor's Manual* . . . , 117–118.

PEDRO HENRÍQUEZ UREÑA

"En Jauja"
Lacau, María H. "Pedro Henríquez Ureña y 'Jauja,' su país de utopía infantil,"
    Sur, 355 (July–December, 1984), 77–101.

FRED URQUHART

"Alicky's Watch"
Baldwin, Dean. "The English Short Story in the Fifties," in Vannatta, Dennis,
    Ed. *The English Short Story, 1945–1980,* 47.

"Maggie Logie and the National Health"
Baldwin, Dean. "The English Short Story . . . ," 36–37.

"Once a Schoolmissy"
Baldwin, Dean. "The English Short Story . . . ," 47.

ARTURO USLAR PIETRI

"The Jack-o'-Lantern"
Parra, Teresita J. "Perspectiva mítica de la realidad histórica en dos cuentos de
    Arturo Uslar Pietri," *Revista Iberoamericana,* 52 (1986), 857–874.

GLEB USPENSKY

"The Intelligentsia of the People"
Moser, Charles A. *The Russian Short Story* . . . , 91–92.

GINA VALDÉS

"This Is a Story"
Sánchez, Rosauro. "Chicana Prose Writers: The Case of Gina Valdés and Sylvia
    Lizárrago," in Herrera-Sobek, María, Ed. *Beyond Stereotypes* . . . , 66–67.

LUISA VALENZUELA

"He Who Searches"
Glantz, Margo. "Luisa Valenzuela's 'He Who Searches,'" *R Contemp Fiction*, 6, iii (1986), 62–66.
Hicks, Emily. "That Which Resists: The Code of the Real in Luisa Valenzuela's 'He Who Searches,'" *R Contemp Fiction*, 6, iii (1986), 55–61.
Maci, Guillermo. "The Symbolic, the Imaginary, and the Real in Luisa Valenzuela's 'He Who Searches,'" trans. Janet Pérez, *R Contemp Fiction*, 6, iii (1986), 67–72.

"Neither the Most Terrifying Nor the Least Memorable"
Marting, Diane. "Female Sexuality in Selected Short Stories by Luisa Valenzuela: Toward an Ontology of Her Work," *R Contemp Fiction*, 6, iii (1986), 51–53.

"Other Weapons"
Marcos, Juan M. "Luisa Valenzuela, más allá de la araña de la esquina rosada," *Prismal/Cabral*, 11 (Fall, 1983), 57–65.
Morello-Frosch, Marta. "'Other Weapons': When Metaphors Become Real," *R Contemp Fiction*, 6, iii (1986), 82–87.

"Rituals of Rejection"
Mull, Dorothy S. "Ritual Transformation in Luisa Valenzuela's 'Rituals of Rejection,'" *R Contemp Fiction*, 6, iii (1986), 88–96.

"Unlimited Rapes United, Argentina"
Marting, Diane. "Female Sexuality . . . ," 50–51.

"The Verb to Kill"
Marting, Diane. "Female Sexuality . . . ," 48–50.

"Where the Eagles Dwell"
Martinez, Zulma. "Luisa Valenzuela's 'Where the Eagles Dwell': From Fragmentation to Holism," *R Contemp Fiction*, 6, iii (1986), 109–115.

RAMÓN VALLE-INCLÁN

"Eulalia"
González del Valle, Luis T. "Una nueva lectura de un cuento olvidado de Ramón del Valle-Inclán," *Insula*, 41 (July–August, 1986), 5, 24.

JACK VANCE [JOHN HOLBROOK VANCE]

"Guyal of Sfere"
Dirda, Michael. "Jack Vance," in Bleiler, E. F., Ed. *Supernatural Fiction Writers . . .* , II, 1108–1109.

"Liane the Wayfarer"
Dirda, Michael. "Jack Vance," 1108.

MARIO VARGAS LLOSA

"The Challenge"
Gerdes, Dick. *Mario Vargas Llosa,* 21–24.
Williams, Raymond L. *Mario Vargas Llosa,* 23–25.

"The Cubs"
Gerdes, Dick. *Mario Vargas Llosa,* 75–91.

"The Grandfather"
Gerdes, Dick. *Mario Vargas Llosa,* 29–31.

"The Leaders"
Gerdes, Dick. *Mario Vargas Llosa,* 20–21.
Williams, Raymond L. *Mario Vargas Llosa,* 20–23.

"On Sunday"
Gerdes, Dick. *Mario Vargas Llosa,* 24–26.
Williams, Raymond L. *Mario Vargas Llosa,* 25–26.

"A Visitor"
Gerdes, Dick. *Mario Vargas Llosa,* 28–29.

"The Younger Brother"
Gerdes, Dick. *Mario Vargas Llosa,* 26–28.
Williams, Raymond L. *Mario Vargas Llosa,* 26–27.

M. G. VASSANJI

"Waiting for the Goddess"
Suganasiri, Suwanda. "Reality and Symbolism in the South Asian Canadian
    Short Story," *World Lit Written Engl,* 26 (1986), 103–104.

ANA LYDIA VEGA

"Pollito chicken"
Vélez, Diana L. "'Pollito chicken': Split Subjectivity, National Identity and the
    Articulation of Female Sexuality in a Narrative of Ana Lydia Vega," *Am
    R,* 14, ii (1986), 68–76.

ALEXANDER VELTMAN

"Erotis"
Moser, Charles A. *The Russian Short Story . . . ,* 13–14.

CÉSAR VERDUGUES

"Hay un grito en tu silencio"
Prada, Ana R. "El cuento contemporáneo de la represión en Bolivia," in
    Sanjinés C., Javier, Ed. *Tendencias actuales . . . ,* 60–64.

GIOVANNI VERGA

"Rosso Malpelo"
Lucente, Gregory L. *Beautiful Fables* . . . , 69–97.

VICKI VIIDIKAS

"The Silk Trousers"
Bennett, Bruce. "Asian Encounters in the Contemporary Australian Short
   Story," *World Lit Written Engl*, 26 (1986), 56–57.

JOAN D. VINGE

"The Crystal Ship"
Law, Richard. "Joan D. Vinge," in Barr, Marleen, Ruth Salvaggio, and Richard
   Law. *Suzy McKee Charnas* . . . , 13–16.

"Exorcycle"
Law, Richard. "Joan D. Vinge," 40–41.

"Eyes of Amber"
Law, Richard. "Joan D. Vinge," 11–13.

"The Hunt of the Unicorn"
Law, Richard. "Joan D. Vinge," 57–59.

"Legacy"
Law, Richard. "Joan D. Vinge," 22–24.

"Mother and Child"
Law, Richard. "Joan D. Vinge," 56–57.

"Phoenix in Ashes"
Law, Richard. "Joan D. Vinge," 52–53.

"Psiren"
Law, Richard. "Joan D. Vinge," 55–56.

"The Storm King"
Law, Richard. "Joan D. Vinge," 53–54.

"Tin Soldier"
Law, Richard. "Joan D. Vinge," 16–18.

"To Bell the Cat"
Law, Richard. "Joan D. Vinge," 18.

"View from the Height"
Law, Richard. "Joan D. Vinge," 18–20.

"Voices from the Dust"
Law, Richard. "Joan D. Vinge," 53.

JOAN D. VINGE and VERNON VINGE

"The Peddler's Apprentice"
Law, Richard. "Joan D. Vinge," in Barr, Marleen, Ruth Salvaggio, and Richard
    Law. *Suzy McKee Charnas . . .* , 54–55.

KARL EDWARD WAGNER

"The River of Night's Dreaming"
Schweitzer, Darrell. "Karl Edward Wagner and the Haunted Hills (and
    Kudzu)," in Schweitzer, Darrell, Ed. . . . *Horror Fiction*, 87.

"220 Swift"
Schweitzer, Darrell. "Karl Edward Wagner . . . ," 88.

"Where the Summer Ends"
Schweitzer, Darrell. "Karl Edward Wagner . . . ," 88–89.

H. RUSSELL WAKEFIELD [HERBERT RUSSELL WAKEFIELD]

"Damp Sheets"
Morgan, Chris. "H. Russell Wakefield," in Bleiler, E. F., Ed. *Supernatural Fiction
    Writers . . .* , II, 617–618.

"The First Sheaf"
Morgan, Chris. "H. Russell Wakefield," 620.

"The Gorge of the Churels"
Morgan, Chris. "H. Russell Wakefield," 620–621.

"He Cometh and He Passeth By!"
Morgan, Chris. "H. Russell Wakefield," 620.

"Jay Walkers"
Morgan, Chris. "H. Russell Wakefield," 619.

"The Red Lodge"
Morgan, Chris. "H. Russell Wakefield," 618–619.

"That Dieth Not"
Morgan, Chris. "H. Russell Wakefield," 618.

"The Triumph of Death"
Morgan, Chris. "H. Russell Wakefield," 620.

ALICE WALKER

"Advancing Luna"
Christian, Barbara. *Black Feminist Criticism* . . . , 83–92.

"The Child Who Favored Daughter"
Christian, Barbara. *Black Feminist Criticism* . . . , 38–42.

"Everyday Use"
Baker, Houston A., and Charlotte Pierce Baker. "Patches: Quilts and Community in Alice Walker's 'Everyday Use,' " *Southern R*, 21 (1985), 706–720.
Byerman, Keith E. *Fingering the Jagged Grain* . . . , 142–146.
Christian, Barbara. *Black Feminist Criticism* . . . , 86–87.
Kane, Patricia. "The Prodigal Daughter in Alice Walker's 'Everyday Use,' " *Notes Contemp Lit*, 15, ii (1985), 7.
Pryse, Marjorie. "Zora Neale Hurston, Alice Walker, and the 'Ancient Power' of Black Women," in Pryse, Marjorie, and Hortense J. Spillers, Eds. *Conjuring* . . . , 16–17.

"1955"
Byerman, Keith E. *Fingering the Jagged Grain* . . . , 159–161.

"Really, Doesn't Crime Pay?"
Christian, Barbara. *Black Feminist Criticism* . . . , 36–38.

"The Revenge of Hannah Kemhuff"
Byerman, Keith E. *Fingering the Jagged Grain* . . . , 140–142.
Pryse, Marjorie. "Zora Neale Hurston . . . ," 15–16.

"Roselily"
Christian, Barbara. *Black Feminist Criticism* . . . , 34–36.

"Strong Horse Tea"
Byerman, Keith E. *Fingering the Jagged Grain* . . . , 139–140.

"A Sudden Trip Home in the Spring"
Byerman, Keith E. *Fingering the Jagged Grain* . . . , 156–159.

"To Hell with Dying"
Bohner, Charles H. *Instructor's Manual* . . . , 118–119.

"The Welcome Table"
Christian, Barbara. *Black Feminist Criticism* . . . , 42–44.

MERVYN WALL

"The Garden of Echoes"
Hogan, Robert. "Mervyn Wall," in Bleiler, E. F., Ed. *Supernatural Fiction Writers* . . . , II, 649–650.

ERIC D. WALROND

"Panama Gold"
Ramchand, Kenneth. "The Writer Who Ran Away: Eric Walrond and Tropical Death," *Savacou*, 2 (1970), 71–74.

"Tropic Death"
Bogle, Enid E. "Eric Walrond," in Dance, Daryl C., Ed. *Fifty Caribbean Writers . . .*, 478, 479–480.

"White Snake"
Bogle, Enid E. "Eric Walrond," 478.

WAN ZHI [CHEN MAIPING]

"Open Terrain"
Duke, Michael S. *Blooming . . .*, 71–72.

SYLVIA TOWNSEND WARNER

"A Kitchen Knife"
Baldwin, Dean. "The English Short Story in the Fifties," in Vannatta, Dennis, Ed. *The English Short Story, 1945–1980*, 45–46.

"The One and the Other"
Crossley, Robert. "A Long Day's Dying: The Elves of J. R. R. Tolkien and Sylvia Townsend Warner," in Yoke, Carl B., and Donald M. Hassler, Eds. *Death and the Serpent . . .*, 64–65.

"Poor Mary"
Stinson, John J. "The English Short Story, 1945–1950," in Vannatta, Dennis, Ed. *The English Short Story, 1945–1980*, 12–13.

ROBERT PENN WARREN

"Blackberry Winter"
Runyon, Randolph. "The View from the Attic: Robert Penn Warren's *Circus Stories*," *Mississippi Q*, 38 (1985), 123–128.
Snipes, Katherine. *Robert Penn Warren*, 64–65.
Watkins, Floyd C. "Following the Tramp in Warren's 'Blackberry Winter,'" *Stud Short Fiction*, 22 (1985), 343–345.

"The Circus in the Attic"
Runyon, Randolph. "The View . . . ," 120–123.
Snipes, Katherine. *Robert Penn Warren*, 61–62.

"The Patented Gate and the Mean Hamburger"
Snipes, Katherine. *Robert Penn Warren*, 62–63.

"Prime Leaf"
Runyon, Randolph. "The View . . . ," 130–133.

"The Unvexed Isles"
Runyon, Randolph. "The View . . . ," 133–134.

EVELYN WAUGH

"Love Among the Ruins"
Berger, Harold L. *Science Fiction* . . . , 186–187.

"Ryder by Gaslight"
Meckier, Jerome. "Evelyn Waugh's 'Ryder by Gaslight': A Postmortem," *Twentieth-Century Lit*, 31 (1985), 399–409.

H. G. WELLS

"The Beautiful Suit"
*Costa, Richard H. *H. G. Wells*, 2nd ed., 35–36.

"The Country of the Blind"
*Costa, Richard H. *H. G. Wells*, 2nd ed., 36–40.

"The Desert Daisy"
*Costa, Richard H. *H. G. Wells*, 2nd ed., 5–6.

"The Door in the Wall"
*Costa, Richard H. *H. G. Wells*, 2nd ed., 35–36.
Gardner, Martin. "H. G. Wells," in Bleiler, E. F., Ed. *Supernatural Fiction Writers* . . . , I, 400.

"A Dream of Armageddon"
Gardner, Martin. "H. G. Wells," 400–401.

"The Grisly Folks"
Costa, Richard H. *H. G. Wells*, 2nd ed., 140–143.

"The Inexperienced Ghost"
Sarkissian, Gisèle. "Ghosts in Tales of the Fantastic," *Mythes, Croyances et Religions*, 3 (1985), 155–163.

"The Lord of the Dynamos"
*Costa, Richard H. *H. G. Wells*, 2nd ed., 32–34.

"The Man Who Could Work Miracles"
*Costa, Richard H. *H. G. Wells*, 2nd ed., 32.
Crossley, Robert. *H. G. Wells*, 64–65.
Gardner, Martin. "H. G. Wells," 399.

"The New Accelerator"
Crossley, Robert. *H. G. Wells*, 61–62.

"The Plattner Story"
Crossley, Robert. *H. G. Wells*, 62–63.

"The Remarkable Case of Davidson's Eyes"
*Costa, Richard H. *H. G. Wells*, 2nd ed., 34.

"The Star"
Crossley, Robert. *H. G. Wells*, 58–59.

"The Stolen Bacillus"
*Costa, Richard H. *H. G. Wells*, 2nd ed., 31–32.

"The Story of the Days to Come"
Crossley, Robert. *H. G. Wells*, 59–60.

"A Story of the Stone Age"
Crossley, Robert. *H. G. Wells*, 60–61.

"The Time Machine"
Abrash, Merritt. "The Hubris of Science: Wells's Time Traveler," in Hassler,
    Donald M., Ed. *Patterns . . . II*, 5–11.
Costa, Richard H. *H. G. Wells*, 31–35; 2nd ed., 12–17.
Crossley, Robert. *H. G. Wells*, 20–29.
Lindsay, Clarence. "H. G. Wells, Viktor Shklovsky, and Paul de Man: The Sub-
    version of Romanticism," in Collins, Robert A., and Howard D. Pearce,
    Eds. *The Scope of the Fantastic . . .* , 130–132.
Showalter, Elaine. "Syphilis, Sexuality, and the Fiction of the Fin de Siècle," in
    Yeazell, Ruth B., Ed. *Sex, Politics . . .* , 104–105.

EUDORA WELTY

"Asphodel"
Manning, Carol S. *With Ears Opening . . .* , 92–97.
Shinn, Thelma J. *Radiant Daughters . . .* , 37–38.
Spacks, Patricia M. *Gossip*, 253–256; rpt. Bloom, Harold, Ed. *Eudora Welty*, 161–
    162.

"At the Landing"
Manning, Carol S. *With Ears Opening . . .* , 90–92.
Shinn, Thelma J. *Radiant Daughters . . .* , 38–39.
*Vande Kieft, Ruth M. "The Mysteries of Eudora Welty," in Bloom, Harold,
    Ed. *Eudora Welty*, 57–59.

"The Bride of Innisfallen"
Toman, Marshall. "Welty's 'The Bride of Innisfallen,'" *Explicator*, 43, ii (1985),
    42–44.
*Vande Kieft, Ruth M. "The Mysteries . . . ," 64–65.

"The Burning"
Bloom, Harold. "Introduction," in Bloom, Harold, Ed. *Eudora Welty*, 6–9.

"Circe"
*Vande Kieft, Ruth M. "The Mysteries . . . ," 65–66.

"Clytie"
Manning, Carol S. *With Ears Opening* . . . , 13–15.
*Vande Kieft, Ruth M. "The Mysteries . . . ," 55–56.

"A Curtain of Green"
*Vande Kieft, Ruth M. "The Mysteries . . . ," 47–48.

"Death of a Traveling Salesman"
*Vande Kieft, Ruth M. "The Mysteries . . . ," 68–69.

"Flowers for Marjorie"
*Vande Kieft, Ruth M. "The Mysteries . . . ," 49–50.

"The Hitch-Hikers"
*Vande Kieft, Ruth M. "The Mysteries . . . ," 54–55.
Walter, James. "The Fate of the Story Teller in Eudora Welty's 'The Hitch-Hikers,'" *So Central R*, 2 (1985), 57–70.

"June Recital"
Manning, Carol S. *With Ears Opening* . . . , 23–24.

"Keela, the Outcast Indian Maiden"
Coulthard, A. P. "'Keela, the Outcast Indian Maiden': A Dissenting View," *Stud Short Fiction*, 23 (1986), 35–41.
Manning, Carol S. *With Ears Opening* . . . , 71–73.

"The Key"
*Vande Kieft, Ruth M. "The Mysteries . . . ," 60–63.

"Kin"
Manning, Carol S. *With Ears Opening* . . . , 51–53.
Spacks, Patricia M. *Gossip*, 251–253; rpt. Bloom, Harold, Ed. *Eudora Welty*, 158–159.

"Livvie"
*Warren, Robert P. "Love and Separateness in Eudora Welty," in Bloom, Harold, Ed. *Eudora Welty*, 25–26.

"Moon Lake"
Manning, Carol S. *With Ears Opening* . . . , 107–116.

"Petrified Man"
Bohner, Charles H. *Instructor's Manual* . . . , 119–120.
Spacks, Patricia M. *Gossip*, 248–249; rpt. Bloom, Harold, Ed. *Eudora Welty*, 155–156.

"Shower of Gold"
Manning, Carol S. *With Ears Opening* . . . , 97–100.

"Sir Rabbit"
Manning, Carol S. *With Ears Opening* . . . , 100–103.

"A Still Moment"
Bloom, Harold. "Introduction," 1–5.
Cluck, Nancy. "Audubon: Images of the Artist in Eudora Welty and Robert Penn Warren," *Southern Lit J*, 17, ii (1985), 41–53.
Gray, Richard. *Writing the South* . . . , 237–238.
Marrs, Suzanne. "John James Audubon in Fiction and Poetry: Literary Portraits by Eudora Welty and Robert Penn Warren," *Southern Stud*, 20 (1981), 378–383.
*Vande Kieft, Ruth M. "The Mysteries . . . ," 51–54.

"The Wanderers"
MacKethan, Lucinda H. "To See Things in Their Time: The Act of Focus in Eudora Welty's Fiction," *Am Lit*, 50 (1978), 270–272.
Manning, Carol S. *With Ears Opening* . . . , 104–106.
Spacks, Patricia M. *Gossip*, 249–251; rpt. Bloom, Harold, Ed. *Eudora Welty*, 156–157.

"Where Is the Voice Coming From?"
Clerc, Charles. "Anatomy of Welty's 'Where Is the Voice Coming From?'" *Stud Short Fiction*, 23 (1986), 389–400.

"Why I Live at the P.O."
Bohner, Charles H. *Instructor's Manual* . . . , 120–121.

"The Wide Net"
*Warren, Robert P. "Love and Separateness . . . ," 24–25.

"A Worn Path"
Bohner, Charles H. *Instructor's Manual* . . . , 121–122.
Sheidley, William E., and Ann Charters. *Instructor's Manual* . . . , 133–134; rpt. Charters, Ann, William E. Sheidley, and Martha Ramsey. *Instructor's Manual* . . . , 2nd ed., 133–134.

ALBERT WENDT

"The Pint-Sized Devil on a Thoroughbred"
Nightingale, Peggy. "All Any Man with a Club Can Do: Albert Wendt and Witi Ihimaera," in Sellick, Robert, Ed. *Myth and Metaphor*, 59–60.

"A Resurrection"
Nightingale, Peggy. "All Any Man . . . ," 55–56.

ANTHONY C. WEST

"Narcissus unto Echo"
Eyler, Audrey S. "'Narcissus unto Echo': Two Stories by Anthony C. West," *Éire*, 20, iii (1985), 130–144.

NATHANAEL WEST

"A Cool Million"
Schulz, Dieter. "Nathanael West's 'A Cool Million' and the Myth of Success," in Dietrich, Maria, and Christoph Schöneich, Eds. *Studien zur englischen und amerikanischen Prosa . . .* , 164–175.

"The Dream Life of Balso Snell"
Long, Robert E. *Nathanael West*, 22–43.

"Miss Lonelyhearts"
Butler, Rebecca R. "Todorov's Fantastic, Kayser's Grotesque, and West's 'Miss Lonelyhearts,'" in Collins, Robert A., and Howard D. Pearce, Eds. *The Scope of the Fantastic . . .* , 42–48.
Laurenson, Diana, and Alan Swingewood. *The Sociology . . .* , 237–244.
Long, Robert E. *Nathanael West*, 44–83.
Nilsen, Helge N. "A Novel of Despair: A Note on Nathanael West's 'Miss Lonelyhearts,'" *Neophilologus*, 70 (1986), 475–478.
Robinson, Douglas. *American Apocalypse . . .* , 213–216.
Slatoff, Walter J. *The Look of Distance . . .* , 54–66.

"The Sun, the Lady, and the Gas Station"
Long, Robert E. *Nathanael West*, 87–88.

REBECCA WEST

"The Abiding Vision"
Orel, Harold. *The Literary Achievement . . .* , 143–145.

"Life Sentence"
Orel, Harold. *The Literary Achievement . . .* , 139–140.

"The Salt of the Earth"
Orel, Harold. *The Literary Achievement . . .* , 141–143.

"There Is No Conversation"
Orel, Harold. *The Literary Achievement . . .* , 137–139.

EDITH WHARTON

"Afterward"
Robillard, Douglas. "Edith Wharton," in Bleiler, E. F., Ed. *Supernatural Fiction Writers . . .* , II, 786–787.

"Expiation"
Kaplan, Amy. "Edith Wharton's Profession of Authorship," *Engl Lit Hist*, 53 (1986), 440.

"The Eyes"
Robillard, Douglas. "Edith Wharton," 786.

"The Fulness of Life"
Robillard, Douglas. "Edith Wharton," 785.

"Kerfol"
Robillard, Douglas. "Edith Wharton," 787–788.

"The Lady's Maid's Bell"
Robillard, Douglas. "Edith Wharton," 786.

"Miss Mary Pask"
Robillard, Douglas. "Edith Wharton," 787.

"The Pelican"
Kaplan, Amy. "Edith Wharton's Profession . . . ," 438–440.

"Roman Fever"
Bohner, Charles H. *Instructor's Manual . . .* , 123–124.
Gerlach, John. *Toward the End . . .* , 58–60.
Sheidley, William E., and Ann Charters. *Instructor's Manual . . .* , 42–44; rpt.
    Charters, Ann, William E. Sheidley, and Martha Ramsey. *Instructor's Manual . . .* , 2nd ed., 52–53.

RUDY WIEBE

"Where Is the Voice Coming From?"
Davidson, Arnold E. "The Provenance of Story in Rudy Wiebe's 'Where Is the Voice Coming From?'" *Stud Short Fiction*, 22 (1985), 189–193.

ELLEN WILBUR

"Wind and Birds and Human Voices"
Mernit, Susan. "The State of the Short Story," *Virginia Q R*, 62 (1986), 306–309.

OSCAR WILDE

"The Birthday of the Infanta"
Elkins, Mary J. "Oscar Wilde," in Bleiler, E. F., Ed. *Supernatural Fiction Writers . . .* , I, 347.

"The Canterville Ghost"
Sarkissian, Gisèle. "Ghosts in Tales of the Fantastic," *Mythes, Croyances et Religions*, 3 (1985), 155–163.

"Lord Arthur Savile's Crime"
Elkins, Mary J. "Oscar Wilde," 346.

"The Model Millionaires"
Roditi, Edouard. *Oscar Wilde*, 105–107; 2nd ed., 71–72.

"The Portrait of Mr. W. H."
Roditi, Edouard. *Oscar Wilde*, 107–110; 2nd ed., 72–74.

WILLIAM CARLOS WILLIAMS

"Country Rain"
Mariani, Paul. "Williams: La Gioconda's Smile," *William Carlos Williams R*, 11,
    ii (1985), 55–60.

"Mind and Body"
Gratto, Joseph M. "An Analysis of William Carlos Williams' 'Mind and Body,'"
    Stud Short Fiction, 22 (1985), 347–351.

"The Use of Force"
Bohner, Charles H. *Instructor's Manual . . .* , 124.

JACK WILLIAMSON

"With Folded Hands"
Berger, Harold L. *Science Fiction . . .* , 29–30.

NATHANIEL PARKER WILLIS

"Kate Crediford"
Gerlach, John. *Toward the End . . .* , 54–55.

"Mabel Wynne"
Gerlach, John. *Toward the End . . .* , 29–30.

ANGUS WILSON

"A Bit off the Map"
Gardner, Averil. *Angus Wilson*, 54–55.

"Et Dona Ferentes"
Gardner, Averil. *Angus Wilson*, 24–26.

"Fresh-Air Fiend"
Gardner, Averil. *Angus Wilson*, 17–18.

"More Friend Than Lodger"
Gardner, Averil. *Angus Wilson*, 53–54.

"Raspberry Jam"
Gardner, Averil. *Angus Wilson*, 21–23.
Stinson, John J. "The English Short Story, 1945–1950," in Vannatta, Dennis,
    Ed. *The English Short Story, 1945–1980*, 14.

EDMUND WILSON

RICHARD WILSON

"The Eight Billion"
Berger, Harold L. *Science Fiction* . . . , 159–160.

ROBLEY WILSON

"The Apple"
Klinkowitz, Jerome. *Literary Subversions* . . . , 81–82.

"Business. 1947"
Klinkowitz, Jerome. *Literary Subversions* . . . , 88–89.

"Loving a Fat Girl"
Klinkowitz, Jerome. *Literary Subversions* . . . , 79–80.

"Paint"
Klinkowitz, Jerome. *Literary Subversions* . . . , 89–90.

"Saying Goodbye to the President"
Klinkowitz, Jerome. *Literary Subversions* . . . , 83–84.

"Thief"
Klinkowitz, Jerome. *Literary Subversions* . . . , 86–87.

OWEN WISTER

"Balaam and Pedro"
Payne, Darwin. *Owen Wister* . . . , 135–137.

"Hank's Woman"
Payne, Darwin. *Owen Wister* . . . , 122–124.

"The Right Honorable the Strawberries"
Payne, Darwin. *Owen Wister* . . . , 311–312.

P. G. WODEHOUSE

"The Nodder"
Flora, Joseph M. *The English Short Story* . . . , 106–107.

GENE WOLFE

"Alien Stones"
Gordon, Joan. *Gene Wolfe*, 58.

"Beautyland"
Gordon, Joan. *Gene Wolfe*, 53–54.

"The Changeling"
Gordon, Joan. *Gene Wolfe,* 59–60.

"The Doctor of Death Island"
Gordon, Joan. *Gene Wolfe,* 62–63.

"The Eyeflash Murders"
Gordon, Joan. *Gene Wolfe,* 63–64.

"The Fifth Head of Cerberus"
Gordon, Joan. *Gene Wolfe,* 20–23.

"Forlessen"
Gordon, Joan. *Gene Wolfe,* 54–57.

"How I Lost the Second World War and Turned Back the German Invasion"
Gordon, Joan. *Gene Wolfe,* 52–53.

"Seven American Nights"
Gordon, Joan. *Gene Wolfe,* 67–72.

"'A Story' by John V. Marsch"
Gordon, Joan. *Gene Wolfe,* 23–25.

"Three Fingers"
Gordon, Joan. *Gene Wolfe,* 57.

"Tracking Song"
Gordon, Joan. *Gene Wolfe,* 64–66.

"V. R. T."
Gordon, Joan. *Gene Wolfe,* 25–27.

THOMAS WOLFE

"The Child by Tiger"
Stutman, Suzanne. "Technique in 'The Child by Tiger': Portrait of a Mature
    Artist," *So Carolina R,* 18, i (1985), 83–88.
Washburn, Delores. "'The Child by Tiger' and Students' Innocent Ignorance,"
    Thomas Wolfe R, 9, ii (1985), 47–52.

"Death, the Proud Brother"
Boyer, James D. "The City in the Short Fiction of Thomas Wolfe," *Thomas Wolfe
    R,* 7, ii (1983), 37; rpt. Phillipson, John S., Ed. *Critical Essays . . . ,* 184.
Salmon, Webb. "Thomas Wolfe's Search to Know Brooklyn," in Phillipson,
    John S., Ed. *Critical Essays . . . ,* 179–180.

"The Lost Boy"
Adams, Timothy D. "The Ebb and Flow of Time and Place in 'The Lost Boy,'"
    Southern Stud, 19 (1980), 400–408; rpt. Phillipson, John S., Ed. *Critical
    Essays . . . ,* 158–166.

"No Door"
Boyer, James D. "The City . . . ," 38; rpt. Phillipson, John S., Ed. *Critical Essays* . . . , 184–185.

"Only the Dead Know Brooklyn"
Boyer, James D. "The City . . . ," 38–39; rpt. Phillipson, John S., Ed. *Critical Essays* . . . , 185.
Salmon, Webb. "Thomas Wolfe's Search . . . ," 174–175.

"The Party at Jack's"
Boyer, James D. "The City . . . ," 39–40; rpt. Phillipson, John S., Ed. *Critical Essays* . . . , 185–186.

"The Train and the City"
Boyer, James D. "The City . . . ," 36–37; rpt. Phillipson, John S., Ed. *Critical Essays* . . . , 182–184.

MRS. HENRY WOOD [ELLEN PRICE WOOD]

"A Curious Experience"
Campbell, James L. "Mrs. Henry Wood," in Bleiler, E. F., Ed. *Supernatural Fiction Writers* . . . , I, 284.

"David Garth's Ghost"
Campbell, James L. "Mrs. Henry Wood," 283–284.

"David Garth's Night-Watch"
Campbell, James L. "Mrs. Henry Wood," 283.

"Reality or Delusion?"
Campbell, James L. "Mrs. Henry Wood," 283.

"The Surgeon's Daughter"
Campbell, James L. "Mrs. Henry Wood," 282.

VIRGINIA WOOLF

"Kew Gardens"
Bohner, Charles H. *Instructor's Manual* . . . , 124–125.

"Lappin and Lapinova"
Flora, Joseph M. *The English Short Story* . . . , 60–61.

"The Mark on the Wall"
Flora, Joseph M. *The English Short Story* . . . , 59–60.

"Moments of Being"
Sheidley, William E., and Ann Charters. *Instructor's Manual* . . . , 76; rpt. Charters, Ann, William E. Sheidley, and Martha Ramsey. *Instructor's Manual* . . . , 2nd ed., 71.

"Monday or Tuesday"
Quéré, Henri. "Transformations et ruptures: Le Roman, forme en question,"
    Fabu, 1 (March, 1983), 115–124.

"The Searchlight"
Flora, Joseph M. *The English Short Story . . .* , 57–58.

"Together and Apart"
Slatoff, Walter J. *The Look of Distance . . .* , 168–170.

"An Unwritten Novel"
Slatoff, Walter J. *The Look of Distance . . .* , 209–217.

CORNELL WOOLRICH [CORNELL GEORGE HOPLEY-WOOLRICH]

"The Light in the Window"
Nevins, Francis M. "Introduction," in Woolrich, Cornell. *The Fantastic Stories . . .* , xxi.

CONSTANCE FENIMORE WOOLSTON

"Felipa"
Rowe, Anne. *The Enchanted Country . . .* , 61.

"King David"
Rowe, Anne. *The Enchanted Country . . .* , 60–61.

"Old Gardiston"
Rowe, Anne. *The Enchanted Country . . .* , 63–64.

"The Street of Hyacinth"
Edwards Kitterman, Mary P. "Henry James and the Artist-Heroine in the Tales
    of Constance Fenimore Woolston," in Nathan, Rhoda B., Ed. *Nineteenth-
    Century Women Writers . . .* , 51–52.

RICHARD WRIGHT

"Big Boy Leaves Home"
Jones, Lola E. "Sex and Sexuality in Richard Wright's 'Big Boy Leaves Home,'"
    in Hollis, Burney J., Ed. *Amid Visions . . .* , 102–108.

"Bright and Morning Star"
Williams, Sherley A. "Papa Dick and Sister-Woman: Reflections on Women in
    the Fiction of Richard Wright," in Fleischmann, Fritz, Ed. *American Novelists
    Revisited . . .* , 398–402.

"Long Black Song"
Williams, Sherley A. "Papa Dick . . . ," 406–410.

"The Man Who Lived Underground"
Gilyard, Keith. "The Sociolinguistics of Underground Blues," *Black Am Lit Forum*, 19 (1985), 158–159.
Nisula, Dasha C. "Dostoevsky and Richard Wright: From Petersburg to Chicago," in Ugrimsky, Alexej, and Valija K. Ozolins, Eds. *Dostoevski and the Human Condition . . .* , 163–170.

"The Man Who Was Almost a Man"
Bohner, Charles H. *Instructor's Manual . . .* , 125–126.
Loftis, John E. "Domestic Prey: Richard Wright's Parody of the Hunt Tradition in 'The Man Who Was Almost a Man,'" *Stud Short Fiction*, 23 (1986), 437–442.
Sheidley, William E., and Ann Charters. *Instructor's Manual . . .* , 129; rpt. Charters, Ann, William E. Sheidley, and Martha Ramsey. *Instructor's Manual . . .* , 2nd ed., 129.

SYDNEY FOWLER WRIGHT

"Choice"
Stableford, Brian. *Scientific Romance . . .* , 192–193.

WU ZUXIANG [WU TSU-HIANG]

"Young Master Gets His Tonic"
Anderson, Marston. "The Morality of Form: Lu Xun and the Modern Chinese Short Story," in Lee, Leo Ou-fan, Ed. *Lu Xun . . .* , 48–49.

RICHARD YATES

"B. A. R. Man"
Klinkowitz, Jerome. *Literary Subversions . . .* , 118.

"The Best of Everything"
Klinkowitz, Jerome. *The New American Novel . . .* , 23–25.

"Doctor Jack-o-Lantern"
Klinkowitz, Jerome. *The New American Novel . . .* , 23.

"A Glutton for Punishment"
Klinkowitz, Jerome. *The New American Novel . . .* , 26–28.

"Jody Rolled the Bones"
Klinkowitz, Jerome. *The New American Novel . . .* , 25.

"Liars in Love"
Klinkowitz, Jerome. *Literary Subversions . . .* , 122–123.

"No Pain Whatsoever"
Klinkowitz, Jerome. *The New American Novel . . .* , 25–26.

"Oh, Joseph, I'm So Tired"
Klinkowitz, Jerome. *Literary Subversions* . . . , 121–122.

"A Wrestler with Sharks"
Klinkowitz, Jerome. *The New American Novel* . . . , 28–29.

STARK YOUNG

"The Land of Juan de Dios"
Makowsky, Veronica A. "Mothers and Inventions in *The Street of the Island*,"
Southern Q, 24, iv (1986), 69–73.

"The Light on the Hills"
Makowsky, Veronica A. "Mothers and Inventions . . . ," 73–74.

"Ora Pro Nobis"
Makowsky, Veronica A. "Mothers and Inventions . . . ," 77–78.

"The Passionate Road"
Makowsky, Veronica A. "Mothers and Inventions . . . ," 74–76.

MARGUERITE YOURCENAR

"Achilles"
Farrell, C. Frederick and Edith R. *Marguerite Yourcenar* . . . , 51–52.

"Clytemnestra"
Farrell, C. Frederick and Edith R. *Marguerite Yourcenar* . . . , 51–52.

"Lena"
Farrell, C. Frederick and Edith R. *Marguerite Yourcenar* . . . , 53–54.

"Mary Magdalene"
Farrell, C. Frederick and Edith R. *Marguerite Yourcenar* . . . , 53.

"Patroclus"
Farrell, C. Frederick and Edith R. *Marguerite Yourcenar* . . . , 52–53.

"Sappho"
Farrell, C. Frederick and Edith R. *Marguerite Yourcenar* . . . , 60–61.

DUILIU ZAMFIRESCU

"To Coteşti"
Stolojan, Sanda. *Duiliu Zamfirescu*, 103–105.

ROGER ZELAZNY

"The Engine at Heartspring's Center"
Sanders, Joseph. "Dancing on the Tightrope: Immortality in Roger Zelazny," in Yoke, Carl B., and Donald M. Hassler, Eds. *Death and the Serpent . . .* , 138–140.

"For a Breath I Tarry"
Sanders, Joseph. "Dancing on the Tightrope . . . ," 140–141.

"Home Is the Hangman"
Sanders, Joseph. "Dancing on the Tightrope . . . ," 140–141.

"The Man Who Loved the Faioli"
Sanders, Joseph. "Dancing on the Tightrope . . . ," 138–140.

"A Rose for Ecclesiastes"
Francavilla, Joseph V. "Promethean Bound: Heroes and Gods in Roger Zelazny's Science Fiction," in Reilly, Robert, Ed. *The Transcendent Adventure . . .* , 214–215.

ZHANG TIANYI

"A Subject Matter"
Anderson, Marston. "The Morality of Form: Lu Xun and the Modern Chinese Short Story," in Lee, Leo Ou-fan, Ed. *Lu Xun . . .* , 47.

ZHU LIN

"The Web"
Duke, Michael S. *Blooming . . .* , 80–82.

ÉMILE ÉDOUARD CHARLES ANTOINE ZOLA

"Adventures of Big Sidoine and Little Médéric"
Walker, Philip. *Zola*, 54–55.

"The Blacksmith"
Walker, Philip. *Zola*, 113–114.

"A Puff of Wind"
Walker, Philip. *Zola*, 37–38.

A CHECKLIST OF BOOKS USED

Aarons, Victoria. *Author as Character in the Works of Sholom Aleichem.* New York: Edwin Heller, 1985.

Abbott, H. Porter. *Diary Fiction: Writing As Action.* Ithaca: Cornell Univ. Press, 1984.

Aberbach, David. *At the Handles of the Lock: Themes in the Fiction of S. J. Agnon.* Oxford: Oxford Univ. Press, 1985.

Abrahams, Cecil A. *Alex La Guma.* Boston: Twayne, 1985.

Agheana, Ion T. *The Prose of Jorge Luis Borges: Existentialism and the Dynamics of Surprise.* New York: Peter Lang, 1984.

Alden, Patricia. *Social Mobility in the English Bildungsroman: Gissing, Hardy, Bennett, and Lawrence.* Ann Arbor: UMI Research Press, 1986.

Aldridge, A. Owen. *The Reemergence of World Literature: A Study of Asia and the West.* Cranbury, N.J.: Associated Univ. Presses [for Univ. of Delaware Press], 1986.

Alexander, Edward. *Isaac Bashevis Singer.* Boston: Twayne, 1980.

Allen, Elizabeth. *A Woman's Place in the Novels of Henry James.* New York: St. Martin's Press, 1984.

Allen, Roger, Ed. *In the Eye of the Beholder: Tales of Egyptian Life from the Writings of Yusuf Idris.* Chicago: Bibliotheca Islamica, 1978.

Alsen, Eberhard. *Salinger's Glass Stories as a Composite Novel.* Troy, N.Y.: Whitston, 1983.

Amirthanayagam, Guy, and S. C. Harrex, Eds. *Only Connect: Literary Perspectives East and West.* Adelaide: Centre for Research in the New Literatures in English, 1981; Am ed. Honolulu: East-West Center, 1981.

Ancona, Francesco A. *Writing the Absence of the Father: Undoing Oedipal Structures in the Contemporary American Novel.* Lanham, Md.: Univ. Press of America, 1986.

Anderson, Roger B. *Dostoevsky: Myth of Duality.* Gainesville: Univ. of Florida Press, 1986.

Andrew, Joe, and Christopher Pike, Eds. *The Structural Analysis of Russian Narrative Fiction.* Keele: Keele Univ. Press, 1984.

Angier, Carole. *Jean Rhys.* New York: Viking, 1985.

Aronne-Amestoy, Lida. *Utopía Paraíso e historia: Inscripciones del mito en García Márquez, Rulfo y Cortázar.* Amsterdam: Benjamins, 1986.

Atiş, Sarah M. *Semantic Structuring in the Modern Turkish Short Story: An Analysis of "The Dream of Abdullah Efendi" and Other Stories by Ahmet Hamdi Tanpinar.* Leiden: Brill, 1983.

Auchard, John. *Silence in Henry James: The Heritage of Symbolism and Decadence.* University Park: Pennsylvania State Univ. Press, 1986.

Averill, Deborah M. *The Irish Short Story from George Moore to Frank O'Connor.* Lanham, Md.: Univ. Press of America, 1982.

Bailey, Peter J. *Reading Stanley Elkin.* Urbana: Univ. of Illinois Press, 1985.

Baker, A. W. *Death Is a Good Solution: The Convict Experience in Early Australia.* Brisbane: Univ. of Queensland Press, 1984.

Balakian, Anna, James J. Wilhelm, Douwe W. Fokkema, Claudio Guillén, and

M. J. Valdés, Eds. *Proceedings of the Xth Congress of the International Comparative Literature Association.* 3 vols. New York: Garland, 1985.

Balbert, Peter, and Phillip Marcus, Eds. *D. H. Lawrence: A Centenary Consideration.* Ithaca: Cornell Univ. Press, 1985.

Barbour, James, and Thomas Quirk, Eds. *Romanticism: Critical Essays in American Literature.* New York: Garland, 1986.

Barclay, Glen St. John. *Anatomy of Horror: The Masters of Occult Fiction.* London: Weidenfeld & Nicolson, 1978; Am. ed. New York: St. Martin's Press, 1979.

Barr, Marleen S., Ruth Salvaggio, and Richard Law. *Suzy McKee Charnas, Octavia Butler, Joan D. Vinge.* Mercer Island, Wash.: Starmont, 1986.

Basler, Roy, Ed. *Literary Lectures Presented at The Houses of Congress.* Washington: Library of Congress, 1973.

Bastian, Katherine. *Joyce Carol Oates's Short Stories Between Tradition and Innovation.* Frankfurt: Peter Lang, 1983.

Beet, Gilliam. *George Eliot.* Bloomington: Indiana Univ. Press, 1986.

Bensick, Carol M. *La Nouvelle Beatrice: Renaissance and Romance in "Rappaccini's Daughter."* New Brunswick: Rutgers Univ. Press, 1985.

Benstock, Bernard. *James Joyce.* New York: Ungar, 1985.

———, Ed. *Art and Crime Writing: Essays on Detective Fiction.* New York: St. Martin's Press, 1983.

Ben-Zvi, Linda. *Samuel Beckett.* Boston: Twayne, 1986.

Bercovitch, Sacvan, Ed. *Reconstructing American Literary History.* Cambridge: Harvard Univ. Press, 1986.

Berendsohn, Walter A. *August Strindberg: Der Mensch und seine Umwelt—Das Werk—Der schöpferische Künstler.* Amsterdam: Rodopi, 1974.

Berger, Alan L. *Crisis and Covenant: The Holocaust in American Jewish Fiction.* Albany: State Univ. of New York Press, 1985.

Berger, Harold L. *Science Fiction and the New Dark Age.* Bowling Green: Bowling Green Univ. Popular Press, 1976.

Berman, Jeffrey. *The Talking Cure: Literary Representation of Psychoanalysis.* New York: New York Univ. Press, 1985.

Berman, Russell A. *The Rise of the Modern German Novel: Crisis and Charisma.* Cambridge: Harvard Univ. Press, 1986.

Bevilacqua, Winifred F. *Josephine Herbst.* Boston: Twayne, 1985.

Biles, Jack I., and Robert O. Evans, Eds. *William Golding: Some Critical Considerations.* Lexington: Univ. Press of Kentucky, 1978.

Bittner, James W. *Approaches to the Fiction of Ursula K. Le Guin.* Ann Arbor: UMI Research Press, 1984.

Black, Michael. *D. H. Lawrence: The Early Fiction.* Cambridge: Cambridge Univ. Press, 1986.

Blackham, H. J. *The Fable as Literature.* London: Athlone Press, 1985.

Bleiler, E. F., Ed. *Supernatural Fiction Writers: Fantasy and Horror, I—Apuleius to May Sinclair.* New York: Scribner, 1985.

———. *Supernatural Fiction Writers: Fantasy and Horror, II—A. E. Coppard to Roger Zelazny.* New York: Scribner, 1985.

Bloom, Harold, Ed. *Edgar Allan Poe.* New York: Chelsea House, 1985.

———. *Joseph Conrad.* New York: Chelsea House, 1986.

———. *Nathaniel Hawthorne.* New York: Chelsea House, 1986.

———. *Franz Kafka.* New York: Chelsea House, 1986.

———. *Ursula K. Le Guin.* New York: Chelsea House, 1986.

———. *Eudora Welty.* New York: Chelsea House, 1986.

Bohner, Charles H. *Instructor's Manual [for] "Classic Short Fiction."* Englewood Cliffs: Prentice-Hall, 1986.

Bold, Alan N. *Muriel Spark.* New York: Methuen, 1986.

Boudreau, H. L., and Luis T. González-del-Valle, Eds. *Studies in Honor of Sumner M. Greenfield.* Lincoln: Soc. of Spanish & Spanish-American Studies, 1985.

Boué, André. *William Carleton, romancier irlandais (1794–1865).* Paris: Sorbonne, 1978.

Boyle, Nicholas, and Martin Swales, Eds. *Realism in European Literature: Essays in Honour of J. P. Stern.* Cambridge: Cambridge Univ. Press, 1986.

Brassell, Tim. *Tom Stoppard: An Assessment.* New York: St. Martin's Press, 1985; Brt. ed. London: Macmillan, 1985.

Brinkmeyer, Robert H. *Three Catholic Writers of the Modern South.* Jackson: Univ. Press of Mississippi, 1985.

Bristol, Evelyn, Ed. *East European Literature.* Berkeley: Berkeley Slavic Specialties, 1982.

Brodetsky, Tessa. *Elizabeth Gaskell.* Leamington Spa, England: Berg, 1986.

Brown, Richard. *James Joyce and Sexuality.* Cambridge: Cambridge Univ. Press, 1985.

Bruyère, Claire. *Sherwood Anderson: L'Impuissance créatrice.* Paris: Klincksieck, 1985.

Buell, Lawrence. *New England Literary Culture: From Revolution Through Renaissance.* Cambridge: Cambridge Univ. Press, 1986.

Burgess, Anthony. *Flame into Being: The Life and Work of D. H. Lawrence.* New York: Arbor House, 1985.

Burt, Forrest D. *W. Somerset Maugham.* Boston: Twayne, 1985.

Byerman, Keith E. *Fingering the Jagged Grain: Tradition and Form in Recent Black Fiction.* Athens: Univ. of Georgia Press, 1985.

Cabibbo, Paola, Ed. *Melvilliana.* Rome: Bulzoni, 1983.

Callary, Edward, Ed. *Festschrift in Honor of Virgil J. Vogel.* DeKalb: Illinois Names Society, 1985.

Cameron, Barry. *John Metcalf.* Boston: Twayne, 1986.

Cameron, Keith. *René Maran.* Boston: Twayne, 1985.

Campbell, Ian. *Lewis Grassic Gibbon.* Edinburgh: Scottish Academic Press, 1985.

Capellán, Angel. *Hemingway and the Hispanic World.* Ann Arbor: UMI Research Press, 1985.

Cardwell, Richard A., Ed. *Essays in Honour of Robert Brian Tate from His Colleagues and Pupils.* Nottingham: Univ. of Nottingham, 1984.

Carey, Glenn O. *Edward Payson Roe.* Boston: Twayne, 1985.

Carlson, Eric W., Ed. *The Recognition of Edgar Allan Poe.* Ann Arbor: Univ. of Michigan Press, 1966.

Carothers, James B. *William Faulkner's Short Stories.* Ann Arbor: UMI Research Press, 1985.

Carton, Evan. *The Rhetoric of American Romance: Dialectic and Identity in Emerson, Dickinson, Poe, and Hawthorne.* Baltimore: Johns Hopkins Univ. Press, 1985.

Cascardi, Anthony J. *The Bounds of Reason: Cervantes, Dostoevsky, Flaubert.* New York: Columbia Univ. Press, 1986.

Castronovo, David. *Edmund Wilson.* New York: Ungar, 1984.

Cattaneo, Mariateresa, and Silvana Serafin, Eds. *Studi de letteratura ibero-americana offerti a Giuseppe Bellini.* Rome: Bulzoni, 1984.

Caws, Mary Ann. *Reading Frames in Modern Fiction.* Princeton: Princeton Univ. Press, 1985.

———, Ed. *Textual Analysis: Some Readers Reading*. New York: Modern Language Association, 1986.

Chametzky, Jules. *Our Decentralized Literature: Cultural Meditations in Selected Jewish and Southern Writers*. Amherst: Univ. of Massachusetts Press, 1986.

Chen, Yo-shih. *Realism and Allegory in the Early Fiction of Mao Tun*. Bloomington: Indiana Univ. Press, 1986.

Chénetier, Marc, Ed. *Critical Angles: European Views of Contemporary American Literature*. Carbondale: Southern Illinois Univ. Press, 1986.

Chevigny, Bell G., and Gari Laguardia, Eds. *Reinventing the Americas: Comparative Studies of Literature of the United States and Spanish America*. Cambridge: Cambridge Univ. Press, 1986.

Chibbett, David G., Ed. *River Mist and Other Stories by Kunikida Doppo*, trans. David G. Chibbett. Tokyo: Kodansha, 1982; Am. ed. New York: Kodansha, 1983.

Child, Lydia Maria. *"Hobomok" and Other Writings on Indians*, ed. with Introd. by Carolyn L. Karcher. New Brunswick: Rutgers Univ. Press, 1986.

Christian, Barbara. *Black Feminist Criticism: Perspectives on Black Women Writers*. New York: Pergamon Press, 1985.

Clews, Hetty. *The Only Teller: Readings in the Monologue Novel*. Victoria, B.C.: Sono Nis Press, 1985.

Cloonan, William. *Michel Tournier*. Boston: Twayne, 1985.

Clyman, Toby W., Ed. *A Chekhov Companion*. Westport, Conn.: Greenwood, 1985.

Coale, Samuel C. *In Hawthorne's Shadow: American Romance from Melville to Mailer*. Lexington: Univ. Press of Kentucky, 1985.

Cockrell, Roger, and David Richards, Eds. *The Voice of a Giant: Essays on Seven Russian Prose Classics*. Exeter: Univ. of Exeter, 1985.

Collins, Max A., and James L. Traylor. *One Lonely Knight: Mickey Spillane's Mike Hammer*. Bowling Green: Bowling Green State Univ. Popular Press, 1984.

Collins, Robert A., and Howard D. Pearce, Eds. *The Scope of the Fantastic— Theory, Technique, Major Authors*. Westport, Conn.: Greenwood, 1985.

Cooke, John. *The Novels of Nadine Gordimer: Private Lives/Public Landscapes*. Baton Rouge: Louisiana State Univ. Press, 1985.

Cooke, Rose Terry. *"How Celia Changed Her Mind" and Selected Stories*, ed. with Introd. by Elizabeth Ammons. New Brunswick: Rutgers Univ. Press, 1986.

Cooney, Seamus, Bradford Morrow, Bernard Lafourcade, and Hugh Kenner, Eds. *Blast 3*. Santa Barbara: Black Sparrow, 1984.

Cope, Jackson I. *Robert Coover's Fiction*. Baltimore: Johns Hopkins Univ. Press, 1986.

Corngold, Stanley. *The Fate of the Self: German Writers and French Theory*. New York: Columbia Univ. Press, 1986.

Costa, Richard H. *H. G. Wells*. New York: Twayne, 1967; 2nd ed. Boston: Twayne, 1985.

Couturier, Maurice, and Regis Durand. *Donald Barthelme*. New York: Methuen, 1982.

Cowdery, Lauren T. *The Nouvelle of Henry James in Theory and Practice*. Ann Arbor: UMI Research Press, 1986.

Cox, Don R. *Arthur Conan Doyle*. New York: Ungar, 1985.

Cox, Gary. *Tyrant and Victim in Dostoevsky*. Columbus: Slavica, 1983.

Coyle, William, Ed. *Aspects of Fantasy: Selected Essays from the Second International Conference on Fantasy in Literature and Film*. Westport, Conn.: Greenwood, 1986.

Crompton, Don, and Julia Briggs. *A View from the Spire: William Golding's Later Novels*. Oxford: Blackwell, 1985.

Crone, Anna V., and Catherine V. Chvany, Eds. *New Studies in Russian Language and Literature*. Columbus: Slavica, 1986.

Crossley, Robert. *H. G. Wells*. Mercer Island, Wash.: Starmont, 1986.

Crowley, John W. *The Black Heart's Truth: The Early Career of W. D. Howells*. Chapel Hill: Univ. of North Carolina Press, 1985.

Current-García, Eugene. *The American Short Story before 1850: A Critical History*. Boston: Twayne, 1985.

Dabydeen, David, Ed. *The Black Presence in English Literature*. Manchester: Manchester Univ. Press, 1985.

Dameron, J. Lasley, and James W. Mathews, Eds. *No Fairer Land: Studies in Southern Literature Before 1900*. Troy, N.Y.: Whitston, 1985.

Dance, Daryl C., Ed. *Fifty Caribbean Writers: A Bio-Bibliographical Critical Sourcebook*. Westport, Conn.: Greenwood, 1986.

Davidson, Arnold E. *Jean Rhys*. New York: Ungar, 1985.

Davis, Ursula B. *Paris Without Regret: James Baldwin, Kenny Clarke, Chester Himes, and Donald Byrd*. Iowa City: Univ. of Iowa Press, 1986.

Day, William P. *In the Circles of Fear and Desire: A Study of Gothic Fantasy*. Chicago: Univ. of Chicago Press, 1985.

Deane, Seamus. *A Short History of Irish Literature*. London: Hutchinson, 1986.

Dietrich, Maria, and Christoph Schöneich, Eds. *Studien zur englischen und amerikanischen Prosa nach dem ersten Weltkrieg*. Darmstadt: Wissenschaftlich Buchgesellschaft, 1986.

Dillingham, William B. *Melville's Later Novels*. Athens: Univ. of Georgia Press, 1986.

Donaldson, William. *Popular Literature in Victorian Scotland*. Aberdeen: Aberdeen Univ. Press, 1986.

Donohue, Agnes M. *Hawthorne: Calvin's Ironic Stepchild*. Kent: Kent State Univ. Press, 1985.

Dooley, Dennis. *Dashiell Hammett*. New York: Ungar, 1984.

Duke, Michael S. *Blooming and Contending: Chinese Literature in the Post-Mao Era*. Bloomington: Indiana Univ. Press, 1985.

Dumouchel, Paul, Ed. *Violence et vérité autour de René Girard*. Paris: Grasset & Centre National de la Recherches Scientifique, 1985.

Duncan, L. Ann. *Voices, Visions, and a New Reality: Mexican Fiction Since 1970*. Pittsburgh: Univ. of Pittsburgh Press, 1986.

DuPlessis, Rachel B. *Writing Beyond the Ending: Narrative Strategies of Twentieth-Century Women Writers*. Bloomington: Indiana Univ. Press, 1985.

Ehre, Milton. *Isaac Babel*. Boston: Twayne, 1986.

Elling, Barbara, Ed. *Kafka-Studien*. New York: York, 1985.

Ermarth, Elizabeth D. *George Eliot*. Boston: Twayne, 1985.

Ernst, Gilles, Ed. *La Mort en toutes lettres*. Nancy: Univ. de Nancy, 1983.

Ettin, Andrew V. *Literature and the Pastoral*. New Haven: Yale Univ. Press, 1984.

Ewell, Barbara C. *Kate Chopin*. New York: Ungar, 1986.

Fairbanks, Carol. *Prairie Women: Images in American and Canadian Fiction*. New Haven: Yale Univ. Press, 1986.

Farrell, C. Frederick and Edith R. *Marguerite Yourcenar in Counterpoint*. Lanham, Md.: Univ. Press of America, 1983.

Ffinch, Michael. *G. K. Chesterton*. San Francisco: Harper & Row, 1986.

Fickett, Harold, and Douglas R. Gilbert. *Flannery O'Connor: Images of Grace*. Grand Rapids: Eerdmans, 1986.

Firchow, Peter E. *The Death of the German Cousin: Variations on a Literary Stereotype, 1890–1920.* Cranbury, N.J.: Associated Univ. Presses [for Bucknell Univ. Press], 1986.

Fitz, Earl E. *Clarice Lispector.* Boston: Twayne, 1985.

Fleischmann, Fritz, Ed. *American Novelists Revisited: Essays in Feminist Criticism.* Boston: Hall, 1982.

Flora, Joseph M. *The English Short Story 1880–1945: A Critical History.* Boston: Twayne, 1985.

Flores, Angel, Ed. *El Realismo mágico en el cuento hispanoamericano.* Tlahuapan, Mexico: Premià, 1985.

Flynn, Elizabeth A., and Patrocinio P. Schweickart, Eds. *Gender and Reading: Essays on Readers, Texts, and Contexts.* Baltimore: Johns Hopkins Univ. Press, 1986.

Fogel, Aaron. *Coercion to Speak: Conrad's Poetics of Dialogue.* Cambridge: Harvard Univ. Press, 1985.

Fowler, Doreen, and Ann J. Abadie, Eds. *Faulkner and Humor: Faulkner and Yoknapatawpha, 1984.* Jackson: Univ. Press of Mississippi, 1986.

———. *Faulkner and Women: Faulkner and Yoknapatawpha, 1985.* Jackson: Univ. Press of Mississippi, 1986.

Frank, Elizabeth. *Louise Bogan: A Portrait.* New York: Knopf, 1985.

Frank, Joseph. *Dostoevsky: The Stir of Liberation.* Princeton: Princeton Univ. Press, 1986.

Frieden, Ken. *Genius and Monologue.* Ithaca: Cornell Univ. Press, 1985.

Friedman, Melvin J., and Beverly L. Clark, Eds. *Critical Essays on Flannery O'Connor.* Boston: Hall, 1985.

Fullbrook, Kate. *Katherine Mansfield.* Bloomington: Indiana Univ. Press, 1986.

Gaiser, Gottlieb, Ed. *International Perspectives on James Joyce.* Troy, N.Y.: Whitston, 1986.

Gallagher, Catherine. *The Industrial Reformation of English Fiction: Social Discourse and Narrative Form, 1832–1867.* Chicago: Univ. of Chicago Press, 1985.

Gardner, Averil. *Angus Wilson.* Boston: Twayne, 1985.

Garfield, Evelyn P. *Women's Voices from Latin America.* Detroit: Wayne State Univ. Press, 1985.

Gargano, James W., Ed. *Critical Essays on Henry James: The Early Novels.* Boston: Hall, 1986.

Garner, Shirley N., Claire Kahane, and Madelon Sprengnether, Eds. *The (M)other Tongue: Essays in Feminist Psychoanalytic Interpretation.* Ithaca: Cornell Univ. Press, 1985.

Gay-Crosier, Raymond, and Jacqueline Lévi-Valensi, Eds. *Albert Camus: Oeuvre fermée, oeuvre ouverte?* Paris: Gallimard, 1985.

Geckeler, Horst, Ed. *Logos Semantikos: Studia Linguistica in Honorem Eugenio Coseriu 1921–1981,* III. Berlin: de Gruyter, 1981.

Geduld, Harry M., Ed. *The Definitive "Dr. Jekyll and Mr. Hyde" Companion.* New York: Garland, 1983.

Geherin, David. *The American Private Eye: The Image in Fiction.* New York: Ungar, 1985.

Gentry, Marshall B. *Flannery O'Connor's Religion of the Grotesque.* Jackson: Univ. Press of Mississippi, 1986.

Gerdes, Dick. *Mario Vargas Llosa.* Boston: Twayne, 1985.

Gerlach, John. *Toward the End: Closure and Structure in the American Short Story.* University: Univ. of Alabama Press, 1985.

Gibian, George, and Stephen Jan Parker, Eds. *The Achievement of Vladimir Na-*

bokov: Essays, Studies, Reminiscences, and Stories from the Cornell Nabokov Festival. Ithaca: Cornell Univ. Press, 1984.

Gidez, Richard B. *P. D. James.* Boston: Twayne, 1986.

Gilbert, Sandra M., and Susan Gubar, Eds. *The Female Imagination and the Modernist Aesthetic.* New York: Gordon & Breach, 1986.

Gilmore, Michael T. *American Romanticism and the Marketplace.* Chicago: Univ. of Chicago Press, 1985.

Ginsburg, Michal P. *Flaubert Writing: A Study in Narrative Strategies.* Stanford: Stanford Univ. Press, 1986.

Gittleman, Sol. *Sholom Aleichem: A Non-Critical Introduction.* The Hague: Mouton, 1974.

Gladstein, Mimi R. *The Indestructible Woman in Faulkner, Hemingway, and Steinbeck.* Ann Arbor: UMI Research Press, 1986.

Goertz, R. O. W., Ed. *Iberia: Literary and Historical Issues: Studies in Honour of Harold V. Livermore.* Calgary: Univ. of Calgary Press, 1985.

Goetz, William. *Henry James and the Darkest Abyss of Romance.* Baton Rouge: Louisiana State Univ. Press, 1986.

Goffin, Roger, Michel Vanhelleputte, and Monique Weyembergh-Boussart, Eds. *Littérature et culture allemandes.* Brussels: Univ. of Brussels, 1985.

Goldman, Leila H. *Saul Bellow's Moral Vision: A Critical Study of the Jewish Experience.* New York: Irvington, 1983.

Gonzalez, N. V. M. *Mindoro and Beyond: Twenty-one Stories.* Quezon City: Univ. of Philippines Press, 1979.

González-del-Valle, Luis T., and Darío Villanueva, Eds. *Estudios en honor a Ricardo Gullón.* Lincoln: Society of Spanish & Spanish-American Studies, 1984.

———, and Catherine Nickel, Eds. *Selected Proceedings of the Mid-America Conference on Hispanic Literature.* Lincoln: Society of Spanish & Spanish-American Studies, 1986.

Goodwin, K. L., Ed. *Commonwealth Literature in the Curriculum.* St. Lucia: South Pacific Association for Commonwealth Literature and Language Studies, 1980.

Gordon, Joan. *Gene Wolfe.* Mercer Island, Wash.: Starmont, 1986.

Gordon, Lois. *Robert Coover: The Universal Fictionmaking Process.* Carbondale: Southern Illinois Univ. Press, 1983.

Grafstein, M. W., Ed. *Sholom Aleichem Panorama.* New York: Jewish Observer, 1948.

Gray, Richard. *Writing the South: Ideas of an American Region.* Cambridge: Cambridge Univ. Press, 1986.

Green, Martin, and John Swan. *The Triumph of Pierrot: The Commedia dell'Arte and the Modern Imagination.* New York: Macmillan, 1986.

Green, Mary J. *Fiction in the Historical Present: French Writers and the Thirties.* Hanover, N.H.: Univ. Press of New England, 1986.

Greene, Gayle, and Coppélia Kahn, Eds. *Making a Difference: Feminist Literary Criticism.* London: Methuen, 1985.

Greiner, Donald J. *Adultery in the American Novel: Updike, James, and Hawthorne.* Columbia: Univ. of South Carolina Press, 1985.

———. *Understanding John Hawkes.* Columbia: Univ. of South Carolina Press, 1985.

Griffin, Joseph. *The Small Canvas: An Introduction to Dreiser's Short Stories.* Cranbury, N.J.: Associated Univ. Presses [for Fairleigh Dickinson Univ. Press], 1985.

Grimes, Larry E. *The Religious Design of Hemingway's Early Fiction.* Ann Arbor: UMI Research Press, 1985.

Grimm, Reinhold, and Jost Hermand, Eds. *Blacks and German Culture.* Madison: Univ. of Wisconsin Press, 1986.

Grübel, Rainer, Ed. *Russische Erzählung—Russian Short Story: Ütrechter Symposium zur Theorie und Geschichte der russischen Erzählung im 19. und 20. Jahrhundert.* Amsterdam: Rodopi, 1984.

Gustafson, Richard F. *Leo Tolstoy: Resident and Stranger.* Princeton: Princeton Univ. Press, 1986.

Gutsche, George J. *Moral Apostasy in Russian Literature.* DeKalb, Ill.: Northern Illinois Univ. Press, 1986.

Hadgraft, Cecil, Ed. *The Australian Short Story Before Lawson.* Melbourne: Oxford Univ. Press, 1986.

Hamilton, Robert. *W. H. Hudson: The Vision of Earth.* London: Dent, 1946; rpt. Port Washington, N.Y.: Kennikat, 1970.

Hanson, Clare. *Short Stories and Short Fiction, 1880–1980.* New York: St. Martin's Press, 1985; Brt. ed. London: Macmillan, 1985.

Harari, Josué, Ed. *Textual Strategies.* Ithaca: Cornell Univ. Press, 1979.

Harkness, Don, Ed. *Design, Pattern, Style: Hallmarks of a Developing American Culture.* Tampa: American Studies Press, 1983.

———. *Ritual in the United States: Acts and Representations.* Tampa: American Studies Press, 1985.

Hartman, Geoffrey H., and Sanford Budick, Eds. *Midrash and Literature.* New Haven: Yale Univ. Press, 1986.

Hasan, Noorul. *Thomas Hardy: The Sociological Imagination.* London: Macmillan, 1982.

Hassall, Anthony J. *Strange Country: A Study of Randolph Stow.* St. Lucia: Univ. of Queensland Press, 1986.

Hassler, Donald M., Ed. *Patterns of the Fantastic II.* Mercer Island, Wash.: Starmont, 1985.

Hayashi, Tetsumaro, Ed. *Steinbeck's Women: Essays in Criticism.* Muncie, Ind.: Steinbeck Society of America, 1979.

———, Yasuo Hashiguchi, and Richard F. Peterson, Eds. *John Steinbeck: East and West.* Muncie, Ind.: Steinbeck Society of America, 1978.

Haywood, John A. *Modern Arabic Literature, 1800–1970.* New York: St. Martin's Press, 1971.

Heller, Thomas C., Morton Sosna, David E. Wellbery, Arnold I. Davidson, Ann Swidler, and Ian Watt, Eds. *Reconstructing Individualism: Autonomy, Individuality, and the Self in Western Thought.* Stanford: Stanford Univ. Press, 1986.

Henderson, Jeff, Ed. *Thor's Hammer: Essays on John Gardner.* Conway: Univ. of Central Arkansas Press, 1985.

Herget, Winfried, Klaus P. Jochum, and Ingeborg Weber, Eds. *Theorie und Praxis im Erzählendes 19. und 20. Jahrhundert.* Tübingen: Narr, 1986.

Hernández de López, Ana María, Ed. *En el punto de mira: Gabriel García Márquez.* Madrid: Pliegos, 1985.

Herrera-Sobek, María, Ed. *Beyond Stereotypes: The Critical Analysis of Chicano Literature.* Binghamton: Bilingual Press, 1958.

Hickman, Hannah. *Robert Musil and the Culture of Vienna.* La Salle, Ill.: Open Court, 1984.

Hillyer, Robert, Richard Wilbur, and Cleanth Brooks. *Anniversary Lectures.* Washington: Library of Congress, 1959.

Hirshberg, Edgar W. *John D. MacDonald.* Boston: Twayne, 1985.

Hochman, Baruch. *Characters in Literature.* Ithaca: Cornell Univ. Press, 1985.

Hokenson, Jan, and Howard Pearce, Eds. *Forms of the Fantastic.* Westport, Conn.: Greenwood, 1986.

Hollis, Burney J., Ed. *Amid Visions and Revisions: Poetry and Criticism on Literature and the Arts.* Baltimore: Morgan State Univ. Press, 1985.

Holquist, Michael. *Dostoevsky and the Novel.* Princeton: Princeton Univ. Press, 1977.

Homans, Margaret. *Bearing the Word: Language and Female Experience in Nineteenth-Century Women's Writing.* Chicago: Univ. of Chicago Press, 1986.

Howard, June. *Form and History in American Literary Naturalism.* Chapel Hill: Univ. of North Carolina Press, 1985.

Howard, Patricia, Ed. *Benjamin Britten: "The Turn of the Screw."* Cambridge: Cambridge Univ. Press, 1985.

Hubbard, Francis A. *Theories of Action in Conrad.* Ann Arbor: UMI Research Press, 1984.

Hughes, Kenneth J. *Signs of Literature: Language, Ideology and Literary Text.* Vancouver, B.C.: Talonbooks, 1986.

Hume, Kathryn. *Fantasy and Mimesis: Response to Reality in Western Literature.* New York: Methuen, 1985.

Humphries, Jefferson. *Metamorphoses of the Raven: Literary Overdeterminedness in France and the South Since Poe.* Baton Rouge: Louisiana State Univ. Press, 1985.

Huss, Roy. *The Mindscapes of Art: Dimensions of Psyche in Fiction, Drama, and Film.* Cranbury, N.J.: Associated Univ. Presses [for Fairleigh Dickinson Univ. Press], 1986.

Ingwersen, Faith and Niels. *Quest for a Promised Land: The Works of Martin Andersen Nexø.* Westport, Conn.: Greenwood, 1984.

Irvine, Lorna. *Sub/version: Canadian Fiction by Women.* Toronto: ECW Press, 1986.

Jain, S. P. *Hemingway: A Study of His Stories.* New Delhi: Arnold-Heinemann, 1985.

Jardine, Alice A. *Gynesis: Configurations of Woman and Modernity.* Ithaca: Cornell Univ. Press, 1985.

Johansen, Ib, and Peter Ronnon-Jessen, Eds. *Inventing the Future: Science Fiction in the Context of Cultural History and Literary Theory.* Aarhus, Denmark: Univ. of Aarhus, 1985.

Jones, Michael P. *Conrad's Heroism: A Paradise Lost.* Ann Arbor: UMI Research Press, 1985.

Kadir, Djelal. *Questing Fictions: Latin America's Family Romance.* Minneapolis: Univ. of Minnesota Press, 1986.

Kalikoff, Beth. *Murder and Moral Decay in Victorian Popular Literature.* Ann Arbor: UMI Research Press, 1986.

Kalinnikova, Elena J. *Indian-English Literature: A Perspective,* ed. K. K. Sharma, trans. Virendra Pal Sharma. Atlantic Highlands, N.J.: Humanities Press, 1982.

Karl, Frederick R. *Modern and Modernism: The Sovereignty of the Artist 1885–1925.* New York: Atheneum, 1985.

Kazin, Alfred. *An American Procession.* New York: Knopf, 1984.

Kent, Thomas. *Interpretation and Genre: The Role of Generic Perception in the Study of Texts.* Cranbury, N.J.: Associated Univ. Presses [for Bucknell Univ. Press], 1986.

Kessler, Edward. *Flannery O'Connor and the Language of Apocalypse.* Princeton: Princeton Univ. Press, 1986.

Kestner, Joseph. *Protest and Reform: The British Social Narrative by Women, 1824–1867.* Madison: Univ. of Wisconsin Press, 1985; Brt. ed. London: Methuen, 1985.

Kim, Seong-Kon. *Journey into the Past: The Historical and Mythical Imagination of Barth and Pynchon.* Seoul, Korea: American Studies Institute, 1985.

Kime, Wayne R. *Donald G. Mitchell.* Boston: Twayne, 1985.

Kinnaird, John. *Olaf Stapledon.* Mercer Island, Wash.: Starmont, 1986.

Kirby, David. *The Sun Rises in the Evening: Monism and Quietism in Western Culture.* Metuchen, N.J.: Scarecrow, 1982.

Klein, Michael, and Sigurd P. Scheichl, Eds. *Thematisierung der Sprache in der österreichischen Literatur des 20. Jahrhundert.* Innsbruck: Univ. of Innsbruck, 1982.

Klinkowitz, Jerome. *The American 1960s: Imaginative Acts in a Decade of Change.* Ames: Iowa State Univ. Press, 1980.

———. *Literary Subversions: New American Fiction and the Practice of Criticism.* Carbondale: Southern Illinois Univ. Press, 1985.

———. *The New American Novel of Manners: The Fiction of Richard Yates, Dan Wakefield, and Thomas McGuane.* Athens: Univ. of Georgia Press, 1986.

Knapp, Bettina L. *Archetype, Architecture, and the Writer.* Bloomington: Indiana Univ. Press, 1986.

Knapp, Mona. *Doris Lessing.* New York: Ungar, 1984.

Knight, Diana. *Flaubert's Characters: The Language of Illusion.* Cambridge: Cambridge Univ. Press, 1985.

Knox-Shaw, Peter. *The Explorer in English Fiction.* New York: St. Martin's Press, 1986.

Kobler, J. F. *Ernest Hemingway, Journalist and Artist.* Ann Arbor: UMI Research Press, 1985.

Köpeczi, Béla, and György Vajda, Eds. *Proceedings of the 8th Congress of the International Comparative Literature Association. II. Twentieth Century Literatures Originating in Different Cultures & Comparative Literature and Theory of Literature.* Stuttgart: Bieber, 1980.

Kroetsch, Robert, and Reingard M. Nischik, Eds. *Gaining Ground: European Critics on Canadian Literature.* Edmonton, Alberta: NeWest Press, 1985.

Kroker, Arthur, and David Cook. *The Postmodern Scene: Excremental Culture and Hyper-Aesthetics.* New York: St. Martin's Press, 1986.

Kunikida Doppo. *River Mist and Other Stories,* trans. and ed. David G. Chibbett. Tokyo: Kodansha, 1982; Am. ed. 1983.

Kutnik, Jerzy. *The Novel As Performance: The Fiction of Ronald Sukenick and Raymond Federman.* Carbondale: Southern Illinois Univ. Press, 1986.

Larsen, Nella. *"Quicksand" and "Passing,"* ed. Deborah E. McDowell. New Brunswick: Rutgers Univ. Press, 1986.

Larson, Randall D. *Robert Bloch.* Mercer Island, Wash.: Starmont, 1986.

Lattin, Vernon E., Ed. *Contemporary Chicano Fiction: A Critical Survey.* Binghamton: Bilingual Press, 1986.

Laurenson, Diana, and Alan Swingewood. *The Sociology of Literature.* London: MacGibbon & Kee, 1971.

Layton, Lynne, and Barbara Ann Schapiro, Eds. *Narcissism and the Text: Studies in Literature and the Psychology of Self.* New York: New York Univ. Press, 1986.

Leclerq, Florence. *Elizabeth Taylor.* Boston: Twayne, 1985.

Lee, A. Robert, Ed. *The Nineteenth-Century American Short Story.* London: Vision Press, 1985; Am. ed. Totowa, N.J.: Barnes & Noble, 1985.

Lee, Leo Ou-fan, Ed. *Lu Xun and His Legacy.* Berkeley: Univ. of California Press, 1985.

Leland, Christopher T. *The Last Happy Men: The Generation of 1922.* Syracuse: Syracuse Univ. Press, 1986.

Lemon, Lee T. *Portraits of the Artist in Contemporary Fiction.* Lincoln: Univ. of Nebraska Press, 1985.

Lewis, Leon. *Henry Miller: The Major Writings.* New York: Schocken, 1986.

Lewis, Peter. *John Le Carré.* New York: Ungar, 1985.

Liptzin, Sol. *The Flowering of Yiddish Literature.* New York: Yoseloff, 1963.

————. *The Maturing of Yiddish Literature.* New York: David, 1970.

Littérature et Psychanalyse: Une Clinique de l'écriture. Nantes: Univ. of Nantes, 1986.

Ljungquist, Kent. *The Grand and the Fair: Poe's Landscape Aesthetics and Pictorial Techniques.* Potomac, Md.: Scripta Humanistica, 1984.

Lo lúdico y lo fantástico en la obra de Cortázar. Madrid: Fundamentos, 1986.

Long, Robert E. *Nathanael West.* New York: Ungar, 1985.

Loveday, Simon. *The Romances of John Fowler.* New York: St. Martin's Press, 1985.

Lucas, John. *Moderns and Contemporaries: Novelists, Poets, Critics.* Brighton, Sussex: Harvester Press, 1985; Am. ed. Totowa, N.J.: Barnes & Noble, 1985.

Lucente, Gregory L. *Beautiful Fables: Self-consciousness in Italian Narrative from Manzoni to Calvino.* Baltimore: Johns Hopkins Univ. Press, 1986.

Lyons, Phyllis I. *The Saga of Dazai Osamu: A Critical Study with Translations.* Stanford: Stanford Univ. Press, 1985.

McCarthy, Patrick A., Ed. *Critical Essays on Samuel Beckett.* Boston: Hall, 1986.

McConkey, James, Ed. *Chekhov and Our Age: Responses to Chekhov by American Writers and Scholars.* Ithaca: Cornell Univ. Center for Int'l Studies, 1985.

McCullen, Maurice L. *E. M. Delafield.* Boston: Twayne, 1985.

McGann, Jerome J. *The Beauty of Inflection: Literary Investigations in Historical Method and Theory.* Oxford: Clarendon Press, 1985.

McGuire, Patrick L. *Red Star: Political Aspects of Soviet Science Fiction.* Ann Arbor: UMI Research Press, 1985.

MacKillop, James. *Fionn mac Cumhaill: Celtic Myth in English Literature.* Syracuse: Syracuse Univ. Press, 1986.

MacLulich, T. D. *Hugh MacLennan.* Boston: Twayne, 1983.

McWilliams, James R. *Brother Artist: A Psychological Study of Thomas Mann's Fiction.* Lanham, Md.: Univ. Press of America, 1983.

Malcolm, William K. *A Blasphemer and Reformer: A Study of James Leslie Mitchell/ Lewis Grassic Gibbon.* Aberdeen: Aberdeen Univ. Press, 1984.

Manlove, C. N. *Science Fiction: Ten Explorations.* Kent, Ohio: Kent State Univ. Press, 1986.

Manning, Carol S. *With Ears Opening Like Morning Glories: Eudora Welty and the Love of Storytelling.* Westport, Conn.: Greenwood, 1985.

Marder, Daniel. *Exiles at Home: A Story of Literature in Nineteenth-Century America.* Lanham, Md.: Univ. Press of America, 1984.

Marling, William H. *Raymond Chandler.* Boston: Twayne, 1986.

Marret-Tising, Carlee. *The Reception of Hermann Hesse by the Youth in the United States: A Thematic Analysis.* Bern: Lang, 1982.

Marsh, Rosalind J. *Soviet Fiction Since Stalin: Science, Politics and Literature.* Totowa, N.J.: Barnes & Noble, 1986.

Martin, Robert K. *Hero, Captain, and Stranger: Male Friendship, Social Critique, and Literary Form in the Sea Novels of Herman Melville.* Chapel Hill: Univ. of North Carolina Press, 1986.

Martínez, Julio A., and Francisco A. Lomelí, Eds. *Chicano Literature: A Reference Guide*. Westport, Conn.: Greenwood, 1985.

Mason, Eve. *Stifter*. London: Grant & Cutlet, 1986.

Melchiori, Barbara A. *Terrorism in the Late Victorian Novel*. London: Croom Held, 1985.

Meldrum, Barbara H., Ed. *Under the Sun: Myth and Realism in Western American Literature*. Troy, N.Y.: Whitston, 1985.

Meyers, Jeffrey. *Disease and the Novel, 1880–1960*. New York: St. Martin's Press, 1985.

———. *Hemingway: A Biography*. New York: Harper & Row, 1985.

Milbauer, Asher Z. *Transcending Exile: Conrad, Nabokov, I. B. Singer*. Miami: Univ. Press of Florida, 1985.

Miller, Christopher L. *Blank Darkness: Africanist Discourse in French*. Chicago: Univ. of Chicago Press, 1985.

Miller, David N. *Fear of Fiction: Narrative Strategies in the Works of I. B. Singer*. Albany: State Univ. Press of New York, 1985.

Miller, Judith, Ed. *The Art of Alice Munro: Saying the Unsayable*. Waterloo, Ont.: Univ. of Waterloo Press, 1984.

Miller, Karl. *Doubles: Studies in Literary History*. New York: Oxford Univ. Press, 1985.

Miller, Robin F., Ed. *Critical Essays on Dostoevsky*. Boston: Hall, 1986.

Mills, Nicolaus. *The Crowd in American Literature*. Baton Rouge: Louisiana State Univ. Press, 1986.

Miyoshi, Masao. *The Divided Self: A Perspective on the Literature of the Victorians*. New York: New York Univ. Press, 1969.

Morrison, John W. *Modern Japanese Fiction*. Salt Lake City: Univ. of Utah Press, 1955.

Moser, Charles A. *The Russian Short Story: A Critical History*. Boston: Twayne, 1986.

Mozejko, Edward, Boris Briker, and Per Dalgard, Eds. *Vasiliy Pavlovich Aksenov: A Writer in Quest of Himself*. Columbus: Slavica, 1986.

Mukherjee, Meenakshi. *Realism and Reality: The Novel and Society in India*. Delhi: Oxford Univ. Press, 1985.

Murfin, Ross C., Ed. *Conrad Revisited: Essays for the Eighties*. University: Univ. of Alabama Press, 1985.

Murphy, Christina. *Ann Beattie*. Boston: Twayne, 1986.

Nagel, Gwen L., Ed. *Critical Essays on Sarah Orne Jewett*. Boston: Hall, 1984.

Naimy, Nadim. *Mikhail Naimy: An Introduction*. Beirut: American Univ. at Beirut, 1967.

Nathan, Rhoda B., Ed. *Nineteenth-Century Women Writers of the English-Speaking World*. Westport, Conn.: Greenwood, 1986.

Natov, Nadine. *Mikhail Bulgakov*. Boston: Twayne, 1985.

Nestor, Pauline. *Female Friendships and Communities*. Oxford: Clarendon Press, 1985.

Newman, Robert D. *Understanding Thomas Pynchon*. Columbia: Univ. of South Carolina Press, 1986.

Norman, Torborg. *Isolation and Contact: A Study of Character Relationships in Joyce Carol Oates's Short Stories 1963–1980*. Gothenburg: Acta Universitatis Gothoburgensis, 1984.

Norris, Margot. *Beasts of the Modern Imagination: Darwin, Nietzsche, Kafka, Ernst and Lawrence*. Baltimore: Johns Hopkins Univ. Press, 1985.

Nye, David E., and Kristen K. Thomsen, Eds. *American Studies in Transition.* Odense: Odense Univ. Press, 1985.

Oldsey, Bernard, and Joseph Browne, Eds. *Critical Essays on George Orwell.* Boston: Hall, 1986.

Orel, Harold. *The Literary Achievement of Rebecca West.* New York: St. Martin's Press, 1986.

———. *The Victorian Short Story: Development and Triumph of a Literary Genre.* Cambridge: Cambridge Univ. Press, 1986.

Owens, Louis. *John Steinbeck's Re-Vision of America.* Athens: Univ. of Georgia Press, 1985.

Page, Norman. *A Conrad Companion.* New York: St. Martin's Press, 1986.

Paolini, Gilbert, Ed. *La Chispa '85: Selected Proceedings.* New Orleans: Tulane Univ., 1985.

Paris, Bernard J., Ed. *Third Force Psychology and the Study of Literature.* Cranbury, N.J.: Associated Univ. Presses [for Fairleigh Dickinson Univ. Press], 1986.

Parnell, Michael. *Eric Linklater: A Critical Biography.* London: Murray, 1984.

Parret, Herman, and Hans-George Ruprecht, Eds. *Exigences et perspectives de la sémiotique: Recueil d'hommages pour Algirdas Julien Greimas/Aims and Prospects of Semiotics: Essays in Honor of Algirdas Julien Greimas.* Amsterdam: Benjamins, 1985.

Paulin, Roger. *The Brief Compass: The Nineteenth-Century German Novelle.* Oxford: Clarendon Press, 1985.

Pavel, Thomas G. *Fictional Worlds.* Cambridge: Harvard Univ. Press, 1986.

Payne, Darwin. *Owen Wister: Chronicler of the West, Gentleman of the East.* Dallas: Southern Methodist Univ. Press, 1985.

Perry, John. *Jack London: An American Myth.* Chicago: Nelson-Hall, 1981.

Phillipson, John S., Ed. *Critical Essays on Thomas Wolfe.* Boston: Hall, 1985.

Pivato, Joseph, Ed. *Contrasts: Comparative Essays on Italian Canadian Writing.* Montreal: Guernica, 1985.

Plumb, Cheryl. *Fancy's Craft: Art and Identity in the Early Works of Djuna Barnes.* Cranbury, N.J.: Associated Univ. Presses [for Susquehanna Univ. Press], 1986.

Pollin, Burton R. *Insights and Outlooks: Essays on Great Writers.* New York: Gordian Press, 1986.

Poole, Richard. *Richard Hughes, Novelist.* Bridgend, Glamorgan: Poetry Wales Press, 1986.

Porter, Laurence M., Ed. *Critical Essays on Gustave Flaubert.* Boston: Hall, 1986.

Pounds, Wayne. *Paul Bowles: The Inner Geography.* New York: Peter Lang, 1985.

Prenshaw, Peggy W. *Elizabeth Spencer.* Boston: Twayne, 1985.

———, Ed. *Women Writers of the Contemporary South.* Jackson: Univ. Press of Mississippi, 1984.

Price, Cecil. *Gwyn Jones.* Cardiff: Univ. of Wales Press, 1976.

Proffer, Carl R., Ed. *Russian Romantic Prose: An Anthology.* Ann Arbor: Translation Press, 1979.

Pryse, Marjorie, and Hortense J. Spillers, Eds. *Conjuring: Black Women, Fiction, and Literary Tradition.* Bloomington: Indiana Univ. Press, 1985.

Przybylowicz, Donna. *Desire and Repression: The Dialectic of Self and Other in the Late Works of Henry James.* University: Univ. of Alabama Press, 1986.

Putt, S. Gorley. *A Preface to Henry James.* London: Longman, 1986.

Putzel, Max. *Genius of Place: William Faulkner's Triumphant Beginnings.* Baton Rouge: Louisiana State Univ. Press, 1985.

Rai, Gangeshwar. *Graham Greene*. New Delhi: Associated Publishing House, 1983.

Rainwater, Catherine, and William J. Scheick, Eds. *Contemporary American Women Writers: Narrative Strategies*. Lexington: Univ. Press of Kentucky, 1985.

Ram, Atma, Ed. *Perspectives on R. K. Narayan*. Ghaziabad: Vimal Prakashan, 1981; Am. ed. Atlantic Highlands, N.J.: Humanities Press, 1982.

Rancour-Lafettiere, Daniel. *Out from Under Gogol's Overcoat: A Psychoanalytic Study*. Ann Arbor: Ardis, 1982.

Raval, Suresh. *The Art of Failure: Conrad's Fiction*. Winchester: Allen, 1986.

Rawson, Claude, Ed. *English Satire and the Satiric Tradition*. Oxford: Blackwell, 1984.

Redpath, Philip. *William Golding: A Structural Reading of His Fiction*. London: Vision, 1986; Am. ed. Totowa, N.J.: Barnes & Noble, 1986.

Reep, Diana C. *Margaret Deland*. Boston: Twayne, 1985.

Regan, Robert, Ed. *Poe: A Collection of Critical Essays*. Englewood Cliffs: Prentice-Hall, 1967.

Reid, Robert, Ed. *Problems of Russian Romanticism*. Aldershot, Hants: Gower, 1986.

Reilly, Patrick. *George Orwell: The Age's Adversary*. New York: St. Martin's Press, 1986.

Reilly, Robert, Ed. *The Transcendent Adventure: Studies in Religion in Science Fiction*. Westport, Conn.: Greenwood, 1985.

Reynolds, Michael. *The Young Hemingway*. London: Blackwell, 1986.

Rice, James L. *Dostoevsky and the Healing Art: An Essay in Literary and Medical History*. Ann Arbor: Ardis, 1985.

Riddle, Mary-Madeleine G. *Herman Melville's "Piazza Tales."* Gothenburg: Acta Universitatis Gothoburgensis, 1985.

Rigaud, Nadia J., Ed. *Le Monstruex dans la littérature et la pensée anglaises*. Aix-en-Provence: Univ. of Provence, 1985.

Robert, Marthe. *As Lonely As Franz Kafka*, trans. Ralph Manheim. New York: Harcourt Brace Jovanovich, 1982.

Robertson, Ritchie. *Kafka, Judaism, Politics, and Literature*. Oxford: Clarendon Press, 1985.

Robinson, Douglas. *American Apocalypse: The Image of the End of the World in American Literature*. Baltimore: Johns Hopkins Univ. Press, 1985.

Roditi, Edouard. *Oscar Wilde*. New York: New Directions, 1947; 2nd ed. 1986.

Rollfinke, Dieter and Jacqueline. *The Call of Human Nature: The Role of Scatology in Modern German Literature*. Amherst: Univ. of Massachusetts Press, 1986.

Rose, Jonathan. *The Edwardian Temperament 1895–1919*. Athens: Ohio Univ. Press, 1986.

Roses, Lorraine E. *Voices of the Storyteller: Cuba's Lino Novás Calvo*. Westport, Conn.: Greenwood, 1986.

Rosowski, Susan J. *The Voyage Perilous: Willa Cather's Romanticism*. Lincoln: Univ. of Nebraska Press, 1986.

Ross, William T. *Weldon Kees*. Boston: Twayne, 1985.

Roth, Phyllis A., Ed. *Critical Essays on Vladimir Nabokov*. Boston: Hall, 1984.

Routley, Erik. *The Puritan Pleasures of the Detective Story*. London: Gollancz, 1972.

Rovit, Earl, and Gerry Brenner. *Ernest Hemingway*, 2nd ed. Boston: Twayne, 1986.

Rowe, Anne. *The Enchanted Country: Northern Writers in the South, 1865–1910*. Baton Rouge: Louisiana State Univ. Press, 1978.

——. *The Idea of Florida in the American Literary Imagination*. Baton Rouge: Louisiana State Univ. Press, 1986.

Royot, Daniel, Ed. *Interface: Essays on History, Myth, and Art in American Literature*. Montpellier: Univ. Paul Valéry, 1985.

Runyon, Randolph. *Fowles / Irving / Barthes: Canonical Variations on an Apocryphal Theme*. Columbus: Ohio State Univ. Press [for Miami University], 1981.

Sacken, Jeannée P. *"A Certain Slant of Light": Aesthetics of First-Person Narration in Gide and Cather*. New York: Garland, 1985.

Sadler, Lynn V. *Margaret Drabble*. Boston: Twayne, 1986.

Sagar, Keith. *D. H. Lawrence: Life into Art*. Athens: Univ. of Georgia Press, 1985.

Saltzman, Arthur M. *The Fiction of William Gass: The Consolation of Language*. Carbondale: Southern Illinois Univ. Press, 1986.

Sanders, Joseph. *E. E. "Doc" Smith*. Mercer Island, Wash.: Starmont, 1986.

Sanjinés C., Javier, Ed. *Tendencias actuales en la literatura Boliviana*. Minneapolis: Institute for the Study of Ideologies & Literature, 1985.

San Miguel, Angel, Richard Schwaderer, and Manfred Tietz, Eds. *Romanische Literaturbeziehungen im 19. und 20. Jahrhundert*. Tübingen: Narr, 1985.

Schiff, Timothy. *Scenarios of Modernist Disintegration: Tryggve Andersen's Prose Fiction*. Westport, Conn.: Greenwood, 1985.

Schneider, Daniel J. *The Consciousness of D. H. Lawrence: An Intellectual Biography*. Lawrence: Univ. Press of Kansas, 1986.

Schneider, Marilyn. *Vengeance of the Victim: History and Symbol in Giorgio Bassani's Fiction*. Minneapolis: Univ. of Minnesota Press, 1986.

Schoolfield, George C. *Elmer Diktonius*. Westport, Conn.: Greenwood, 1985.

Schubnell, Matthias. *N. Scott Momaday: The Cultural and Literary Background*. Norman: Univ. of Oklahoma Press, 1985.

Schweitzer, Darrell, Ed. *Discovering Modern Horror Fiction*. Mercer Island, Wash.: Starmont, 1985.

Searles, George J. *The Fiction of Philip Roth and John Updike*. Carbondale: Southern Illinois Univ. Press, 1985.

Seidel, Kathryn L. *The Southern Belle in the American Novel*. Tampa: Univ. of Southern Florida Press, 1985.

Seidel, Michael. *Exile and the Narrative Imagination*. New Haven: Yale Univ. Press, 1986.

Sekine, Masaru, Ed. *Irish Writers and Society at Large*. Gerrards Cross, Bucks: Smythe, 1985; Am. ed. Totowa, N.J.: Barnes & Noble, 1985.

Sellick, Robert, Ed. *Myth and Metaphor*. Adelaide: Centre for Research in the New Literatures in English, 1982.

Seltzer, Mark. *Henry James and the Art of Power*. Ithaca: Cornell Univ. Press, 1984.

Sharma, K. K., Ed. *Perspectives on Mulk Raj Anand*. Ghaziabad: Vimal Prakashan, 1978; Am. ed. Atlantic Highlands, N.J.: Humanities Press, 1982.

Sharma, R. K. *Isolation and Protest: A Case Study of J. P. Donleavy's Fiction*. New Delhi: Ajanta Publications, 1983; Am. ed. Atlantic Highlands, N.J.: Humanities Press, 1983.

Shaw, Donald L. *Alejo Carpentier*. Boston: Twayne, 1985.

Sheidley, William E., and Ann Charters. *Instructor's Manual to Accompany "The Story and Its Writer: An Introduction to Short Fiction."* New York: St. Martin's Press, 1983.

Sherry, Norman, Ed. *Joseph Conrad: A Commemoration*. London: Macmillan, 1976; Am. ed. New York: Barnes & Noble, 1977.

Shinn, Thelma J. *Radiant Daughters: Fictional American Women*. Westport, Conn.: Greenwood, 1986.

Shorley, Christopher. *Queneau's Fiction: An Introduction*. Cambridge: Cambridge Univ. Press, 1985.

Sicher, Efraim. *Style and Structure in the Prose of Isaac Babel*. Columbus: Slavica, 1985.

Siegel, Adrienne. *The Image of the American City in Popular Literature, 1820–1870*. Port Washington: Kennikat, 1981.

Siegel, Mark. *James Tiptree, Jr.* Mercer Island, Wash.: Starmont, 1985.

Silberschlag, Eisig. *From Renaissance to Renaissance: Hebrew Literature from 1492–1970*. New York: KTAV, 1973.

Silet, Charles L., Robert E. Welch, and Richard Boudreau, Eds. *The Critical Reception of Hamlin Garland, 1891–1978*. Troy, N.Y.: Whitston, 1985.

Simmonds, Roy S. *The Two Worlds of William March*. University: Univ. of Alabama Press, 1984.

Simons, Kenneth. *The Ludic Imagination: A Reading of Joseph Conrad*. Ann Arbor: UMI Research Press, 1985.

Simpson, Mark S. *The Officer in Nineteenth-Century Russian Literature*. Washington: Univ. Press of America, 1981.

Skaggs, Peggy. *Kate Chopin*. Boston: Twayne, 1985.

Skei, Hans H. *William Faulkner: The Novelist as Short Story Writer*. Oslo: Universitetforlaget, 1985.

Slatoff, Walter J. *The Look of Distance: Reflections on Suffering & Sympathy in Modern Literature—Auden to Agee, Whitman to Woolf*. Columbus: Ohio State Univ. Press, 1985.

Sloan, Barry. *The Pioneers of Anglo-Irish Fiction 1800–1850*. Gerrard Cross, Bucks, England: Colin Smythe, 1986; Am. ed. Totowa, N.J.: Barnes & Noble, 1986.

Slusser, George E., and Eric S. Rabkin, Eds. *Hard Science Fiction*. Carbondale: Southern Illinois Univ. Press, 1986.

Smock, Ann. *Double Dealing*. Lincoln: Univ. of Nebraska Press, 1985.

Snipes, Katherine. *Robert Penn Warren*. New York: Ungar, 1983.

Société des Anglicistes de l'Enseignement Supérieur, Ed. *Actes du Congrès de Poitiers*. Paris: Didier Erudition, 1984.

Sojka, Gregory S. *Ernest Hemingway: The Angler as Artist*. New York: Lang, 1985.

Sollors, Werner. *Beyond Ethnicity: Consent and Descent in American Culture*. New York: Oxford Univ. Press, 1986.

Spacks, Patricia M. *The Adolescent Idea: Myths of Youth and the Adult Imagination*. New York: Basic Books, 1981.

———. *Gossip*. New York: Knopf, 1985.

Spanier, Sandra W. *Kay Boyle: Artist and Activist*. Carbondale: Southern Illinois Univ. Press, 1986.

Spivack, Charlotte. *Ursula K. Le Guin*. Boston: Twayne, 1984.

Spivey, Ted R. *Revival: Southern Writers in the Modern City*. Gainesville: Univ. of Florida Press, 1986.

Sprague, Claire, and Virginia Tiger, Eds. *Critical Essays on Doris Lessing*. Boston: Hall, 1986.

Stableford, Brian. *Scientific Romance in Britain 1890–1950*. New York: St. Martin's Press, 1985.

Stauffer, Helen W., and Susan J. Rosowski, Eds. *Women and Western American Literature*. Troy, N.Y.: Whitston, 1982.

Stead, C. K. *In the Glass Case: Essays on New Zealand Literature*. Auckland: Auckland Univ. Press, 1981.

Steinecke, Hartmut, Ed. *Zu Gottfried Keller*. Stuttgart: Klett, 1984.

Stephens, Michael. *The Dramaturgy of Style: Voice in Short Fiction.* Carbondale: Southern Illinois Univ. Press, 1986.

Stern, J. P., and J. J. White, Eds. *Paths and Labyrinths: Nine Papers Read at the Franz Kafka Symposium Held at the Institute of Germanic Studies on 20 and 21 October 1983.* London: Univ. of London, 1985.

Sternlicht, Sanford. *Padraic Colum.* Boston: Twayne, 1985.

Stevenson, Robert Louis. *The Strange Case of Dr. Jekyll and Mr. Hyde,* 1886; rpt. Edinburgh: Canongate, 1986.

Stolojan, Sanda. *Duiliu Zamfirescu.* Boston: Twayne, 1980.

Stolz, Benjamin A., I. R. Titunik, and Lubomír Doležel, Eds. *Language and Literary Theory.* Ann Arbor: Univ. of Michigan Press, 1984.

Strickland, Charles. *Victorian Domesticity: Families in the Life and Art of Louisa May Alcott.* University: Univ. of Alabama Press, 1985.

Struthers, J. R., Ed. *The Montreal Story Tellers: Memoirs, Photographs, Critical Essays.* Montreal: Véhicule Press, 1985.

Strutz, Joseph, and Johann Strutz, Eds. *Robert Musil: Literatur, Psychologie.* Munich: Fink, 1984.

Taiwo, Oladele. *Female Novelists of Modern Africa.* New York: St. Martin's Press, 1984.

Tanner, Tony. *Henry James: The Writer and His Work.* Amherst: Univ. of Massachusetts Press, 1985.

Tarrow, Susan. *Exile from the Kingdom: A Political Rereading of Albert Camus.* University: Univ. of Alabama Press, 1985.

Thiher, Allen. *Words in Reflection: Modern Language Theory and Postmodern Fiction.* Chicago: Univ. of Chicago Press, 1984.

Timmerman, John H. *John Steinbeck: The Aesthetics of the Road Taken.* Norman: Univ. of Oklahoma Press, 1986.

Tobin, Ronald W., Ed. *Littérature et gastronomie.* Paris: Papers on French Seventeenth Century Literature, 1985.

Todd, William M. *Fiction and Society in the Age of Pushkin.* Cambridge: Harvard Univ. Press, 1986.

Torchiana, Donald T. *Backgrounds for Joyce's "Dubliners."* Boston: Allen & Unwin, 1986.

Toth, Emily, Ed. *Regionalism and the Female Imagination: A Collection of Essays.* New York: Human Sciences, 1985.

Touponce, William F. *Ray Bradbury and the Poetics of Reverie: Fantasy, Science Fiction, and the Reader.* Ann Arbor: UMI Research Press, 1984.

Tretjakow, Pirjo, and Elisabeth Lübcke, Eds. *Russische Autoren des XIX. Jahrhundert: Beiträge und Lesertexte.* Hamburg: Buske, 1982.

Tymieniecka, Anna-Teresa, Ed. *Poetics of the Elements in the Human Condition: The Sea: From Elemental Stirrings to Symbolic Inspiration, Language, and Life-Significance in Literary Interpretation and Theory.* Dordrecht: Reidel, 1985.

Tymn, Marshall B., and Mike Ashley, Eds. *Science Fiction, Fantasy, and Weird Fiction Magazines.* Westport, Conn.: Greenwood, 1985.

Udoff, Alan, Ed. *Kafka's Contextuality.* New York: Gordian Press & Baltimore Hebrew College, 1986.

Ueda, Matoro, Ed. *Explorations: Essays in Comparative Literature.* Lanham, Md.: Univ. Press of America, 1986.

Ugrimsky, Alexej, and Valija K. Ozolins, Eds. *Dostoevski and the Human Condition after a Century.* New York: Greenwood, 1986.

Unrue, Darlene H. *Truth and Vision in Katherine Anne Porter's Fiction.* Athens: Univ. of Georgia Press, 1985.

Vannatta, Dennis, Ed. *The English Short Story, 1945–1980.* Boston: Twayne, 1985.

Von Frank, Albert J. *The Sacred Game: Provincialism and Frontier Consciousness in American Literature, 1630–1860.* Cambridge: Cambridge Univ. Press, 1985.

Vos, Luk de, Ed. *Just the Other Day: Essays on the Suture of the Future.* Antwerp: EXA, 1985.

Walker, Philip. *Zola.* London: Routledge & Kegan Paul, 1985.

Walkiewicz, Edward P. *John Barth.* Boston: Twayne, 1986.

Ward, Bruce K. *Dostoyevsky's Critique of the West: The Quest for the Earthly Paradise.* Waterloo, Ont.: Wilfrid Laurier Univ. Press, 1986.

Weber, Horst. *Beiträge zur neueren Literatur.* Heidelberg: Carl Winter, 1985.

Wedel, Erwin, Ivan Galabov, and Herbert Schelesniker, Eds. *Symposium Slavicum 1977: Referate der III. Tagung bayerischer und österreichischer Slavisten an 22./ 23. Oktober 1977 in Innsbruck.* Innsbruck: Univ. of Innsbruck, 1980.

Weedman, Jane, Ed. *Women Worldwalkers: New Dimensions of Science Fiction and Fantasy.* Lubbock: Texas Tech Press, 1985.

Westling, Louise. *Sacred Groves and Ravaged Gardens: The Fiction of Eudora Welty, Carson McCullers, and Flannery O'Connor.* Athens: Univ. of Georgia Press, 1985.

White, Barbara A. *Growing Up Female: Adolescent Girlhood in American Fiction.* Westport, Conn.: Greenwood, 1985.

Williams, Raymond L. *Mario Vargas Llosa.* New York: Ungar, 1986.

Williams, Rhys W. *Carl Sternheim: A Critical Study.* Berne: Lang, 1982.

Woodcock, George, Ed. *A Place to Stand On: Essays By and About Margaret Laurence.* Edmonton, Alberta: NeWest Press, 1983.

Yoke, Carl B., and Donald M. Hassler, Eds. *Death and the Serpent: Immortality in Science Fiction and Fantasy.* Westport, Conn.: Greenwood, 1985.

A CHECKLIST OF JOURNALS USED

Acme	*Acme: Annali della Facoltà di Lettere e Filosofía*
Acta Germanica	*Acta Germanica: Jahrbuch des Südafrikanischen Germanistenverbandes*
	Acta Literaria
Acta Litteraria	*Acta Litteraria Academiae Scientiarum Hungaricae*
	Acta Orientalia
Adalbert Stifter Institut	*Adalbert Stifter Institut des Landes Oberösterreich: Vierteljahrsschrift*
Africana Journey	*Africana Journey: A Bibliographic Library Journal and Review Quarterly*
Afro-Hispanic R	*Afro-Hispanic Review*
Alabama R	*Alabama Review: A Quarterly Journal of Alabama History*
Aligarh J Engl Stud	*The Aligarh Journal of English Studies*
Am J Semiotics	*American Journal of Semiotics*
Am Lit Realism	*American Literary Realism, 1870–1910*
Am Lit	*American Literature: A Journal of Literary History, Criticism, and Bibliography*
Am Transcendental Q	*American Transcendental Quarterly: A Journal of New England Writers*
Anales de la Literatura Española	*Anales de la Literatura Española Contemporánea*
Anglia	*Anglia: Zeitschrift für Englische Philologie*
Anglo-Welsh R	*The Anglo-Welsh Review*
	L'Année Balzacienne
	Arbeiten aus Anglistik und Amerikanistik
Archiv	*Archiv für das Studium der Neueren Sprachen und Literaturen*
	Archiv für Kulturgeschichte
Arizona Q	*Arizona Quarterly*

Baker Street J	*The Baker Street Journal: An Irregular Quarterly of Sherlockiana*
Black Am Lit Forum	*Black American Literature Forum* [formerly *Negro American Literature Forum*]
	Boletín Editorial (El Colegio de México)
Boundary	*Boundary 2: A Journal of Postmodern Literature*
Bucknell R	*Bucknell Review: A Scholarly Journal of Letters, Arts and Sciences*
Bull Hispanic Stud	*Bulletin of Hispanic Studies*
Bull Hispanique	*Bulletin Hispanique*
Cahiers du Monde Hispanique	*Cahiers du Monde Hispanique et Luso-Brésilien*
Cahiers du Monde Russe	*Cahiers du Monde Russe et Sovietique*
	Cahiers Gérard de Nerval
Cahiers Victoriens et Edouardiens	*Cahiers Victoriens et Edouardiens: Revue du Centre d'Études et de Recherches Victoriennes et Edouardiennes de l'Université Paul Valéry, Montpellier*
Callaloo	*Callaloo: A Black South Journal of Arts and Letters*
Canadian J Italian Stud	*Canadian Journal of Italian Studies*
Canadian Lit	*Canadian Literature*
Canadian Mod Lang R	*Canadian Modern Language Review*
Canadian R Comp Lit	*Canadian Review of Comparative Literature*
	Caribe
	Carleton Newsletter
	Casa de las Americas
Celfan R	*Revue Celfan/Celfan Review*
	Central Asian Survey
Chasqui	*Chasqui: Revista de Literatura Latinoamericana*
Children's Lit	*Children's Literature: An International Journal*
Christianity & Lit	*Christianity and Literature*
	Ciencia & Sociedad (Santo Domingo)
Cithara	*Cithara: Essays in the Judaeo-Christian Tradition*

Clio	*Clio: A Journal of Literature, History, and the Philosophy of History*
Clues	*Clues: A Journal of Detection*
Colby Lib Q	*Colby Library Quarterly*
Coll Engl	*College English*
Coll Engl Assoc Critic	*CEA Critic: An Official Journal of the College English Association*
Coll Lang Assoc J	*College Language Association Journal*
Coll Lit	*College Literature*
Colloquia Germanica	*Colloquia Germanica, Internationale Zeitschrift für Germanische Sprach- und Literaturwissenschaft*
Comparatist	*The Comparatist: Journal of the Southern Comparative Literature Association*
Comp Lit	*Comparative Literature*
Comp Lit Stud	*Comparative Literature Studies*
Conference Coll Teachers Engl	*Conference of College Teachers of English of Texas Proceedings*
Confluencia	*Confluencia: Revista Hispánica de Cultura y Literatura*
The Conradian	*The Conradian: Journal of the Joseph Conrad Society [U.K.]*
Conradiana	*Conradiana: A Journal of Joseph Conrad*
	Co-textes
	Crítica Hispánica
Criticism	*Criticism: A Quarterly for Literature and the Arts*
Critique	*Critique: Studies in Modern Fiction*
	Cuadernos Americanos
Cuadernos Hispanoamericanos	*Cuadernos Hispanoamericanos: Revista Mensual de Cultura Hispanica*
	Cycnos
D. H. Lawrence R	*The D. H. Lawrence Review*
Delta	*Delta: Revue du Centre d'Études et de Recherche sur les Écrivains du Sud aux États-Unis*

Deutsche Vierteljahrsschrift	*Deutsche Vierteljahrsschrift für Literaturwissenschaft und Geistesgeschichte*
	Deutschunterricht in Südafrika
Dieciocho	*Dieciocho: Hispanic Enlightenment, Aesthetics, and Literary Theory*
Discurso Literario	*Discurso Literario: Revista de Temas Hispánicos*
	Doris Lessing Newsletter
Edebiyat: J Middle Eastern Lit	*Edebiyat: A Journal of Middle Eastern Literatures*
Éire	*Éire-Ireland: A Journal of Irish Studies*
Engl Lang Notes	*English Language Notes*
Engl Lit Hist	*English Literary History* [formerly *Journal of English Literary History*]
Engl Lit Transition	*English Literature in Transition*
Engl Stud	*English Studies: A Journal of English Language and Literature*
Engl Stud Africa	*English Studies in Africa: A Journal of the Humanities*
Engl Stud Canada	*English Studies in Canada*
Escritura	*Escritura: Teoría y Crítica Literarias*
ESQ: J Am Renaissance	*Emerson Society Quarterly: Journal of the American Renaissance*
Essays Arts & Sciences	*Essays in Arts & Sciences*
Essays Canadian Writing	*Essays on Canadian Writing*
Essays Lit	*Essays in Literature* (Western Illinois)
	Estudos Anglo-Americanos
	Études Germaniques
	Études Germano-africaines
	Études Irlandaises
	Études Philosophiques
Euphorion	*Euphorion: Zeitschrift für Literaturgeschichte*
	Explicación de Textos Literarios
	Explicator

	Extrapolation
Fabu	*Fabula*
Flannery O'Connor Bull	*Flannery O'Connor Bulletin*
Folio	*Folio: Papers on Foreign Languages and Literature*
Foreign Lit Stud	*Foreign Literary Studies* (China)
Forum Mod Lang Stud	*Forum for Modern Language Studies*
Foundation	*Foundation: Review of Science Fiction*
	French Forum
French Lit Series	*French Literature Series*
French R	*French Review: Journal of the American Association of Teachers of French*
Georgia R	*Georgia Review*
Germ Life & Letters	*German Life and Letters*
Germ Notes	*Germanic Notes*
Germ Q	*German Quarterly*
Germ R	*Germanic Review*
Germanisch-Romanische Monatsschrift	*Germanisch-Romanische Monatsschrift*, Neue Folge
Great Plains Q	*Great Plains Quarterly*
Hartford Stud Lit	*University of Hartford Studies in Literature: A Journal of Interdisciplinary Criticism*
Henry James R	*Henry James Review*
	Heresies
Hispamerica	*Hispamerica: Revista de Literatura*
Hispania	*Hispania: A Journal Devoted to the Interests of the Teaching of Spanish and Portuguese*
Hispanic J	*Hispanic Journal*
Hispanic R	*Hispanic Review*
Hispano	*Hispano: Hispanofilia*
	Hollins Critic
	Homines

Horen	*Die Horen: Zeitschrift für Literatur, Kunst und Kritik*
Illinois Q	*Illinois Quarterly*
Insula	*Insula: Revista de Letras y Ciencias Humanas*
Inti	*Inti: Revista de literatura Hispánica*
Int'l Fiction R	*International Fiction Review*
Int'l J Middle East Stud	*International Journal of Middle East Studies*
Iowa J Lit Stud	*Iowa Journal of Literary Studies*
Irish Slavonic Stud	*Irish Slavonic Studies*
Italian Q	*Italian Quarterly*
Italian Stud	*Italian Studies*
	Jack London Newsletter
James Joyce Q	*James Joyce Quarterly*
J Am Stud	*Journal of American Studies*
J Arabic Lit	*Journal of Arabic Literature*
J Australasian Univs Lang & Lit Assoc	*Journal of the Australasian Universities Language and Literature Association: A Journal of Literary Criticism, Philology & Linguistics*
J Commonwealth Lit	*The Journal of Commonwealth Literature*
J Engl & Germ Philol	*Journal of English and Germanic Philology*
J Evolutionary Psych	*Journal of Evolutionary Psychology*
J Kafka Soc Am	*Journal of the Kafka Society of America*
J Midwest Mod Lang Assoc	*Journal of the Midwest Modern Language Association*
J Mod Lit	*Journal of Modern Literature*
J Narrative Technique	*Journal of Narrative Technique*
J Pop Culture	*Journal of Popular Culture*
Judaism	*Judaism: A Quarterly Journal of Jewish Life and Thought*
Kentucky Romance Q	*Kentucky Romance Quarterly*
Kenyon R	*Kenyon Review*
Kipling J	*The Kipling Journal*

Kleist-Jahrbuch

Kyushu Am Lit	*Kyushu American Literature*
Lamar J Humanities	*Lamar Journal of the Humanities*
Lang & Style	*Language and Style: An International Journal*
Lang Q	*The University of Southern Florida Language Quarterly*
Lang Sci	*Language Sciences*
Les Langues Néo-Latines	*Les Langues Néo-Latines: Bulletin Trimestrial del Société de Langues Néo-Latines*
Latin Am Lit R	*Latin American Literary Review*
Legacy	*Legacy: A Journal of Nineteenth-Century American Women Writers*
	Letras de Deusto
	Letras Femeninas
	Il Lettore di Provincia
	Les Lettres Romanes
Lexis	*Lexis: Revista de Lingüística y Literatura*
Licorne	*La Licorne*
Lit Criterion	*Literary Criterion*
Lit R	*Literary Review: An International Journal of Contemporary Writing*
Lit & Hist	*Literature and History*
Lit & Psych	*Literature and Psychology*
Luso-Brazilian R	*Luso-Brazilian Review*
Malahat R	*Malahat Review: An International Quarterly of Life and Letters*
Markham R	*Markham Review*
Melville Soc Extracts	*Melville Society Extracts* [supersedes *Extracts: An Occasional Newsletter*]
Merkur	*Merkur: Deutsche Zeitschrift für Europäisches Denken*
	México en el arte (Mexico City)
Michigan Germ Stud	*Michigan Germanic Studies*

Midamerica	*Midamerica: The Yearbook of the Society for the Study of Midwestern Literature*
Mid-American R	*Mid-American Review*
Mid-Hudson Lang Stud	*Mid-Hudson Language Studies* (Bulletin of the Mid-Hudson Modern Language Association)
Midwest Q	*Midwest Quarterly: A Journal of Contemporary Thought*
Mississippi Q	*Mississippi Quarterly: The Journal of Southern Culture*
Missouri R	*Missouri Review*
Mitteilungen der E. T. A. Hoffmann	*Mitteilungen der E. T. A. Hoffmann-Gesellschaft-Bamberg*
Mod Austrian Lit	*Modern Austrian Literature: Journal of the International Arthur Schnitzler Research Association*
Mod Fiction Stud	*Modern Fiction Studies*
Mod Hebrew Lit	*Modern Hebrew Literature*
Mod Lang Notes	*Modern Language Notes* [retitled *MLN*]
Mod Lang Q	*Modern Language Quarterly*
Mod Lang R	*Modern Language Review*
Mod Lang Stud	*Modern Language Studies*
Mod Philol	*Modern Philology: A Journal Devoted to Research in Medieval and Modern Literature*
Monatshefte	*Monatshefte: Für Deutschen Unterricht, Deutsche Sprache und Literatur*
Mosaic	*Mosaic: A Journal for the Comparative Study of Literature and Ideas for the Interdisciplinary Study of Literature*
Mythes	*Mythes, Croyances et Religions dans le Monde Anglo-Saxon*
Nassau R	*The Nassau Review: The Journal of Nassau Community College Devoted to Arts, Letters, and Sciences*
Nathaniel Hawthorne J	*Nathaniel Hawthorne Journal*
Neohelicon	*Neohelicon: Acta Comparationis Litterarum Universatum*

	Neophilologus
	Neue Germanistik
	New Criterion
New Germ Stud	*New German Studies*
New Lit Hist	*New Literary History*
New Orleans R	*New Orleans Review*
	Nineteenth-Century Fiction
Nineteenth-Century French Stud	*Nineteenth-Century French Studies*
Notes Contemp Lit	*Notes on Contemporary Literature*
Notes Mississippi Writers	*Notes on Mississippi Writers*
Notes Mod Am Lit	*NMAL: Notes on Modern American Literature*
Novel	*Novel: A Forum on Fiction*
Orbis Litterarum	*Orbis Litterarum: International Review of Literary Studies*
Oxford Germ Stud	*Oxford German Studies*
Pacific Q	*Pacific Quarterly (Moana): An International Review of Arts and Ideas*
La Palabra y el Hombre	*La Palabre y el Hombre: Revista de la Universidad Veracruzana*
Panjab Univ Research Bull	*Panjab University Research Bulletin (Arts)*
Papers Lang & Lit	*Papers on Language and Literature: A Journal for Scholars and Critics of Language and Literature*
Paragraph	*Paragraph: The Journal of the Modern Critical Theory Group*
Pennsylvania Engl	*Pennsylvania English*
Perspectives Contemp Lit	*Perspectives on Contemporary Literature*
Philol Q	*Philological Quarterly*
Philosophy & Lit	*Philosophy and Literature*
Plaza	*Plaza: Revista de Literatura*
PMLA	*PMLA: Publications of the Modern Language Association of America*

Poetics Today	Poetics Today: Theory and Analysis of Literature and Communication (Tel Aviv, Israel)
Poétique	Poétique: Revue de Théorie et d'Analyse Littéraires
Post Script	Post Script: Essays in Film and the Humanities
Prismal/Cabral	Prismal/Cabral: Revista de Literatura Hispánica/ Caderno Afro-Brasileiro Asiático Lusitano
Prooftexts	Prooftexts: A Journal of Jewish Literary History
Pubs Mississippi Philol Assoc	Publications of the Mississippi Philological Association
Pubs Missouri Philol Assoc	Publications of the Missouri Philological Association
	Pynchon Notes
Quaderni Ibero-Americani	Quaderni Ibero-Americani: Attualità Culturale nella Penisola Iberica e America Latina
	Quadrant
	RE: Artes Liberales
	Recherches Anglaises et Américaines
Regionalism & Female Imagination	Regionalism and the Female Imagination
Renascence	Renascence: Essays on Value in Literature
Rendezvous (China)	Rendezvous: A Chinese-English Translation Magazine
Research African Lit	Research in African Literature
R Contemp Fiction	Review of Contemporary Fiction
	Revista Canadiense de Estudios Hispánicos
Revista Canaria	Revista Canaria de Estudios Ingleses
	Revista Chicano-Riqueña
	Revista Chilena Literatura
	Revista de Estudios Hispánicos (Puerto Rico)
	Revista de Estudios Hispánicos (Univ. Alabama)
	Revista di Studi Anglo-Americani
	Revista Iberoamericana
	Revista Revenar (Costa Rica)

R Interamericana	Revista/Review Interamericana
R Lettres Modernes	La Revue des Lettres Modernes Histoire des Idées des Littératures
	Romance Notes
Romance Q	Romance Quarterly
Romanic R	Romanic Review
	Round Table
Russian Lang J	Russian Language Journal
	Salmagundi
San José Stud	San José Studies
Saul Bellow J	Saul Bellow Journal [formerly Saul Bellow Newsletter]
Savacou	Savacou: A Journal of the Caribbean Artists Movement
Scandinavian R	Scandinavian Review
Scandinavian Stud	Scandinavian Studies
Scandinavica	Scandinavica: An International Journal of Scandinavian Studies
	Schriften der Theodor-Storm-Gesellschaft
Sci-Fiction Stud	Science-Fiction Studies
Selecta	Selecta: Journal of the Pacific Northwest Council on Foreign Languages [formerly Proceedings of the Pacific Northwest Conference on Foreign Languages]
Seminar	Seminar: A Journal of Germanic Studies
Sewanee R	Sewanee Review
Slavic & East European J	Slavic and East European Journal
Slavonic & East European R	Slavonic & East European Review
Sophia Engl Stud	Sophia English Studies
So Atlantic Q	South Atlantic Quarterly
So Carolina R	South Carolina Review
So Central R	South Central Review
Southern Hum R	Southern Humanities Review

Southern Lit J	*Southern Literary Journal*
Southern Q	*The Southern Quarterly: A Journal of the Arts in the South*
Southern R	*Southern Review* (Baton Rouge)
Southern R (Adelaide)	*Southern Review: Literary and Interdisciplinary Essays* (Adelaide)
Southern Stud	*Southern Studies: An Interdisciplinary Journal of the South*
Southwest R	*Southwest Review*
SPAN	*SPAN: Newsletter of the South Pacific Association for Commonwealth Literature and Language Studies*
SPELL	*Swiss Papers in English Language and Literature*
Sphinx	*The Sphinx: A Magazine of Literature and Society*
Sprachkunst	*Sprachkunst: Beiträge zur Literaturwissenschaft*
Stanford French R	*Stanford French Review*
Steinbeck Q	*Steinbeck Quarterly*
Stud Afro-Hispanic Lit	*Studies in Afro-Hispanic Literature*
Stud Am Fiction	*Studies in American Fiction*
Stud Am Jewish Lit	*Studies in American Jewish Literature*
Stud Canadian Lit	*Studies in Canadian Literature*
Stud Hum	*Studies in the Humanities*
Stud Lang & Lit (Taiwan)	*Studies in Language and Literature* (Taiwan)
Stud Novel	*Studies in the Novel*
Stud Scottish Lit	*Studies in Scottish Literature*
Stud Short Fiction	*Studies in Short Fiction*
Stud Weird Fiction	*Studies in Weird Fiction*
	Style
Sur	*Revista Sur*
Sydney Stud Engl	*Sydney Studies in English*
Texas Stud Lit & Lang	*Texas Studies in Literature and Language: A Journal of the Humanities*
	Textes et Langages

Thesaurus	*Thesaurus: Boletín del Instituto Caro y Cuevo*
Thought	*Thought: A Review of Culture and Ideas*
	TriQuarterly
Twentieth Century Lit	*Twentieth Century Literature: A Scholarly and Critical Journal*
Univ Mississippi Stud Engl	*University of Mississippi Studies in English*
Univ Toronto Q	*University of Toronto Quarterly*
Univ Windsor R	*University of Windsor Review*
Virginia Q R	*Virginia Quarterly Review: A National Journal of Literature and Discussion*
Weimarer Beiträge	*Weimarer Beiträge: Zeitschrift für Literaturwissenschaft, Ästhetik und Kulturtheorie*
West Virginia Univ Philol Papers	*West Virginia University Philological Papers*
Westerly	*Westerly: A Quarterly Review*
Western Am Lit	*Western American Literature*
William Carlos Williams R	*William Carlos Williams Review*
Wirkendes Wort	*Wirkendes Wort: Deutsche Sprache in Forschung und Lehre*
Women's Stud	*Women's Studies: An Interdisciplinary Journal*
World Lit Today	*World Literature Today: A Literary Quarterly of the University of Oklahoma*
World Lit Written Engl	*World Literature Written in English*
Yale French Stud	*Yale French Studies*
Yale R	*The Yale Review: A National Quarterly*
	Zeitschrift für Deutsche Philologie

INDEX OF SHORT STORY WRITERS